Oxford Bibliographical Society Publications

NEW SERIES VOLUME XXIII

Plate I.   *Vol. I. facing the general Title.*

Blakey del.   Major Sculp.

Plate 1. Frontispiece to Pope's *Works*, vol. 1, edited by Warburton (1751).

POPE'S LITERARY LEGACY:

THE BOOK-TRADE CORRESPONDENCE
OF WILLIAM WARBURTON
AND JOHN KNAPTON

with other letters and documents

1744–1780

Edited by

DONALD W. NICHOL

1992

THE OXFORD BIBLIOGRAPHICAL SOCIETY

Published by the Oxford Bibliographical Society
care of the Bodleian Library, Oxford OX1 3BG

© 1992 Oxford Bibliographical Society
ISBN 0 901420 48 4

Inquiries about the Society and its publications should be addressed to the
Honorary Secretary

Printed in Great Britain at The Alden Press, Oxford

TO
SUSAN,
SUSANNAH,
LEILA (*fille et belle-mère*)
and
ROBBIE

CONTENTS

LIST OF PLATES

Plate 1. Frontispiece: Pope's *Works*, edited by Warburton (1751), vol. 1, plate 1, facing general title-page, designed by Nicholas Blakey and engraved by Thomas Major, showing Pope above and Warburton as the central figure (National Library of Scotland, Ak. 7. 15; frontispiece border 84 × 130 mm.; block 95 × 160 mm.; page app. 125 × 200 mm.), reproduced courtesy of the Trustees of the National Library of Scotland.

Plate 2. General title-page: Pope's *Works*, edited by Warburton (1751), vol. 1 (National Library of Scotland, Ak. 7. 15; app. 125 × 200 mm.), reproduced courtesy of the Trustees of the National Library of Scotland.

Plate 3. Letter: Warburton to Knapton, 14 March [1751?], with Knapton's note to Bowyer (Egerton 1954, f.15; 186 × 235 mm.), reproduced courtesy of the British Library (actual size).

Plate 4. Warburton's policy: Sun Insurance Office (16 June 1753), as requested in his letter to Knapton of 9 June 1753, reproduced courtesy of the Sun Alliance Insurance Group (enlarged).

Plates 5–9. A Catalogue of Books in Quires, and Copies: Knapton trade sale (25 September 1755), showing buyers and prices paid; Longman no. 67 (British Library C.170.aa.1(67); app. 276 × 417 mm.).

ACKNOWLEDGEMENTS

A project of this nature depends upon mercies large and small from many sources. The letters and documents below are reproduced by courtesy of the following owners, libraries and institutions: the Bath Reference Library; the British Library; the Trustees of Boston Public Library; the Master and Fellows, Trinity College, Cambridge University; Edinburgh University Library; the Folger Shakespeare Library; Gloucestershire Record Office; the Right Reverend Philip Goodrich, Bishop of Worcester, Hartlebury Castle; the Harvard Theatre Collection and the Houghton Library, Harvard University; the Historical Society of Pennsylvania; the Huntington Library; Mary Hyde, Viscountess Eccles, the Hyde Collection; the Lilly Library, Indiana University; the University Library, University of Michigan; the National Library of Scotland; the Principal Archivist, Nottinghamshire Archives Office; the Bodleian Library, Oxford; the Pierpont Morgan Library; Princeton University Library; the Lewis Walpole Library, and the James M. and Marie-Louise Osborn Collection in the Beinecke Rare Book and Manuscript Library, Yale University. Thanks also are due to the Public Record Office, London; the Harry Ransom Humanities Research Center, University of Texas at Austin; the New York Public Library; McGill University; McMaster University; and the University of Toronto.

David Fleeman sparked my interest in the Knaptons from an early stage. David Foxon's 1975–6 Lyell Lectures, which were published as this book was going to press – *Pope and the Early Eighteenth-Century Book Trade*, revised and edited by James McLaverty (Oxford, 1991) – have considerably influenced my research. Without the patient guidance of John Valdimir Price, my research would have foundered. Pat Rogers inflamed this project with early praise. Maynard Mack encouraged my foragings into 'the whole posthumous business'. John Feather, H. R. Woudhuysen and James McLaverty oversaw the editing of this book for the Oxford Bibliographical Society and made many vital suggestions which have been adopted in its final form. This edition has depended on a network of correspondents including Hugh Amory, John Baird, Martin Battestin, Kathryn L. Beam, Terry Belanger, Ben Benedikz, Sarah Brewer, Graham Cartwright, Julian Conway, Marlies Danziger, Rodney G. Dennis, Marie Devine, Donald Eddy, David Fairer, Kenneth Graham, Charles Greene, the late Robert Halsband, Sarah S. Hodson, Diana Howard, John V. Howard, Mervyn Jannetta, Catherine J. Johnson, M. Joyce, Bill Kinsley, David McKitterick, Robin Myers, Robert Nikirk, Enid Nixon, Geoffrey F. Nuttall, Philip Oldfield,

Robert E. Parks, Mary Parsons, Clive Probyn, David Raynor, John Riely, Betty Rizzo, Anne-Marie T. Schaaf, Peter Seary, D. J. H. Smith, Margaret M. Smith, Bruce Stovel, Michael Thompson, Steven Tomlinson and Elspeth Yeo.

Warburton's recent biographer, Robert M. Ryley, who once with Thomas Gilmore planned a full edition of the correspondence, generously entrusted me with his extensive card index and other invaluable material. Michael Crump supplied me with useful data from the Eighteenth-Century Short Title Catalogue. Keith Maslen provided me with details concerning the Knaptons from the Bowyer ledgers. James Tierney forwarded transcripts from his edition of the Dodsley correspondence. Michael Treadwell has shared his considerable knowledge of the book trade with me. Laetitia Yeandle very kindly checked all Folger material for me. D. L. Hill of the Sun Alliance Insurance Group tracked down Warburton's policy. Kenneth Roberts of Barclays Bank allowed me to pore over Gosling's ledgers.

At Edinburgh University, I wish to thank Ken Fielding, Jonquil Bevan, Geoffrey Carnall, Harry Dickinson, Colin Nicholson, Michael Phillips and Nick Phillipson. Margot Butt kindly allowed me access to her late husband's library and papers. Funding for two trips to Britain was provided by the Vice-President's Research Fund of Memorial University. At Memorial, I would like to thank the Dean of Arts, Michael Staveley, Dean of Research, Niall Gogan, Malcolm MacLeod, Philip and Averil Gardner, Gordon Jones, Patrick O'Flaherty, George Story, Ron Rompkey, Robert Hollett, William Barker, Rob Pitt, Sue Sexty, Vic Hancock and the staff of the English department and Queen Elizabeth II Library, colleagues and students.

Tom Bell, Angus Calder, James and Alma Cullen, Steve Ellis and Joanna Porter, Robin Fincham and Anita Rafferty, David Ketterer, Charles and Marion Nichol, Tim Ochitwa, Ian Rankin and Miranda Harvey, Phil Sheldrake and Elaine Robertson, Stephen Walsh, Carol Gibson-Wood and Paul Wood have all helped in various ways. Under the Challenge/SEED programme, sponsored by Employment and Immigration Canada, I was able to enlist Jim Quilty and Donna Lynn Davis as proofreaders. The Social Sciences and Humanities Research Council of Canada enabled me to travel to several conferences and has supported this project with a research grant. As the prototype of this edition was dedicated to my parents, Dr. Walter and Evelyn Nichol, I would like to extend the dedication of this present work to my wife, Susan, our two daughters, Leila and Susannah, and Robbie and Leila Aitken of North Berwick, Scotland, all of whom have given their love and support.

DONALD W. NICHOL

SHORT FORMS AND ABBREVIATIONS

Add. MS(S).	Additional Manuscript(s), British Library
AP	Alexander Pope (in Chronology, Biographical Appendix and Index)
BL	British Library
Boyce	Benjamin Boyce, *The Benevolent Man: a Life of Ralph Allen of Bath* (Cambridge, Mass., 1967)
BPL	Boston Public Library
BRL	Bath Reference Library
Correspondence	*The Correspondence of Alexander Pope*, ed. George Sherburn, 5 vols. (Oxford, 1956)
CSR	*The Correspondence of Samuel Richardson*, ed. Anna Lætitia Barbauld, 6 vols. (London, 1804; rpt. New York, 1966)
CTCL	Cambridge, Trinity College Library
DNB	*Dictionary of National Biography*
Dodsley	*The Correspondence of Robert Dodsley 1733–1764*, ed. James E. Tierney (Cambridge, 1988)
E-C	*The Works of Alexander Pope*, ed. Whitwell Elwin and W. J. Courthope, 10 vols. (London, 1871–89)
Eg.	Egerton Manuscripts, British Library
ESTC	Eighteenth-Century Short Title Catalogue
EUL	Edinburgh University Library
Evans	A. W. Evans, *Warburton and the Warburtonians* (Oxford and London, 1932)
Foxon	David Foxon, *English Verse 1701–1750*, 2 vols. (Cambridge, 1975)
FSL	Folger Shakespeare Library
GM	*The Gentleman's Magazine*
Griffith	R. H. Griffith, *Alexander Pope: a bibliography*, 1 vol. in 2 pts. (Austin, 1922–7)
GRO	Gloucestershire Record Office
Guerinot	J. V. Guerinot, *Pamphlet Attacks on Alexander Pope, 1711–1744* (London, 1969)
HC	Hartlebury Castle
HCS	The Hyde Collection, Somerville, New Jersey
HL	Huntington Library
HSP	Historical Society of Pennsylvania
HTC	Harvard Theatre Collection, Harvard College Library
HUHL	Harvard University, Houghton Library
ILH	*Illustrations of the Literary History of the Eighteenth Century*, ed. John Nichols, 8 vols. (London, 1817–58)

IULL	Indiana University, Lilly Library
JK	John Knapton (in Chronology, Biographical Appendix and Index)
Johnson, *Dict.*	Samuel Johnson, *A Dictionary of the English Language*, 2 vols. (London, 1755)
Johnson, 'Pope'	Samuel Johnson, *Lives of the English Poets*, ed. G. Birkbeck Hill, 3 vols. (Oxford, 1905)
LA	*Literary Anecdotes of the Eighteenth Century*, ed. John Nichols, 9 vols. (London, 1812–15)
LDG	*The Letters of David Garrick*, ed. David M. Little and George M. Kahrl, 3 vols. (Cambridge, Mass., 1963)
LLEP	*Letters from a Late Eminent Prelate to One of his Friends*, ed. Richard Hurd (Kidderminster, [1808])
LLS	*Letters of Laurence Sterne*, ed. Lewis Perry Curtis (Oxford, 1935)
LM	*The London Magazine*
LWL	Lewis Walpole Library, Yale University
Mack, *Collected*	Maynard Mack, *Collected in Himself: Essays Critical, Biographical, and Bibliographical on Pope and Some of His Contemporaries* (Newark, 1982)
Mack, *Life*	Maynard Mack, *Alexander Pope: a Life* (London and New York, 1985)
McKenzie (*a; b*)	D. F. McKenzie, (*a*) *Stationers' Company Apprentices 1641–1700*, OBS, ns vol. 17 (1974); and (*b*) *Stationers' Company Apprentices 1701–1800*, OBS, ns vol. 19 (1978)
Maslen	K. I. D. Maslen, 'New Editions of Pope's *Essay on Man* 1745–48', *PBSA*, 62 (1968): 177–88
NAO	Nottinghamshire Archives Office
NLS	National Library of Scotland
N&Q	*Notes and Queries*
ns	new series
n.s.	no signature
OB	Oxford, Bodleian Library
OBS	Oxford Bibliographical Society
OED	*Oxford English Dictionary*
PBSA	*Papers of the Bibliographical Society of America*
PCDG	*Private Correspondence of David Garrick*, ed. James Boaden, 2 vols. (London, 1831–2)
Plomer	H. R. Plomer *et al.*, *A Dictionary of the Printers and Booksellers who were at work in England, Scotland and Ireland from 1726 to 1775* (London, 1932; rpt. 1968)
PML	Pierpont Morgan Library
PRO	Public Record Office, London

PUL	Princeton University Library
Ryley	Robert M. Ryley, *William Warburton* (Boston, 1984)
Spence	Joseph Spence, *Observations, Anecdotes, and Characters of Books and Men*, ed. James M. Osborn, 2 vols. (Oxford, 1966)
Stowe	Stowe Manuscripts, British Library
SUP	*A Selection from Unpublished Papers of the Right Reverend William Warburton, D.D.*, ed. Francis Kilvert (London, 1841)
TE	*The Twickenham Edition of the Poems of Alexander Pope*, ed. John Butt *et al.*, 11 vols. in 12 (London, 1939–69)
TLS	*Times Literary Supplement*
UMUL	University of Michigan, University Library
Wimsatt	W. K. Wimsatt, *The Portraits of Alexander Pope* (New Haven and London, 1965)
Works (1751)	*The Works of Alexander Pope Esq.*, ed. William Warburton, 9 vols. (London: J. and P. Knapton *et al.*, 1751)
WW	William Warburton (in Chronology, Biographical Appendix and Index)
WWW	*The Works of William Warburton*, ed. Richard Hurd, 7 vols. (London, 1788–94; rpt. Hildesheim, 1978–80)
YB	Yale University, Beinecke Library

POPE, WARBURTON AND KNAPTON:
A CHRONOLOGY

1688 Birth of Pope [AP] (May 21), 2 Plough Court, Lombard Street, London.

1696 Birth of John Knapton [JK] (baptized, St. Faith, Apr. 23), London.

1698 Birth of Warburton [WW] (Dec. 24), Newark-on-Trent, Nottinghamshire.

1703 Birth of Paul Knapton (baptized, St. Faith, Jan. 20), London.

1714 WW articled as attorney in East Markham, Notts., for five years.

1717 AP's *Works*, vol. 1.

1719 WW practised law (until 1722).

1723 WW ordained deacon (Dec. 22).

1724 WW's *Miscellaneous Translations, in Prose and Verse.*

1725 AP's 6-vol. ed. of Shakespeare.

1726 Lewis Theobald's *Shakespeare Restored.*

1727 WW criticized AP in letter to Matthew Concanen (Jan. 2); ordained priest (Mar. 1); presented to living of Greaseley, Notts.; *Critical and Philosophical Inquiry*; assisted Samuel Burroughs with *Legal Judicature in Chancery Stated* in dispute with Sir Philip Yorke.

1728 AP's *Dunciad*; WW awarded M.A. on King's visit to Cambridge; presented by Sir Robert Sutton to living of Brant Broughton, Lincolnshire; JK co-published AP's ed. of Shakespeare.

1729 AP's *Dunciad Variorum*; WW began lengthy correspondence with Theobald and attacked AP in three anon. *Daily Journal* articles.

1731 WW began writing *Divine Legation of Moses* (vol. 1, 1738; vol. 2, 1740).

1733 AP published first three epistles of *Essay on Man* (anon.); WW's anon. *Apology for Sir Robert Sutton*, concerning Charitable Corporation scandal.

1734 AP published fourth and last epistle of *Essay on Man*; Theobald's Shakespeare ed., citing WW (dated 1733; 2nd ed., 1741).

1735 AP's *Works*, vol. 2, including *Essay on Man*; WW began to correspond with Sir Thomas Hanmer.

1736 WW's *Alliance between Church and State*; death of James Knapton; Étienne de Silhouette's French prose translation of *Essay on Man*.

1737 First AP-JK imprint, *Letters*; JK acted as arbitrator in Dodsley's dispute with Watson over piracy of AP's *Letters*; Jean Pierre de Crousaz's *Examen* (based on Silhouette translation) attacked AP's *Essay on Man*.

1738 Crousaz's *Commentaire* (based on Du Resnel translation); WW defended AP in *General Evening Post* and wrote first of seven letters defending *Essay on Man* in *History of the Works of the Learned* (Dec.).

1739 AP's first letter to WW (Feb. 2); WW's *Vindication of Mr. Pope's Essay on Man* (dated 1740); Samuel Johnson's *Annotations to Crousaz.*

1740 AP met WW (late Apr.); WW appointed Chaplain to the Prince of Wales; *A Seventh Letter* (end of his letters defending *Essay on Man*).

1741   WW met Ralph Allen; *Divine Legation*, vol. 2; AP recommended JK to
       WW (Nov. 12) upon the death of his bookseller Fletcher Gyles.
1742   *The New Dunciad* with WW's commentary; *A Critical and Philosophical
       Commentary on Mr. Pope's Essay on Man*; 'Supplement to the Translator's
       Preface' in Jervas's translation of *Don Quixote*; Orator Henley's gibes on
       AP and WW began to appear in *Daily Advertiser*; Louis Racine attacked
       Essay on Man in *La religion*, and Chevalier Ramsay mediated between
       them.
1743   AP and WW worked on quarto editions of *Essay on Criticism* and *Essay on
       Man*; AP revised *Dunciad* with WW as editor; Prior Park rift (July).
1744   Colley Cibber's *Another Occasional Letter* (Jan.) attacking AP and WW;
       death of Pope (May 30); WW named literary executor, but Bolingbroke
       left in charge of AP's unpublished MSS; *Patriot King* copies found; WW
       supplied notes for Zachary Grey's edition of *Hudibras*.
1745   First of several small octavo WW eds. of *Essay on Man* published by JK.
1746   WW married Gertrude Tucker (Apr. 25); 'Atossa' portrait released;
       WW preacher of Lincoln's Inn; John Brown's *Essay on Satire* (included in
       WW eds. of AP's *Works*).
1747   'AP'-WW Shakespeare ed. in 8 vols. published by J. and P. Knapton
       (and 11 others); AP's *Ethic Epistles*, WW's anon. *Letter from an Author, to a
       Member of Parliament, concerning Literary Property*; William Mason's
       Musæus mourned the death of AP.
1748   *Epistles to Several Persons* (printed in 1744); WW's 'Editor to the Reader'
       in vol. 4 of Richardson's *Clarissa* (later removed). Attacks on WW's
       Shakespeare ed. included John Upton's *Critical Observations on Shakes-
       peare* (2nd ed.), Thomas Edwards' *Supplement* (rev. as *Canons of Criticism*,
       7th ed. 1765) and Theophilus Cibber's *Serio-Comic Apology*.
1749   *Dunciad*; *Patriot King* controversy began in *LM* (Jan.); WW's *Letter to the
       Editor of the Letters on the Spirit of Patriotism*; Joseph Spence's *Apology for the
       late Mr. Pope*; Bolingbroke/Mallet's anon. *Familiar Epistle to the Most
       Impudent Man Living*; WW began corresponding with Richard Hurd.
1750   WW's *Julian*; Zachary Grey's *Free and Familiar Letter to that Great Refiner of
       Pope and Shakespear*; Christopher Smart's anon. *Horatian Canons of
       Friendship*; William Dodd's anon. *New Book of the Dunciad*.
1751   AP's *Works* in 9 vols., large octavo (1500 sets) published on June 18;
       crown octavo edition (3000 sets) published in October; John G.
       Cooper's *Cursory Remarks*; *Verses Occasioned by Mr. Warburton's Late Edition
       of Mr. Pope's Works*.
1752   AP's *Works*, 9 vols., large octavo (750 sets).
1753   AP's *Works*, 9 vols., crown octavo (2500 sets); *A Familiar Epistle to Mr.
       Warburton from Theophilus Cibber*.
1754   AP's *Works*, 10 vols., pot octavo (3000 sets); WW's *View of Lord
       Bolingbroke's Philosophy*.

1755   WW appointed to a prebend at Durham; death of Paul Knapton (June 12); JK's financial crisis and trade sale (Sept. 25); Andrew Millar became WW's bookseller.

1757   WW appointed Dean of Bristol; Hurd's *Remarks on Mr. David Hume's Essay on the Natural History of Religion*; *A Supplement to the Works of Alexander Pope* printed for Mary Cooper without WW's approval.

1760   WW consecrated Bishop of Gloucester (Jan. 20).

1761   Knapton, Rivington, Johnston and Law trade sale (Sept. 29).

1762   *An Enquiry into the Nature and Origin of Literary Property* (anon. refutation of WW's 1747 *Letter . . . concerning Literary Property*).

1763   WW's speech on John Wilkes' *Essay on Woman* in House of Lords (Nov. 15). *The Castrated Sheet of Sir Thomas Hanmer* accused WW of deception over Shakespeare ed.

1764   Charles Churchill's *Duellist* irked WW; death of Ralph Allen (June 27).

1768   Death of Millar (June 8); succeeded by Thomas Cadell (*d.* 1802).

1769   Owen Ruffhead's *Life of Pope* in quarto ed. of *Works*, 5 vols. (vol. 6, 1807).

1770   Death of John Knapton (Sept. 26; will proved Oct. 6).

1775   Death of WW's only son Ralph Allen from consumption.

1779   Death of Warburton (June 7; will proved in London July 6).

1780   Gertrude Warburton disposed of WW's papers; Hurd bought WW's books.

1788   WW's *Works*, 7 vols., quarto ed. Hurd.

1794   Hurd's *Discourse*, preface to WW's *Works*.

1797   AP's *Works*, 9 vols., ed. Joseph Warton.

TABLE OF CORRESPONDENCE

From:	To:	Date:	Source:
1751			
Warburton	Knapton	14 March [1751?]	BL: Eg. 1954, f.15
John Jortin	Thomas Birch	22 April 1751*a*	*ILH*, 1: 822
Warburton	Thomas Birch	22 April 1751*b*	BL: Add. MS. 4320, f.180
Warburton	William Bowyer	6 May 1751	*LA*, 2: 229
Warburton	William Bowyer	3 June 1751*a*	*LA*, 2: 229
Warburton	[Knapton]	3 June 1751*b*	BL: Eg. 1954, f.19
Warburton	Knapton	19 June 1751	BL: Eg. 1954, f.20
Warburton	[Anon]	27 June 1751	BPL: Ch.G.12.56
Warburton	[John Nourse?]	10 July 1751	FSL: Art Vol. a9, p.128
Warburton	[Knapton]	3 August 1751	BL: Eg. 1954, f.22
Warburton	[Knapton]	13 August 1751	BL: Eg. 1954, f.23
Warburton	[Knapton]	24 August 1751	BL: Eg. 1954, f.25
Warburton	Knapton	31 August 1751	BL: Eg. 1954, f.26
Warburton	[Knapton]	9 September 1751	BL: Eg. 1954, f.29
Warburton	Knapton	[September 1751?]	BL: Eg. 1954, f.28
Warburton	Robert Dodsley	28 September 1751	NAO: M9659, f.15
Knapton	Thomas Birch	1 October 1751	BL: Add. MS. 4312, f.41
Warburton	Knapton	14 October 1751	BL: Eg. 1954, f.31
Warburton	[Knapton]	19 October 1751	BL: Eg. 1954, f.32
Warburton	[Knapton]	1 December 1751	BL: Eg. 1954, f.33
Warburton	Knapton	9 December 1751	BL: Eg. 1954, f.34
Warburton	Knapton	22 December 1751	BL: Eg. 1954, f.37
[Warburton]	Knapton	[late 1751?]	BL: Eg. 1954, f.36
1752			
Warburton	[Thomas Comber]	11 January 1752	BRL: A.L. 2314
Warburton	[William Hogarth]	28 March 1752	BL: Add. MS. 27995, f.7
Warburton	[Knapton]	17 June 1752	BL: Eg. 1954, f.30
Warburton	[Knapton]	6 July 1752	BL: Eg. 1954, f.40
Warburton	[Knapton]	22 July 1752	BL: Eg. 1954, f.41
Warburton	[Knapton]	27 July 1752	BL: Eg. 1954, f.43
Warburton	[Knapton]	3 August 1752	BL: Eg. 1954, f.45
Warburton	[Knapton]	19 August 1752	BL: Eg. 1954, f.47
Warburton	[Knapton]	2 September 1752	BL: Eg. 1954, ff.48–9
Warburton	[Knapton]	8 October 1752	BL: Eg. 1954, ff.50–1
Warburton	[John Nourse?]	14 October 1752	IULL
Warburton	[Knapton]	15 October 1752	BL: Eg. 1954, f.52
Warburton	[Knapton]	26 October 1752	BL: Eg. 1954, f.53
Robert Horsfield	Thomas Birch	7 November 1752	BL: Add. MS. 4310, f.165
Warburton	[Knapton]	4 December 1752	BL: Eg. 1954, f.55
Warburton	[Knapton]	19 December 1752	BL: Eg. 1954, f.56
Warburton	[John Nourse?]	[late 1752?]	HTC: TS 937.3.2 (I: 212
1753			
Warburton	[Sir John Hill]	28 January [1753]	BL: Stowe MS. 155, f.129
Warburton	Philip Yorke	19 March 1753	BL: Add. MS. 35592, f.48
Warburton	[Thomas Pelham-Holles]	21 March 1753	BL: Add. MS. 32731, f.29
Warburton	Knapton	25 April 1753	BL: Eg. 1954, f.58
Warburton	Knapton	6 May 1753	BL: Eg. 1954, f.59

From:	To:	Date:	Source:
Warburton	Paul Knapton	30 May 1753	BL: Eg. 1954, f.60
Warburton	[John Nourse]	[mid-1753?]	PUL: John Wild Autographs, 3: 113
Warburton	[Knapton]	9 June 1753	BL: Eg. 1954, f.62
J. and P. Knapton	Warburton	10 July 1753	BL: Eg. 1954, f.63
Warburton	Knapton	17 July 1753	BL: Eg. 1954, f.64
Warburton	Knapton	28 July 1753	BL: Eg. 1954, f.65
Warburton	Knapton	9 August 1753	BL: Eg. 1954, f.66
Warburton	Knapton	3 September 1753*a*	BL: Eg. 1954, f.67
Warburton	James Leake	3 September 1753*b*	PUL: Robert H. Taylor Collection
Warburton	Knapton	24 September 1753	BL: Eg. 1954, f.69
Warburton	[Knapton]	17 October 1753	BL: Eg. 1954, f.70
Warburton	[Knapton]	22 October 1753	BL: Eg. 1954, f.71
Warburton	[Knapton]	30 December 1753	BL: Eg. 1954, f.72
[Warburton]	[Andrew Millar]	[late December 1753]	BL: Eg. 1959, f.16*v*.

1754

From:	To:	Date:	Source:
Andrew Millar	[Warburton]	1 January 1754	BL: Eg. 1959, f.15
Warburton	Andrew Millar	3 January 1754	BL: Eg. 1959, f.16
Warburton	[Knapton]	7 January 1754	BL: Eg. 1954, f.73
Warburton	[Knapton]	19 January 1754	BL: Eg. 1954, f.74
John Sayer	Warburton	26 January 1754	BL: Eg. 1954, ff.76–7
Warburton	John Sayer	28 January 1754*a*	BL: Eg. 1954, f.78
Warburton	Knapton	28 January 1754*b*	BL: Eg. 1954, f.75
Warburton	Knapton	7 February 1754	BL: Eg. 1954, f.79
Warburton	Knapton	11 February 1754	BL: Eg. 1954, f.80
Warburton	Knapton	16 February 1754	BL: Eg. 1954, f.82
John Sayer	Warburton	22 February 1754	BL: Eg. 1954, ff.85–6
Warburton	[Knapton]	4 March 1754*a*	BL: Eg. 1954, f.84
Warburton	John Sayer	4 March 1754*b*	BL: Eg. 1954, f.87
Warburton	Andrew Millar	20 March 1754	BL: Add. MS. 4320, f.183
Warburton	[Knapton]	1 June 1754	BL: Eg. 1954, f.88
Warburton	[Knapton]	19 June 1754	BL: Eg. 1954, f.89
Warburton	[Knapton]	23 June 1754	BL: Eg. 1954, f.90
Warburton	Knapton	2 July 1754	BL: Eg. 1954, f.92
Warburton	Knapton	28 July 1754	BL: Eg. 1954, f.93
Warburton	[Knapton]	20 August 1754	BL: Eg. 1954, f.97
Warburton	Knapton	25 August 1754	BL: Eg. 1954, ff.95–6
Warburton	[Knapton]	1 September 1754	BL: Eg. 1954, f.98
Warburton	Knapton	7 September 1754	BL: Eg. 1954, f.99
Warburton	[Knapton]	14 September 1754	BL: Eg. 1954, f.100
[William Murray?]	[Warburton]	[late 1754?]	BL: Eg. 1959, ff.31–4
[Warburton]	[Knapton]	[November 1754]	BL: Eg. 1959, f.25
Robert Foulis	[Warburton]	27 November 1754	BL: Eg. 1959, f.17
Ronald Crawfurd	George Ross	28 November 1754	BL: Eg. 1959, ff.23–4
Warburton	[Knapton]	6 December 1754	BL: Eg. 1954, f.102
Robert Foulis	[William Murray]	20 December 1754	BL: Eg. 1959, f.20
William Murray	[Warburton]	28 December 1754	BL: Eg. 1959, f.18
Warburton	[Knapton]	30 December 1754	BL: Eg. 1954, f.104

From:	To:	Date:	Source:
1755			
Warburton	Knapton	12 January 1755	BL: Eg. 1954, ff.105–06
Warburton	[Knapton]	18 January 1755	BL: Eg. 1954, f.107
[Anon]	[Anon]	[early 1755?]	BL: Eg. 1959, f.22
Warburton	[John Nourse]	11 August 1755	YB: Osborn Files, fc 76/2
William Bowyer	Knapton	20 September 1755	*LA*, 2: 278–9
Warburton	Richard Hurd	24 September 1755	FSL: Y.c.1451 (4)
Warburton	[Henry Lintot?]	31 October 1755	BL: Eg. 1959, f.27
Warburton	Joseph Atwell	9 December 1755	BL: Eg. 1955, f.34
Warburton	[Knapton]	[December 1755?]	BL: Eg. 1954, ff.3–4
Warburton	[Knapton]	[December 1755?]	BL: Eg. 1954, f.5
Warburton	[Knapton]	[December 1755?]	BL: Eg. 1954, ff.6–7
Warburton	Robert Dodsley	26 December 1755	EUL: La.II.153
Warburton	[Anon]	28 December 1755	FSL: Y.c.1451 (9)
1756–1759			
Robert Dodsley	[Warburton]	[*c*. 6 January 1756]	HCS
Robert Dodsley	[Warburton]	6 January [1756]	HCS
Warburton	John Nourse	15 March 1756	UMUL
Warburton	[John Nourse?]	5 May 1756	YB: Osborn Files
Warburton	[Mercy Doddridge]	6 May 1756	PML
R. and A. Foulis	Andrew Millar	25 September 1756	EUL: Dc.4.102
Warburton	Andrew Millar	7 February 1757	*SUP*, pp.309–10
Warburton	John Nourse	9 September 1758	BRL: A.L.2312
Warburton	John Nourse	14 December 1758	YB: Osborn Files
Warburton	[Mercy Doddridge]	8 March 1759	HSP: Dreer Collection
Warburton	David Garrick	[*c*. 2 April 1759]	FSL: W.b.114
Warburton	(memorandum)	18 May 1759	BL: Eg. 1959, f.29*v*.
1760–1765			
Warburton	[Samuel Richardson?]	26 January 1760	FSL: W.b.474
Warburton	David Garrick	7 March 1760	*PCDG*, 1: 115–16
Laurence Sterne	Warburton	9 June 1760	*LLS*, p.112
Warburton	[Laurence Sterne]	15 June 1760	FSL: W.b. 481, p.149
Warburton	David Garrick	16 June 1760	*PCDG*, 1: 117
Laurence Sterne	Warburton	19 June 1760	*LLS*, pp.115–16
Warburton	Laurence Sterne	26 June 1760	*LLS*, pp.118–19
Warburton	[John Nourse]	2 October 1760	FSL: Art. Vol. a10, p.25
Warburton	[A bookseller]	29 January 1761	*European Magazine*, 24: 2
Warburton	John Nourse	8 June 1761	HSP: Dreer Collection
Warburton	Richard Hurd	27 December 1761	*LLEP*, pp.246–7
Warburton	[Thomas Newton]	17 April 1762	PML
Warburton	Thomas Becket	9 May 1762	HSP: Gratz Collection
Warburton	[John Nourse]	28 July 1762	YB: Osborn Files
Warburton	[Sir Edward Littleton]	15 May 1763	FSL: W.a.57 (3)
Warburton	Ralph Allen	16 November 1763	*SUP*, pp.224–7
Warburton	Ralph Allen	17 November 1763	*SUP*, pp.227–31
Warburton	Ralph Allen	26 November 1763	BRL: A.L. 367
Warburton	Ralph Allen	1 December 1763	YB: Osborn Files
Warburton	[James Harris]	16 February 1765	YB: Osborn Files
Warburton	John Nourse	25 May 1765	BL: Add. MS. 12113, ff.

From:	*To*:	*Date*:	*Source*:
1766–1780			
Warburton	[John Nourse]	1 May 1766	YB: Osborn Files
Jonathan Toup	John Nourse	24 October 1766	EUL: La.II.646, 255
Warburton	[John Nourse]	16 December 1766	YB: Osborn Files
Warburton	[John Nourse]	30 November 1767	HSP: Gratz Collection
George Lyttelton	Warburton	20 January 1768	LWL
Warburton	[Isaac H. Browne]	7 February 1768	CTCL: MS. R.4.57[27]
Warburton	John Nourse	24 May 1768	PML
Warburton	[Charles Bathurst?]	22 December 1768	PML
[Charles Bathurst?]	(memorandum)	*c.* 22 December 1768	PML
Warburton	[Richard Hurd]	23 September 1769	FSL: Y.c.1451 (5)
Warburton	[Jeremiah Milles?]	9 July 1770	LWL
Warburton	[Thomas Cadell?]	24 October 1770	GRO: D1361/2
Warburton	William Mason	24 January 1771	FSL: Y.c.1451 (6)
Warburton	Thomas Cadell	1772	FSL: Y.c.1451 (1)
Warburton	Gosling & Clive	22 December 1772	NLS: MS. 968, f.74
David Garrick	Warburton	21 April 1774	FSL: Y.c.2600 (181)
Warburton	[A bookseller]	23 January 1775	OB: MS. Montagu d. 10, f.282
Warburton	Catherine Malet	23 July 1777	BL: Eg. 1960, ff.11–12
Gertrude Warburton	[Richard Hurd]	3 May 1780	HC: Hurd MS. 16, ff.10–11

INTRODUCTION

THE LETTERS

This edition of book-trade correspondence grew from an interest in the relationship between Alexander Pope (1688–1744), his editor William Warburton (1698–1779) and their London bookseller John Knapton (1696–1770). Pope liked to form 'triumvirates', as he had done with Swift and Bolingbroke, and his last major one was formed with Knapton and Warburton.[1] The culmination of this triumvirate's efforts was the 1751 edition of *The Works of Alexander Pope Esq.*, edited by Warburton and published by John Knapton.[2] Warburton's extant correspondence with Knapton starts in 1747, continues through the first five posthumous editions of Pope's *Works* (1751–4) and ends with the near-failing of the Knapton business in 1755. Other letters coinciding with and overlapping the Warburton-Knapton correspondence have been added to shed light on the book trade at a time of change. In an era of uncertainty over copyright legislation, Warburton and Knapton had to consider carefully the problems of Scottish reprints and translation rights. My overall intention has been to explore a hitherto unexamined relationship between an editor and his bookseller and to give a broader impression of Warburton as an editor, a book buyer and an author in his own right. Warburton's letters shed light on the preparation, publication and reception of one of the most important, controversial and lucrative editions of the mid-eighteenth century.

The publication of Warburton's correspondence in *Literary Anecdotes* shocked one pious reviewer into wishing that John Nichols 'had swept these letters into the fire, as soon as they reached his shop'.[3] Francis Kilvert's *A Selection from Unpublished Papers of the Right Reverend William Warburton* met with a more favourable response from Robert Chalmers in 1841.[4] In 1863, John Selby Watson noted a regret 'that none of Warburton's letters to Pope have been preserved'.[5] Mark Pattison posed a series of questions in his long review of Watson's *Life of William Warburton*:

Warburton's own letters are understood to have been almost all destroyed by his widow. One cannot help asking, Where are those which were not destroyed? Where are the letters of Warburton's correspondents? Where are the papers from which Mr. Kilvert printed a 'Selection' in 1841? and where are the collections which Mr. James Crossley has been many years making? No *subsidia* from these sources are to be found in the present biography.[6]

This edition goes some way towards answering Pattison's questions, although tracing the provenance of many manuscripts, or proving the destruction of others, has been impossible. Like George Sherburn's edition of *The Correspondence of Alexander Pope*,[7] this gathering of letters derives for the most part from the Egerton Manuscripts in the British Library.

During the period of Warburton's correspondence with Knapton, the publishing of Pope's works was at a peak. Between February 1745 and February 1748, William Bowyer printed 5,000 copies of *An Essay on Man*, and the 10,750 sets making up the five Warburton editions of Pope's *Works* published between 1751 and 1754 comprise almost 100,000 single volumes.[8] After his death, Pope kept a small but complex industry thriving; the main recipient of this correspondence was at the heart of the British book trade. Warburton's letters to Knapton tell us, for example, that Somerset Draper (a close friend of Garrick) was expected to deliver the copy for the 1747 Shakespeare edition, that Andrew Millar visited Prior Park (perhaps with an offer to buy a share of Pope's *Works*), and that Nathaniel Cole, who once helped Pope settle a copyright dispute, occasionally browsed in Knapton's Ludgate Street bookshop.

Like Pope, Warburton was the first editor of his own correspondence.[9] The 1751 edition of Pope's *Works* contained twenty-five letters from Pope to his editor. Sherburn increased that number to sixty-six (thirty-seven of which were published for the first time), but found only one letter from Warburton to Pope. This is a disappointing rate of survival given that so many of Warburton's letters to others remain. Robert M. Ryley has estimated, 'Of the roughly 1,000 Warburton letters that have survived, about 600 have found their way into print in eighteen scattered sources, where they are inadequately annotated, often carelessly printed, and sometimes expurgated.'[10] At least thirty libraries and repositories around the world hold Warburton manuscripts.

This present edition represents approximately one-tenth of Warburton's extant correspondence. Of the 189 letters that follow, 159 were written by Warburton and 30 were written by others: Charles Bathurst (1); Bolingbroke (1); William Bowyer (1); Ronald Crawfurd (1); Robert Dodsley (2); Henry Etough (1); Robert Foulis (2); Robert and Andrew Foulis (1); David Garrick (1); Robert Horsfield (1); John Jortin (1); John Knapton (2); John and Paul Knapton (1); George Lyttelton (2); David Mallet (1); Andrew Millar (1); William Murray (2); Samuel Richardson (1); John Sayer (2); Laurence Sterne (2); Jonathan Toup (1); Gertrude Warburton (1); and anonymous (1).

Recipients include: a bookseller (2); Ralph Allen (4); Joseph Atwell (1); Charles Bathurst (1); Thomas Becket (1); Thomas Birch (4); William Bowyer (12); John Brown (1); Isaac Hawkins Browne (1); Thomas Cadell (2); Catharine Cockburn (1); Thomas Comber (1);

Mercy Doddridge (2); Philip Doddridge (1); Robert Dodsley (3); Henry Etough (2); David Garrick (3); Gosling & Clive (1); James Harris (1); John Hill (1); William Hogarth (1); Richard Hurd (4); John Knapton (75); Paul Knapton (1); James Leake (1); Henry Lintot (1); Sir Edward Littleton (1); Catherine Malet (1); David Mallet (1); William Mason (1); Andrew Millar (5); Jeremiah Milles (1); William Murray (1); the Duke of Newcastle (1); Thomas Newton (1); John Nourse (19); Samuel Richardson (2); George Ross (1); John Sayer (2); Laurence Sterne (2); Warburton (16); Philip Yorke (1); anonymous (3); and memoranda (2).[11]

One hundred and sixty-two letters have been transcribed from manuscripts; twenty-six have been taken from printed sources (the manuscripts having either eluded discovery or vanished entirely); and one from a facsimile. Nichols, for one, used many of Warburton's letters, some of which survive, but others may have been lost in his fire of 1808. Most of the manuscript letters presented here have never been printed in full, although several biographers and scholars have made use of those in the Egerton Manuscripts.[12]

As Pope's editor and a controversial author, Warburton would have been aware that his letters too might one day become publishable, even valuable.[13] Pope had effectively managed to get his own letters into print in 1737. And while Knapton kept his letters from Warburton (presumably they were returned for Owen Ruffhead's *Life of Pope*, 1769), Warburton apparently did not keep Knapton's replies. Only one item – a receipt dated 10 July 1753 from John and Paul Knapton to Warburton – remains of the scores of letters that must have been sent, many of which are referred to by Warburton. As with the Pope-Warburton correspondence, letters of the dominant personality in the relationship survive: Warburton's seventy-three letters to John Knapton (and one to Paul Knapton) in the present edition. Warburton's correspondence offers an outsider's view of the complex world of the eighteenth-century book trade, 'embracing a vast range of interlocking activity: from type-founders and paper-makers to hack authors, from prosperous business men to destitute entrepreneurs, and from complicated commercial structures to low-key personal operations.'[14]

According to one collector, an early edition of Warburton's letters was much in demand:

I take it for granted, you have got Bp Hurd's volume of Warburton's letters, which I read with great avidity some months ago. There were but 250 of the quarto edition, which had been printed in 1793 or 1794 under Bp Hurd's immediate inspection; they were of course very quickly bought up, so quickly that the Queen could not purchase the book, and the Archbishop of Canterbury, finding that to be the case, very gallantly presented his own copy to her majesty. —— Cadell and Davies took care that the market should be soon supplied, by having a large impression of an octavo edition ready to follow the other in succession.[15]

So wrote Thomas Percy to Edmond Malone on 21 March 1809 in an age when such a correspondence might sell out before the Queen could obtain a copy. G. S. Rousseau put Warburton in the same class of letter-writers as Gay and Arbuthnot, a grouping which suggests Warburton might be considered belatedly as a Scriblerian in view of his involvement in the final form of the *Dunciad*.[16] The essential businesslike nature of this correspondence – what Pope liked to call 'the dull duty of an Editor'[17] – seems to have subdued Warburton's verbal flair, although he did, on one or two occasions, make an attempt to enliven his letters. With the Earl of Sandwich, he allegedly engaged in word-play: 'Orthodoxy is my doxy; heterodoxy is another man's doxy.'[18] While Warburton held Knapton in high esteem, his letters show that he could be a demanding author and a petulant editor.

Without Pope's impetus the following correspondence would not have begun. When Warburton's bookseller Fletcher Gyles died on 8 November 1741, Pope was quick to advise his editor that of all the London booksellers, 'I know none who is so worthy, & has so good a title in that Character to succeed him, as Mr Knapton' and repeated his recommendation in his next letter (4: 370, 373).[19] Charles Bathurst expressed an interest in gaining this new author, but he was too late. Initially reticent, Knapton finally yielded to Pope's encouragement and became Warburton's bookseller. Thus began the association out of which emerged the first, 'complete', uniform edition of Pope's *Works*.[20] Although Pope and Warburton had prepared many of the works for a definitive edition, the poet's death left many matters still to be put in order. First and foremost was what he referred to (with a deferential use of upper- and lower-case letters) as 'the Great Edition of my things with your Notes' (4: 491). To this end, he actively engaged Warburton's services from September 1741. It took ten years to publish 'the Great Edition'.

POPE AND WARBURTON

The repercussions of *An Essay on Man* in Europe were responsible for creating the debt Pope felt he owed Warburton. Had Jean Pierre de Crousaz, a professor of mathematics and philosophy in Lausanne, not taken offence at the Abbé du Resnel's French verse translation of *An Essay on Man* (which had been preceded by Étienne de Silhouette's 1736 prose translation), Warburton might not have found his *métier* as a vindicator. Pope first wrote to Warburton on 2 February 1739, thanking

him for his 'Animadversion on Mr Crousaz' (4: 163). Fifteen months
elapsed between first letter and first meeting. During this time
Warburton continued his *Vindication of Mr. Pope's Essay on Man* and Pope
actively supported him (4: 361). Their introduction took place on or
about 26 April 1740 in Lord Radnor's garden, near Pope's Twickenham
villa. 'Let us meet', Pope wrote, 'like Men who have been many years
acquainted with each other, & whose Friendship is not to begin, but
Continue... I insist on my making You the first Visit' (4: 233). Pope
even offered to put his waterman at Warburton's disposal. According to
Joseph Warton, 'Dodsley was present; and was, he told me, astonished
at the high compliments paid him [Warburton] by Pope as he
approached him.'[21] There can be no doubt that their first meeting was
favourable. Although he thwarted Pope's attempts to ply him with
lobster and Cyprus wine, Warburton received invitations to dine with
Oxford, Bathurst and Lyttelton within a fortnight.[22] From Twickenham, Warburton wrote to his friend Charles Yorke at Cambridge that
he was filled with the 'strains of rapturous commendation'. Returning to
his home at Brant Broughton by way of Cambridge, he followed up the
success of his first visit by attempting to engage Christopher Smart as
translator for a Latin *Essay on Man* (4: 252). Pope continued to write
letters of unrestrained praise: 'You Understand my Work better than I
do myself' (4: 288). By August 1741, Pope was seeking preferment for
Warburton.

What Pope knew at their first meeting of Warburton's earlier alliance
with Matthew Concanen and Lewis Theobald is not certain, but had
Warburton cut a more prominent figure a dozen years earlier, he might
well have been pilloried in the 1728 *Dunciad*. On 2 January 1727, at a
time when Pope's edition of Shakespeare provided a butt for their
zealous editorial humour, Warburton wrote to Concanen, 'Dryden I
observe borrowed for want of leisure, and Pope for want of genius.'[23]
Warburton must have regretted committing such a slur to paper,
although Pope never set eyes on it. Still, there was a more solid
indication of Warburton's earlier views in print. If Pope's memory failed
him, Colley Cibber reminded the world:

that the very Person, who had so judiciously assisted Mr. *Tibbald* in his Edition
of *Shakespear* (wherein the idle Guesses and Errors of Mr. *Pope*, in the same
Undertaking, are so justly exposed and refuted) should now, almost in the same
Breath, blow Hot and Cold, and enter into so unexpected an Alliance with Mr.
Pope, whose Labours he had so unluckily disgraced![24]

Pope may well have come across Warburton's name for the first time in
Theobald's *Shakespeare* edition (1733/4) – the logical extension of his

attack on Pope in *Shakespeare Restored* (1726). As a collector of tirades printed about himself, Pope must have winced upon reading:

In this miserably mangled Condition is this Passage exhibited in the first *Folio*. All the Editions since have left out the last Couplet of it; I presume, as too hard for them. Mr. *Pope*, who pretends to have collated the first *Folio*, should have spar'd us the Lines, at least, in their Corruption. —— I communicated my Doubts upon this Passage to my Friend Mr. *Warburton*; and to his Sagacity I owe, in good part, the Correction of it.[25]

Warburton's first patron, Sir Robert Sutton, had fallen victim to Pope's satire. In the wake of the 1732 Charitable Corporation scandal, Warburton published a defence of Sutton, whose 'meeker air' and '*small Neglects*' Pope played upon in *An Epistle to Bathurst* (1733) and *Dialogue I* (1738). Warburton's one extant letter to the poet raised this delicate subject; and Pope agreed to change these lines. This gesture was one of many in recognition of Warburton's unsolicited defence of *An Essay on Man*, a poem he had supposedly earlier condemned before his Newark literary club.[26] Yet Warburton's *Vindication of Mr. Pope's Essay on Man* won Pope's esteem. Samuel Johnson found nothing unusual in Warburton's apparent volte-face:

The arrogance of Warburton excited against him every artifice of offence, and therefore it may be supposed that his union with Pope was censured as hypocritical inconstancy; but surely to think differently at different times of poetical merit may be easily allowed. Such opinions are often admitted and dismissed without nice examination. Who is there that has not found reason for changing his mind about questions of greater importance?[27]

Perhaps Warburton's change of allegiance was all the more valuable to Pope: he had won over a potential Dunce, a convert.

Pope's first public acknowledgement of his alliance with Warburton appeared in a notice on the verso of the 1743 *Dunciad* title-page, and the initials 'W.W.' were given at the foot of the 'Advertisement to the Reader' which explained the transformation of the central figure from Theobald to Cibber. Warburton had encouraged Pope to revise the *Dunciad*, but his role was hardly as crucial as readers may have been led to believe. On 27 November 1742, Pope wrote of his editorial stratagem:

A Project has arisen in my head to make you in some measure the Editor of this new Edit. of the Dunc. if you have no scruple of owning some of the *Graver Notes* which are now added to those of Mr Cleland & Dr Arb... I have scratched out a sort of *Avis au Lecteur*, which I'l send you to this effect, which if you disapprove not, you'l make your own. (4: 427–8)

Warburton might have wished his début as Pope's editor otherwise. Pope's announcement to his readership of his new editor, later confirmed in his will, was to bring Warburton into the kind of controversial mud-slinging which Pope had experienced much of his life. Whether Warburton welcomed this role, he nonetheless adopted it. The decision was to change his life and career in many remarkable ways.

Pope's relationship with Warburton was tested on a number of occasions; and not all of Pope's circle were taken with Warburton. Marchmont declared that, 'it is manifest from your close connexion with your new commentator you want to show posterity what an exquisite poet you are, and what a quantity of dullness you can carry down on your back without sinking under the load.'[28] When Oxford University offered the poet an honorary degree in August 1741, but decided against awarding one to his editor, Pope declared his loyalty: 'I will be Doctor'd with you, or not at all' (4: 357), turning down an honour few Roman Catholics could expect. Five weeks later, on 20 September 1741, Pope reminded Warburton of this gesture of solidarity in the context of a growing weariness from revising the *Dunciad* and preparing his *Works*:

> If I can prevail on myself to complete the Dunciad, it will be publishd at the Same time with a General Edition of all my Verses (for Poems I will not call them) and I hope Your Friendship to me will be then as well known, as my being an Author, & go down together to Posterity; I mean to as much of posterity as poor Moderns can reach to, where the Commentator (as usual) will lend a Crutch to the weak Poet to help him to limp a little further than he could on his own Feet. We shall take our Degree together in Fame, whatever we do at the University: And I tell you once more, I will not have it, there, without you. (4: 362)

However, shortly before he died, Pope must have felt strong reservations about his choice of editor and literary executor. After a quarrel at Prior Park in the summer of 1743, in which Warburton sided with the Allens against Martha Blount, Pope wrote to her, 'W. is a sneaking Parson, & I told him he flatterd' (4: 464). Yet within a matter of weeks, Pope was back writing to his editor and Allen as if nothing had happened. The rift perhaps strengthened the poet's relationship with his editor; or perhaps Pope felt it was too late to consider another candidate. Whatever resentment may have been felt, Warburton's name remained in Pope's will.

Sherburn's *Correspondence* ends with accounts of Pope's death. Bolingbroke wept at Pope's death-bed, but Warburton was not present. Two days after Pope's death on 30 May 1744, David Mallet conveyed his deep sense of sorrow to the Earl of Orrery:

> At last, my Lord, we have lost that excellent Man! His Person I loved, his Worth I knew, & shall ever cherish his Memory with all the Regard of Esteem, with all the Tenderness of Friendship... It brings the Tears afresh into my Eyes. (4: 523–4)

The sentiments of Bolingbroke and Mallet (who later became Bolingbroke's editor) soon changed with the revelation of Pope's surreptitious printing of *The Idea of a Patriot King*.

Pope's will turned out to be a disappointing document for some. Ralph Allen called him 'a bad accomptant', while Martha Blount, who ostensibly received the lion's share of Pope's fortune, said, 'Everybody thought Mr. Pope worth a great deal more than he left behind him.'[29] In the long run, however, Warburton, who received no actual money from Pope's will, stood to gain the most. Johnson said that the poet left his editor 'a legacy which may be reasonably estimated at four thousand pounds'.[30] The relevant clause in Pope's will read:

I also give and bequeath to the said Mr. Warburton the property of all such of my Works already printed, as he hath written, or shall write Commentaries or Notes upon, and which I have not otherwise disposed of, or alienated; and all the profits which shall arise after my death from such editions as he shall publish without future alterations.[31]

Warburton's legacy was by no means clear-cut. The laws on literary property, as set out in the Copyright Act of 1710, were still unsettled in the 1750s. Warburton had to contend with issues such as translation rights with John Sayer, and Scottish publication with Robert Foulis. As John Feather has observed:

The Scottish courts had never been entirely happy in dealing with copyright cases. A number of such cases had been heard in the Court of Session in the 1750s and 1760s, but no coherent body of practice had emerged. In general the Scots judges had ruled against perpetual copyright, because there was an underlying feeling that Scots law did not recognise the existence of copyright at all. The problem was that the Roman basis of Scots law did not admit of the concept of 'incorporeal' property: to be a legal entity, a property had to have real, or physical, existence. Thus, although a book or a manuscript was certainly a piece of property, Scots lawyers were generally very doubtful whether the same could be said of the text.[32]

Warburton's control extended to choosing which booksellers could have a share in Pope's copyright. He also decided on matters of format, titles and the 'cuts' or illustrations – including the frontispiece which accentuated Warburton's image at the expense of Pope's.[33] But Warburton's principal labours were the sedentary activities of proofreading the poet's text as well as furnishing the prefatory Advertisement and all editorial annotation under five headings – 'variations', 'imitations', 'commentary', 'notes' and 'remarks'. There is little distinction between Warburton's three kinds of textual notes: the 'commentary' was essentially a spliced essay; the 'notes' varied from Pope's brief references to Warburton's slices of longer commentaries; and the 'remarks' were the equivalent of 'notes' in the *Dunciad*. Above all, the clause in the will seems to have stressed that Warburton was not to do what Pope had done to Bolingbroke's *The Idea of a Patriot King*: launder, alter or in any way attempt to 'improve' the text. Nothing, however, prevented Warburton from padding his edition with extraneous matter like Brown's 'Essay on Satire' and retaining Parnell's imitation of Donne's third satire along with a note suggesting Pope would have done a better job on it had he found the time.

Pope understood more than most the vicissitudes of editing. In October 1718, he inherited the literary estate of his friend, Thomas Parnell, 'almost with his dying Breath' and performed his duties discreetly: 'What he gave me to publish, was but a small part of what he left behind him, but it was the best, and I will not make it worse by enlarging it' (2: 24). For his edition of Parnell's *Poems on Several Occasions*, which appeared without a preface or annotation in 1722, he was paid £15. Pope's name appeared on the title-page, but apart from the dedication, list of errata and index, his presence was undetectable. As he intimated to John Caryll, the business of collating, proof-reading and setting points 'exactly right' took its toll on creativity:

I must again sincerely protest to you, that I have wholly given over scribbling, at least any thing of my own, but am become, by due gradation of dulness, from a poet a translator, and from a translator, a mere editor. (2: 140)

Pope learned early that the views contained in a controversial work could be imputed to its editor: his edition of Buckingham's *Works*, published on 24 January 1723, was suppressed within a matter of days. Had he not edited Shakespeare, Pope might never have written the *Dunciad*. The amount he was paid, £217 12*s*. (*LA*, 5: 597), must have seemed hardly commensurate with the attack he later suffered. As the first writer to earn a successful living from the sale of his books, Pope left behind an estate valued at roughly £4000. At the time of his death, editing remained a highly sensitive occupation. For his edition of Samuel Butler's *Hudibras* (1744), in which Warburton assisted, Zachary Grey was 'ridiculed and attacked for deigning to edit a modern author in such a manner, not least by Warburton and Fielding; but on the other hand it was reported that he earned no less than £1,500 from the work.'[34] By 1775, Thomas Newton had earned £735 for editing Milton's *Paradise Lost* and *Paradise Regain'd*. Warburton's profits from the first five posthumous *Works* rose to £2626 0*s*. 9*d*. Yet, his wealth was hard won.

Warburton's literary reputation has been rising and falling ever since Pope named him as his editor. A 'pachydermatous defender' of 'illimitable pugnacity', a 'feeble-jointed and knock-kneed giant' were some of Sir Leslie Stephen's well-peppered descriptions of Warburton.[35]

In the 1932 edition of *The Oxford Companion to English Literature*, Sir Paul Harvey concluded his entry on Warburton, 'He was a bad scholar, a literary bully, and a man of untrustworthy character.' George S. Fraser went so far as to describe Warburton as 'loathsome' and 'in some ways the evil genius of Pope's last years'.[36] When F. W. Bateson considered the odd transformation of titles from *Epistles to Several Persons* to *Moral Essays* in the 1751 edition, he declared, 'Indeed for Warburton the editor there is almost nothing to be said.' Much of his editorial duty, Bateson thought, was 'to relieve the poems as far as possible from the load of Warburtonian incrustation' (*TE*, 3.ii: xv; xvi). At least one satirical analogy has circulated involving a chimney-sweep riding a white horse: 'Ah! Warburton on Shakespeare.'[37] However, several scholars have offered more sympathetic opinions of Pope's editor.[38] His works have recently been published in French, prompting Jacques Derrida to ask, '*Comment lire*, ici, *Warburton?*'[39]

Like all polemical writers, Warburton fell in and out of favour with major and minor literary figures of his day. At Warburton's consecration his learning was praised by Thomas Newton. In the privacy of a letter, Henry Fielding once told James Harris:

We have here the *great* Warburton, Who resides at Mr Allen's, but sometimes visits Leake's where he harangued yesterday near two Hours: His Reading and Memory seem both very extraordinary, and his Knowledge of Things seems as extensive as Young's of Words. As to the rest, Pride, Arrogance, Self Sufficiency and some other such Ecclesiastical Qualities compose his Character.[40]

Yet, in spite of this unflattering impression, Harris later sent Warburton a copy of his *Hermes*. In *Tom Jones* Fielding praised Warburton in the same company as George Lyttelton, to whom the novel was dedicated, and Ralph Allen, who served as the model for Squire Allworthy. Private and public judgements, like literary reputations, are subject to change.

Samuel Johnson is another case in point. Johnson, who had played a part in the *Essay on Man* controversy by translating and annotating Crousaz's *Commentary* in 1739, bowed to Warburton's superior reading in his interview with George III, although at a different time he also admitted, 'The worst of Warburton is, that he has a rage for saying something, when there's nothing to be said.'[41] In an entry for Saturday 21 August 1773, shortly after hearing the great lexicographer recite Macbeth's speech upon meeting the three witches, Boswell recorded a conversation between Johnson and Monboddo:

JOHNSON. 'Learning has decreased in England, because learning will not do so much for a man as formerly. There are other ways of getting preferment. Few bishops are now made for their learning. To be a bishop, a man must be learned in a learned age, factious in a factious age; but always of eminence. Warburton is an exception; though his learning alone did not raise him. He was first an antagonist to Pope, and helped Theobald to publish his *Shakspeare*; but, seeing Pope the rising man, when Crousaz attacked his *Essay on Man*, for some faults which it has, and some which it has not, Warburton defended it in the *Review* of that time. This brought him acquainted with Pope, and he gained his friendship. Pope introduced him to Allen, Allen married him to his niece: so, by Allen's interest and his own, he was made a bishop. But then his learning was the *sine qua non*: he knew how to make the most of it; but I do not find by any dishonest means.' MONBODDO. 'He is a great man.' JOHNSON. 'Yes; he has great knowledge, great power of mind. Hardly any man brings greater variety of learning to bear upon his point.'[42]

Yet Pope's choice of Warburton over other prospective editors has baffled many critics since 1744. Several members of Pope's circle – John Gay, Thomas Dancastle, the younger Jonathan Richardson – had served occasionally as editorial assistants or amanuenses. Spence might have been a more likely choice, but perhaps Pope (like Johnson, who once expressed an unfavourable opinion of Spence) thought his scholarship fell short of the mark.[43] Pope may have felt a sense of betrayal when Bolingbroke, the dedicatee of *An Essay on Man*, left for France at the same time as Warburton defended the poem against the charge of deism.

Within a short span of time, Pope decided that Warburton could be trusted to fulfil his wishes that his works be given an enduring form. Yet can Pope have been so blind as to misjudge Warburton? The answer probably lies somewhere in the *Essay on Man* controversy in the late 1730s. When the two Crousaz attacks – the *Examen* followed by the *Commentaire* – threatened the reputation of the *Essay on Man* in London late in 1738, Pope's confidence in the poem he had regarded as the foundation of his 'opus magnum' was shaken. Although both translated attacks – Elizabeth Carter's *Examination* and Samuel Johnson's *Commentary* which vied with Charles Forman's – were covertly sympathetic towards the poet, Pope perhaps felt he had been misled by his mentor, Lord Bolingbroke. The *Essay on Man* controversy coincided with a prolonged barrage of criticism of his satires.[44] Whatever artistic paranoia he may have then been experiencing, Pope was more than grateful when an anonymous writer rose to his defence in December 1738 in the *History of the Works of the Learned*, from whose publisher, Jacob Robinson, Pope probably discovered Warburton's name.[45] Within a year, Pope was able to distribute copies of *A Vindication of Mr. Pope's Essay on Man, from the Misrepresentations of Mr. Crousaz* to Ralph Allen and Henry Brooke (the latter called Warburton 'the Newton of your system').[46]

Pope's personal acquaintance with Warburton lasted little more than four years – from late April 1740 up until the time of his death on 30 May 1744. Throughout this association Warburton held a living at Brant Broughton near Newark in Nottinghamshire, where he lived with his mother and sisters: if he had moved to London, there might not have been a need for a correspondence between the two men.

Up until this time Warburton's career as a man of letters had been undistinguished. His first book, *Miscellaneous Translations, in Prose and Verse: from Roman poets, orators, and historians* (London: printed for Anthony Barker, and sold by G. Strahan, A. Bettesworth and J. Isted, 1724 [1723]; rpt. W. Reeve, 1745) proved embarrassing in its faulty Latin dedication to Sir Robert Sutton. Warburton's second book, *A Critical and Philosophical Enquiry into the Causes of Prodigies and Miracles* (London: Thomas Corbett, 1727) contained 'an audacious plagiarism' of *Areopagitica*; Warburton was later forced to buy back the copyright from Edmund Curll.[47] In the late 1720s Warburton sent three anonymous anti-Pope letters to the *Daily Journal* and swapped sneering comments with Lewis Theobald about Pope's Shakespeare edition. Before defending Pope's *Essay on Man*, Warburton had evidently been one of that poem's harshest critics.[48] As literary history has ironically witnessed, Warburton was instrumental in prodding Pope to revise the *Dunciad*, which installed Cibber in Theobald's place.

Pope's involvement in Warburton's *Vindication* is hinted at in his first known letter to his future editor where he parenthetically suggests '... much might be said on the article of the Passions in the Second Book' (4: 164). Soon after Warburton's third letter was published in *The History of the Works of the Learned*, Pope responded enthusiastically: 'I know I meant just what you explain, but I did not explain my own meaning so well as you: You understand me as well as I do myself, but you express me better than I could express myself' (4: 171–2). In this second letter, Pope's eagerness was obvious: 'I cannot but wish these Letters were put together in a book, & intend (with your leave) to procure a Translation of part at least of them into French.' Two steps ahead, Pope not only wanted Warburton's *Vindication* published in book form in Britain, he wanted his French translator Étienne de Silhouette to relay Warburton's message to Crousaz on the continent. Between compliments ran a remarkable degree of enterprise. Warburton's initial willingness to participate in Pope's publishing manoeuvres must have been a deciding factor in Pope's later choice of him as editor. By May 1739, Pope felt sufficiently at ease with this Anglican clergyman to describe 'The Dissipation in which I am obliged to live' (4: 182). Pope was now taking an active interest in Warburton's *Vindication*, proof-reading the letters, making suggestions as to their arrangement and asking Warburton, as diplomatically as possible, to curb his habit of 'too great Complaisance' towards himself. With an ironic gift of prophecy, Pope prayed: 'May that Independency, Charity & Competency attend you, which sets a Good Priest above a Bishop, & truly makes his Fortune, that is his Happiness...'

One is ineluctably drawn back to the curious chemistry which brought Pope and Warburton together and kept these two men of such diverse characters, temperaments and backgrounds from falling out after their first discord. The desire to lend one another sorts of immortality was an obvious motive. The law of attracting opposites may well pertain here. Perhaps Pope felt Warburton was the only suitable, or the most efficient, candidate for the job of assembling his literary effects into a lasting form. Maynard Mack and Robert M. Ryley have modified some of the harsher interpretations of their friendship which adjudged it mercenary,[49] but any psychological 'reading' of their relationship must be approached with caution, treated tentatively, and regarded ultimately as incomplete.

The main narrative available is epistolary, hence fragmented, and an interpretation of Pope's relationship with Warburton through their correspondence will be subject to such difficulties as hiatus (non-extant letters), imbalance (more of Pope's letters have been preserved than Warburton's), irretrievable conversations and tonal inference (is the writer sneering behind his pen or is he serious?). It is difficult for the modern reader to gauge mid-eighteenth-century manners, customs of hospitality, forms of patronage, and hyperbolic adulation. Judging the tone of correspondence presents obvious problems: when Pope wrote, 'W. is a sneaking Parson, & I told him he flatterd', was he expressing an honest opinion or attempting to appease Martha Blount after the unpleasant episode at Prior Park? When Warburton added his note to the 1751 *To a Lady* (*Works*, 3: 193) which states that '*no one character in it was drawn from the life*', he was following Pope's request to maintain a sense of anonymity, although Bateson conjectured that Warburton stressed the point 'partly to deprive Martha Blount (his principal rival in Pope's affections) of literary glory; and partly to propitiate Mrs Allen, whose niece Warburton had married and who had quarrelled with Martha.'[50]

We will never know exactly why Pope chose Warburton to be his editor, but some inferences can be made on the basis of the external realities of their situation. Pope, acutely aware (especially after 1740) of the prospect of death, needed someone to tend his works: the job was vacant. He had tried to exert control over every aspect of his publishing life, even to the extent of setting up his own printers and booksellers, but his dealings with John Wright and Lawton Gilliver proved troublesome. An editor might act as a buffer – or, to use Maynard Mack's metaphor, 'breakwater' – against the distracting exigencies of publishing. Warburton had defended Pope at a time when no-one else seemed inclined to help him out. Pope's gratitude survived the Oxford degree test and the temporary breach at Prior Park in the summer of 1743. Warburton's defection from the Theobald camp might have counted in his favour. Pope had at least one excellent reason to curtail his association with Warburton: Martha Blount disliked him. Perhaps Pope thought that if he dismissed his defender, Warburton might retract his vindication, causing the poet an even greater problem.

On the positive side, Warburton possessed qualities which Pope must have admired: his devotion to his mother, his polemical candour, and his prodigious memory. His book orders to Knapton, John Nourse, Thomas Becket and Thomas Cadell suggest he maintained his voracious appetite for reading until late in life. Warburton came into the limelight just as Bolingbroke was leaving for France; Pope naively hoped to bring his two mentors together, but they were to become locked in dispute after Pope's death.[51] There is a sense of self-effacement which shines through in Pope's diminutive 'my things' in contrast to Warburton's commanding 'Notes'; beyond both the poet and his editor stood the imposing 'Great Edition'. Hard-working, ten years younger, full of the flattery of upward mobility, Warburton satisfied Pope's requirements for being the inheritor and editor of his works. The final truth is that Pope regarded Warburton as the best candidate for the job, and against much adversity, Warburton fulfilled his obligation. Pope's faith in Warburton was not unfounded. Warburton had to abandon the completion of his own 'opus magnum', *The Divine Legation of Moses*. While George III remarked to Johnson during their conversation of February 1767, 'that Pope made Warburton a Bishop', editing Pope made Warburton a small fortune and many enemies.

BACKGROUND OF THE 1751 *WORKS*

Pope's legacy to the man who rose to his defence during the *Essay on Man* controversy proved to be a mixed blessing. From the moment he became Pope's editor, Warburton found himself besieged from various quarters for the rest of his life. Warburton's success – he died a far wealthier man than Pope – provoked considerable envy. 'Orator' Henley (1692–1756) made a number of barbs at Pope and Warburton in the *Daily Advertiser* announcements: 'Alliance of Church and State, i.e. Pope and W – – b – – n; and Scheme for a Funeral Sermon on the Death of Mr. Pope's Reputation' (4 September 1742); 'Mr. P* and W*b*n married?' (31 December 1743) and 'Friend P*pe's Funeral Sermon, the fifth Dunciad' (9 June 1744). Henley claimed that Pope had promised to remove satirical references to himself, but the 1749 edition of the *Dunciad* went ahead without the desired changes and, in spite of Henley's protests, his 'gilt tub' remained in the *Works*. Within a month of Pope's death, *Discord* (Foxon D326) appeared in the form of a poetical dialogue, with Warburton unctuously awaiting Pope's last effort. In 1745 *The Review* (Foxon R171) asked, 'Has Friendship not bedawb'd Pope's brilliant Page?' In March 1750, the *Gentleman's Magazine* printed 'A Simile' in three verses, comparing Warburton to 'a muzzel'd Bear' who had been 'teaz'd to death' (20: 135).

By 1751 – the last full year of the Julian calendar – there were few signs that augured well for the public reception of Warburton's edition of Pope's *Works*. Recent publications attacking Warburton far outnumbered those sympathetic towards him, especially in the wake of the resounding condemnation of his Shakespeare edition in 1747 and the *Patriot King* controversy of 1749. As an editor of Shakespeare, Warburton shared much the same fate as Pope did twenty-two years earlier. While Warburton was paid £500 for his labours by Tonson,[52] the edition fared poorly in the market-place: listed originally at £2 8s. in 1747, it was being sold off at eighteen shillings within a year. Had his Shakespeare edition been more favourably received, the 1751 *Works* might have been introduced and edited differently. In spite of its shortcomings, Warburton's Shakespeare edition has had its uses.[53] At least Warburton was not so entrenched that he overlooked Samuel Johnson's early work on *Macbeth*.

One note in Pope's *Works* (1751), to the *Epistle to Arbuthnot* (line 169), summed up Warburton's response to a mountain of criticism against his Shakespeare edition:

Our Poet had the full pleasure of this amusement soon after the publication of his *Shakespear*. Nor has his Friend been less entertained since the appearance of his edition of the same poet. The liquid *Amber* of whose Wit has lately licked up, and enrolled such a quantity of these *Insects*, and of tribes so grotesque and various, as would have puzzled *Reaumur* to give names to. Two or three of them it may not be amiss to preserve and keep alive. Such as the Rev. Mr. *J. Upton, Thomas Edwards*, Esq. and, to make up the Triumvirate, their learned Coadjutor, that very respectable personage, Mr. THEOPHILUS CIBBER. (4: 23)

Warburton took exception to John Upton's *Critical Observations on Shakespeare* (London: G. Hawkins, 1746) in the preface to his 1747 edition of Shakespeare, whereupon Upton (1707–60) added a preface to the second edition of *Critical Observations* in 1748 in which he expressed his astonishment at Warburton's edition: '*He has* launched forth on the immense ocean of criticism with no compass or card to direct his little skiff. . . *yet all this fig-leave covering will but the more serve to discover the nakedness of the commentator to the discerning eye of the real Critic*' (p.xlvi). Warburton, unlike Upton, had not attended university, hence his credentials as a scholarly editor were called into question.

Warburton replied with a derogatory note in the 1749 *Dunciad* (pp.28–9 n.; book 4, lines 237–8) which he cancelled in the 1751 edition, although Upton's name (described as 'a Renegado Scholiast, writes notes on the FIRE-SIDE') remained in the index. Warburton decided to substitute Upton's name for that of Aristarchus in a note that had been published under Pope's supervision in 1743 (*Works*, 1751, 5: 295 n.). Such a change stretched the 'without future alterations' clause in Pope's will, signifying a lack of distinction between annotating Shakespeare and Pope: the critic of one might be answered in the other, as though critical apparatuses were interchangeable. Warburton consigned his enemies to damning epithets in the footnotes to Pope's works.

Like Upton, Thomas Edwards (1699–1757) earned an unfavourable mention in the 1749 *Dunciad* notes (book 4, line 568) and was subsequently attacked in three different footnotes in the 1751 Pope edition.[54] His reason for being mocked by Warburton as 'Fungoso of Lincoln's Inn' was his anonymous *A Supplement to Mr. Warburton's Edition of Shakespear*, published by Mary Cooper in 1748, which, revised as *The Canons of Criticism* and now published by Charles Bathurst, ran to a third edition by 1750 and a seventh by 1765. Edwards had corresponded with Pope concerning minerals for his grotto (4: 342, 349, 351–2) and challenged Warburton's knowledge of Greek at Prior Park. Under the initials T.E., he wrote *A Letter to the Author of a late Epistolary Dissertation addressed to Mr. Warburton* in 1744. Their rift coincided with Warburton's falling out of favour with Samuel Richardson and Edwards' elevation to the novelist's circle. Signed 'By another Gentleman of Lincoln's Inn', *The Canons of Criticism* enumerated the errors committed by Warburton, reducing them to satirical principles. In the seventh edition Edwards added a sonnet, which began 'Tongue-doughty Pedant' and bade Warburton stop writing commentaries: 'Much hast thou written – more than will be read.' Another was addressed directly 'To the Editor of Mr. POPE's Works', casting Warburton as one 'Whom impious *Lauder* blushes to accuse'.

The last member of the triumvirate who criticised Warburton's Shakespeare was Theophilus Cibber (1703–58). He briefly slighted the edition in *A Serio-Comic Apology* which was appended to his revamping of *Romeo and Juliet* (London: C. Corbett and G. Woodfall, 1748). Cibber later returned to attack Warburton's Pope edition in much the same way as Edwards treated his Shakespeare: by examining Warburton's commentaries under a critical microscope. Cibber's scrutiny of Warburton's notes in *A Familiar Epistle to Mr. Warburton* (London: R. Griffiths, 1753), prefixed to *The Lives and Characters of the most Eminent Actors and*

Actresses, revealed many editorial inconsistencies, although the serious nature of his verbal criticism was undercut by his satirical hyperbole. Still, Cibber compiled a considerable number of examples of Warburton's idiosyncrasies, especially in notes where he pointed out Pope's apparent shortcomings. Of all the critics of Warburton's Pope edition, Cibber was the only one to devote space to an examination of Warburton's commentaries. Textual evidence gave Cibber's case all the more force and may actually have had some effect: in the following year, 1754, many of Warburton's notes were dropped from the pot octavo edition of Pope's *Works*.

Warburton later revised his triumvirate in the *Epistle to Arbuthnot* footnote, replacing Upton with Zachary Grey, and in 1770 upset the balance by adding Edward Capell whose edition of Shakespeare had come out two years earlier. Grey had previously acknowledged Warburton's help in his edition of *Hudibras* (Cambridge: printed by J. Bentham for W. Innys, A. Ward, J. and P. Knapton *et al.*, 1744), but upbraided Warburton anonymously in *A Word or Two of Advice to William Warburton* (London: printed for J.L. and sold by J. Fuller, R. Baldwin and Co., 1746), *An Answer to Certain Passages in Mr. W – – 's Preface to his Edition of Shakespear* (London: H. Carpenter, 1748) and *A Free and Familiar Letter to that Great Refiner of Pope and Shakespear* (London: G. Jones, 1750), after Warburton had dismissed Grey's editorial efforts as 'so execrable a heap of nonsense'.[55] Grey later briefly referred to Warburton in the preface to his two-volume *Critical, Historical, and Explanatory Notes on Shakespeare* (London: R. Manby, 1754) and proceeded to ignore his edition. 1749 was possibly the worst year for Pope's editor. Although Bolingbroke was armed with the story of Pope's apparent treachery over the surreptitious printing of *The Idea of a Patriot King*, he had remained silent, concerned that Warburton would cast him in a bad light in his projected life of Pope. Lyttelton interceded with Warburton, pointing out the danger of offending Pope's friends. Yet early in 1749, the disaster Lyttelton and others had hoped to avert happened: Pope's surreptitious printing of *The Idea of a Patriot King* was revealed in the January number of the *London Magazine* which carried 'Of the Private Life of a Prince'. Further instalments were printed in the March and April issues. Three pamphlets in support of Pope were advertised in the May issue of the *Gentleman's Magazine*: *A Letter to Lord V. B ——* ; Joseph Spence's *Apology for the late Mr. Pope*; and Warburton's anonymous *A Letter to the Editor of the Letters on the Spirit of Patriotism, &c.* In the same month the *London Magazine* printed an announcement of Bolingbroke's forthcoming authorized edition. The new *Monthly Review* devoted a thirteen-page spread to the *Spirit of Patriotism* and promised more in later issues. Warburton's *Letter* was counter-attacked by another anonymous pamphlet, *To the Author of a Libel, entitled, A Letter to the Editor, &c.* (London: W. Webb, 1749) which asked, 'Whether you [Warburton] are a wrangling *Wapping* Attorney, a pedantic pretender to Criticism, an impudent paradoxical Priest, or an Animal yet stranger, an heterogenous Medley of all three (as your farraginous Stile seems to confess) there are few, I believe, would trouble themselves to determine, had you confined your Insolence to your own stercoracious Rank' (p.1). By far the most vicious attack against Warburton on this pamphlet battlefield was *A Familiar Epistle to the Most Impudent Man Living* which condemned his edition of Pope's *Works* two years before its publication.

In the 'Advertisement' to the authorized edition of *The Idea of a Patriot King*, Bolingbroke and his editor David Mallet, struck deeply at Pope's integrity, leaving Warburton in an awkward defensive position:

You signalized yourself by affecting to be the Bully of Mr. *P.*'s Memory, into whose acquaintance, at the latter End of the poor Man's life, you was introduced by your nauseous Flattery; and whose admirable Writings you are about to publish, with Commentaries worthy of Scriblerus himself; for we may judge of them beforehand, by the Specimens we have already seen of your Skill in Criticism.[56]

The *Patriot King* scandal had, on the face of it, nothing to do with Warburton as an editor, but because it struck the most devastating blow to Pope's reputation, Warburton had to attempt some form of damage control – which was not his strongest point. Pope would have made his editor's task much easier had he simply asked the printer John Wright to destroy the impression, but his last months were crowded with other preparations.

Several other critics tackled Warburton: John Gilbert Cooper in *The Life of Socrates* in 1749 and *Cursory Remarks on Mr. Warburton's New Edition of Mr. Pope's Works* in 1751; Christopher Smart (under the pseudonym of Ebenezer Pentweazle) feebly rebuked Warburton in *The Horatian Canons of Friendship* (1750); William Dodd published a parody, complete with rhyming couplets and mock-Warburtonian annotation, called *A New Book of the Dunciad: occasion'd by Mr. Warburton's new edition* (1749–50), in which Warburton took Cibber's throne.

In the midst of Warburton's Shakespeare and *Patriot King* controversies, Fielding paid tribute to Pope's editor in his burlesque of Juvenal's *Sixth Satire*, *A Journey from this World to the Next* and, more importantly, in the invocation to Book XIII of *Tom Jones* where the novelist asked the goddess of Learning to 'give me a-while that key to all thy treasures, which to thy Warburton thou hast entrusted.'[57] The popularity of *Tom Jones* (10,000 sets sold in 1749) must have whetted the public appetite for a new Pope edition. Warburton repaid the favour in the 1751 footnotes by reworking a note from his preface to volume 4 of the 1748 edition of Samuel Richardson's *Clarissa* which Richardson decided to drop from the second edition of 1749. Warburton replaced Richardson's name with Fielding's as the novelist who brought 'Amatory' fiction 'to its perfection' (*Works*, 4: 169 n., 'Epistle to Augustus', line 146). Here was another example of Warburton's indiscriminate transference of notes between one edition and another.

From the printer's point of view, Warburton must have seemed an exasperating customer. The presswork for the 1751 edition was done in the shop of the 'learned printer', William Bowyer II, son of the printer of Pope's 1717 *Works*. Unlike the 1717 and 1735 editions of Pope's *Works*, the printer was not named on the title-page, although Bowyer's ornaments appeared in the 1751 edition. Relations between Bowyer and Warburton gradually deteriorated. Warburton once sent his regards to 'Mrs. Bill', but later criticized standards and demanded that work be done promptly. On 12 December 1748, Warburton complained to Bowyer of the 'miserable work' he was seeing in the printed sheets and asked why Brown's *Essay on Satire* (which was to preface the *Essay on Man* in the third volume) and the Index to the *Dunciad* at the end of the fifth volume were not printed. By 15 September 1750, considerable progress had been made. Warburton wrote to Knapton asking him to 'send me by the Carrier stitched the 8 Vs. of Pope that are printed (the last is in the press) that I may examine the errata &c. and prepare every thing for compleating the Edn.' He also peppered him with questions: 'Pray in what forwardness are the decorations for the vols? Is the little Edn gone to the press? And when you think we shall be ready, & when will it be proper for the publication?' Warburton put a great deal of trust in the printer, allowing him to make editorial decisions without scruple: 'As to that letter of Dr. Arbuthnot to Mr. Pope in Curll's Edition, if you are sure it be genuine, I would have it in; and what else there is there that is genuine and modest' (14 October 1749). Relations with Bowyer were further strained by Warburton's many cancels, corrections and demands for quick delivery of revised sheets to Prior Park. Eventually, Warburton began to send proofs via Knapton. By March 1750, he had seen the first volume of the 1751 *Works* and was waiting to proof-read volumes 3, 4 and 5 which carried most of his notes and commentaries. He complained about being 'very ill used' by not having revised proofs. The next letter was worse: 'Had you *condescended* to do what I desired, which was, to have the first sheet re-composed with speed, the compositor would now have had nothing to do but fall to work on this [*Julian*]'. On 6 May 1751, within six weeks of publication, Warburton wrote to Bowyer in peremptory fashion, telling him to hurry with 'the cancelled leaves, contents, title-pages, &c. And let them be done out of hand, and have Mr. Knapton's final direction about the title-pages directly, and without any more put-offs.' Finally, on June 3, he complained: 'I take it extremely ill of you for not sending me two copies of all the reprinted leaves, prefaces, title-pages, &c. before I left town, as I ordered.' On the same day, June 3, he sent Knapton a list of names for gift sets. Volume 6 was the last to be printed. Once this nine-volume edition was completed and out of the shop, much of the type would have been stored for the second large octavo edition. But before either of these editions was published, Warburton was asking about the small octavo edition (15 September 1750).

Bowyer's ledgers record the various stages of production from June 1748. Like most multi-volume works, the Warburton edition arrived in piecemeal fashion: the final 1480 sets of volumes 3, 4 and 5 were delivered to Knapton on 22 May 1751; the remaining 20 sets arrived on June 5. The next day, 20 sets of volumes 1, 2, 6, 7, 8 and 9 were sent, followed on the tenth by '25 Setts of Vol. 1 & Cancelled Leafs'. The big consignment came the following day: 1474 sets of volumes 6, 7, 8 and 9. Finally on June 19, sixty pairs of the first two volumes with cancelled leaves were delivered to Knapton. Altogether, Bowyer printed 1500 sets of the large octavo edition. Titles in red and black, contents and cancels, which were itemized volume by volume, came to £272 1s. 6d. The printing costs amounted to £1094 10s. 7d.; the wholesale price (or selling price to other booksellers) was £2475, leaving a profit of £1380 9s. 5d.

At least three of the booksellers in the 1751 imprint – Henry Lintot, Jacob and Richard Tonson – had long been known to Pope. An older Jacob Tonson ushered Pope into the world of publishing with the *Miscellanies* in 1709; Bernard Lintot first published *The Rape of the Lock* in 1712; and both had been lampooned in the *Dunciad*. Henry Lintot published Pope's works off and on from 1736 to 1764 and proved troublesome over the copyright to Pope's *Dunciad* in 1755. Somerset Draper, the last name in the imprint, may have been the Draper who delivered a letter to Hugh Bethel in Yorkshire from Pope in 1736 (4: 21). A long-time associate of the Tonsons, Draper handled the accounts of the 1751–4 *Works*. Charles Bathurst, who had once helped Pope find minerals for his grotto, was a silent partner in the 1751 *Works* although his name appeared in the 1752 edition. Bathurst published Swift's *Imitation of the sixth satire of the second book of Horace* (including additions by Pope) with Benjamin Motte (whom he succeeded) and J. and P. Knapton in 1738, and *The Works of Mr. Alexander Pope, in Prose. Vol. II* with the Knaptons and Dodsley in 1741. Bathurst's dealings with Thomas Edwards, whose popular, Warburton-bashing *The Canons of Criticism* he published from 1750, may have had something to do with his initial absence from the Warburton-Pope imprint. However, he received almost £65 when the profits were calculated for the 1751 edition.

Two booksellers who conducted business with Pope later fell out of favour with his editor. Dodsley, who had been set up in business by Pope, helped perpetuate his memory by publishing James Kirkpatrick's *Celeberrimi Popii Tentamen* (1745), a Latin translation of *An Essay on Criticism*, and Mason's *Musaeus* (1747) in praise of the departed poet. When Warburton read John Brown's anonymous *Essay on Satire*, he wrote to Dodsley to find out the author's name, so that he might include it in his edition of Pope's *Works*. Dodsley complied, but was later passed over by Warburton when Knapton was forced to sell off his share in Pope's copyright. Dodsley had published John Gilbert Cooper's *The Life of Socrates* in 1749 and was the silent partner behind Mary Cooper's imprint in *Cursory Remarks on Mr. Warburton's New Edition of Mr. Pope's Works* in 1751, both of which had insulted Warburton.

Mary Cooper, whose name appeared on the 1743 *Dunciad* and whose late husband Thomas appeared in the imprints of several Pope volumes, was relegated to a minor role. Her name appeared as the 'publisher' (i.e. trade publisher) of John Jackson's *Treatise on the Improvements Made in the Art of Criticism. Collected out of the Writings of a Celebrated Hypercritic* (1748), written under the pseudonym of Philocriticus Cantabrigiensis, which concluded by declaring: 'Hence it is demonstrable that those Schools which produced the Scaligers, Casaubons, Bentley, Wasse, Davis, Hody, Mill, and Potter, and many more, could never have produced one Warburton' (p.58). The 1751 *Works* occasioned a number of anonymous, scurrilous responses which were published by Mary Cooper in a 24-page pamphlet, *Verses Occasioned by Mr. Warburton's Late Edition of Mr. Pope's Works*. A favoured tactic was to contrast the beauty of Pope's text with the dross of Warburton's subtext: 'To Dulness sacred POPE a Temple rear'd,/And Warburton with notes the work besmear'd' (p.13). In 1757, Mary Cooper also published *A Supplement to Mr. Pope's Works*, containing *Three Hours after Marriage*, 'Sober Advice from Horace' and other risqué verses, which Warburton chose not to include in his edition: 'The motives for the reverend publisher of his works omitting them, are best known to himself; and which ... he has declined communicating' (v–vi). Curiously, in the same year *Remarks on Mr. David Hume's Essay on the Natural History of Religion: Addressed to the Rev. Dr. Warburton*, by Hurd was printed for M. Cooper. In all, Mary Cooper did well out of both Pope and attacks on his editor.

Not even Warburton knew exactly when his edition of Pope's *Works* would be issued. To Balguy he wrote a week before the expected date, 'Mr. Pope's Works ... will be published on the 1st., 2nd. or 3rd. of June.'[58] Two weeks later, Horace Walpole was still waiting to see what

Warburton would say about 'the famous piece of prose on Lord Hervey, which he formerly suppressed at my uncle's desire'. He wrote to Montagu, 'I am told the edition has waited, because Warburton has cancelled above a hundred sheets, (in which he had inserted notes) since the publication of the *Canons of Criticism*.'[59] A hundred sheets is an exaggeration – the entire nine-volume edition takes up under two hundred sheets. Still, there is ample evidence of late or last-minute changes in the cancelled note on Mallet on the opening page of the *Epistle to Arbuthnot*.[60] In the 1751 Advertisement, Warburton mentioned delaying his edition in order to allow the executors time to sell the 'large impressions' left by Pope at his death. The publication was announced in the June issue of the *London Magazine* under 'Entertainment *and* Poetry': 'The Works of Alexander Pope, Esq; compleat in 9 Vols. 8vo. pr. 2*l.* 2*s.* in Sheets. Knapton.' An advertisement in the *London Evening Post* pins down the publication date to 18 June 1751.[61] Two guineas would have been a substantial outlay for a set of books, although when compared with the cost in 1755 of Johnson's two-volume *Dictionary* at £4. 10*s.*, it was not so staggering a sum. Those too frugal to spend two guineas on their posthumous Pope could save about a third of the cost by waiting until autumn for the small octavo edition priced at twenty-seven shillings. In a letter dated 27 June 1751, Warburton explained the delay, saying that the Pope edition had 'waited for ornaments'.

He no doubt felt the sting of Edwards' *Canons*, especially as it spurred other writers to sharpen their quills. Barely six weeks after the Pope edition was issued, Warburton complained to his bookseller John Knapton, 'If one had one's choice one would wish such execrable papers as the Magazines would meddle only with their own trash. But since they do what they please in this blessed Land of Liberty one had better see them impertinent than scurrelous. The Public is a strange machine, which by fits is as easily wound up by the veriest dunce or idiot as by the best Artist...' (3 August 1751). By the end of the year, Warburton claimed indifference: to Knapton he wrote 'You need not have given your selfe the trouble to send the Pamphlet of Cooper [i.e. John Gilbert Cooper's *Cursory Remarks*], for I have never read any of the trash wrote agt me of several years' (9 December 1751).

THE 1751 FRONTISPIECE, TITLE-PAGE, MOTTO AND ADVERTISEMENT

The 1751 general title-page conveyed a good deal of information for the would-be buyer, combining a sense of definitiveness with the urgency of a poet's last breath (see Plate 2). Facing this, the frontispiece pictorially mirrored the names in the title: medallions of the poet and his editor are

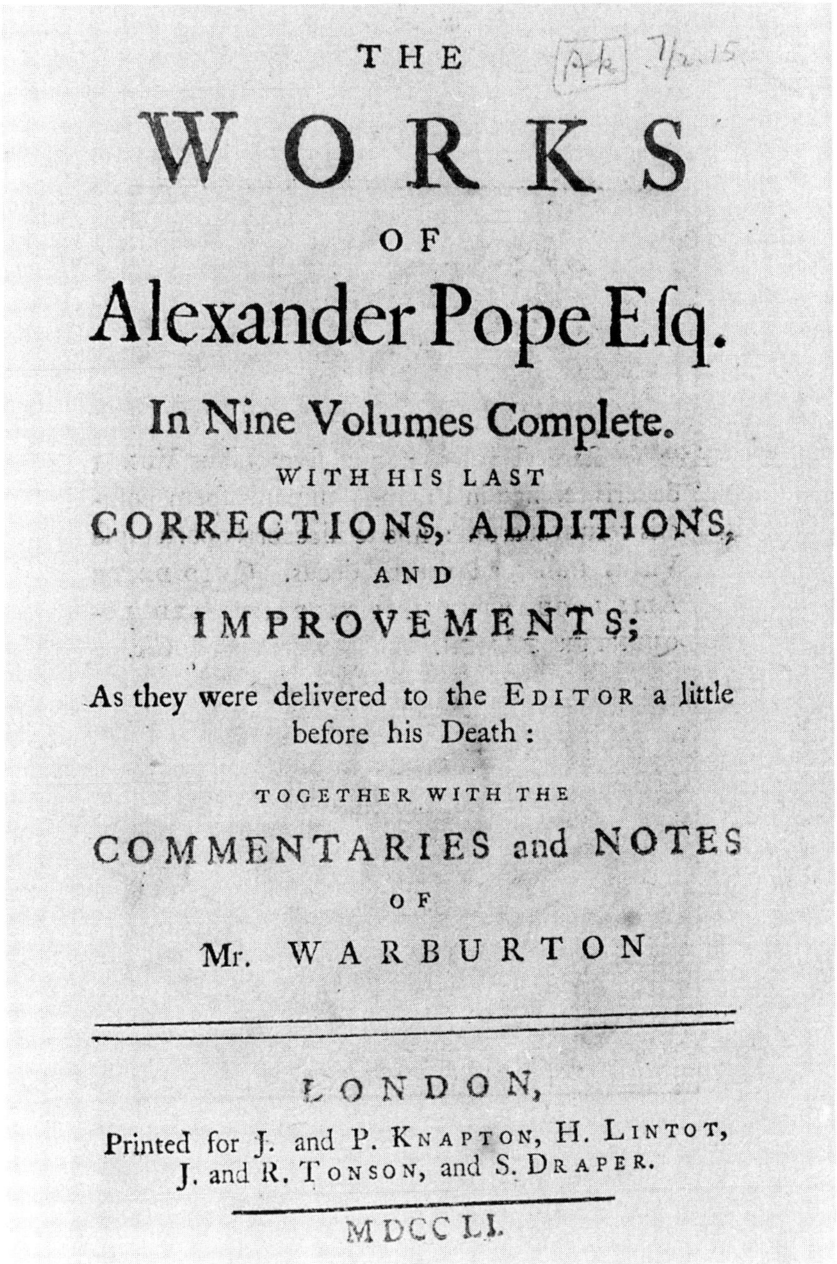

THE

WORKS

OF

Alexander Pope Efq.

In Nine Volumes Complete.

WITH HIS LAST

CORRECTIONS, ADDITIONS,

AND

IMPROVEMENTS;

As they were delivered to the EDITOR a little
before his Death :

TOGETHER WITH THE

COMMENTARIES and NOTES

OF

Mr. WARBURTON

LONDON,

Printed for J. and P. KNAPTON, H. LINTOT,
J. and R. TONSON, and S. DRAPER.

MDCCLI.

Plate 2. General title-page to Pope's *Works*, vol. 1, edited by Warburton (1751).

linked by a putto (see Plate 1). Together, the 1751 title-page and frontispiece form an implicit statement about Warburton's view of his own importance in relation to the Pope edition. Malone recorded one anecdote from the designer Nicholas Blakey:

Mr. Burke, who avowed he knew little of art, though he admired it and knew many of the professors, was acquainted with Blakey the artist, who made the drawing for the frontispiece to Warburton's edition of Pope's works. He told him it was to Warburton's particular desire that he made him the principal figure, and Pope only secondary; and that the light, contrary to the rules of art, goes upward from Warburton to Pope. A gentleman who was present when Mr. B. mentioned this circumstance, remarked that it was observable the poet and his commentator were looking different ways.[62]

Had Warburton felt compelled to justify his glowing presence in such an image, he could have produced one of Pope's letters to his editor:

... You have made my System as clear as I ought to have done & could not. It is indeed the Same System as mine, but illustrated with a Ray of your own, as they say our Natural Body is the same still, when it is Glorifyed. (4: 171; 11 April [1739])

Yet Pope might have been taken aback by a frontispiece which placed Warburton in the central point and made the editor the source of creative light while the poet appeared distinctly shaded.

Plate I was more than likely the last of the 'cuts' or illustrations to be commissioned. In his letter to Knapton of 20 December 1750, Warburton mentioned bumping into Robert Dingley who knew the engraver, Thomas Major: 'I desired that he would use his interest with him to engrave what you think fit to put into his hands with care & expedition.' At this time, volume 6, the last to have been printed of the nine, had just gone through Bowyer's press. 'No Prints have been thought of for this Vol:', Warburton wrote, 'The last two tracts in it are Mr P's Prefaces to his Homer & to his Shakespear. Would not the heads of those two Poets be Proper?' In the end, Hayman and Grignion executed the frontispiece to volume 6 depicting Homer, Shakespeare and Apollo overseeing Pope's efforts, while the task of engraving the new frontispiece fell to Thomas Major. This late commission may have ruffled a few feathers and pushed back the publication of the edition to mid-June (when many book-buyers vacated London for Bath). It may have caused some reshuffling: plate XVII was shifted at a late stage.[63] While Warburton's chance meeting with Dingley led to yet another delay in the return for the booksellers' investment, the Major frontispiece did not escape without comment. John Gilbert Cooper paused to deride it in *Cursory Remarks* (pp.25–6); and Theophilus Cibber made a satirical flourish: 'Behold the Frontispiece! – what a Parade! How modest the Design too! See there poor Pope lifted towards the Skies not by his own Works, but by his Legatee EDITOR ... why did he not call in more Company? – the more the merrier.'[64] The 1751 frontispiece by Major and Blakey was retained in later editions of the *Works*, and by 1770 it had been re-engraved so as to look like a grotesque parody of its former state.

The illustrators of the 1751 *Works* are not now particularly well known, although an extensive study has been made of Francis Hayman who, together with Charles Grignion the elder, executed nine of the twenty-four illustrations: plates XVI-XXIV in volumes 4 (3 illusts.), 5 (5 illusts.) and 6 (1 illust.).[65] Nicholas Blakey was the designer for all eight of the volume 3 illustrations, with Simon François Ravenet as the engraver for five (VIII–XI; XV) and G. Scotin for three (XII–XIV). Plate IX in volume 3 is dated 1748. Of the remaining seven plates in volumes 1 and 2, two are by Samuel Wale and J.S. Müller (II, IV); two are by Wale and C. Mosley (VI, VII); two are by the Yorkshireman Anthony Walker on his own (III, V); and the last is the frontispiece, designed by Blakey and engraved by Major.[66]

In his Advertisement, Warburton apologized for the delay of the edition, although he had been far from indolent: between the time of the poet's death and the publication of the *Works* on 18 June 1751, he had married and become involved in several literary projects in addition to his duties as a clergyman. Seven years does not seem an overlong period in which to bring out a nine-volume edition, but Warburton made apologies in his Advertisement. 'Together with his Works,' Warburton complained, 'he hath bequeathed me his DUNCES' (*Works*, 1: xii) and concluded with a curious statement, 'And though Rome permitted her Slaves to calumniate her best Citizens on the day of Triumph, yet the same petulancy at their Funeral would have been rewarded with execration and a gibbet.' In the 1752 edition, Warburton further alienated his readership by adding a more sarcastic conclusion which began, 'The Public may be malicious: but it is rarely vindictive or ungenerous.' He ended bitterly:

It would abhor these insults on a writer dead, tho' it had born with the ribaldry, or even set the ribalds on work, when he was alive. And in this there was no great harm: for he must have a strange impotency of mind whom such miserable scribler [*sic*] can ruffle. Of all that gross Beotian phalanx who have written scurrilously against me, I know not so much as one whom a writer of reputation would not wish to have as his enemy, or whom a man of honour would not be ashamed to own for his friend. I am indeed but slightly conversant in their works, and know little of the particulars of their defamation. To my Authorship they are heartily welcome. But if any of them have been so abandoned by Truth as to attack my moral character in any instance whatsoever, to all and every one of these, and their abettors, I give the LYE in form, and in the words of honest Father Valerian, MENTIRIS IMPUDEN-TISSIME. (*Works*, 1752, 1: xii–xiii)

Another slight but perhaps telling change in the Warburton edition lay in the choice of mottoes. The title-pages of both the 1717 and 1735 *Works* carried the same motto from Cicero. Translated, this reads:

These studies are an impetus to youth, and a delight to age; they are an adornment to good fortune, refuge and relief in trouble; they enrich private and do not hamper public life; they are with us by night, they are with us on long journeys, they are with us in the depths of the country. (*Pro Archia*, VII.xvi).

This motto obviously meant much to Pope; otherwise he would not have included it in two editions some eighteen years apart. No motto appears on the 1751 general title-page; there was no room for one. However, Warburton chose a motto, again from Cicero, which was printed on the verso of the title-page:

[Therefore,] if you will only look on high [and contemplate this eternal home and resting place,] you will no longer attend to the gossip of the vulgar herd or put your trust in human rewards for your exploits. Virtue herself, by her own charms, should lead you on to true glory. Let what others say of you be their own concern; whatever it is, they will say it in any case. (*De Republica*, VI.xxiii).

This advice from Cicero is ironically apposite in view of the attacks on Warburton's editorial reputation and his inappropriate replies to his critics in the footnotes to the 1751 Pope edition.

OWNERS OF POPE'S WORKS

A list of contemporary owners of the Warburton edition can be compiled from library catalogues, auction records, book plates, private correspondence and guess-work. Warburton sent a list of names for complimentary sets to John Knapton on 3 June 1751. This list has not survived, although in the letter to which it was attached Warburton questioned whether George Arbuthnot, one of Pope's main executors, should have been included. Heading Warburton's list would have been Ralph Allen, William Murray and the two proof-readers, John Jortin and Thomas Birch; Charles Yorke would have been another likely recipient. William Mason, who had asked Warburton if writing poetry might interfere with his intended religious vocation, received a set of the 1751 edition. Warburton's protégé and eventual editor, Hurd, received sets of both the 1751 and 1753 editions, the latter of which has been preserved in the Hartlebury Castle collection. On 30 June 1753, soon after forwarding the crown octavo edition, Warburton wrote to Hurd:

It may be just worth your while to tell you, before I conclude, that the small edition of Pope which I sent you, is the correctest of all; and I was willing you should always see the best of me. (*LLEP*, p.104)

By this time Warburton had taken into account the recent publication of Hurd's Horatian translations dedicated to him. Hurd eagerly acknowledged Warburton's gift in a letter dated 2 July 1753:

...my curiosity had not suffered me to neglect comparing the second edition of Pope in 8vo. with the first, which you gave me. And I had transcribed into it the most material corrections and alterations. But this smaller set is most acceptable to me, both for its being a proof of your kind remembrance of me; and also for the neatness and convenient size of the volume, so proper for that constant pocket use, which such a poet improved by such a critic deserves. (*LLEP*, p.105)

After the complimentary sets were dispatched, the remaining sets would have been left to the Knaptons and their associates to retail and distribute throughout the country. The Warburton edition would have been required reading for the literati of the latter half of the eighteenth century: Spence, Fielding, Johnson and Boswell, Mrs Piozzi, Elizabeth Carter, Horace Walpole, Garrick, the Wartons, to name but a few likely and illustrious buyers.[67] Theophilus Cibber must have had a well-thumbed set. Some sets, like the small octavo 1751 set bearing Adam Smith's book-plate, survive,[68] while others, like William Murray's set (which went up in flames during the mob violence of June 1780), do not.[69] Riding on the success of *Tristram Shandy*, Laurence Sterne wrote to his bookseller, Thomas Becket, from Paris asking him to send a shipment of books including 'All The Works of Pope – the neatest & cheapest Edition – (therefore I suppose not Warburtons)' (*LLS*, p.166 (12 [May] 1762)). When Sterne's library was put up for sale, one of the items listed was the 1754 Warburton edition of Pope's *Works* in ten volumes, priced at sixteen shillings; 1754 was the most stripped of annotation, and least expensive, of the first five Warburton editions.[70] William Shenstone wrote to Lady Luxborough on 25 January 1752, 'I have since glanc'd upon Mr. Warburton's Edition of Pope's Works; which abounds in scurrilities thrown upon his *own* Enemies & in perversions of his Author's Meaning.'[71]

The practical solution for those critical readers most offended with Warburton's edition of Pope was to re-edit the works themselves. Yet Thomas Edwards resisted the suggestion put to him by Samuel Richardson that he should undertake this task; and John Wilkes, although he had his set of Pope's *Works* specially bound with extra leaves for addenda, never got further with his editorial labours than assembling material.[72] The next edition – Warton's – did not appear for almost twenty years after Warburton's death in 1779.

It is perhaps in the nature of editors to sow the seeds of their own future embarrassment. As Warburton once recorded unkind words about Pope, so too did Hurd reflect an unfavourable impression of the man whose works he would later edit: writing to William Mason in June or July 1747, two years before he met Warburton, Hurd offered a 'new Canon of Criticism ... I am just come from the reading of the new Edition of Shakespeare by Mr. Warburton, a Gentleman, you know, in whose company one does not usually pick up much civility.'[73] Warburton rose to the task of defending and editing Pope; Hurd eventually oversaw Warburton's posthumous works and reputation. In many ways, Warburton was the author (and, more to the point, the editor) of his own critical misfortune. His edition of Pope's *Works* was a major achievement which ought not to be judged too harshly by twentieth-century notions of objectivity, but rather should be considered within the context of its time. If, as Pope had declared in the preface to his 1717 *Works*, 'The life of a Wit is a warfare upon earth', so too was the life of his editor.

A monument to book-trade continuity, the 1751 *Works* embodied some of the finest talents in the eighteenth-century publishing world – from the vital spark of the poet's imagination to the craftsmen who set thousands of rhyming couplets in type. Pope's and Warburton's association as poet and editor must have been the first of its kind in literary history: never before had a poet made a successful living from the sale of his own books; and never before had an editor directly inherited a literary estate of such financial consequence. Pope's bequest was to make Warburton a wealthy, but embattled, man. Whatever might be said against him, Pope's editor had to work hard for his legacy.

THE KNAPTONS

John Knapton was born into bookselling. His father, James Knapton, founder of the business, was the son of William Knapton of Brockenhurst, Southampton, Hampshire. James Knapton was bound to Henry Mortlock from 2 August 1680 to 5 September 1687.[74] At the end of his apprenticeship, he opened his first bookshop at the Queen's Head in St. Paul's Churchyard and soon moved to the nearby Crown in 1690,[75] where he remained until shortly before his death on 24 November 1736.[76] His wife Hester bore him twelve children between 1693 and 1709, all of whom were christened at St. Faith under St. Paul, the local parish church.[77] The two Knaptons we are concerned with here were born seven years apart: John, the third child and first son to survive infancy, was baptized on 23 April 1696; and Paul, the eighth child, was baptized on 20 January 1703.

James Knapton became a leading member, second in seniority to Daniel Browne, of the wholesaling conger, a group of about fifteen booksellers which began to exert control over the scattered trade in the 1690s. The wholesaling conger could afford to buy expensive copyrights normally beyond the means of a single bookseller. Sharing ownership also reduced the risk of piracy.[78] In the first decade of the eighteenth century, the name of James Knapton appeared in 265 imprints; and from 1701 to 1776 the Knaptons figured in some 2148 imprints.[79] He was the sole bookseller of such diverse works as Marcus Zuerius Boxhorn's *Arcana imperii detecta: or, divers select cases in government* (1701), William Dampier's *New Voyage round the World* (1703), *Sir Giddy Whim, or, the lucky amour. A comedy* (1703), *Dictionarium sacrum seu religiosum: A dictionary of all religions, ancient and modern,* attributed to Defoe (1704); and an abridgement of Samuel von Pufendorf's *De jure naturae et gentium* (7th ed., 1708). John Dunton characterized James Knapton as a shrewd bookseller with a reputation for sobriety and sound judgement, especially when it came to acquiring copyrights:

He is a very accomplished person; not that thin sort of animal that flutters from Tavern to Playhouse, and back again; all his life made up with wig and cravat, without one dram of thought in his composition; —— but a person made up with sound worth, brave, and generous; and shews, by his purchasing of 'Dampier's Voyages', he knows how to value a good Copy.[80]

Frequent reprinting of works for which no authors' fees had to be paid, such as Edmund Wingate's *Arithmetique Made Easie* (18th ed., J. and P. Knapton and J. Hodges, 1751), was a key to success in publishing. With John Nicholson and Benjamin Tooke, James Knapton published Boccaccio's *Decameron* in English (1702) and built up a number of titles with John Stephens at Oxford (which were printed by Leonard Lichfield III)[81] and with Edmund Jeffery at Cambridge (printed at the University Press). Knapton's most prolific authors of the earlier part of the century were theologians: Edward Wells (whose controversial treatises were gathered in 1707 and supplemented in 1710), Samuel Clarke (a one-time apprentice to Knapton who became the rector of St. James's in Westminster) and Thomas Bennet. Knapton worked in various lines, including historical biographies – David Jones' *Life of James II* (1702) and *The Life of Leopold, late Emperor of Germany* (1706); drama – the sixth edition of Dryden's *Conquest of Granada* (1704) and George Farquhar's *The Inconstant* ([1710?]); and law – *Considerations Touching our Way of Tryal by Juries; and the true difference between murder and manslaughter* ([1702]).

As the member of an oligopoly, James Knapton sought to protect literary property. In 1734, when the Dublin printer, Samuel Powell, printed an edition of Clarke's *Sermons* for the bookseller Stearne Brock, who sent a shipment to London and undercut Knapton's price of £2 by fourteen shillings, Knapton 'was one of those who petitioned the House of Commons for an alteration of the Copyright Act of 8 Anne and appeared before the Committee of the House' (Plomer, p.398). James Knapton's name appeared in the list of subscribers to Pope's six-volume edition of Shakespeare's *Works* (1725). He became the senior member of the Castle Conger when the wholesaling conger began to break up in the 1720s. His name appears in first position in the imprint of at least fourteen books published by the Castle Conger between 1728 and 1737, including Wilford's *Monthly Catalogue* in 1729 and the fifth edition of Bailey's *Universal English Dictionary* in 1731.[82] Knapton was influential in advertising book titles and their prices in the magazines of the day. He also advertised his stock in one out of every ten books he published. McKenzie's *Stationers' Company Apprentices* records that James Knapton was elected Renter Warden in 1710, Under Warden in 1721 and 1722, Upper Warden in 1725 and 1726, and finally Master in 1727 and 1728. During his last guild year as Master, the printer James Bettenham, in May 1728, entered the *Dunciad* in the Stationers' Register.[83]

John Knapton's name first appeared on the title-page of the second edition of William Camden's two-volume *Britannia*, translated by Edmund Gibson (London: J. and J. Knapton, J. Darby, A. Bettesworth, F. Fayram, J. Osborn, T. Longman *et al.*, [1722?]). In the following year, James and John Knapton, with John Clarke, began the third edition of *Miscellanea curiosa: Containing a collection of some of the principal phænomena in nature* in three volumes for the Royal Society of London, printed by William Bowyer (1723–7). An advertisement for books printed for James and John Knapton appeared on the final leaf of George Lavington's *Influence of Church-music* in 1725. James, John and Paul Knapton appeared together for the first time in the imprint to the fourth edition of William Hawney's *The Compleat Measurer* (London: J., J. and P. Knapton, D. Midwinter, A. Bettesworth and C. Hitch, J. Pemberton, R. Ware *et al.*, [1730?]). An advertisement in the *Daily Courant* of 3 January 1735 for *Monuments of Kings of England*, printed for James, John and Paul Knapton, gave their new premises as the Crown in Ludgate Street (Plomer).

Nine apprentices were bound to James Knapton between 1696 and 1738 (the last presumably completed his training under a new master), one of whom was his son, John, whose apprenticeship lasted from 4 February 1712 to 2 March 1719.[84] As the master's son, John did not have to pay for his apprenticeship. In the Inland Revenue apprentice registers, taxes (at a shilling in the pound for premiums over £50) are recorded for five of James Knapton's apprentices, although one name –

that of Paul Knapton – is duplicated under Arthur Bettesworth. Three of James Knapton's apprentices predated the 1709 Act when the tax was levied; no amounts are entered for two others, one having had two previous masters and the other being John Knapton.[85]

Paul Knapton was apprenticed to Bettesworth from 1 May 1721 until 7 March 1728 at a charge of £70. His term overlapped with that of Charles Hitch, who left Bettesworth in 1725; Hitch's name would later follow Knapton's in the imprint of the first edition of Johnson's *Dictionary*. Why John Knapton served under his father, but Paul, nine years later, went to a shop in nearby Paternoster Row might be explained by the fact that James Knapton had taken on an apprentice the year before; or possibly James Knapton, now more affluent, thought his younger son could improve family business by learning the trade in a different shop.

John Knapton remained single, while his brother Paul married Elizabeth Chalwell of Coleman Street at Stevenage in Hertfordshire on St. Valentine's Day 1741.[86] She brought with her an ample dowry of £5000; they had no children. Warburton later called on her advice when he needed to find a new maid for his Bedford Row residence.[87] John Knapton was elected Renter Warden to the Stationers' Company in 1723. He was later elected Under Warden for 1735 and 1736, Upper Warden for 1739 and 1740, and, following in his father's foot-steps, Master for 1742, 1743 and 1744. Paul Knapton seems to have held no position with the Stationers' Company. If Warburton's letters are any indication, Paul had little to do with the day-to-day running of the bookshop. When it came to acting as a go-between for truculent editor and overworked printer, shipping books to Prior Park or Germany, or keeping an eye out for scurrilous satires, John Knapton was the one Warburton addressed. Paul perhaps led a life of moderate luxury and let his brother manage most of the family business.

Pope evidently had a long acquaintance with the Knapton family. George Knapton, who studied under Pope's friend Jonathan Richardson, made an oil painting of Pope after Kneller.[88] James Knapton published the Richardsons' (*père et fils*) *Account of Some of the Statues, Bas-reliefs, Drawings and Pictures in Italy, &c. with Remarks* (1722) and *Explanatory Notes and Remarks on Milton's Paradise Lost* (1734/5). For the latter publication, James Knapton was joined by his two sons in the imprint. Charles Knapton collaborated with Arthur Pond in the *Essay on Man* medallion and on a series of sixty-nine engravings from 1732 to 1736.[89] The Knaptons thus played an integral part not only in publishing Pope's works but also in the creation of his image.

Pope's professional association with James and John Knapton began in 1728 when they headed the imprint of his Shakespeare edition in ten volumes duodecimo. A decade later, on 13 April 1737, Pope wrote to Samuel Buckley to ask 'Mr Knapton to send me word what number of Second Vols. of my Works, Quarto or folio, are in his hands?' (4: 66). Pope was becoming increasingly concerned with the business side of the poet's lot. He had already set up his own printer and bookseller – John Wright and Lawton Gilliver – to print and sell his works from 1729 in an effort to gain more authorial control as well as profits, but their arrangements became strained.[90] Ten years after Pope quarrelled with Bernard Lintot over the *Odyssey* in 1725, he had a falling-out with Gilliver over the equal division of profits between poet and bookseller.[91] Pope, undeterred, helped set up Dodsley as a bookseller with £100. The year 1736 was a period of transition marked by the deaths of Bernard Lintot on February 3 (succeeded in business by his son Henry), of his chief rival, the first Jacob Tonson (who was predeceased by his nephew of the same name), on April 2, and of James Knapton on November 24. It was also the year the New Conger was formed.

Pope thus renewed his dealings with the Knaptons at a time of readjustment. Surveying Pope's publishing career from his 1709 debut in the sixth volume of Tonson's *Miscellanies* up to his 'death-bed' editions, Nicolas Barker concluded, 'Finally, as a sharp contemporary put it, Pope "turned Bookseller to himself, selling all his own Pieces by means of a Publisher, without giving his Bookseller any share of them". The distributor, as we should say, was Thomas Cooper, employed (in fairness to Pope) through Dodsley.'[92] Knapton collaborated with Gilliver, Brindley and Dodsley on two editions of the *Epistles of Horace Imitated*. Curiously, although Dodsley's name appeared on different occasions either independently or in conjunction with Cooper (as distributor) or with Knapton (as co-publisher), Knapton and Cooper never shared the same imprint in Pope's works.[93]

Frequent variations in Pope imprints of the late 1730s coincide with threats and recourse to Chancery over breaches of copyright. Mack has uncovered twenty-two items relating to Dodsley's proceedings against James Watson in Chancery.[94] Gilliver had sued Watson in 1729 over the *Dunciad*, and now Watson printed an octavo edition of the *Letters* under the name of Thomas Johnson. Sherburn noted that Pope wrote to the solicitor to the Stationers' Company, Nathaniel Cole, on the advice of William Murray (4: 87–8). Mack's seventh item in this sequence now positively dates Cole's reply to Pope; and the eleventh item, a letter from Watson to Knapton dated 30 November 1737, pinpoints Sherburn's date of Pope's invitation to Samuel Buckley for a business dinner.[95] Pope also invited Knapton and Cole to dine with him on the following Saturday. If the poet's meeting with his solicitor and bookseller was meant to agitate Watson, it seems to have achieved the desired effect.

Watson's letter to Knapton maintained he had not infringed copyright. The most Pope could 'expect in Equity, is an Injunction'. However, Watson was more than anxious to make an out-of-court settlement, and he wanted Knapton to mediate:

His folio Edition is not the same Book he complains against, and his Octavo was not Enter'd till October 31. last past, which was at least a full Month after the Publication of the Edition complain'd of, and his own first Edition entirely sold before the Octavo was Enter'd. I should be glad, if you could be any Instrument of stopping any further Proceedings in this Affair, and if that Gentleman who claims the Property will yield a little to my Necessities, I will submit a great deal to his supposed Right. You shall have an Account of the Paper, and the Printing is easily computed, and I am willing to deliver everything upon your Determination, if Mr. Pope is willing likewise, that you should be the Arbitrator.[96]

An agreement was reached fairly quickly: Pope dined at Knapton's house in Marsh-gate, now the Sheen Road, on November 29 and by December 1 Watson was arranging to put the books in Knapton's hands 'as soon as they can be press'd and ty'd up'.[97] In the wake of the suit against Watson, Pope no doubt foresaw the sort of copyright problems which his future editor might one day face. Four years later, Pope evidently thought John Knapton was the most capable bookseller to manage Warburton's publications as well as his own literary estate.

Pope probably introduced Warburton to John Knapton in the early days of their friendship. The first work directly connected with Pope's reputation which the Knaptons published was Joseph Spence's anonymous *An Essay on Pope's Odyssey: in which some particular beauties and blemishes of that work are consider'd.*[98] James and John Knapton headed the long list of booksellers on the general title-page to *The Works of Mr. William Shakespear. In ten volumes. Publish'd by Mr. Pope and Dr. Sewell.*[99] A year after his father's death, John Knapton co-published his first book with the poet, the authorized text of the *Letters of Mr. Alexander Pope, and several of his friends* (London: printed by J. Wright for J. Knapton, L. Gilliver, J. Brindley, and R. Dodsley, 1737).

Having proved himself a capable and respected arbitrator in the Watson case, Knapton began to serve as a go-between for Pope and Warburton: 'I shall be obliged to Mr Warburton, if he would read over the Preface & Life of Homer; and if he finds some Objections to any part (as I think he may, especially in the Life) to communicate them to me to be amended: there being a new Edition preparing, in which I would alter any Errors I can' (4: 384 and n.2). Meetings were arranged in hastily written notes: 'we'l go together to Mr Knapton's about ten' (4: 386). Pope invited Knapton to Twickenham on a number of other occasions (4: 285, 417), although no direct correspondence has survived between the two. Pope no doubt had occasion to write to Knapton concerning details of publication as he had done with other booksellers; yet if Knapton kept Warburton's letters, he would have saved Pope's. Pope employed the Knaptons for folio and quarto editions; Dodsley (who shared several of these imprints) may have been groomed for larger projects. The Knaptons had ample experience of handling the myriad details involved in large projects which tied up considerable amounts of capital over a number of years.

The Knapton account with their main printers, the two William Bowyers, stretches from 1725 (when James Knapton was running the business) to 1764 (when John Knapton may have retired). The elder William Bowyer died in 1737, and subsequently 'entries in all three ledgers begin to fall off in quality, and towards the end of the period in quantity as well'.[100] Thus, for the duration of Warburton's editorship, the ledgers, the source of the Knapton account, are neither neatly kept nor exhaustive. Time has taken its toll as well, in the form of fire damage and crumbling.

However, what has survived of Bowyer's ledgers gives us a sufficient idea of the mounting debts which the Knaptons incurred with their printer around the time of the posthumous Pope editions. During the late 1740s Bowyer printed the works of various authors for the Knaptons: Pope and Warburton, obviously, and sermon-writers like Hoadly, Clarke and Sharp. By the early 1750s, Bowyer's printing ledger 'B' begins to show a sharp accumulation of unpaid bills. The Knaptons' account at Gosling's Bank shows a payment of £50 to Bowyer on 15 April 1755, although few other payments were made to Bowyer through the bank. Around this time, the Knaptons were falling behind with their payments to William Strahan for printing Johnson's *Dictionary*. The Knaptons missed their first payment to Strahan and were late on their instalment of £38 on 9 November 1753.[101] By 9 June 1755, just three days before Paul Knapton's death, the Knaptons owed Bowyer the staggering sum of £1470 6s. – more than the Knaptons made in profits from all five Warburton editions of Pope's *Works*.

The Knaptons were part of the original group of booksellers which presented the written agreement to Johnson on 18 June 1746: in exchange for the overall sum of £1575 the lexicographer was to prepare a comprehensive dictionary within three years. Johnson's *Dictionary* was perhaps the Knaptons' swan-song. Its full imprint read: 'London, Printed by W. Strahan, For J. and P. Knapton; T. and T. Longman; C. Hitch and L. Hawes; A. Millar; and R. and J. Dodsley. MDCCLV.' The *Dictionary* was published by 15 April 1755. Nine years after signing the initial agreement, Johnson wrote to Thomas Warton, 'two of our partners are dead'.[102] One was Paul Knapton who died on 12 June 1755;

the other was the first Thomas Longman who died six days later.[103] Shortly after his brother's death, John Knapton faced financial ruin.

Rumours circulated that Bowyer was planning to sue Knapton, which would have ensured his bankruptcy, but Bowyer wrote on 20 September 1755 to assure his old fellow tradesman of his good will, although he declined to act as one of Knapton's trustees. (When the elder William Bowyer's printing-house was destroyed by fire on 30 January 1713, James Knapton contributed three guineas to a relief fund.[104]) Still, the printer had to be paid his outstanding debt or risk facing bankruptcy himself. Warburton, who maintained that he was Knapton's biggest creditor, told Hurd in his letter of 24 September 1755 that Knapton was generally 'thought the richest Bookseller in Town'. After collaborating on five editions of Pope's *Works* with Knapton, Warburton would have been shocked to hear that the publishing house verged on disaster. The Knaptons' account at Gosling's Bank in Fleet Street (now Barclays) shows that they juggled thousands of pounds in credits and debits (as most booksellers did), but their balance rarely rose over £100. Shortly before Paul Knapton died, their debt to Bowyer shot up to £1470 6s. A few days after his death, Gosling's ledger records that two dozen members of the book trade made transactions totalling £475 4s. with Knapton. The account was audited by Gosling who, having been a bookseller, knew the nature of the trade.

Knapton's bank account shows that he escaped the bailiff's reach. As Paul Knapton had died intestate and the creditors preferred to rescue the business rather than force the surviving brother into bankruptcy, a trusteeship, made up of John Knapton, the Longmans, Hitch, Millar and Dodsley, was formed. Bowyer's debt was soon reduced to £1010. The bookshop seems to have remained open, but John Knapton was forced to part with the bulk of his copyrights and stock at a trade sale on 25 September 1755. Knapton's copyrights alone realised more than £4600 (according to the total of the annotations on the catalogue in Appendix B). The money raised by the sale, which was enough to settle the amounts owing to Bowyer and Warburton, helped to alleviate Knapton's financial problems, but at the same time his future in the trade was curtailed. Once he gave up his copyrights, many of which had been acquired by his father, John Knapton in effect ceased to function as a bookseller.

Knapton managed to find his way out of the near-collapse. The trusteeship was dissolved by 23 March 1757. On 4 May 1757 he paid Bowyer £463 in cash and £294 19s. 6d. in notes drawn on several booksellers. The remainder of his debt was paid off at regular intervals. Between 4 November 1757 and 17 November 1758, Knapton gave Bowyer notes worth £245 (plus £7 13s. in cash). Bowyer was thus eventually paid in full and continued to serve as Knapton's printer. Through the patience and good will of his creditors, Knapton recovered. It meant losing his quarter share of Pope's works to Andrew Millar, but his will (in the Public Record Office) suggests that he made enough money to retire in modest comfort.

Without specifying the cause of Knapton's financial upset, Warburton simply told Hurd it was 'a business of years' (24 September 1755). Several factors could have contributed to Knapton's collapse as a copyright-owning bookseller: mismanagement, breakdown in distribution, fraud, inept accounting, overextending capital in too many slow-selling publications, or falling too far behind on printing and storage payments. Perhaps Knapton simply wished, as he approached sixty, to ease into a less complicated, less cluttered, less competitive retirement. Throughout the first half of the eighteenth century, the Knapton imprint was associated with the kind of diversity a modern publisher might emulate: dictionaries, educational texts, fiction, practical guides, historical tomes, medical treatises, new authors like William Mason and Laurence Sterne, extravagant picture books like Birch's *Heads of Illustrious Persons*, philosophy, plays and poetry (large collected editions of Pope and Shakespeare), sermons and travel books. The map of literature and the economic structure of publishing had changed considerably in his time.

When the Ludgate Street bookshop changed hands is not precisely known. Knapton auctioned off more of his stock in 1761 and assigned a one-third share in the copyright of *The Fair Quaker of Deal* to Thomas Loundes for two guineas on 8 April 1761.[105] The bookseller who took over the premises had a trade card made up that read, 'Robert Horsfield in Ludgate Street Successor to Mr. Knapton'.[106] Following the trade sale, Knapton still published the odd play – *Hamlet* in 1756, *The Alchemist* in 1770 – and retained William Mason's *Elfrida* (5th ed., 1757; 6th ed., 1759) and *Caractacus* (3rd ed., with R. and J. Dodsley, and R. Horsfield, in 1760). Editions of Rapin's *History of England* and Nicholas Tindal's *Continuation of Mr. Rapin's History of England* were 'printed by assignment from Mr. Knapton' for a long list of booksellers. In 1776, six years after his death, Knapton's name made its last appearance in the twenty-fourth edition of Nathan Bailey's *Universal Etymological English Dictionary*.

Warburton referred to 'my accts with Mr Knapton, and his selling his share (which was the 3d pt of Pope) to Messrs Tonson & Millar' in a memorandum of 18 May 1759 and in her inventory of 3 May 1780, his widow listed 'Papers fm. Mr. Knapton's Executors & Millar's Account' which have not been traced. Knapton's share in Pope's works was sold privately under Warburton's direction to Millar and Draper. Millar, who had done well by Thomson and Fielding, earned Johnson's commendation: 'I respect Millar, Sir; he has raised the price of literature.'[107] Son of a Paisley clerk, Millar maintained his Scottish connections, co-publishing numerous works with the Foulis press from 1742. In 1756, he purchased paper through Robert and Andrew Foulis for the printing of Pope's works. Between 1756 and 1780, Millar's name appeared on eleven editions of Pope's *Works*, four editions of *An Essay on Man* and a miscellaneous gathering. In spite of Warburton's prejudice against the publication of Bolingbroke's and Hume's works, he too became a Millar author. He had gained a reputation for fighting piracy in the courts: 'if Millar has had redress, I may', Pope wrote to Warburton, pleased at the precedent Millar had set in protecting his rights in *Joseph Andrews* (4: 425). Millar took Robert Taylor to court over a pirated edition of Thomson's *Seasons* and won, but he died before the decision was handed down in 1768. Millar based his success on the economic logic of the market-place: 'Your plain English reader loves his pennyworth for a penny.'[108] Editions published during Millar's proprietorship were accompanied with poor re-engravings of the 1751 illustrations and tended to avoid extravagances of wide margins, large letters and red ink splashed on the title-page. Not until 1769 was the sumptuous quarto edition with Owen Ruffhead's *Life of Pope* published, although its final volume did not arrive until 1807. Millar's apprentice and successor, Thomas Cadell, made his first appearance on a Pope imprint in this edition and collaborated with William Strahan on three *Essays on Man* in the 1770s. The firm of Cadell and Davies continued to publish Pope's and Warburton's works well into the nineteenth century.

NOTES ON THIS EDITION AND PRINCIPLES OF TRANSCRIPTION

Provenance: Most of the following letters and documents have been transcribed from volumes 1954 and 1959 of the Egerton Manuscripts in the British Library, Department of Manuscripts. Egerton 1954 and 1959 were acquired by the British Museum in 1864 in the sale of Egerton Manuscripts 1946 to 1960. These fifteen volumes mainly comprise letters and papers of Pope, Warburton, Hurd and others from 1713 to 1799. Warburton supplied Ruffhead with these manuscripts in preparation for his 1769 *Life of Pope*. On the flyleaf to Egerton 1946, Sir Frederic Madden inscribed, 'The Nos. 1946 to 1960 inclusive, were purchased of the Rev. John Mill Chanter of Ilfracombe, 12 Feby. 1864.' In a letter to Madden dated 3 February 1864, Chanter explained how he came by the manuscripts: Warburton died without an heir; his widow Gertrude married her husband's chaplain, the Rev. Martin Stafford Smith, who inherited the papers. The manuscripts then passed on to Smith's second wife (née Plaisted) who in turn left them to her nearest relative, Miss Hester Wolfustan, of Tamworth Castle in Staffordshire. When Miss Wolfustan died in 1862, the manuscripts passed into the possession of her nephew, Chanter.[109] Other letters have been selected from Additional Manuscripts in the British Library and other libraries, institutions and private owners as listed in the acknowledgements. Previously published letters have been added where they might help fill a gap or contribute to the literary or antiquarian side of Warburton's life.

Selection of Letters: This is by no means a complete edition, even of Warburton's correspondence with booksellers and printers. My first interest in Warburton's letters to Knapton was raised by what they had to say about the background to the publication of Pope's works. Gradually, it became apparent that other letters, relating to printing, publishing, editing or the book trade in general, helped fill in gaps. Hence, this edition comprises a 'book-trade correspondence': many letters concern Pope's works, others give minute details about problems arising out of Warburton's editorship and Knapton's financial stake. A full edition of Warburton's letters must remain a project for future consideration.

What has been selected here will, I hope, give the reader a deeper insight into the decisions involved in the production of the first posthumous Pope edition. Warburton is more often than not criticized for his editorial interference in the Pope canon; yet as Pope's editor he found himself in a position without precedent, one which, while financially rewarding, invited attack from various quarters.

Physical state of manuscripts: In general, Warburton's letters have been fairly well preserved; John Knapton evidently took good care of them. Occasionally where the text has been impaired by mutilation, ink blotting or ravages of time, conjectural matter has been put in square brackets, with a footnote to identify the problem. Warburton's hand can be difficult at times to make out, but it is much easier to read than Andrew Millar's.

Identification: All letters addressed to 'Mr Knapton' are assumed to be directed to John Knapton unless otherwise specified. Warburton's letter of season's greetings on 1 January 1749 concludes, 'All here join with me in our best respects to your selfe & Mr & Mrs Knapton.' Since Paul was married and John remained a bachelor, we may assume this letter was intended for John. Later, when Warburton asks to have Ralph Allen's name put down for two sets of 'Montfalcon's Antiquities of France', we might further assume that John took charge of other book orders. Again, on 22 December 1751, Warburton pays his respects to 'you & Mr & Mrs Knapton' after expressing his intention of forwarding his 'copy' for an edition of his sermons. The only letter addressed specifically to Paul Knapton (30 May 1753) is a request for Mrs Knapton's advice on finding a new servant. Warburton adds, 'Pray tell Mr J. Knapton I recd his favour at Gloucester & was in hopes of receiving a specimen of the little Edn. of Pope.'

As time drew on, the nature of Warburton's and Knapton's relationship changed: Warburton wrote to Knapton as an editor, a polemical writer, a clergyman, a reader, someone in need of honey, of insurance or of a new maid; but in the more important letters, he addressed his bookseller as a friend and adviser, someone who might temper legal opinion on interpretations of copyright with the wisdom of the market-place. Warburton had his own literary career to pursue, and his letters often rake over the dry terrain of the professional author. Some letters help to connect patterns which might otherwise remain completely indiscernible. Bolingbroke, Robert Dodsley, David Mallet, Andrew Millar, William Murray and the 'learned' printer William Bowyer are but a few of the people who knew Pope and wrote about him after his death. Warburton's letters record the editor's executorial management of Pope's literary estate in the fluctuating world of the mid-eighteenth-century book trade.

Arrangement and dating: The order of letters is chronological with one or two slight exceptions. In the case of two letters bearing the same date (or enclosed letters), I have placed them in the order in which the recipient would probably have read them.

In the case of undated letters or ones that have apparently been misplaced by the original archivist, I have given a note of explanation. Most problematic are the three undated letters (Eg. 1954, ff.3–7) which I have shifted to 1755 as they appear to concern Warburton's selling his share at a loss to Knapton's gain.

All dates in headings have been normalized and are given in the New Style, with the new year beginning on January 1 instead of March 25. This correspondence overlaps the great change from the Julian to the Gregorian calendar which necessitated the eleven-day jump ahead in 1752 from Wednesday, September 2, to Thursday, September 14. Warburton alluded to the forthcoming change in calendars in his letter of 19 June 1751 and offered a dual date. The Calendar Bill, which brought England in line with the Continent and Scotland, was brought in by Chesterfield (who once offered to take Warburton to Ireland as his chaplain) and supported by Henry Pelham.

Arrangement of text: No attempt has been made to preserve the lineation of the main body of the letters, although dates, locations, opening and closing salutations, and post-scripts have been set more or less as they appear on the page. Similarly, no notes have been made of when the writer has turned the page to write along the margin. Paragraph indentations have been followed, but their length has been standardized.

Orthography: In an age of verbal criticism, not long after Martinus Scriblerus had satirically belaboured the spelling of 'Dunceiade' in the light of the disputed number of 'e's in 'Shakespeare',[110] Warburton was not the most consistent of spellers. Warburton's spelling is subject to change from one line to the next. I have endeavoured to reproduce all spellings, alternate spellings and misspellings as accurately as possible. The ideal of a standardized spelling eluded him as it did most of his contemporaries. Misspellings (e.g. 'Leak' for 'Leake', the Bath bookseller; '*literrary Propy*' for 'literary property') are given as they appear. *Sic* has been used sparingly, mainly where doubt might arise between what Warburton wrote and my transcription. Warburton's idiosyncrasies as a letter-writer might be of interest to some readers. When, for example, he intends 'thing' but writes 'think', his verbal misfiring may have some philological or psychological significance.

One owner of an early letter from Warburton to Concanen, Mark Akenside, noted its provenance and spelling:

This Letter was found, about the year 1750, by Dr. Gawin Knight, First Librarian to the British Museum, in fitting up a house which he had taken in Crane-court, Fleet-street. The house had, for a long time before, been let in lodgings, and in all probability Concanen had lodged there. The original Letter has been many years in my possession, and is here most exactly copied with its several little peculiarities in grammar, spelling, and punctuation.[111]

When the first letter or part of a word is given, I have on occasion hazarded a guess and filled in the gap using square brackets for the sake of common sense and the reader's convenience.

Punctuation and capitals: All original punctuation and capital letters have been retained. A sentence may begin without a capital and end without punctuation. Occasionally it has been difficult to distinguish between upper- and lower-case letters. In such instances, I have relied on a combination of context and customary practice.

Stylistic idiosyncrasies: These have been preserved wherever possible, but for practical reasons, undotted *i*'s and *j*'s, uncrossed *t*'s, and crossed *d*'s and *l*'s have been normalized.

Diacritical marks and special characters: Diacritical marks, frequently used to denote ordinal number suffixes '-st', '-nd', '-rd', '-th' (e.g. '10^') for '10th') in dates, have been omitted.

Marginalia: These have been kept wherever relevant, or their omission has been noted. Someone – Knapton, Bowyer or their messengers – occasionally used a letter to jot down numbers: these have generally been noted, but not recorded.

Words crossed out, repeated words and other slips of the pen: These have generally been omitted unless they have some special significance, in which case they appear within angle brackets.

Underlining: It has not been possible to reproduce double or triple underlining. All single underlining has been presented in italics; double, triple or multiple underlining has been treated as single underlining. Occasionally, when the writer has underlined only part of a word or title, the underlining has been extended to the full word.

Pound signs: The sign for pounds sterling (£), usually represented in Warburton's hand by a superscript '*l*' or '*ll.*', has been lowered and put in italics to avoid confusion with the footnote number '1'. In the eighteenth century, twelve pence (*d.*) was the equivalent value of one shilling (*s.*); twenty shillings made one pound; and twenty-one shillings (or £1 1*s.*) made a guinea.

Square brackets: These are used in headings to indicate the absence of the name of the sender, recipient, date or address in the manuscript. In many cases the name of the recipient does not appear on the manuscript, although his identity may be assumed from the context of the letter. Square brackets are also used in the text of letters to fill in missing matter or to denote editorial additions.

Questions marks: These indicate difficulty in transcribing the manuscript or when an exact spelling or sense is in doubt. Where there is room for reasonable doubt in headings, a question mark has been added in conjunction with square brackets.

Superscriptions and subscripts: Raised and lowered letters or words have been normalized.

Postmarks, franks and wax seals: Most of Warburton's letters were franked under the name of Ralph Allen, his wife's uncle. Allen was largely responsible for the efficient service between Prior Park and London. Wherever given, addresses, franks and postmarks are noted. Envelopes which are detached, and therefore may not have accompanied the preceding or following letter in the folio, are noted as such. Wax seals have not been noted, although several are still intact.

Manuscript abbreviations and short forms: Like all letter-writers, Warburton used codes to expedite his writing which he expected his recipient to understand. He also often employed initials to denote a person's name. The following is a list of the most commonly used abbreviations and short forms:

B. *or* Ld. B.	(Lord) Bolingbroke
Bp	Bishop
B.R.	Bedford Row [London]
D.L. *or* Div. Leg.	*The Divine Legation of Moses*
Ed. *or* Edn.	edition

G.S.	Grosvenor Square [London]
M.	Andrew Millar; William Mason
P.	Pope
P.P.	Prior Park
Servt.	Servant
solr	solicitor
V. *or* vol.	volume(s)

References: Wherever possible, Pope editions have been identified by their Foxon, Griffith or Gaskell numbers. The *Eighteenth-Century Short Title Catalogue* (ESTC) has also been an invaluable source. As this edition concerns the eighteenth-century book trade, full imprints have generally been given for printed works relating to Pope, Warburton and the Knaptons.

Knapton's Replies: As with the Pope-Warburton letters, the Warburton-Knapton correspondence is virtually one-sided, this time in Warburton's favour. The fate of Knapton's many letters (often referred to by Warburton) is not known. Warburton's widow informed Hurd that 'The poor Bishop himself destroyd numbers of Letters & other papers before his Death', although he spared 'small promiscuous Papers, wch. seem of no Consequence' including 'Papers fm. Mr. Knapton's Executors & Millar's Account' (3 May 1780). What became of Warburton's box of manuscripts itemized by his widow also remains a mystery. According to Kilvert, Gertrude Warburton destroyed a 'vast mass' of his correspondence, although Boyce modified this: 'back in Prior Park in 1780, [she] tried to dispose of Warburton's papers properly, sending bundles to Hurd, to old Lord Mansfield, to Charles Yorke's polite son, and destroying others'.[112] Warburton obviously kept a great number of his letters, but perhaps his bookseller's letters were discarded because he thought they were too inconsequential or, after the 1755 collapse, too embarrassing a reminder of his losses.

One would expect that John Knapton's replies relayed information about business and friendship. As a recipient of Warburton's letters, he might occasionally have felt the sting of peremptory criticism, but he also received the rare compliment. He seems to have shared the contents of at least one of Warburton's letters with their mutual acquaintance Nathaniel Cole.[113] As a prominent London bookseller with hundreds of pressing matters in a day, Knapton probably kept his written messages to Warburton brief. Knapton's letters to Thomas Birch, which survive in the British Library, are short and to the point; his letters to Warburton would no doubt have been similarly concise.

Book Orders: As well as being a writer, editor and subject of books, Warburton was a voracious reader, frequent buyer and eclectic collector. He inherited half of Pope's library in 1744 (after Bolingbroke took back his own books and Martha Blount selected 'three score'). As Pope left the rest of his library to Ralph Allen, the two halves were rejoined when Allen died in 1764. Warburton's book orders to Knapton and John Nourse have been followed up wherever possible. In two of his biggest book orders (5 May 1756 and 25 May 1765), he referred to numbered items in Nourse's catalogues which have eluded discovery and made the task of reconstructing his book purchases difficult. Warburton left his library to the Gloucester Infirmary to be sold off, and Hurd, one of the three trustees of Warburton's will, acquired it.[114]

For their assistance in checking titles, I am grateful to Ben Benedikz, Graham Cartwright and especially to Mary Parsons, the Honorary Archivist of the Hurd Library at Hartlebury Castle.

NOTES TO INTRODUCTION

[1] See his letter to Swift of 28 June 1728 (2: 503) – here and below, when the context is understood, volume and page number in parentheses refer to *The Correspondence of Alexander Pope*, edited by George Sherburn.

[2] The other booksellers who had smaller shares and played a minor role in Pope's *Works* were his brother Paul Knapton, Henry Lintot, Jacob and Richard Tonson, Somerset Draper and (not appearing in the 1751 imprint) Charles Bathurst.

[3] 'Warburton's letters', *The Wesleyan Journal, the Methodist Magazine*, 41 (1818): 35–8, p.35.

[4] In a letter from Claverton Lodge, Bath, dated 8 May 1841, Kilvert replied to Chalmers, 'It is very gratifying to me to find my own estimate of the value & importance of the Papers I have been enabled to give to the world, confirmed by the judgment of one so competent to speak as ex cathedrâ on the subject' (New College Library, Edinburgh: CHA 4.299.36).

[5] John Selby Watson, *The Life of William Warburton, D.D., Lord Bishop of Gloucester, from 1760 to 1779: with Remarks on his Works* (London, 1863), p.189. With one exception, Warburton's undated letter defending Sir Robert Sutton (*WWW*, 1: 143; *Correspondence*, 4: 492–4), the case remains unchanged.

[6] *Essays by the late Mark Pattison*, 2 vols., ed. Henry Nettleship (Oxford, 1889), 2: 119–20. Crossley's transcriptions of Warburton's letters are now to be found at the University of Texas at Austin: 50 letters from Warburton to Robert Taylor, 1728–40; 121 letters from Warburton to Balguy, 1750–76; abstracts of Warburton's correspondence with Balguy, 1750–76; and an abstract of one letter to Balguy's widow. I am grateful to Cathy Henderson of the Harry Ransom Humanities Research Center for this information.

[7] For a recent study of Pope's involvement in the publication of his correspondence, see Wendy L. Jones, *Talking on Paper: Alexander Pope's Letters*, English Literary Studies, no. 50 (Victoria, B.C., 1990).

[8] For the print run of the *Essay on Man*, see Maslen, p.184; for Pope's *Works*, see Appendix A.

[9] Warburton was known to splice letters Pope sent him: Sherburn notes that 'Warburton indulged in this conflation of letters more than once' (4: 234 n.4; e.g., 4: 427–8, cited below).

[10] Ryley, p.91. Warburton's letters have been included in: *WWW* (London, 1788–94; rpt. 1811); *A Discourse by Way of General Preface to the Quarto Edition of Bishop Warburton's Works*, ed. Richard Hurd (London, 1794); *LLEP* (Kidderminster, [1808]; 2nd ed., London, 1809); *Letters to and from the Rev. Philip Doddridge*, ed. Thomas Stedman (Shrewsbury, 1790); *CSR* (London, 1804; rpt. New York, 1966); *Biographical Memoirs of the Late Revd. Joseph Warton, D.D.*, ed. John Wooll (London, 1806); *Letters from the Reverend Dr. Warburton, Bishop of Gloucester, to the Hon. Charles Yorke, from 1752 to 1770* (London, 1812); *LA* (London, 1812–15) and *ILH* (1817–58); *Literary and Miscellaneous Memoirs*, ed. Joseph Cradock (London, 1824); *SUP*, ed. Francis Kilvert (London, 1841); Francis Kilvert, *Memoirs of the Life and Writings of the Right Rev. Richard Hurd* (London, 1860); miscellaneous collections of correspondence such as *Epistolarum Sylloge: or, Elegant Epistles*, book 3 (London, 1790); journals such as the *European Magazine*; biographies by Watson (1863); Evans (1932) and Ryley (1984); editions of Pope's works (from 1751); Sherburn's *Correspondence* (1956); biographies of contemporaries – Boyce; Frederic T. Blanchard, *Fielding the Novelist* (New Haven, 1927); other editions of correspondence – *CSR*, *Dodsley*, *LDG*, *LLS* and *PCDG*; and bibliographical studies – Eddy (see Short Forms and Abbreviations).

[11] The authorship of all but seven letters (noted in the Table of Correspondence and letter headings by square brackets) is clear from the signature or handwriting. However, seventy-eight addressees are not specified in the letter or by a surviving envelope, although in most cases their identity may be divined by context and custom.

[12] For example, early biographers and editors – Owen Ruffhead, Richard Hurd, Samuel Parr, Francis Kilvert and John Selby Watson – have pored over Warburtoniana; and more recently, A. W. Evans, Maynard Mack, Robert M. Ryley and John Feather have referred to the Egerton Manuscripts in their published researches. In *Lewis Theobald and the Editing of Shakespeare* (Oxford, 1990), Peter Seary suggested at the start of chapter 7, 'Theobald's Correspondence with Warburton', that Warburton destroyed his letters to Theobald after they were returned as a result of a quarrel around 4 May 1736, although five stray letters were later reprinted in *ILH*, 2: 634–54 (p.102 n.2).

[13] On 30 August 1798 the Rev. John Oldisworth of Nortonville offered to sell seventeen Warburton letters to John Sewell for twenty pounds and gave a sample transcription:

Sir

The Letters in Question were addressed to the late Revd Mr Sparkes who was many years Master of ye Grammar School at Glocester and Chaplain to the Bp. upon what terms of Friendship, the Letters will sufficiently evince, they were written between ye years 1763 & –69– Seventeen of which are now before me – all I have found out of a Number from other Literary Characters of which hereafter –

The following being very short I'll transcribe – to shew that ye beginning of each was generally on something relating to ecclesiastical business –

P.P. Jany 9 1769[?]

Dear Sir/

I have the favour of yours of the 6 I have enclosed a [Commission?] for Mr Hasting, which I beg the favour of you to execute.

I have inclosed under another cover, some of...

I hear you have had an Earthquake lately: They are good awakening things. One at Westminster might rouse the Constitution, which tho' it never sleeps, yet sometimes slumbers. We have been long lost to the Voice of God: The Voice of Nature may possibly restore us to our Senses.

Dear Sir, ever faithfully
yours
W. Gloucester

I am obliged to hasten – post waits. Twenty Pounds – I presume will not be considered as exorbitant for the whole – if so – I will send you a few more, which will be equally interesting from another Hand – that you may have a proper opinion of me in this transaction, Character &c I can refer you to many whom if I mistake not you know – Dr White, Oxford can advise

yours – in haste
John Oldisworth

direct if you please – to ye Revd J. Oldisworth [YB: Osborn Files].

[14] Michael Harris, 'Periodicals and the Book Trade', *Development of the English Book Trade, 1700–1899*, ed. Robin Myers and Michael Harris (Oxford, 1981), pp.66–89; p.66.

[15] *The Correspondence of Thomas Percy and Edmond Malone*, ed. Arthur Tillotson, in *The Percy Letters*, gen. ed. D. N. Smith, C. Brooks *et al.*, 9 vols. (New Haven, 1944–88), 1: 249–

50. This refers to *LLEP*. The quarto edition was listed at £1 7s. and was published on December 21, shortly after Hurd's death.

[16] *The Letters and Papers of Sir John Hill 1714–1775*, ed. G. S. Rousseau (New York, 1982), p.xiv.

[17] Pope used the phrase in his 1725 'Preface of the Editor to *The Works of Shakespear*', *The Prose Works of Alexander Pope*, vol. 2, ed. Rosemary Cowler (Oxford, 1986), pp.24, 39 n.72. James R. Sutherland borrowed the quotation for the title of his article in *Review of English Studies*, 21 (1945): 202–15; rpt. *Essential Articles for the study of Alexander Pope*, ed. and rev. Maynard Mack (Hamden, Conn., 1968).

[18] Cited in *The Oxford Dictionary of Quotations*, 2nd ed. (Oxford, 1953).

[19] Knapton and Gyles, among others, published John Colbatch, *An Examination of the late Archdeacon Echard's Account of the Marriage-treaty* (1733); Philip Bearcroft, *An Historical Account of Thomas Sutton Esq;* (1737); Vincent Perronet, *Some Enquiries, chiefly Relating to Spiritual Beings* (1740); and John Ward, *The Lives of the Professors of Gresham College* (1740).

[20] The title-page carried the phrase 'In Nine Volumes Complete' which might refer to the set or the *œuvre*. Warburton left out many minor pieces, some of which were published in the 1757 *Supplement*, apparently against his wishes.

[21] Pope, *Works*, ed. Joseph Warton, 9 vols. (London, 1797), 9: 342.

[22] Spence, 1: 216–17. Warburton soon introduced Charles Yorke to George Lyttelton and offered to assist him 'in an abridged Account of the Ancient History of Ireland'; see Lyttelton's letter to Warburton, dated 12 April 1745 (NLS: MS. 1002, f.176).

[23] *ILH*, 2: 195; also cited in Leslie Stephen's article on Warburton in *DNB*. Evans pointed out that Akenside referred to, but did not quote, this letter in a note to his 'Ode to Thomas Edwards' (1766); this letter was in fact first printed in Malone's *Supplement to the Edition of Shakespeare's Works* (1780), in the year after Warburton's death (p.21 n.1).

[24] *Another Occasional Letter from Mr. Cibber to Mr. Pope… With An Expostulatory Address to the Reverend Mr. W. W—— n., Author of the new Preface, and Adviser in the curious Improvements of that Satire* (London: printed: and sold by W. Lewis, 1744), pp.35–6.

[25] Shakespeare, *Works*, ed. Lewis Theobald, 7 vols. (London, 1733 [1734]), 3: 15n. (*Comedy of Errors*, II.i. [109–13]). In his introduction Theobald amply acknowledged Warburton's 'indefatigable Zeal and Industry' (1: lxvi).

[26] Sir James Prior, *The Life of Edmond Malone, Editor of Shakespeare. With Selections from his Manuscript Anecdotes* (London, 1860), p.430. This story is also cited in the *DNB* article on Warburton.

[27] Johnson, 'Pope', 3: 167.

[28] Prior, *Life of Edmond Malone*, p.386; cited in Evans, p.92.

[29] Spence, 1: 158–9.

[30] Johnson, 'Pope', 3: 170. Mack wrote '[Warburton] received the property of all the poet's works in print – a legacy that over the editions of his lifetime cannot have been worth less to him than four or five thousand pounds – eighty to a hundred thousand pounds in today's money' (*Life*, p.744).

[31] Pope's will was widely published: first by Charles Corbett in 1744; again in the same year by Weaver Bickerton; and also in *GM*, 14 (June 1744): 313–14. Warburton reprinted it in his edition of Pope's *Works* (1751), 9: 369, and gave the cited clause relating to his editorial bequest as a footnote on the first page of the advertisement in volume 1.

[32] John Feather, *A History of British Publishing* (London, 1988), p.81.

[33] One vigilant contemporary reader queried in *GM*, 21 (August 1751): 344, the absence of Pope's own frontispiece to the *Essay on Man*, which had appeared in several small octavo editions after Pope's death.

[34] David McKitterick, *Four Hundred Years of University Printing and Publishing in Cambridge 1584–1984* (Cambridge, 1984), p.92.

[35] *History of English Thought in the Eighteenth Century*, 3rd ed., 2 vols. (London, 1902; rpt. New York, 1962), 1: 294–6.

[36] George S. Fraser, *Alexander Pope* (London, 1978), pp.11, 105.

[37] I am grateful to Professor David Pitt, former head of the English department at Memorial University, for relating this anecdote, which he recalls having heard at a lecture in the University of Toronto in the 1940s.

[38] See, for example, Elise F. Knapp, 'Community Property: the Case for Warburton's 1751 Edition of Pope', *Studies in English Literature*, 26 (1986): 455–68.

[39] *Essai sur les hiéroglyphes des Égyptiens*, traduit par Léonard des Malpeines, édition et notes par Patrick Tort, précédé de SCRIBBLE (pouvoir/écrire) par Jacques Derrida (Paris, 1977). This is a preface to a 1744 translation of book 4, sections 2–6, of Warburton's *The Divine Legation of Moses*.

[40] Martin Battestin with Ruth Battestin, *Henry Fielding: a Life* (London and New York, 1989), pp.355–6 (24 September 1742).

[41] James Boswell, *Life of Johnson*, ed. R. W. Chapman, rev. J. D. Fleeman, introd. Pat Rogers (Oxford, 1980), p.234.

[42] Boswell, *The Journal of a Tour to the Hebrides*, ed. Peter Levi (Harmondsworth, 1984), pp.199–200.

[43] Boswell, *Journal*, pp.354–5. Boswell modified this slur on Spence's scholarship with a footnote of Johnson's commendations of his *Essay on Pope's Odyssey* and *Anecdotes*.

[44] Mack, *Life*, p.736.

[45] Robinson had previously figured in the legal fracas over the publication of Pope's *Letters*; see *Correspondence*, 4: 87–8.

[46] *Correspondence*, 4: 207–08, 213. Brean Hammond sets the publication date of Warburton's *Vindication* as August 1742 in *Pope and Bolingbroke: a Study of Friendship and Influence* (Columbia, Miss., 1984), pp.106–07.

[47] See Leslie Stephen's account of Warburton in *DNB*; and *LLEP*, p.218.

[48] Mack, *Life*, p.744.

[49] Mack, *Life*, pp.736–45, *passim*; Ryley, chapters 1 and 4.

[50] *Correspondence*, 4: 516 and n.1; *TE*, 3.ii: 46–7 and n.1.

[51] Although Pope attempted to introduce Warburton to Bolingbroke – Ruffhead reported a quarrel between them at Murray's residence in Lincoln's Inn Fields shortly before Pope's death – it remains uncertain whether the poet's two mentors actually met (*Correspondence*, 4: 488).

[52] For Warburton's copyright assignment with Tonson, see Appendix D.

[53] In the Introduction to *Samuel Johnson on Shakespeare* (London, 1989), H. R. Woudhuysen mentions that 'Johnson annotated it [Warburton's edition of Shakespeare] for use while he worked on the *Dictionary*. He turned to it again when he was editing Shakespeare. Some time after 1753 he borrowed from Sir Edward Walpole a copy of this same edition which contained manuscript notes and annotations by Styan Thirlby' (p.17). Warburton's edition was used as the copy-text for the 1753 Edinburgh edition; and it was later cross-bred with William Dodd's *Beauties of Shakespeare* (1752) for a Pope-Warburton-Dodd *Beauties* in 8 vols. (London and Edinburgh: printed for A. Donaldson, 1771), which was how many German readers were introduced to Shakespeare.

[54] *Works*, 1: 188 (*Essay on Criticism*, line 463 n.); 4: 23 (*Arbuthnot*, line 169 n.); and 5: 288 (*Dunciad*, book 4, line 567 n.).

[55] Arthur Sherbo, *The Birth of Shakespeare Studies* (East Lansing, 1986), p.14.

[56] *A Letter to the Editor* and *A Familiar Epistle to the Most Impudent Man Living*, ed. Donald T. Siebert, Jr., Augustan Reprint Society, no. 192 (Los Angeles, 1978), pp.22–3. Siebert identifies Bolingbroke as the author of the latter pamphlet (v–vi), although some passages have the malicious tone of Mallet's Scottish flyting.

[57] Henry Fielding, *Tom Jones*, ed. R. P. C. Mutter (Harmondsworth, 1966), p.609. Fielding also cites Pope in his dedication, opening chapter and throughout (pp.36, 52, 241, 257, 340, 361, 532, 657).

[58] Griffith, 2: 524. The source for this unpublished letter is not given, although it was sent from Bedford Row on 23 May 1751.

[59] *The Yale Edition of Horace Walpole's Correspondence*, ed. Wilmarth S. Lewis *et al.*, 48 vols. (New Haven, 1937–83), 9: 116–17 (13 June 1751).

[60] E-C, 3: 534–5.

[61] *Dodsley*, p.213.

[62] James Prior, *Life of Malone*, pp.370–1; cited in Wimsatt, p.340.

[63] D. W. Nichol, 'A Misplaced Plate in Warburton's *Pope* IV', *N&Q*, 228 (1983): 34–5.

[64] Theophilus Cibber, *A Familiar Epistle to Mr. Warburton* (London, 1753), p.xiv.

[65] Brian Allen, *Francis Hayman* (New Haven and London, 1987).

[66] Blakey worked on a series of prints of English history with Hayman. Grignion assisted Hogarth with the 1746 print of Garrick as Richard III. Major became engraver to the King and to the Stamp Office. Wale was elected a member of the Royal Academy in 1768 and became its first professor of perspective as well as its first pensioner. See Wimsatt, *passim*; and H. A. Hammelmann, 'Eighteenth-Century English Illustrators: Samuel Wale, R.A.', *Book Collector*, 1 (1952): 150–65.

[67] *Sale Catalogues of Libraries of Eminent Persons*, gen. ed. A. N. L. Munby, 12 vols. (London, 1971–5), records numerous owners of Warburton's Pope edition: Joseph Spence's set of the 1751 large octavo was offered for £2 10s. at the fixed-price sale of his library; Spence also owned sets of the 1760 edition bound in vellum (£2 14s.), the 1764 duodecimo in six volumes, the 1766 crown octavo in nine volumes, and the 1766 edition (5: 227; see also the introduction by Stephen Parks, p.89). Fielding's set of the 1751 *Works* fetched £2 2s. (7: 154). Mrs Piozzi's 9-volume set (as well as sets of the *Iliad* and *Odyssey*) sold for £7 15s. (5: 402). David Garrick owned both the 1751 and 1757 editions (12: 139). Hugh Blair owned an incomplete set of the 1759 edition (7: 205). William Dodd had a nine-volume duodecimo edition (5: 377). No Warburton editions are listed for Lady Mary Wortley Montagu (although she kept her 1717 quarto edition of Pope's *Works* and a 1738 edition of *Essai sur l'homme* [7: 98, 71]), Goldsmith, Wordsworth or Browning.

[68] Smith's crown octavo set is in EUL (JA 1900–8).

[69] Pat Rogers, *Hacks and Dunces: Pope, Swift and Grub Street* (London, 1972; abridged 1980), pp.119–20.

[70] *Sale Catalogues*, 5: 323. This set is listed as duodecimo (although it is presumably the pot octavo edition of 1754), 'with Cuts, fine Paper, neatly gilt'. Other Pope items in the collection included a cobbled-together set of works published between 1742 and 1745, vols. 1, 2, 6, 7, 8, 9 (notably including the *Memoirs of Scriblerus*); a 1745 edition of *An Essay on Man*, bound together with Warburton's *Commentary*; the 1729 edition of *The Dunciad* in octavo; and the 1727 Pope-Swift *Miscellanies*.

[71] *The Letters of William Shenstone*, ed. Marjorie Williams (Oxford, 1939), p.331 (BL: Add. MS. 28958).

[72] BL: G. 12850–8. Butt referred to this set of 1751a in *TE*, 4: ix, 307n. Wilkes' set of the 1751 *Works* was listed in two different auctions in *Sale Catalogues*: in the sale beginning 3 May 1764 Wilkes apparently paid £3 15s. for his own set (8: 108); and in the sale beginning on 29 November 1802 it was purchased by Clarke for £3 18s. (8: 165). Writing to Wilkes in Calais in 1764, the bookseller Thomas Bonell offered to print anything Wilkes cared to submit, including a new edition of Pope which might be entitled 'Wilkes *v*. Warburton', *Royal Commission on Historical Manuscripts*, 4th Report, part 1 (London, 1874), p.401.

[73] *The Correspondence of Richard Hurd & William Mason*, introd. E. H. Pearce, ed. Leonard Whibley (Cambridge, 1932), p.7.

[74] McKenzie (*a*), p.115.

[75] Ambrose Heal, 'London Booksellers and Publishers, 1700–1750', *N&Q*, 5th ser., 161 (1931): 328.

[76] Reported in *GM*, 6 (Nov. 1736): 685; *LA*, 3: 607.

[77] They were: Hester I (21 Feb. 1693); John I (26 Mar. 1695); John II (23 Apr. 1696); James I (8 Apr. 1697); Hester II (5 Aug. 1698); James II (16 Apr. 1701); William I (28 Aug. 1702); Paul (20 Jan. 1703); Rebeckah (17 June 1705); James III (28 Oct. 1706); Cisilia (13 Feb. 1707), William II (22 Apr. 1709), *International Genealogical Index (IGI)*, Genealogical Society of the Church of Jesus Christ of Latter Day Saints, 1980; updated August 1981. There has been some confusion about the Knapton family tree. Plomer followed Nichols' error that James Knapton 'was succeeded by two of his brothers, John and Paul Knapton' (*LA*, 1: 236), as did F. T. Wood and Ambrose Heal in their concurrent listings, 'London Booksellers and Publishers, 1700–1750', 186 (Wood); 328 (Heal). In *The Life of William Warburton*, Watson mixed up the brothers (p.473); and Evans compounded the error by stating that John Knapton (rather than Paul) died in 1755.

The two painters, George (1698–1778) and Charles (1700–60) Knapton, are not listed under baptisms in the *IGI*, although the *DNB* entry for George Knapton mistakenly states that 'he assisted his brothers, John and Paul...'. As Hester Knapton (named after her mother) was born in August 1698, it would seem most unlikely that she gave birth to another child – George – in the same year. A cousin, George Knapton, is named in John Knapton's will. The only Charles Knapton listed in *IGI* was born in 1728, possibly the son of the artist, Charles, and Elizabeth Knapton of Westminster. It is possible that Charles I and George were cousins of John and Paul; the family of booksellers and artists had strong ties and various reasons to be connected with Pope.

These discrepancies have not greatly affected recent scholarship. Norma Hodgson and Cyprian Blagden correctly pointed out that John and Paul Knapton succeeded their father in the Castle (or 'New') Conger in 1737 in *The Notebook of Thomas Bennet and Henry Clements (1686–1719)*, OBS, ns vol. 6 (Oxford, 1956), App. 13, and *passim*, as did Terry Belanger, 'Booksellers' Trade Sales, 1718–1768', in *The Library*, 5th ser., 30 (1975): 281–302; p.291. However, Wimsatt assumed that the booksellers and artists were brothers (pp.63, 140), although he rightly questioned Plomer's accuracy (p.188). In *Selling Art in Georgian England: the rise of Arthur Pond* (New Haven, 1983), Louise Lippincott suggested that John and Paul were 'either brothers or cousins' of George and Charles (p.130).

[78] See Terry Belanger, 'Publishers and writers in eighteenth-century England', *Books and their Readers in Eighteenth-Century England*, ed. Isabel Rivers (Leicester, 1982), pp.5–25; p.14.

[79] I am grateful to Michael Crump, Managing Editor of the Eighteenth-Century Short Title Catalogue, based in the British Library, for assisting me with information on Knapton imprints. Figures here and below are based on an ESTC list compiled on 31 May 1990. The Knapton list is virtually complete, but as the ESTC is ongoing, figures may be subject to slight fluctuation as repetitions are uncovered and new items entered. Items can range from a broadside to a multi-volume edition.

[80] *The Life and Errors of John Dunton*, 2 vols. (London, 1818; rpt. New York, 1969), 1: 217–18; also cited in *LA*, 1: 236.

[81] Stephens was forced out of business by his brother in 1709 (Plomer), which may have caused Knapton some difficulty, although a number of later items were printed by Lichfield.

[82] *The Notebook of Thomas Bennet and Henry Clements*, App. 13; *passim*.

[83] Foxon, P765.

[84] McKenzie (b).

[85] Ian Maxted, *The British Book Trades 1710–1777* (Exeter, 1983).

[86] *GM*, 11 (March 1741): 108.

[87] Eg. 1954, f.60; 30 May 1753.

[88] Wimsatt, pp.62–4; 79 n.31; 140 n.17. He also designed the line engraving of Pope for the second volume of Thomas Birch's *Heads of Illustrious Persons*, published by the Knaptons in 1751.

[89] Wimsatt, pp.328–9; 190–1; 329 n.4. For Pond and the Knaptons, see Lippincott, *Selling Art in Georgian England*, pp.36–8; 149–58.

[90] J. McLaverty, 'Lawton Gilliver: Pope's Bookseller', *Studies in Bibliography*, 32 (1979): 101–24; p.101.

[91] See also McLaverty's introduction to the catalogue of ornaments, *Pope's Printer, John Wright: a preliminary study*, OBS Occasional Publication no. 11 (1977), pp.1–8; and 'A Study of John Wright and Lawton Gilliver, Alexander Pope's printer and bookseller' (unpublished B.Litt. thesis, University of Oxford, 1974), pp.58–9 and appendices A–G, pp.90–166.

[92] Nicolas Barker, 'Pope and his publishers', *TLS* (3 September 1976), p.1085 (review of David Foxon's Lyell lectures).

[93] 'Some of the later trade publishers were more prosperous than this [John Morphew, who left assets of £300] (Thomas Cooper's obituarist in the *Daily Advertiser* believed he had acquired 'a handsome Fortune'), but even they did not have the kind of money which could finance the more than one-hundred titles a year which Mrs Cooper advertised in the years following her husband's death, a period in which great booksellers like Andrew Millar or the Knaptons issued only a small fraction of this number', Michael Treadwell, 'London Trade Publishers 1675–1750', *The Library*, 6th ser., 4 (1982): 99–134; p.115. Using advertisements from *LM*, Treadwell notes that 51% of the Knaptons' advertised stock was priced at 2s. 6d. or more (compared to 7% of the Coopers' stock). As trade publishers, the Coopers dealt mainly in ephemera, priced one shilling or less (p.122).

[94] Mack, *Collected*, pp.491–501.

[95] *Correspondence*, 4: 88–9 [23 November 1737].

[96] Mack, *Collected*, p.496. Mack's slashmarks denoting lineation have been omitted.

[97] Mack, *Collected*, pp.519–20, n.3; 497.

[98] [London:] printed for J. and J. Knapton, R. Knaplock, W. and J. Innys, J. Wyatt, D. Midwinter, London: and S. Wilmot, Oxford, 1726–7.

[99] London: printed for J. and J. Knapton, J. Darby, A. Bettesworth, J. Tonson, F. Fayram, W. Mears, J. Pemberton, J. Osborn and T. Longman, B. Motte, C. Rivington, F. Clay, J. Batley, Ri., Ja. and B. Wellington, 1728. Nine of the ten volumes are a re-issue of the Tonson edition of the same year, and the Knaptons are listed only in the imprint to the last volume which mixes Shakespeare's poems with works of his contemporaries.

[100] K. I. D. Maslen, *The Bowyer Ornament Stock*, OBS Occasional Publication no. 8 (1973), p.2. I am indebted to Professor Maslen for information about the Knaptons' account in the Bowyer ledgers. His facsimile edition of Bowyer's ledgers is forthcoming.

[101] See J. A. Cochrane, *Dr. Johnson's Printer: the life of William Strahan* (London, 1964), pp.26–7.

[102] James L. Clifford, *Dictionary Johnson* (London, 1979), pp.46, 137, 151.

[103] Dates from *GM*, 25 (June 1755): 284; and Philip Wallis, *At the Sign of the Ship: notes on the house of Longman, 1724–1974* (Harlow, 1974), p.12.

[104] *LA*, 1: 62. Jacob Tonson gave five guineas, Edmund Curll one. Damages amounted to £5146; Bowyer received a total of £2539 15s. 2d. from sixty-one subscribers.

[105] BL: Add. MS. 38730, f.10.

[106] British Museum, Department of Prints and Drawings, Banks and Heal Collections, box 1, Banks, 17.49. 'Mr. Horsfield died March 4, 1798, aged 75. —— He had been for several years a Bookseller in Ludgate-street; where he succeeded to the extensive business of Messrs. Knapton' (*LA*, 3: 607). He served as treasurer of the Stationers' Company from 1785 to 1797.

[107] Boswell, *Life of Johnson*, pp.205–06.

[108] [Richard Hurd,] *Moral and Political Dialogues* (London, A. Millar; Cambridge, W. Thurleborne and J. Woodyer, 1759), pp.x–xi. This line occurs in a lively, satirical interlude in the attention-grabbing preface, between a lofty-minded editor and a pragmatic bookseller, and seems to sum up Millar's key to success.

[109] I am indebted to Julian Conway of the Department of Manuscripts, the British Library, for furnishing me with this information and a transcript of Chanter's letter of 15 February 1864.

[110] *TE*, 5: 59, 267.

[111] *ILH*, 2: 195 (2 Jan. 1727).

[112] Kilvert, *Memoirs of... Richard Hurd*, p.40; Boyce, p.297.

[113] See 4 May 1749; and Donald W. Nichol, 'Pope, Warburton, Knapton, and Cole: a longstanding connection', *N&Q*, 234 (1989): 54–6.

[114] See Graham Cartwright, 'Pope's Books: a postscript to Mack', *N&Q*, 231 (1986): 56–8.

CORRESPONDENCE

1744

On January 12, Pope alerted Warburton to Colley Cibber's *Another Occasional Letter* in response to the revised *Dunciad* of October 1743. While Pope's name did not appear on his final work, Warburton's was given in the notice on the verso of the title-page for quarto editions of the *Essay on Criticism* and the *Essay on Man*; and the initials 'W.W.' were given in the 'Advertisement to the Reader' concerning Cibber's substitution. Had Cibber's pamphlet, announcing Warburton's earlier alliance with Theobald to the public, come sooner, it might have driven a wedge between the poet and his editor, but Pope was determined to continue working with Warburton on 'the Great Edition of my things with your Notes' (*Correspondence*, 4: 491).

Warburton last visited Pope at Twickenham in March, but went to Prior Park with Ralph Allen in early May. Pope still hoped to introduce Warburton to Bolingbroke, but the accuracy of Ruffhead's account of their heated meeting at Murray's house is doubtful. In his last illness, Pope gave friends copies of the 'deathbed' *Epistles to Several Persons* which he and Warburton had been preparing since the autumn of 1743. Publication of this edition was delayed because of passages in *Epistle to a Lady*. Bolingbroke asked Marchmont, 'Is it worth while to suppress the edition?' (*TE*, 3.ii: xi).

Pope died on May 30. His will named Warburton as literary executor. Warburton returned for the funeral on June 5. Bolingbroke held control over his manuscripts and soon learned of Pope's surreptitious edition of the *Patriot King*. Henry Lintot may have wanted to revive his father's claim to *An Essay on Criticism* or reprint one of his editions of Pope's *Works* containing the *Dunciad* in order to benefit from sales after Pope's death. Lintot would later prove troublesome over the copyrights to Pope's works.

Warburton supplied notes for Zachary Grey's edition of *Hudibras*, and the first part of his *Remarks on Several Occasional Reflections* was published. Initially amicable, dealings with Bowyer gradually deteriorated.

Warburton *to* William Bowyer[1]   29 January 1744
Nichols, *Literary Anecdotes*, 2: 164   [Newark?][2]

Jan. 29, 1743[/4].

Dear Mr. Bowyer,

I have read over Colley. He is all you say of him, and more. But I love the rogue when he reasons. He is then a delightful ass, indeed. In a word, is it possible there can be buyers for such a pamphlet?[3] ——Never fear but I will get the better of all my adversaries at last.——And then——as Pyrrhus said to his counsellor, we will sit down and drink your raisin wine.[4] Do but decypher my MS. cleverly, and see if I don't make a rogue and an ass of *Dr. Anonimous*.[5] I should have told you, the reason why the inclosed came no sooner was, because your letter, which sent it, was put into a wrong bag, and went farther North, and came back again before I had it, either by the negligence or design of the clerks of the Post-office. I think the Dutch frugality never appeared in a more signal instance than what I have just now seen in the newspapers. They have appointed a *fast* and *thanksgiving* in one, and to be observed together.

Ever yours,
W.W.

[1] Nichols introduces this and the following two letters from Warburton to Bowyer with the note, 'Whilst these volumes were in the press, Mr. Bowyer received the following letters from the learned Commentator.' These three letters appear in a footnote to Bowyer's printing of 'The Works of Mr. Pope, in two volumes, 4to', i.e., *An Essay on Criticism* issued with *An Essay on Man* (Foxon P819; P865) and *Epistles to Several Persons* (Griffith 591). Nichols' transcriptions are often selective (long dashes denoting omissions or new paragraphs) and sometimes in error. The location of the original MSS is a mystery; those printed before the fire of 1808 may not have survived. For a list of 'Nichols Source Material', see Robin Myers, 'John Nichols (1745–1826), Chronicler of the Book Trade', *Development of the English Book Trade, 1700–1899*, ed. Myers and Harris, p.35.

[2] Pope's letter to Warburton on 15 November 1743 was sent to Newark (where his mother still lived and close to his parish of Brant Broughton), although Pope's letter to Ralph Allen on 3 January 1744 suggests Allen's planned trip to London in March will delay Warburton's next – and ultimately last – visit (*Correspondence*, 4: 480–1, 489).

[3] *Another Occasional Letter from Mr. Cibber to Mr. Pope* was advertised in the *London Daily Post and General Advertiser* on 19 January 1744 (Guerinot 316–19). In this first attack on Pope's association with Warburton, Cibber exploited the irony of Warburton's earlier collaboration with Theobald. Pope gave his editor advance warning on January 12: 'He threatens You; but I think you will not fear, or love, him so much as to answer him . . .' (*Correspondence*, 4: 491–2).

[4] Possibly an allusion to Plutarch's Life of Pyrrhus: 'When some advised him [Pyrrhus] to banish a certain ill-tongued Ambracian, who abused him behind his back, "Let the fellow stay here," said he, "and speak against me to a few, rather than ramble about, and give me a bad character to all the world." And some young men having taken great liberties with his character in their cups, and being afterwards brought to answer for it, he asked them whether they really had said such things? "We did, Sir," answered one of them "and should have said a great deal more, if we had had more wine." Upon which he laughed and dismissed them', *Plutarch's Lives*, trans. John and William Langhorne (London, 1890), p.276. It is appropriate that Warburton should identify with the man whose name survives in Pyrrhic victory.

[5] As Cibber's pamphlet was not anonymous, Warburton may have had one of his many unknown detractors in mind.

Warburton *to* William Bowyer   9 March 1744
Nichols, *Literary Anecdotes*, 2: 164 (fragment)   [Twickenham?]

March 9, 1743–4

Mr. Pope thinks that his Works will be comprehended in two volumes of 60 sheets each. But he is unwilling that the paper should be at all worse than the other.—— No. 1000 of that paper, and 100 royal.[1]

Ever yours,
W.W.

[1] These figures are consistent with the printing of *Epistles to Several Persons*, which comprised $12\frac{1}{2}$ sheets in quarto. Pope had written to Bowyer six days earlier: 'On Second thoughts, let the Proof of the Epistle to Lord Cobham, I, be done in the *Quarto*, not the *Octavo*, size: contrive the Capitals & evry thing exactly to correspond with that Edition. The first proof send me, the Number of the whole but *1000*, & the Royal *over* & above' (*Correspondence*, 4: 504). *An Essay on Criticism* and *An Essay on Man* had been entered to Pope in Bowyer's ledgers on 18 February 1744, 1500 copies and 100 Royal (Foxon P819; P865).

Keith Maslen's entry, based on Bowyer's ledger, records: 'Epistles to several persons. (sub-title). (1744). 4°. $12\frac{1}{2}$ sh[ee]ts. . . . "four 4° epistles", 100 FP [fine paper], 1000 ord[ered]., d[elivere]d 28 Nov. 1744–28 Jan. 1745 (3 FP, 5 ord., to Knapton), dd 3 Dec. 1748 93 FP, 986 ord., to Knapton. Griffith 591, "Pope distributed a few copies about 3 weeks before his death". B.M. copy bound with Essay on criticism, and Essay on man' ('Works from the Bowyer Press (1713–1765): a supplement to John Nichols', unpublished B.Litt. thesis, University of Oxford, 1952, p.194). Maslen's edition of the Bowyer archives is forthcoming.

Warburton *to* William Bowyer[1]   20 June 1744
Nichols, *Literary Anecdotes*, 2: 165   Brant Broughton

B. Broughton, June 20, 1744

Dear Sir,

I thank you for both your last. You will oblige me with telling me that beast Lintot's steps.[2] I would do him all reason while he acts with decency and justice, and shall never print any part of his property with my Notes and Commentary without his leave; but if he acts like a rogue, I have but one word with him, the Chancery and Mr. Murray. This *inter nos*. —— If the executors[3] inquire of you, and when they do, about the state of Mr. Pope's Works in your hands yet unfinished (that is to say, of the Epistles),[4] I then desire you would let Mr. Murray have a copy of all those Epistles; and you may tell him I desired you would do so: but say nothing till then. Pray preserve all the Press Copy, to the least scrap. —— I have looked over the corrected proof of the half-sheet, title, &c. and of the leaf that was ordered to be cancelled,[5] and find them right: so desire they may be printed off, and one sent me by the first opportunity. My best respects to Mrs. Bill.

I am, dear sir, your very affectionate friend and servant,

W.W.

[1] Bateson cites part of this letter (*TE*, 3.ii: xii; and 26 n.143).
[2] Pope made notes on the copyright of his works in response to a letter from Henry Lintot on 29 January 1740 (*Correspondence*, 4: 222–4). Pope later sued Lintot in Chancery on 16 February 1743 (PRO: C 11/549/39) for the copyright of the *Dunciad* (4: 425 n.5). A few months before his death, Pope asked Bowyer to 'minute down what Mr Lintot has said to you of printing any thing of mine' (4: 502). Lintot laid claim to Pope's early

poetical works and the *Key to the Lock* (Mack, *Collected*, pp.515–16). Lintot published various editions of Pope's works, including the small octavo *Works* of 1736, 1740, and 1743 (Griffith 417, 510, 582), and the 1749 edition of *An Essay on Criticism* (Foxon P821) with Warburton's notes. He also had a 12·9% share in Pope's *Works* from 1751 to 1754.

[3] Pope named Bathurst, Marchmont, William Murray and George Arbuthnot as his executors; manuscripts and unprinted papers were left in Bolingbroke's care.

[4] The 'deathbed' *Epistles to Several Persons*: Griffith (no. 591) was not able to examine a copy of this edition. Bateson used the BL copy of the *Epistles*, C.59.e.1(2), as the basis for his edition (see *TE*, 3.ii: xiii n.1).

[5] 'Leaf A4 in all the copies of the edition now extant is an insert and the suppression of these lines is the most probable explanation of the cancel' (*TE*, 3.ii: 26 n.143). Bateson surmises that Pope's friendship with the Duchess of Marlborough in 1744 may have led to the suppression of lines in the *Epistle to Cobham* which were unfavourable to the memory of her late husband and also observes, 'It is not clear if it was Pope or Warburton who "ordered" the cancel' (27).

1745

Warburton completed the second and final part of *Remarks on Several Occasional Reflections*. In response to the Jacobite threat, he delivered sermons designed to restore faith in the Anglican church, and by extension Hanoverian rule, in Allen's chapel at Prior Park and at St. James's Church, Westminster.

Bolingbroke was concerned that Warburton might attempt to publish a biographical account of Pope casting him in a bad light, although he was armed with the story of Pope's apparent treachery over the surreptitious printing of *The Idea of a Patriot King*. Lyttelton interceded, pointing out that mutual friends of Warburton and Bolingbroke might take offence.

Three small octavo editions of *An Essay on Man* with Warburton's notes came out under the Knapton imprint, although one may have been a piracy. These editions have a frontispiece designed by Pope, with an explanatory note by Warburton, and a vignette of the poet on the title-page. George Faulkner published a duodecimo edition of *An Essay on Man* in Dublin.

Dr. James Kirkpatrick's Latin translation of *An Essay on Criticism*, *Celeberrimi Popii Tentamen*, appeared under Dodsley's imprint.

Warburton *to* Catharine Cockburn[1]   26 January 1745
WWW, 1: 147–50   Newark

Newark, Jan. 26, 1744–5.

GOOD MADAM,

I HAD the honour of your obliging letter of the 25th of last August, sent me to Bath, where I then was. After some stay there, where my time was taken up more than I could have wished, I went to London, where I was still less in my own power. I am just now returned home; and the first thing I thought of was to make my acknowledgements for that favour.

I do not wonder that the goodness of your heart, and your love of letters, should make you speak with so much tenderness of poor Mr. Pope's death; for it was a great loss both to the literary and moral world. In answer to your obliging question, what works of Mr. Pope have been published with my commentaries and notes? I am to inform you, they are the *Dunciad* in quarto, and the *Essay on Man* and on *Criticism*,[2] in the same size.[3] Which affords me an opportunity to beg the favour of you to let me know into whose hands in London I can consign a small parcel for you: For I have done myself the honour of ordering these two volumes to be sent to you, as I believed you would with difficulty get them of your booksellers so far North;[4] and I hope you will forgive this liberty.

Towards the conclusion of your letter, you have sent me one of the politest cartels[5] imaginable. I think, his answer was generally commended, who told the Emperor, when he pressed him, that he never would dispute with a man who had twenty legions at his beck. And do you think I will enter the lists with a lady, whose writings have twenty thousand charms in them? If I confided in myself, and aimed at honour, I could not indeed do better: for the case is there, as in the works of the Italian poets; who have, with great decorum, when they introduced female warriors, made the overcoming one of them the highest point of valour and address in their heroes. Besides, to speak out of a figure, we differ in what is the true foundation of morality. I have said all I have to say on the subject. And though it be hard to guess when a writer so much the mistress of her subject has said all, yet if I believed what you have said was *all*, I might perhaps be in some measure excuseable; as I see you say so much more than any writer of your side the question had done before you.

One thing, and only one, you will give me leave, Madam, to observe: that I am a little surprized at the consequence drawn from my position – "that, as without a GOD there could be no obligation, therefore the Atheist who believes there is none (and might deduce that truth concerning obligation from the principles of right reason) would have no *tye* upon him."

Hence I concluded, and I thought rightly, that Atheism was highly injurious to society. But how any one could conclude from this (for this is the amount of what I said on that subject) that, on my principles (for as to my opinion, I believe no one would question that) *an atheist is not accountable in a future state for any enormities he may commit here*, I do not see. And my reason for saying so is this. It is a principle, I suppose, agreed on, "That crimes committed *upon wrong principles* are equally punishable with those committed *against right*; for that the falling into this wrong principle was occasioned by some punishable fault in the conduct." Now I have not said one single word, throughout the discourse, that tends to invalidate this principle: Consequently all I have said cannot affect the truth, That *an Atheist is accountable*. I ask your pardon, Madam, for this trouble. It is what I have not given to any other; though several have made the same objection. They deserved nothing at my hands; and you deserve every thing.

You inquire with great civility concerning the third volume of the Divine Legation. Several offices of friendship, several offices of domestic piety and duty, weariness with contradiction of *sinners* both against sense and grammar (for such have been my adversaries) have prevented me doing any thing at the last volume, since the publication of the second. But now being just upon the point of, not washing, but drying, my hands of controversy, I am about to sit down in earnest to the conclusion of the work.

I beg, Madam, not only my best respects and services to Mr.

Cockburn, who, I presume, is your spouse, but, in that case, my congratulations with him, for his honour and happiness in such a consort.

I am, Madam,
With the greatest regard and esteem,
Your very obliged and obedient humble servant,
W. WARBURTON

[1] This letter was appended by Richard Hurd to *A Discourse, by Way of General Preface to the Quarto Edition of Bishop Warburton's Works* (1794) which was intended to preface Hurd's 1788 edition of Warburton's *Works*. In the Advertisement, Hurd announced, 'the purchaser of this edition will be entitled to a Copy of the Discourse, whenever it comes out, on his producing a ticket, which for that purpose will be delivered to him by the Bookseller' (*WWW*, 1: iii).

[2] Foxon P796, P865, and P819 respectively.

[3] The first part of this paragraph is printed with changes to accidentals in *LA*, 5: 586.

[4] Mrs Cockburn lived in Longhorsley, Northumberland, from 1737.

[5] 'A writing containing, for the most part, stipulations between enemies', Johnson, *Dict.*; 'a written challenge, a letter of defiance', *OED*.

Bolingbroke *to* David Mallet[1]   25 July 1745
BL: Add. MS. 4948.A, f.419   Battersea

Battersea July the 25th 1745.
Dear Sr
    since I send to enquire after yr health, and Mrs Mallets, of both which I hope to have a good account, I cannot help mentioning to you what I hear from many different quarters. they say that Warburton talks very indecently of yr humble Servant, and threatens him with the terrible things he shall throw out in a life he is writing of our poor friend Pope.[2] I value neither the good nor ill will of the man, but if he has any regard for the man he flattered living, and thinks himself obliged to flatter dead, he ought to let a certain proceeding dye away in silence, as I endeavour it should.[3] Whenever you have a day of leisure, you will be extreamly welcome

to Dear Sr yr most faithful humble servt.
H St J L B

Address: To Mr Mallet

[1] An incomplete copy was made of this letter (BL: Add. MS. 35,588, f.91).

[2] Warburton announced his intention of writing Pope's biography in a 1745 edition of the *Essay on Man*: '*There is preparing for the Public* the LIFE of Mr. *POPE, with a Critical

Account of his Writings, by Mr. *WARBURTON*.' Warburton renewed this promise in the Advertisement to the 1751 edition of Pope's *Works*, although he left the job to Owen Ruffhead whose *Life* prefaced the 1769 quarto edition, by which time the Warburton-Bolingbroke quarrel had faded from public memory. See George Sherburn, *The Early Career of Alexander Pope* (Oxford, 1934), pp.8–13.

[3] A veiled reference to Pope's surreptitious printing of Bolingbroke's *Idea of a Patriot King*: Bolingbroke left his manuscript with Pope and agreed to a private edition for 'five or six Persons'. Shortly after Pope's death, the printer John Wright approached Bolingbroke, asking what he wanted done with the 1500 copies Pope had ordered. Bolingbroke felt betrayed by his dead friend, but held off making Pope's action public until 1749 when the controversy was sparked off in the *London Magazine*. For Bolingbroke's letter to Marchmont (22 October 1744) on the destruction of copies, see BL: Add. MS. 37,994, f.46; also cited in Henry Hume, *A Selection from the Papers of the Earls of Marchmont*, ed. Sir G. H. Rose, 3 vols. (London, 1831), 2: 338–9.

For the growing body of scholarship relating to the *Patriot King* affair, see Fannie E. Ratchford, 'Pope and the *Patriot King*', *University of Texas, Studies in English*, 6 (1926): 157–77; Giles Barber, 'Bolingbroke, Pope, and the *Patriot King*', *The Library*, 5th ser., 19 (1964): 67–89; H. T. Dickinson, *Bolingbroke* (London, 1970), pp.280–2; Frank T. Smallwood, 'Bolingbroke *vs.* Alexander Pope: the Publication of the *Patriot King*', *PBSA*, 65 (1971): 225–41; J. McLaverty, *Pope's Printer, John Wright*, p.6; Brean S. Hammond, *Pope and Bolingbroke*, pp.77, 109; Mack, *Life*, pp.748–52.

George Lyttelton *to* Warburton[1]   2 September 1745
SUP, pp.207–08   Bath

                                                           Bath, Sept. 2, 1745
Dear Sir,

I came hither for a couple of days to see Mr. Pitt, and go to-morrow to London. I wish I could have been so fortunate as to find you and Mr. Allen here, or in town; but as I understand you are upon a tour that will soon bring you back to this place, and that I am not likely to meet you in London, I take the liberty to leave this for you at Mr. Allen's.

The occasion of my troubling you with it, is a report which I lately heard very confidently asserted of your designing speedily to publish a Life of Mr. Pope, in which you animadvert by way of a vindication upon the affair of Lord Bolingbroke's Papers.[2] Now, as I know more of that matter than I believe you do, and am very sure the stirring it more will not turn out to our friend's advantage, I earnestly advise you not to publish anything upon that delicate subject till you have had some talk with me. You will also consider how many friends you have that are also friends to Lord Bolingbroke, particularly Lord Chesterfield and Mr. Murray; and how disagreeable it would be to them to have you two engaged in an angry dispute upon a point of this nature.

I hope you will excuse my taking this freedom, and impute it to the sincere friendship and great esteem with which I am,

Dear Sir,

Your most faithful humble

servant,

G. Lyttelton

I beg my best compliments to Mr. and Mrs. Allen.

[1] The second paragraph of this letter is cited in Dickinson, *Bolingbroke*, p.281.

[2] The story of Pope's clandestine edition of the *Idea of a Patriot King* was revealed in the Advertisement to the authorized edition, published in May 1749 by Andrew Millar, after extracts began to appear from January in the *London Magazine*. Warburton heeded Lyttelton's advice and set aside the biography.

1746

In his forty-eighth year, Warburton married Gertrude Tucker, the eighteen-year-old niece of Ralph Allen, on April 25. He became a preacher of Lincoln's Inn.

He published *An Apologetical Dedication to the Reverend Dr. Henry Stebbing* as well as two sermons: *The Nature of National Offences Truly Stated: a sermon preached on the general Fast day* and *A Sermon Preach'd on the Thanksgiving appointed to be Observed the Ninth of October.*

Another small octavo editon of *An Essay on Man* with the frontispiece designed by Pope and with Warburton's notes was published by the Knaptons.

Warburton *to* William Bowyer[1]   20 January 1746
Yale University, Beinecke Library: Osborn Files   [Prior Park]

Dear Mr Bowyer

In confidence that you have survived & got the better of all alarms for the constitution & frights from the highlanders that have so lately filled this Country with confusion, I beg the favour of you to do me the following commissions, to receive the money on this bill, to pay to Mr Caryl's order (Fellow of Jesus) 6.17. 9½ when it is called for and to pay Jack Whiston 3*l*: 10*s* 0*d*. He tells me he is got perfectly well again. What strange Heteroclites are the Whiston Family.[2] When he had no occasion to be otherwise than well he was ill, and is well now there is cause enough to be otherwise. But well or ill I could never catch him setting a low price on his books. —— I have subscribed 30*l*. to the Lincolnshire Association (which is more than any other[3] Clergyman in the county) and I have published 3 Sermons.[4] Have I not now fairly contributed my quota both in temporals & spirituals. I will neither be a civil nor Ecclesiastical Slave but don't be surprised if I soon submit to the vinĉ[u]la jugalia.[5] To offer up my freedom to one of the finest women in England is being more than free. In the mean time, whether bond or free depend upon my being always yours

                                                            W. Warburton
pray let me know of ye receipt of this   Jan. 20 1745/6

Address (verso): To Mr. W. Bowyer Printer in White-Friars[6]

---

[1] Boyce quotes from this letter (p.164 n.7). Part of this letter appears as a footnote to the printing of Warburton's sermons in 1746 in 'Annals of Mr. Bowyer's Press, from 1732 to 1765' (*LA*, 2: 189–90).

[2] William Whiston (1667–1752) succeeded Sir Isaac Newton as Lucasian Professor of Mathematics at Cambridge; his *Astronomical Principles of Religion* was published in 1717. See G. S. Rousseau, 'Science Books and their Readers', *Books and their Readers in*

Eighteenth-Century England, ed. Rivers, pp.197–255; 217–18; and *LA*, 8: 375–6. The bookseller John Whiston (1711–80), with his partner Benjamin White, specialized in natural history; he is mentioned in *LA*, 8: 260; 9: 424, 491, 781.

[3] There is a slight tear in the manuscript at this point; Nichols reads 'other'.

[4] Warburton delivered these sermons, all published by the Knaptons (see Appendix C), between 9 October and 18 December 1745: *A Faithful Portrait of Popery* (1745); *A Sermon Occasioned by the Present Unnatural Rebellion* (1745; 2nd ed., 1746); *The Nature of National Offences Truly Stated* (1746). Warburton later added *A Sermon preach'd on the Thankgiving* (1746). A Scottish edition was also published: *Two Sermons, viz. I. A faithful portrait of popery: by which it is seen to be the reverse of christianity; . . . II. An earnest exhortation to a manly defence of our happy constitution in church and state* (Edinburgh: reprinted, and sold by G. Crawfurd, 1746).

[5] Nichols (*LA*, 2: 190) and the *DNB* err in dating Warburton's 'matrimonial chains' as 5 September 1745. The marriage settlement was signed on 25 March 1746 and the marriage between Warburton and Gertrude Tucker took place on the following April 25 (Boyce, p.165). Then eighteen, she was thirty years his junior. The Jacobite invasion ended when Prince Charles Edward gave the order to retreat at Derby on 6 December 1745.

[6] This leaf has been used for various numerical notations, perhaps by Bowyer.

Warburton *to* Robert Dodsley[1]   [7 December 1746?]
Yale University, Beinecke Library: Osborn Files   Bath

Mr Dodsley

I saw, by accident, on ye road a poem called an *Essay on Satire occasioned by the death of Mr Pope*[2] & was surprised to see so excellent a piece of poetry & what was still more uncommon, so much good reasoning. I find it has been published some time. If it be not a secret, I should be glad to know the Author. If I have leasure I shall give some acct of it for the litterary news of your Museum.[3] It will be a better ornam[en]t to it than ye dull book of travels in ye 2d No.

I am your very humble Servant
W. Warburton

Address and postmark: To Mr R. Dodsley   Bookseller at Tully's Head in Pall Mall   London   7/[?]   BATH

[1] Printed in *LA*, 5: 587, as a footnote to Pope's death in the biographical account of Warburton; and Eddy, p.9. Tierney dates this letter [6 or 7 April 1746], noting that 'The exact day on which this letter was written poses some difficulty' (*Dodsley*, p.94 n.1). While the number 7 is clear from the postmark, the month is not, although a stamped 'A' of uncertain derivation appears beside the postmark. The problem with assigning the date of this letter to April is that, as Tierney points out, the second number of the *Museum* did not appear in London until April 12. While Warburton may somehow have received an advance copy, I have dated this letter later in the year, closer to Warburton's follow-up letter to John Brown below, dated December 24.

[2] [John Brown], *An Essay on Satire: Occasion'd by the Death of Mr. Pope* (London: Robert Dodsley, 1745); Foxon B502. Initially anonymous, this took a year to come to Warburton's attention. A second edition came out in 1749 with the addition to the title: *Inscribed to Mr. Warburton . . . Corrected and Enlarged by the Author, in the same manner which it is inserted in the new edition of Mr. Pope's Works, now in the press* (Foxon B503). Warburton included a revised version, which added lines in praise of himself, in the third volume of Pope's *Works* in 1751. This prefaced the *Essay on Man* in successive editions of Pope's *Works*, although it did not appear in separate editions of the *Essay*. See the following letter and the letter of 12 December 1748, below.

[3] Dodsley's fortnightly magazine, *The Museum; or, Literary and Historical Register* (1746–7), published works by Johnson, Garrick, Horace Walpole and the Wartons among others. See James E. Tierney, '*The Museum*, the "Super-Excellent Magazine"', *Studies in English Literature*, 13 (1973): 503–15; and Tierney, '*Museum* Attributions in John Cooper's Unpublished Letters', *Studies in Bibliography*, 27 (1974): 232–5.

Warburton *to* [John Brown][1]   24 December 1746
OB: MS. Eng. misc. c. 390, f.398 (copy)   Bedford Row

Sir,
   It is not long since yt. by accident I met with a Poem intit: An Essay on Sat⟨ire⟩ occasioned by Mr. Pope's death. I own I was much surprized at ye. Performance. To say it is the only piece of poetry that has appeared since his Death wd. be giving it a very low & invidious comendation. For I think it a masterpiece. The long note on Ridicule is admirable. I am preparing a compleat & very fine Edn. of all Mr. Pope's works, & wd. by yr. leave, & if it be agreeable to yr. inclinations, place it before his works, & discard those insipid pieces wrote in his comendation, to give it room.[2] Had poor Mr. Pope been alive I know how much he wd. have esteem'd such a poem & ye. author of it. & in this I shd. be glad to supply his place, & take any opportunity of shewing how much

                                                    I am, Sir,
                                    Yr. most faithfull humble Servt.
                                                  W. Warburton
Bedford Row Decr. 24 1746

[1] Printed in Donald D. Eddy, *A Bibliography of John Brown* (New York, 1971), pp.9–10; and in William Darby Templeman, 'Warburton and Brown Continue the Battle Over Ridicule', *Huntington Library Quarterly*, 17 (1953): 17–36; p.22 and n.15 (which traces the provenance of this letter).

[2] Of the seven prefatory poems in Pope's 1717 *Works*, Warburton decided to keep six (omitting one by Anne Finch, Countess of Winchilsea) and added two later poems by Broome and Lyttelton in the first volume of the 1751 edition.

1747

Warburton wrote prefaces to Catharine Cockburn's *Remarks upon the Principles and Reasonings of Dr. Rutherforth's Essay on the Nature and Obligations of Virtue* and John Towne's *A Critical Inquiry into the Opinions and Practice of the Ancient Philosophers.*

After signing a copyright assignment with Tonson for £500, Warburton finally produced his edition of Shakespeare. This was attacked by a number of critics.

Warburton applied his legal background in defence of perpetual copyright in the anonymous *A Letter from an Author, to a Member of Parliament, concerning Literary Property.*

A small octavo editon of Pope's *Ethic Epistles* was published; the 'Philomedé', 'Atossa' and 'Cloe' passages were excluded from 'To a Lady'. Presented as a Warburton edition, this did not contain the editor's notes and reinstated Pope's satirical reference to Sutton in spite of Warburton's vindication. Pope's frontispiece and the title-page vignette were re-engraved.

Usher Gahagan's Latin translation of *An Essay on Criticism, Tentamen de re critica,* was published by Mary Cooper, although its publication may have been delayed for two years.

Warburton *to* [Knapton]   26 August 1747
BL: Egerton 1954, f.1   [Prior Park]

Dear Sir

There is one Mrs Long[1] a Col.s Wid. living in Park Street beyond Grovener Square a friend of Mr Allen's who some time ago took her money of her, but now intends to pay it in. it is 2500*l*. 1000*l*. at Mich[ael]mas & the remainder at Christmas. Mr Allen will send you a Bill on Shelvoke[2] soon after Michmas for 1000*l*. which when you have recd he begs the favour of you to pay to Mrs Long at her house & take a receipt for it & see it indorsed on the Bond.

I am putting my last hand to *the Alliance between Church & State*[3] which I propose to give a new Edn. of & would willingly have it ready before the busy time comes on.[4] I desire it may be printed exactly in the same manner in all respects with the letter concerning *litterary Prop:y* Both as to paper letter & form.[5] I shall send up part of the Copy next week by Leake's parcel,[6] & only wait for some papers from Mr Yorke[7] to finish the rest. I think to dedicate it to Ld Chest.[8]

I am Dr Sr ever yours
W. Warburton
Augt 26 1747

I have corrected a copy of my Shakespear which you may tell Mr Draper is at his service whenever he requires.[9]

[1] Untraced.

[2] George Shelvocke or Shelvock (*d.* 1760), a circumnavigator, translator and contributor to the *Antient Universal History*, was the secretary of the Post-office General (*LA*, 2: 554; 6: 111).

[3] *The Alliance between Church and State, or, The Necessity and Equity of an Established Religion and a Test-law demonstrated, from the Essence and End of Civil Society, upon the fundamental Principles of the Law of Nature and Nations. In Three Parts* (London: Fletcher Gyles, 1736; 2nd ed., corrected and improved, 1741; 3rd ed., corrected and enlarged, J. and P. Knapton, 1748). Bowyer's ledger records 25 sets (out of 500) of the third edition were delivered to the Knaptons on 24 December 1747, 100 sets on 9 January 1748 and another 226 sets on 16 February 1750, Keith Maslen, 'Works from the Bowyer Press', p.251.

[4] The 'busy time' would have coincided with the return to Westminster of members of parliament for the autumn sitting. Lists of new books in *GM* and *LM* tended to be longer between December and May (depending on the year), with March generally being the peak time for advertising.

[5] [Warburton], *A Letter from an Author, to a Member of Parliament, concerning Literary Property* (London: John and Paul Knapton, 1747). The main text of this 23-page anonymous pamphlet in octavo is printed in Caslon Two Lines Pica. It is reprinted in *Horace Walpole's Political Tracts 1747–1748 with Two by William Warburton on Literary Property 1747 and 1762*, in *The English Book Trade 1660–1853*, ed. Stephen Parks (New York, 1974). The second tract, *An Enquiry into the Nature and Origin of Literary Property* (1762), which is a refutation of the 1747 *Letter*, is misattributed to Warburton.

[6] James Leake was a bookseller and the proprietor of Bath's first circulating library. He organized a parcel service between Bath and London with Charles Hitch at Holborn bridge. According to Dr Cheyne, Leake had 'One of the finest bookshops in Europe', R. S. Neale, *Bath 1680–1850: A Social History* (London, 1981), p.24. Leake and Hitch are listed in Plomer.

[7] Presumably Charles Yorke.

[8] The 1748 edition was dedicated to Lord Chesterfield, whom Dr Johnson chided as a 'patron' in 1755.

[9] The full imprint of Warburton's edition of Shakespeare is given in Appendix C. Warburton dedicated his edition to Mrs Allen. Somerset Draper had a share in Pope's *Works* from 1751 to 1756.

1748

About this time, unsold copies of Pope's works were sold to Warburton by his executors. Pope's 'death-bed' *Epistles to Several Persons* with Warburton's commentary was finally published with a new title-page.

Warburton's edition of Shakespeare was attacked from various quarters. John Upton substantially revised his *Critical Observations on Shakespeare*, first published in 1746, in the light of Warburton's edition. Thomas Edwards' satirical enumeration of Warburton's flaws, *A Supplement to Mr. Warburton's Edition of Shakespear*, came out in two editions published by Mary Cooper. After Warburton responded in the 1749 *Dunciad* footnotes, Edwards expanded his work, calling it *The Canons of Criticism* from 1750: it ran to seven editions by 1765. Charles Bathurst, who had a share in Warburton's edition of Pope, also published this formidable and popular attack on Pope's editor. Theophilus Cibber appended a brief *Serio-Comic Apology* to his revamping of *Romeo and Juliet*.

Warburton furnished Samuel Richardson with the preface to the fourth volume of *Clarissa*; it was later dropped, in part owing to the novelist's friendship with Edwards.

Two more small octavo editons of *An Essay on Man* with Warburton's notes were published by the Knaptons.

Samuel Richardson *to* Warburton[1]   14 April 1748
Indiana University, Lilly Library   London

London, April 14, 1748

Reverend Sir,

   Most heartily do I condole with you the heavy Loss you so affectingly deplore.[2] I have made my poor Clarissa[3] say that the finer Sensibilities make not happy. Who can wonder that Mr. Warburton should most sensibly feel so severe a stroke ⟨as this⟩ however apprehensive he might be of it, not only the good Ladys Illness, but from her advanced Life since to *apprehend* and to *know* must have very different Effects on the Mind; as the one admits of Hope; (the other not) But it would he highly impertinent in me to offer any thing ⟨more⟩ on this awful Subject to You——

   I am infinitely obliged to you, Sir, for your ⟨charming⟩ Paper.[4] But how shall I take it upon myself? I must, if put to me, by Particulars, suppose it to be suggested to me, at least, by some learned Friend, so disguising as You may not be suggested to be the Person. And I have transcribed it, that not even my Compositor may ⟨not⟩ guess at the Author. —— But it is really so much above my Learning and my Ability, that it will not be supposed mine by anybody.

   Will you, good Sir, allow me to mention, that I could wish that the *Air* of Genuineness had been kept up, tho' I want not the Letters to be *thought* genuine; only so far kept up, I mean, as that they should not prefatically be owned *not* to be genuine; and this for fear of weakening their Influence where any of them are aimed to be exemplary; as well as to avoid hurting that kind of Historical Faith which Fiction itself is generally read with, tho' we know it to be Fiction.[5]

Then as to what you are pleased to hint, that I pursued in my former Piece the excellent Plan fallen upon lately by the French Writers, I would only observe that all that know me, know, that I am not acquainted in the least either with the French Language or Writers; And that it was Chance and not Skill or Learning, that made me fall into this way of Scribbling.

But these Points I absolutely submit to your Determination. If they could be easily alter'd, and you were of Opinion that they *should* be alter'd, I then will hope for that Favour. But if you are not of that Opinion, it shall go just as you have favoured me with it. And in either case, I repeat my most hearty Thanks to you for the Favour, and Condescension, as I shall always think it, in bestowing your Thoughts on so light a Subject.

⟨I forbore any acknowledgements of this Favour till one could be composed, which I inclose, lest you should have no copy – But on Second Thought, it will perhaps be more to your own Satisfaction that I inclose your own MS.⟩

I hope that all the good Family of Prior Park are in ⟨good⟩ Health. God preserve yours to you, together with Freedom of Spirit, the greatest Blessing in this Life is the Prayer of Reverend Sir,

Your most obliged and faithful Servant
S. Richardson

Endorsed: Mine to Mr Warburton on Pref. to Vol. III, IV. Apr. 14. 1748 Clarissa

---

[1] Listed in T. C. Duncan Eaves and Ben D. Kimpel, *Samuel Richardson: A Biography* (Oxford, 1971), this letter appears in truncated form and is misdated 19 April 1748 in *Selected Letters of Samuel Richardson*, ed. John Carroll (Oxford, 1964), pp. 85–6. The endorsement suggests this was a rough draft kept by Richardson.

[2] Possibly referring to the declining health of Warburton's mother who died in March 1749.

[3] Richardson's *Clarissa. Or, the History of a Young Lady*, 7 vols. (London: printed for S. Richardson: and sold by John Osborn, Andrew Millar, J. and Ja. Rivington, and J. Leake, at Bath, 1748). The title-page belied the anonymity of the author: '*Published by the* EDITOR *of* PAMELA'. Volumes 1 and 2 were published on 1 December 1747; volumes 3 and 4 were published on 28 April 1748. Volume 5 was printed by October 1; volumes 6 and 7 were printed by November 7; and these three concluding volumes were published on 8 December 1748.

[4] Warburton evidently sent Richardson a draft of 'The Editor *to the* Reader' (i–vi)

which prefaced the first edition of the fourth volume of *Clarissa*, but was dropped from subsequent editions.

[5] In retrospect, Richardson may still have considered Warburton's points too negatively stated. As his preface concluded:

THIS is the nature and purport of his Attempt. Which, perhaps, may not be so well or generally understood. For if the Reader seeks here for Strange Tales, Love Stories, Heroical Adventures, or, in short, for any thing but a *Faithful Picture of Nature* in *Private Life*, he had better be told beforehand the likelihood of his being disappointed. But if he can find Use or Entertainment; either *Directions for his Conduct*, or *Employment for his Pity*, in a HISTORY *of* LIFE *and* MANNERS, where, as in the World itself, we find Vice, for a time, triumphant, and Virtue in distress, an idle hour or two, we hope, may not be unprofitably lost [v–vi] .

Warburton *to* Samuel Richardson[1]   25 April 1748
The Correspondence of Samuel Richardson, 6: *inter* 288–9   Prior Park

Dear Sir

I heartily thank you for the 2d & 3d Vs. of Clarissa[2] I suppose 2 more will finish the work and to those another advertisement of the same length which you have affixed to these may not be improper.[3] This *was* but a general criticism on the *spirits of the Fable*. That will afford a more particular examination of the conduct of this work in which we find that too great a sensibility & impatience under the force put on her selfe satisfaction necessarily & fatally drew after it that long & terrible attack & combat on her Virtue which now so entangled her in the miseries of life that nothing could free her from or make her tryumphant over them, but divine grace which now comes, like the God in the catastrophe of the Ancient fable, to clear up all difficulties. The valid & necessary connexion of all these parts on one another will afford occasion – of remarks advantageous to the conduct of your work – explain the fineness of the moral – and remove that silly objection agt the *too tragical* catastrophe. Tis not so tis happy if an overflow of divine grace upon the human mind to make the close of life (from whence happiness accor[ding?] to the ancient sage is to take its denomination) happy But the objection arose both from want of sense & of religion. I give you this hint that you may work up the concluding scene of her life as seraphicly as you can   cast over it that sunshine that may be able to dispell all the misreforms that the foregoing had made upon minds really & not pretendly tender for as these last only pride themselves in what they have not they will never be brought to own that an author's address can ravish from them what they think it an honour to pretend to – So good a

work as yours deserves a sensible defense rather than a childish revery of
a cake-house vision.

Dear Sr ever most affectionately
yours. W. Warburton

P.P Apr 25 1748

[1] This facsimile appears in a group of letters without annotation.
[2] Warburton received an advance copy of volume 3 of *Clarissa*.
[3] Warburton miscalculated both the final length of *Clarissa*, which ran to seven
volumes, and Richardson's desire for more editorial assistance from him. There were no
prefaces to vols. 5–7, although Richardson added a 'Postscript' (7: 425–32).

Warburton *to* [Knapton]   11 May 1748
BL: Egerton 1954, f.2   [Prior Park]

Dear Sir

I desire you would receive the inclosed Bill for my use. only letting Mr
Allen know this is come safe to hand for I am just setting out for
Lincolnshire

I am extremely surprised at your long silence, and can account no
otherwise for it than your ill health. in which however I hope I am
mistaken Being

your very assured friend &
humble Servant
W. Warburton
May 11 1748

Mr Allen desires that ye two copies of Anson's Voiages[1] may be bound &
gilt, and if they are not sent already I desire you would send his by
Leake's parcel & keep mine till I come to Towne.

[1] George Anson (1697–1762), Baron Anson of Soberton, *A Voyage Round the World, in
the Years MDCCXL, I, II, III, IV*, . . . *Illustrated with forty-two copper-plates*, compiled by
Richard Walker with Benjamin Robins (London: printed for the author; by John and
Paul Knapton, 1748). The Knaptons published another three editions in 1748 and
another two dated 1749.

Warburton *to* William Bowyer[1]   12 December 1748
Nichols, *Literary Anecdotes*, 2: 228   [Prior Park]

Dec. 12, 1748

Dear Sir

I have examined the Volume printed off, as to the press-work; and I
must needs tell you it is miserable work, and I cannot bear to have an

edition appear so badly done. Look into the books printed at Cambridge and Oxford, and you will see other sort of work. Look particularly into a very foolish book of Wood's, just printed at Oxford, on Stonehenge.[2] But your rascals, what between knavery and villainous *newspapers*, do their work never fit to be read, and sometimes incapable of being read.

Mr. Knapton tells me he has given Mr. Bowyer Brown's Poem on Satire.[3] Why is it not yet printed? It is to be put at the head of that volume in which the Essay on Man is. Why is not the Index to the Dunciad yet printed? Send it to me by the bearer.

[1] The note to this and the six following letters from Warburton to Bowyer about Pope's 1751 *Works* reads: 'The extreme care which was taken of this edition, with its progress through the press, will appear from the following curious and expostulatory letters of the learned Editor to his Printer.'

[2] John Wood (1704–54), *Choir Gaure, Vulgarly Called Stonehenge; Described, Restored, and Explained* (Oxford, 1747). Wood was the main architect of Ralph Allen's – later the Warburtons' – residence at Prior Park. See H. M. Colvin, *A Biographical Dictionary of English Architects* (London, 1954), p.688.

[3] See 24 December 1746 and n.1, above.

Warburton *to* [Knapton][1]   17 December 1748
BL: Egerton 1954, f.8   [Prior Park]

Don't you think that Mrs Cockbourn's book agt Rutherforth should be advertised again?[2] I never saw Mr Comber's letter advertised above once or twice.[3] But it might be in papers that do not come here. It is well wrote.

I am most affectionately yours
W. Warburton
Decr 17 1748

It is unreasonable to expect long letters from you who have such variety of Business. But do not forget that I always hear from you with great Pleasure, as there is no friend I more esteem & love.

[1] The opening salutation has been cut off.

[2] Catharine Cockburn, *Remarks upon the Principles and Reasonings of Dr. Rutherforth's Essay on the Nature and Obligations of Virtue*. This was listed in *GM*, 17 (April 1747): 204; and in *LM*, 16 (April–May 1747): 247. Her *Works* were published in two volumes by the Knaptons in 1751.

[3] Possibly referring to *Modest and candid reflections on Dr. Middleton's examination of the Right Reverend the Lord Bishop of London's use and intent of prophecy: in a letter to the Honourable G. Lyttelton, Esq; from Thomas Comber, A.B.* (Malton: printed by J. N. for Messrs. Knapton booksellers in St. Paul's Churchyard [London], 1750). Also, 'The heathens rejection of

christianity in the first ages consider'd. By *Tho*. Comber, A.B. pr. 4*s*. 6*d*. *Knapton'* was advertised in *GM*, 17 (June 1747): 300. See Warburton's letter to Comber of 11 January 1752, below; Gertrude Warburton listed a letter from Comber in her inventory of her late husband's papers, dated 3 May 1780, below.

Warburton *to* [Knapton][1]   *c*. 22 December 1748
Nichols, *Literary Anecdotes*, 9: 624 (fragment)   [Prior Park]

    I desire Bowyer may cancel one Leaf, and reprint it; it is p.160.[2] Instead of the words 'It hath been shewn that they make no distinct Estate there; and consequently are not Representatives but Agents only of the Church' – to be read thus: "It hath been shewn that they make no distinct Estate there; and consequently are not Representatives of the Clergy, but Agents only of the Church."

W.W.

[1] This incomplete letter is printed together with the following under the heading 'Mr. Knapton and Mr. Warburton to Mr. Bowyer'. Warburton's letter giving his cancellation was enclosed in Knapton's curt note to Bowyer.

[2] *The Alliance between Church and State*, 3rd ed. (London: J. and P. Knapton, 1748).

Knapton *to* Willliam Bowyer   22 December 1748
Nichols, *Literary Anecdotes*, 9: 624   [London]

Dec. 22, 1748

SIR,

    A Leaf of Mr. Warburton's "Alliance" must be canceled. I send also Mr. Warburton's alteration, and desire it may be done as soon as you can.——The Press-work of the Volumes now printing wants some care; Mr. Warburton does not like it; and I shall be glad that you will take all possible care about it, that it may be in the best manner possible.

I am, &c. JOHN KNAPTON

1749

After more than four years of strained relations between Warburton and Bolingbroke, the *London Magazine* published an account of Pope's surreptitious printing of *The Idea of a Patriot King* in the January number which also carried 'Of the Private Life of a Prince'. Further instalments appeared in the March and April issues.

Three pro-Pope accounts were advertised in the May issue of the *Gentleman's Magazine*: *A Letter to the Lord Viscount B[olingbro]ke*; Joseph Spence's *Apology for the late Mr. Pope*; and Warburton's anonymous *A Letter to the Editor of the Letters on the Spirit of Patriotism*. In the same month, the *London Magazine* printed an announcement of Bolingbroke's forthcoming authorized edition of *The Idea of a Patriot King*, published by Andrew Millar. The new *Monthly Review* devoted thirteen pages to lengthy quotations from the *Spirit of Patriotism*, with more in subsequent issues. Warburton was attacked in *A Familiar Epistle to the Most Impudent Man Living*, penned most likely by Mallet under Bolingbroke's direction.

Warburton's mother died in March. He began his lengthy correspondence with Richard Hurd and supplied notes for Thomas Newton's edition of *Paradise Lost*.

Henry Lintot published *An Essay on Criticism* with Warburton's notes. Fielding's *Tom Jones*, published by Millar, frequently alluded to Pope and paid Warburton a high, but possibly ironical, compliment.

Warburton *to* Knapton 1 January 1749
BL: Egerton 1954, f.9 [Prior Park]

Dear Sir

Mr & Mrs Allen desire their respects to you. They have sent a Turkey & a Chine directed to you which they beg your acceptance of. They will be at the Carriers at Holborne bridge on Wednesday.

Mr Allen has order'd me to subscribe for two sets of Montfalcon's Antiquities of France one for himselfe, the other for me. So pray put down the Subscription to his account.[1]

All here join with me in our best respects to your selfe & Mr & Mrs Knapton

And I am Dr Sr your very affectionate
friend & humble Servt
W. Warburton
Jan 1 1748/9

A happy new year to you all.

Address and frank (f.11*v*.): To Mr Knapton Bookseller in Ludgate Street London   Free R: Allen

¹ Bernard de Montfaucon (1655–1741), *Monumens de la Monarchie Françoise*, 5 vols. (1729–33); *A Collection of Regal and Ecclesiastical Antiquities of France*, 2 vols., illust. (London: printed for W. Innys, J. and P. Knapton, R. Manby and H.S. Cox, 1750); noted in Boyce, p.177.

Warburton *to* Knapton   9 April 1749
BL: Egerton 1954, f.12   [Prior Park]

Dear Sir

I return the proofe sheet corrected. You are very good in your solicitude for poor Mrs Cockbourn's success. If those who most urged her to this expedient of a subscription do not slacken their zeal, it will succeed.

Any small parcels that come to you directed to me till my return I beg you will order to be sent to Mr Hitch, for Leake's parcel. All the family desire their best compliments particularly my Wife's to Mrs Knapton. Mr Allen thanks you for your last note to him concerning Dobbs book;[1] which he perceives is an old think [*sic*] which he is already in possession of.

I beg as soon as the remaining sheets of ye Dunciad[2] are worked off they may be sent to me, in Leak's parcel. God preserve your health till I see you again & believe me to be

Dear Sr most affectionately yours
W. Warburton
Apr. 9 1749

Address: (*verso*; incomplete): [Kn]apton [Stre]et   [Lo]ndon

¹ Arthur Dobbs (1689–1765). His *Account of the Countries adjoining to Hudson's Bay* was published by Knapton's neighbour in Ludgate Street, Jacob Robinson, in 1744; other publications include: *Remarks upon Captain Middleton's Defence* (1744); *Reasons to Shew, that there is a Great Probability of a Navigable Passage to the Western American Ocean through Hudson's Streights* (1749); *A Short Narrative and Justification of the Proceedings of the Committee Appointed by the Adventurers* (1749). Dobbs also wrote on Anglo-Irish trade.
² *The Dunciad*, London: J. and P. Knapton, 1749 [1750].

Warburton *to* [Knapton]   4 May 1749
BL: Egerton 1954, f.13   Prior Park

Dear Sir

I thank you for the favour of the preface to L. B.'s tracts.[1]
The fact must be deemed as he relates it, because he has in his custody

(by Mr Pope's own designment) all Mr Pope's papers; by which perhaps it might be contradicted, or, at least, seen in a very different light.[2]

However so much must be evident to every impartial Man, that Mr Pope could have no other possible end in this indiscretion (for if Ld. B.'s fact be true, an indiscretion it was) than Ld. B.'s honour. This appears from the nature of the work, which is calculated to do the Author that sort of credit he most affects;——from Mr Pope's not destroying the impression, which he might have done with the same secrecy he had it printed, when his desperate & lingering illness gave him time to, & shewed him the necessity of, destroying it, had he been conscious to himselfe of any oblique[3] or lucritave views:——And lastly the idolatrous fondness he had for the Author. All this, and what ever more I think necessary in justice to my dear friend, shall certainly be laid before the Public in his life:[4] & let them judge between Mr Pope & *this his guide, philosopher & Friend.*[5] I for my part think him justly punished for that extravagant veneration he bore him, which led him, in support of that Ld's quarrels, to abuse many honester men, because hated by him.[6]

He passes a most severe censure p.94 on Dr Clark's *Being & Attr. of God*[7] which I shall vindicate agt him in the 3d Vol. of the Div. Leg:[8]

I am Dear Sir your most affectionate
Friend & humble Servant
W. Warburton
P.P. May 4 1749

Address (f.14; detached): To Mr: John Knapton   Bookseller in Ludgate Street   London   Free R: Allen.

[1] In the Advertisement to the 1749 edition of Bolingbroke's *The Idea of a Patriot King*, Pope was maligned for having 1500 copies printed without the author's knowledge or consent.

[2] Warburton used Bolingbroke's custodianship of Pope's private manuscripts as a mitigating factor in his *Letter to the Editor*, published within a month of this letter. If Pope had wanted to deceive Bolingbroke, Warburton argued, why would he have chosen Bolingbroke to be one of his literary executors?

[3] A tear in the leaf obscures this word.

[4] As he had mentioned in his letter of 25 July 1745 above, Warburton was still planning to write a biography of Pope.

[5] Warburton ironically applied these epithets, formerly ascribed to the dedicatee of *An Essay on Man*, on the title-page of his anonymous *A Letter to the Editor of the Letters on the Spirit of Patriotism.*

[6] Warburton might have had his former patron, Sir Robert Sutton, in mind.

[7] Samuel Clarke, *A Discourse Concerning the Being and Attributes of God* (London: James Knapton, 1705–06; 8th ed. James and John Knapton, 1732). On 11 May 1749, Nathaniel Cole wrote to James Brockman about the *Patriot King*: 'Here is a book lately published by Lord Bolingbroke. It seems to be approved and abuses Mr. Pope in his preface and the late Dr. Clarke in fo. 94' (BL: Add. MS. 42591, f.84); see Jeremy Black,

'Bolingbroke's Attack on Pope: a Lawyer's Comment', *N&Q*, 231 (1986): 513–14; and Donald W. Nichol, 'Pope, Warburton, Knapton, and Cole'. Cole, solicitor to the Stationers' Company, had acted for Pope and Dodsley against the piratical printer James Watson in 1737–8, and knew both Warburton and Knapton (*Correspondence*, 4: 87–8, 335, 345, 425; Mack, *Collected*, pp.492–501). It is likely that Cole picked up the reference to p.94 of Clarke's *Being and Attributes of God* from this letter in Knapton's shop. Warburton mentioned Cole in his letter of 4 December 1752, below.

⁸ Book 5, section 2, of the third volume of *The Divine Legation of Moses* ends with 'Lord Bolingbroke's accusation of the Law of Moses examined and exposed' (*WWW*, 3: 16, 54–69).

[Warburton] *to* [Knapton]¹   [May 1749]
BL: Add. MS. 4948.A, f.446 (transcript)   [Prior Park?]

With regard to Mr Mallet's declaration, there is only one way to convince me he is not the author of that infamous Libel² which is by taking an opportunity of disowning it publickly. —— I think my honour concerned that it be publickly known I had no hand in ye Letter to Ld B.³ merely on account of the Apollo Story;⁴ and I shall do it on the first occasion. If Mr M. does not do the same with regard to this Libel I shall consider him as the author of it and act in consequence of that Belief. This I desire you would let Mr Millar⁵ know, and if he chuses let him have a Transcript⁶ of what I here say.

[n.s.]

¹ This unsigned and undated letter was presumably sent at Warburton's bidding via Knapton or Millar to Mallet during the *Patriot King* controversy in 1749. Mallet's reply, in which he denies his authorship of a pamphlet, at the same time condemns Warburton, thereby suggesting he had a strong motive for writing *A Familiar Epistle to the Most Impudent Man Living* (1749). See *A Letter to the Editor* and *A Familiar Epistle*, ed. Siebert, who assumes Bolingbroke wrote *A Familiar Epistle* (pp.v–vi), although, according to a contemporary report in the *Monthly Review*, it was 'universally attributed to Mr. Mallet' (*LA*, 9: 624; H. T. Dickinson, *Bolingbroke*, pp.280–2). 'A Letter to the Editor' appeared in the *London Evening Post* of 23 May 1749 (Brean S. Hammond, *Pope and Bolingbroke*, p.77).

² Possibly *To the Author of a Libel, entitled, A Letter to the Editor*, printed by W. Webb in reply to Warburton's defence of Pope in *A Letter to the Editor of the Letters on the Spirit of Patriotism, &c*. If 'Libel' refers to tone rather than title, Warburton might be referring to *A Familiar Epistle to the Most Impudent Man Living*.

³ The anonymous *A Letter to the Lord Viscount B[olingbro]ke* was advertised in the May 1749 issue of *GM*. Mallet suspected Warburton's authorship.

⁴ 'It is in this pamphlet [*A Letter to the Lord Viscount B[olingbro]ke*, 1749] that we have the account of the "Apollo Vision" . . . Mallet, so the story goes, had heard that Warburton was preparing a Life of Pope, and in conversation with the biographer recounted a dream which he had had. He was sitting one day with Pope in his last illness when Pope suddenly came out of a reverie, and looking steadfastly at Mallet, said: "Mr Mallet, I have had a strange kind of vision. Methought I saw my own head open and

Apollo come out of it; I then saw your head open and Apollo went into it; after which our heads closed up again." Unimpressed, Warburton remarked: "Why, sir, if I had an intention of writing *your* life, this might perhaps be a proper anecdote; but I don't see that in Mr Pope's it will be of the slightest consequence at all" ', W. L. MacDonald, *Pope and his Critics: a Study in Eighteenth Century Personalities* (London, 1951), pp.218–19; also cited in *The Oxford Book of Literary Anecdotes*, ed. James Sutherland (Oxford, 1976), p.77.
   Warburton later intended to use the 'Apollo story' in a satiric footnote to *Arbuthnot* in the *Works* (1751), 4: 9, but cancelled the leaf; see E-C, 3: 534–5.
   [5] Andrew Millar published an edition of Lord Bolingbroke's *Works*, much against Warburton's advice, in 1754. Two years later, Millar's name appeared in the imprint of Pope's *Works*.
   [6] This may well be the transcript Warburton asked Millar to make for Mallet.

David Mallet *to* [Knapton?][1]   [May 1749]
BL: Add. MS. 4948.A, f.446 (transcript)   [London]

   N.B. I never took the slightest notice of this impudent and silly threatning from Warburton. The writer I had no reason to be afraid of: the man I abhorred A head filled with paradoxes, unproved and unproveable: a heart overflowing with virulences and the most slanderous malice. N.B. I never wrote a pamphlet, nor a sentence in any pamphlet concerning this wrong-headed, dogmatical pedant.

                                                               D. Mallet

   [1] After reading the above transcript of Warburton's letter, presumably passed on from Knapton to Millar, Mallet appended this note intended to serve as the kind of denial of authorship of *A Familiar Epistle to the Most Impudent Man Living* that Warburton could not make public. Knapton may have communicated the message of Mallet's denial without the insults.

Warburton *to* [Henry Etough][1]   28 September 1749
BL: Add. MS. 4326.B, f.31   Prior Park

                                               Prior Park Sepr 28 1749
Revd Sir
   All who have regard to Mrs Cockbourn's memory, or would promote the wellfare of her favorite surviving Daughter, can never say enough in commendation of your zeal & generosity. I have the favour of yours of the 23 and am extremly pleased to find you have put things in so good a train.
   I esteem Mr Birche's kindness in this affair as a favour done to my selfe, both as it eases me, who have indeed at present my hands full, and as I shall have the pleasure of se[e]ing justice done to Mrs Cockbourn's

memory, as well in the memoirs of her life as in the selection of her works. I shall be always ready to continue any assistance of any kind to promote that service we concurr in. I hope to be in London the latter end of next month. When nothing shall be wanting on my part. And indeed you, who have taken the lead in this affair with so much generosity, & success, have a right to all the assistance that every common friend of Mrs C. can lend you.

I am Sir with great regard your
very obedient humble Servant
W. Warburton

[1] Etough sent this letter to Thomas Birch on 7 October 1749 from Therfield, Hants., with the note 'I herewith inclose ye Great Warburtons Letter' (BL: Add. MS. 4326.B, f.29). Before doing so, he drafted his reply to the above letter on its verso, which Warburton answered on October 12.

[Henry Etough] *to* [Warburton][1]   7 October 1749
BL: Add. MS. 4326.B, f.31*v*.   Therfield

Therfield 8ʳ 7 1749

Sir

Your approbation of what has been done in ye Affair of Mrs Cockburns works is highly agre[e]able & pleasing. Mr Birchs goodness in what he has undertaken is a most lucky circumstance. He is both able & willing we are not only eased of much trouble but are sure of having ye work well executed. If You have any thing with You in ye Country You will be so good as to bring it up to Town. When Mr Birch heareth of Your arrival he will be ready to wait on you in order to have every thing in his possession. We are very thankfull for ye kind assurances you have given us of ye continuance of Your good Offices. Your superior skill & merit will be of great advantage; & all your condescentions & services will ever be gratefully acknowledged by

[n.s.]

[1] This would appear to be a draft of Etough's answer to Warburton's letter of 28 September 1749 to which Warburton replied on October 12.

Warburton *to* [Henry Etough]   12 October 1749
BL: Add. MS. 4326.B, f.34   Prior Park

Revd Sir

I have the favour of yours of the 7   I agree with you that it is a lucky circumstance in favour of Mrs Cockborne & her family that Mr Birch will take the trouble of writing her memoirs & taking care of the Edition of her works.

All her papers are in London   And I shall be glad to wait on Mr Birch at my house to deliver them up to him &c I propose to be in Town by the begining of this Michmas term. And am with great respect

Revd Sir your
very obedient humble Servant
W. Warburton
Prior Park   Octr. 12 1749

Warburton *to* William Bowyer   14 October 1749
Nichols, *Literary Anecdotes*, 2: 228   [Prior Park]

Oct. 14, 1749.

As to that letter of Dr. Arbuthnot to Mr. Pope in Curll's Edition,[1] if you are sure it be genuine, I would have it in; and what else there is there that is genuine and modest.

[1] *Works* (1751), 8: 239–41; *Correspondence*, 3: 416–17 (17 July 1734).

1750

Warburton's relations with Bowyer were becoming strained by his many cancels, corrections and demands for quick delivery of corrected sheets to Prior Park. He began to send proofs via Knapton. Volume 6 was the last to be printed of the 1751 *Works*. In September he was enquiring about the small octavo edition of Pope's *Works*, which would not be published for another twelve months. Shortly before Christmas, Warburton asked Knapton to commission Thomas Major, recently returned from the continent, to do an engraving for the 1751 *Works*. This turned out to be the frontispiece to the edition.

The Knaptons published *The Dunciad* (dated 1749), which contained derogatory notes on critics of Warburton's Shakespeare edition. William Dodd published his parody, *A New Book of the Dunciad: Occasion'd by Mr. Warburton's New Edition*, installing Warburton in Cibber's throne.

Warburton's *Julian* was published by the Knaptons.

Warburton *to* William Bowyer   9 March 1750
Nichols, *Literary Anecdotes*, 2: 228   [Prior Park]

March 9, 1749–50.
The inclosed is the conclusion of the Introduction corrected. I would have it worked off. To fasten the concluding loose leaf I have sent the title-page, for there will be no advertisement to make another leaf to that I once proposed——And to make these two leaves half a sheet, I have sent two leaves to be reprinted. I am surprized I have not yet had a proof of the first sheet, which I delivered when I was in London to be reprinted; and think myself very ill used by the neglect.——I expect what I order to be done, to be done out of hand.

Warburton *to* William Bowyer   12 March 1750
Nichols, *Literary Anecdotes*, 2: 228–9   [Prior Park]

March 12, 1749–50.
I have sent the inclosed, that the work may go on with all expedition. What is yet to print will make about four sheets. This (and the little copy you had before) is part. I shall insist on having two sheets composed, and sent me to correct; for I am resolved to have the book out before the end of the month.[1] Had you *condescended* to do what I desired, which was, to have the first sheet re-composed with speed, the compositor would now have had nothing to do but fall to work on this. You need not fear waiting for the rest of the copy.

[1] *Julian* (London: J. and P. Knapton, 1750).

Warburton *to* William Bowyer 23 March 1750
Nichols, *Literary Anecdotes*, 2: 229 [Prior Park]

March 23, 1749–50.
I have sent the conclusion of the book, with a leaf to be reprinted, which is the last I shall cancel.[1] I expected more proof this day. Sure you know the post comes every day.

[1] *Julian.*

Warburton *to* John Nourse 2 April 1750
Harvard University, Houghton Library: Prior Park
fMS. Eng. 1336 (21)

Sir
If there be any vols yet published of that new work of Crevier's of the History of the Emperors I desire you would send them to me. (I do not mean the vols I want of his continuation of Rolin which you was to get bound for me.[1] let those stay till I come to town) If you have the 4 Vols of Racine[2] mentioned in the inclosed advertismt I desire too you would send those with *Orosius* Havercamp's Ed. in 4°. Lug. Bat. 1738.[3] Be ⟨so good to subscribe for me for Hughe's Hist. of Barbadoes Fol.[4] there is no money to be pd till the book be delivered,⟩ and to get me a Cat. of Lady Sunderlands Houshold goods &c. which is to be had at Langford's in the great piazza Covent Garden[5]

Your very humble Servt
W. Warburton
Prior Park Apr. 2d 1750

Address: To Mr: Nurse Bookseller in the Strand London Free R: Allen.

[1] Jean Baptiste Louis Crevier, *Histoire des empereurs romains*, 6 vols. (Paris, 1650–6); Charles Rollin, *Histoire romaine*, 9 vols., continued by Crevier from 1738. The Knaptons published Rollin's *History* from 1734 and were preparing for Crevier's continuation, *The Roman History from the Foundation of Rome*, 2nd ed., 16 vols. (London: J. and P. Knapton, 1754).
[2] Racine, *Oeuvres*, 3 vols. (Amsterdam and Leipzig, 1750).
[3] Paulus Orosius, *Pauli Orosii. Adversus paganos historiarum . . . illustravit Sigebertus Havercampus* (Lugduni Batavorum, 1738).
[4] Griffith Hughes, *The Natural History of Barbados* (London: printed for the author; and sold by most booksellers in Great Britain and Ireland, 1750).

⁵ Lady Sunderland (née Judith Tichborne), wife of Charles Spencer (1674–1722), 3rd Earl of Sunderland. She married Warburton's patron, Sir Robert Sutton (1672–1746), and died in 1749. Plomer lists J. Langford as a pamphlet-seller with a shop opposite St. Clement's Church in the Strand, 1756–65.

Warburton *to* Philip Doddridge[1]   11 June 1750
Huntington Library: HM 20438   Bedford Row, London

Letter 207[2]

Dear Sir

Your favour of the 17 of May was sent me to London where I then was & yet am till tomorrow when I return to P.P.

I am greatly flattered by your thoughts of Julian: because I know the sincerity of your Professions.

Some people of consideration would persuade me to take to task at the end of the 2d pt of Julian a Chapter of one Hume on Miracles in a rank atheistical book called *Phil: Essays*.[3] And as the subject of the 2d part may be a little ticklish, perhaps it may be prudent to conciliate warm tempers by such a conclusion.

I was very sincere in the hint, which you are pleased to call advise, of my last Letter. As I am in saying that I do not know of any thing which your Abilities & application are not capable of.

You are very good to inquire after my motions. I shall not be in Towne either in June or July. Towards the decline of Summer I have some thoughts of taking a Journey into Lincolnshire. If I do I may take Northampton in my way & will take my chance of finding you at home.

As to the *Disquisitions* I will only say that the temper, candour & charity with which they are wrote are very edifying & exemplary. I wish success to them as much as you can do. But I can tell you of certain science, that not the least alteration will be made in the Ecclesiastical System. The present Ministers were bred up under and act entirely on the maxims of the last. And one of the principal of his was *not to stir what is at rest*. He took a medicine for the stone that killed him. And on his deathbed he said he fell by the neglect of his own maxim. Those at the head of affairs find it as much as they can do to govern things as they are & they will never venture to set one part of the Clergy agt another, the consequence of which would be, that in the briques [?] of political contests one of the two parties would certainly fall in with the faction (if we must call it so) agt the Court.

Your truly divine Labours are not only more excellent, but will certainly prove more fruitfull.

But above all I join with your Friends in encouraging you to a subscription which I make no doubt will turn out a considerable benefit. Books of infinitely less importance have lately done so. And I ardently wish that one who has d[eserve?]d so greatly of our common Christianity, may not have the whole of his reward to wait for, in another life.

To understand that all your good family are well, gives me extreme pleasure. My truest respects to all. and particularly to the young Gentle man who is begining his studies.[4] I must now begin to call him my learned friend & have sent him a magnificent Edn. which no money will buy (I mean they are not to be sold) of the Essay on Man & Essay on Criticism.[5]

> Dear Sir believe me ever with
> the truest esteem your most
> Affectionate friend & Brother
> W. Warburton
> Bedford Row   June 11 1750

Address and postmark: To The Revd. Docr: Doddridge at Northampton 12 IV [June]
Endorsed (in another hand): 1750   Mr Warburton   June 31   11——— 38 No. 15th

---

[1] For a list of Warburton's correspondence with this recipient, see Geoffrey F. Nuttall, *A Calendar of the Correspondence of Philip Doddridge, D.D. (1702–1751)* Historical Manuscripts Commission, JP 26 (London, 1979).

[2] In another hand.

[3] David Hume's 'Essay on Miracles' was included in *Philosophical Essays concerning Human Understanding* (London: A. Millar, 1748).

[4] Doddridge had one son who survived infancy, also named Philip.

[5] The quarto editions of the 1743 *Essay on Man* (Griffith 589) and 1744 *Essay on Criticism* (Griffith 590) edited by Warburton. He presumably meant that both editions had sold out.

Warburton *to* [Knapton]   15 September 1750
BL: Egerton 1954, f.16   Prior Park

Sept. 15 1750

Dear Sir

I beg the favour of you to let your correspondent at York Mr Hilyard[1] the Bookseller to pay ten pounds, as he has done before to Mrs Hayes.[2] And as I have given her no notice of it, that he would send to her, I suppose she lives in Yorke or near and that he may know where to send to her.

I had a fifty pounds bank note, and a *bank* post bill for 20 each of them cut in two and in paying away the 20*l.* to I don't know whom I gave away with the left hand part of the sola[3] bill the right hand part of the 50*l.* note. The business is how I shall get this matter remedyed, so as to receive my 50 note of the bank. The two halfs I have in my custody only they shew that the one is a note for *fifty* pounds – and the other a bank post bill payable to Benj. Mendes. But in my pocket book I find the two notes entered thus.

No. B. 24 pay to James Cotebrooke & Co. 50*l.* 26. Octr. 1749 sign. Rich. Handes

No. B. 2154 Bank post bill pay to Mr Benj. Mendes 7 days sight 20*l.* 28 Sept. 1748. sign. Rich. Handes.[4]

I desire you would send me by the Carrier stitched the 8 Vs. of Pope that are printed (the last is in the press) that I may examine the errata &c. and prepare every thing for compleating the Edn.[5] Pray in what forwardness are the decorations for the vols?[6] Is the little Edn gone to the press?[7] And when you think we shall be ready, & when will it be proper for the publication?

> I am Dear Sir ever most affectionately yours
> W. Warburton

Prior Park   I am at present here alone. Mr A's family & a good part of mine are now drinking the fashionable liquor, I mean seawater at Weymouth. But it is not my fortune to be in the fashion.

---

[1] John Hildyard, bookseller in York (1731–57); listed in Plomer.

[2] Possibly a relation, Mrs Hayes is mentioned intermittently throughout Warburton's letters.

[3] 'Of bills . . . A "sola" bill of exchange is a single bill as distinguished from bills drawn in "sets"' (*OED*). Pope used the word 'sola' in his letters (*Correspondence*, 3: 122 and 173).

[4] Untraced.

[5] The 1751 large octavo edition of Pope's *Works*, Griffith 643–51. Bowyer's ledger records volumes 1 (18¼ sheets), 2 (17⅛ sheets), 3 (21 sheets), 4 (21⅝ sheets), 5 (21¼ sheets), 6 (26¾ sheets), 7 (25⅛ sheets), 8 (18¼ sheets) and 9 (24½ sheets). With 5½ sheets of cancels, the total rounded off to 199 sheets. The 1500 nine-volume sets were delivered between 22 May and 12 June 1751. Sets of cancelled leaves to volumes 1–2 and 6–9 were delivered on May 31 and June 5 (Maslen, 'Works from the Bowyer Press', p.197).

[6] There are twenty-four illustrations in the 1751 Pope edition (none for volumes 7–9): Volume 1: plate I: N. Blakey, del., T. Major Sculp.; plate II: S. Wale, inv. et del., J. S. Müller, Sc.; plate III: Anthony Walker del. et sculpt.

Volume 2: plate IV: S. Wale inv. et del., J. S. Müller, Sc.; plate V: Anthony Walker inv., del. et sculpt.; plates VI–VII: S. Wale, delin., C. Mosley, sculp.

Volume 3: plates VIII–XI, XV: N. Blakey, inv. et del., Ravenet, sculp.; plates XII–XIV: N. Blakey, inv. et del., G. Scotin, sculp.

Volumes 4–6: plates XVI–XXIV: F. Hayman, inv. et del., C. Grignion, sculp. ('Inv.' and 'del.' denote the designer, while 'Sc.' or 'Sculp.' indicates the engraver.)

[7] Griffith 653. The 1751 small octavo edition was printed by Bowyer and Strahan.

Bowyer's ledger records volumes 2 ($14\frac{1}{2}$ sheets) and 5 ($20\frac{5}{8}$ sheets), received 21 March–12 July [1751?]. Strahan's ledger for April 1749 records volumes 1 and 6–9 ($85\frac{1}{2}$ sheets) at £2 2s. per sheet, with a total of 3,000 nine-volume sets (Maslen, 'Works from the Bowyer Press', p.197).

Warburton *to* [Knapton]   20 December 1750
BL: Egerton 1954, f.17   Prior Park

Dear Sir

I saw Mr Dingley[1] the other day who has an influence with Major the ingraver who he says is come back to England.[2] I desired that he would use his interest with him to engrave what you think fit to put into his hands with care & expedition; he promised he would write to him immediately, and I dare say would be glad to oblige me in this matter.

I wish the Prints wanting may be expidited all they can. I believe Bowyer has by this time finished the Last Vol. that was to print. It consists of Misc. poetry & Prose.[3] No Prints have been thought of for this Vol: The two last tracts in it are Mr P's Prefaces to his Homer & to his Shakespear. Would not the heads of those two Poets be Proper?[4]

I am Dear Sir your most
faithfull humble Servt
W. Warburton

P.P. Decr 20 1750

Address (f.18; detached): To Mr: Knapton Bookseller in Ludgate Street London

[1] Robert Dingley was a member of the Dilettanti; see Louise Lippincott, *Selling Art in Georgian England*, pp.45, 130, 176 n.76.

[2] Thomas Major (1720–99) engraved the Blakey design for the frontispiece of the 1751 edition of Pope's *Works*, depicting Warburton as the principal figure. See *DNB* and Wimsatt, pp.339–41.

[3] Volume 6 of the 1751 *Works*.

[4] The result of Warburton's suggestion may be seen in plate 24 of volume 6 of the 1751 *Works*, although this frontispiece is by Francis Hayman and Charles Grignion.

1751

Seven years after the poet's death, Warburton was finally ready to publish his edition of Pope's *Works*. On May 23, he wrote to Balguy, tentatively mentioning 'Mr. Pope's Works, which will be published on the 1st., 2nd. or 3rd. of June' (Griffith, 2: 524).

However, a fortnight later Horace Walpole was still waiting. Warburton made numerous last-minute changes: the first page to *Arbuthnot* which carried a satiric reference to Mallet was cancelled; and plate XVII was shifted at a late stage of production. According to Warburton, the edition 'waited for ornaments'. The publication date, according to the *London Evening Post*, was June 18. Bowyer printed 1500 sets of the large octavo edition of Pope's *Works* which sold at £2 2s. in sheets. A small octavo edition, listed at 27s., came out in October. The Warburton edition of Pope's *Works* was attacked by John Gilbert Cooper, Thomas Edwards, Theophilus Cibber and many anonymous hacks.

Warburton also helped see Mrs. Cockburn's works through the press. His long-time correspondent Philip Doddridge died in Lisbon on October 26, followed by his major opponent Bolingbroke on December 12.

Warburton *to* Knapton   14 March [1751?][1]
BL: Egerton 1954, f.15   Prior Park

Dear Sir

I have the favour of yours of the 7   I desire you would send Bowyer the inclosed proofe sheet. I have inclosed too, a little more copy.

I shall be glad to see Mr Mason's Trag:[2] If there be any thing left for me with you to make up a packet you may send it the usual way. I have looked over the 1st vol. of Pope large 8°. now printing.   if the 3d 4th & 5th vols. (in which there are the most notes) be printed off you may send me those th[r]ee stitched for the same purpose

> I am Dear Sir, with the
> most regard your most affect.
> friend & faithfull Servt
> W. Warburton

P.P. March 14.

Addendum (probably in Knapton's hand): Recd 3 MS. Sheets. Page 31. to 42 Incl and send them to Mr Bowyer Mar 16
Address, postmark and frank (*verso*): To Mr: Knapton Bookseller in Ludgate Street London   Free R: Allen   16 MR

---

[1] The year is difficult to pin down as William Mason's *Elfrida: a Dramatic Poem. Written on the model of the antient Greek tragedy* (London: J. and P. Knapton, 1752) circulated in manuscript a year before it was published (a notice appeared in the *Daily Advertiser* on 21 March 1752). Thomas Gray mentioned the tragedy in a letter to Horace Walpole on 20

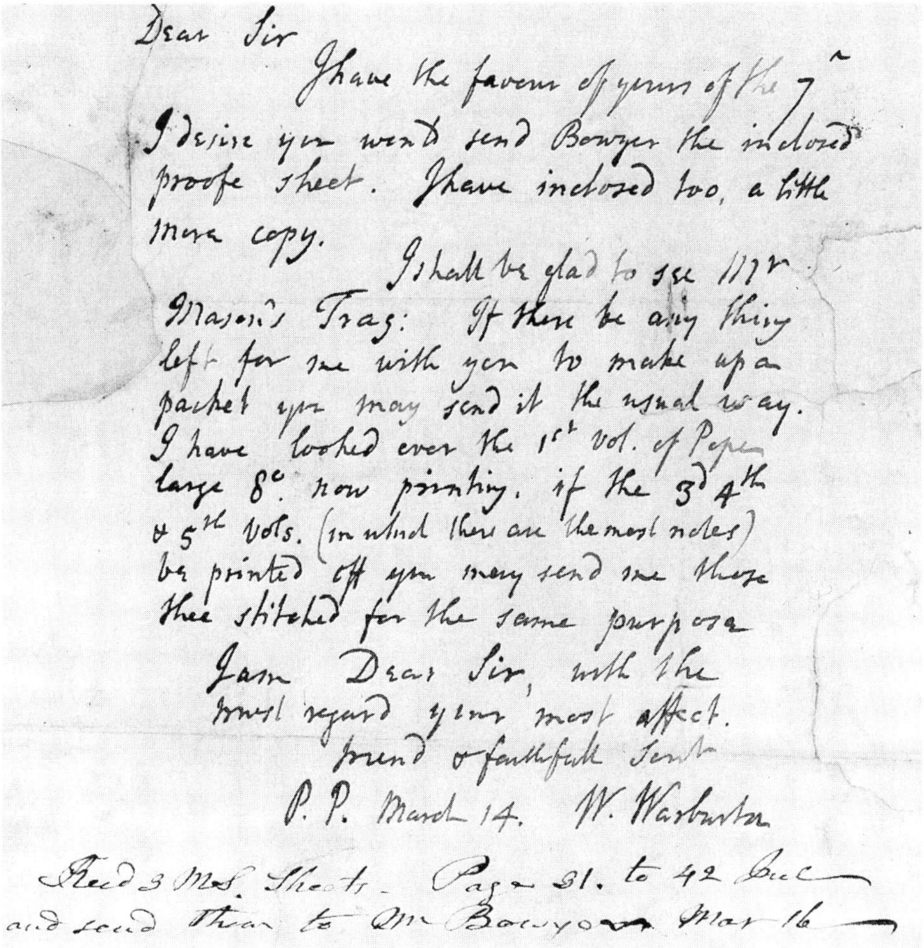

Dear Sir

I have the favour of yours of the 7.

I desire you wou'd send Bowyer the inclosed proofe sheet. I have inclosed too, a little more copy.

I shall be glad to see Mr. Mason's Trag: If there be any thing left for me with you to make up a packet you may send it the usual way. I have looked over the 1st vol. of Pope large 8o. now printing. if the 3d 4th & 5th vols. (in which there are the most notes) be printed off you may send me these thee stitched for the same purpose

I am Dear Sir, with the most regard your most affect. friend & faithfull servant

P. P. March 14.   W. Warburton

Recd 3 Ms. Sheets. Page 31. to 42 incl and send them to Mr Bowyer.   Mar 16

Plate 3. Warburton to Knapton, 14 March [1751?], with Knapton's note.

February 1751 and again on March 3 when he wrote from Cambridge, 'Elfrida... and her author are now in town together', *Horace Walpole's Correspondence*, ed. Lewis *et al.*, 1: 343; 14: 47. Gray also sent Walpole a copy and advised discretion as Mason was planning to publish it. Mason may well have sent his manuscript to Knapton at this time. Knapton, in turn, may have asked for Warburton's advice on whether to publish *Elfrida*. Yet in a transcript of a letter dated 5 November 1751, Warburton advised Mason, 'It is a good Point for a young Author to have a bookseller of Eminence. The person I mean is Mr Knapton not only the most eminent in the trade but of as great integrity & honesty as any man I know. as he has very great dealings I asked him if he chose to be involved in such a work' (BL: Add. MS. 32563, ff.125*v*.-7). On 29 December 1751 Warburton wrote to Hurd, 'Pray what is Mr. Mason doing? Mr. Knapton wrote me word not long since that he had received no copy from him' (*LLEP*, p.68).

Warburton referred to 'the 8 Vs. of Pope that are printed (the last is in the press)' in his letter of 15 September 1750, above, although he made a number of last-minute changes to the 1751 large octavo *Works*. As Warburton did not make his corrections to the second large octavo *Works* until 15 October 1752 (below) – long past March 14 –1751 seems the more likely year for this letter. The three sheets sent to Bowyer on March 16, mentioned in the addendum, may in part correspond with the entry dated 27 March [1751] in Bowyer's ledger for the first large octavo edition: 'To Mr Knapton 1 of D° Vol. 6' (f.127).

[2] For the textual history of *Elfrida*, see Philip Gaskell, *The First Editions of William Mason*, Cambridge Bibliographical Society, monograph no. 1 (Cambridge, 1951), p.3.

John Jortin *to* Thomas Birch 22 April 1751*a*
Nichols, *ILH*, 1: 822 [London]

Monday, April 22, 1751.

Dear Sir,

You and I have sought one another very often to no purpose, being both of us afternoon-ramblers, and street-walkers. Mr. Warburton is in town, and would be very glad to see you; therefore, this is to invite and summon you to meet me at his house on Wednesday morning, to breakfast there, and to settle such points as may arise.[1]

Your most obedient, &c.
J. Jortin

[1] Jortin and Birch helped proof-read the 1751 edition of Pope's *Works* for Warburton and edited Mrs Cockburn's works. Jortin's editorial assistance is mentioned in Warburton's letters of April 22, June 27, August 13 and 31, and September 9, below.

Warburton *to* Thomas Birch 22 April 1751*b*
BL: Add. MS. 4320, f.180 Bedford Row, London

Dear Sir

Mr Knapton just gave me a sight of Mrs Cockbourn's works. In the 2d Vol. at p. 339. 1. 7 there is a particularity that you may imagine I should be well pleased to have omitted.[1] If this leaf could be cancelled and reprinted without it, which is fitter for a news-paper, it would give me much pleasure Tho' I am sorry to give you the trouble being

Dear Sir your most
affectionate & faithfull Servant
W. Warburton
B.R. Apr. 22 1751

Address: To The Revd Mr Birch at his house in Norfolk Street

[1] This refers to a passage at the end of a letter from Catharine Cockburn to her niece on 16 October 1747: 'You ask me, what Mr. *Warburton* has been doing this long time. I can only tell you, he is often at the *Bath* for his health, married Mr. *Allen's* niece near | that place, was called to the preachership of *Lin-* | *coln's-Inn*, has published an edition of *Shakespeare* with critical notes, at Mr. *Pope's* request, for which he refers us in the margin to some letters from him, but I know not where they are to [be] found for I never heard of them before' (*Works*, 2: 339, lines 3–12). As line 7 runs from 'that' to '*Lin-*' (as indicated by upright strokes), Birch has presumably acceded to Warburton's wishes by removing a possibly embarrassing clause.

Warburton *to* William Bowyer   6 May 1751
Nichols, *Literary Anecdotes*, 2: 229   [London]

May 6, 1751

I am resolved to have Pope finished before I go out of town. Therefore I desire you to proceed with all expedition on the cancelled leaves, contents, title-pages, &c. And let them be done out of hand, and have Mr. Knapton's final direction about the title-pages directly, and without any more put-offs.

Warburton *to* William Bowyer   3 June 1751*a*
Nichols, *Literary Anecdotes*, 2: 229   [Prior Park][1]

June 3, 1751.

Mr. Bowyer,
    I take it extremely ill of you for not sending me two copies of all the reprinted leaves, prefaces, title-pages, &c. before I left town, as I ordered. If I thought what I said would be any way regarded by you, I would have them sent by Leake's parcel.

W.W.

[1] The following letter of the same date suggests Warburton left London for Prior Park towards the end of May.

Warburton *to* [Knapton][1]   3 June 1751*b*
BL: Egerton 1954, f.19   Prior Park

Dear Sir
    I have the favour of yours of the 1st. We have been in great alarm here for poor Mrs Allen. We thought her dying for several days. She is yet in a very dangerous way.[2]
    I am sorry Hobracken has served you so rascally.[3] But there is no remedy. I have inclosed the list of presents. I have not put down *Arbuthnot*.[4] The question is whether you think proper he should have one.
    I have nothing more to add at present. Nor do I know of any thing to hinder the intended publication. I hope the Letter to Bolingbroke at the end of the last Vol. is laid by carefully to be used on a proper occasion.[5]

I am Dear Sir most
Affectionately yours
W. Warburton
P.P. June 3d 1751

[1] Warburton returned to Prior Park three weeks before the publication of the Pope edition in London.
    [2] Reports of Mrs Allen's illness were given on June 19, August 3 and August 24, by which time she had been taken to Weymouth.
    [3] Jacobus Houbraken engraved the portrait of Pope which appeared at the end of the second volume of Thomas Birch's *The Heads of Illustrious Persons of Great Britain: engraven by Mr. Houbraken, and Mr. Vertue. With their lives and characters*, 2 vols. (London: printed for John and Paul Knapton, 1743–51). (Another volume 1 appeared in 1747; another volume 2 was published in 1752; the two volumes were combined in 1756.) Dated 1747, this line engraving, after Arthur Pond and based on the Van Loo type, was done in Amsterdam. The nature of Houbraken's treatment of Knapton (who announced the subscription of *Heads* in 1737) is unknown. See Wimsatt, pp.327–9; for Houbraken's dealings with Arthur Pond and the Knaptons, see Louise Lippincott, *Selling Art in Georgian England*, pp.150–3.
    [4] George Arbuthnot, son of Pope's Scriblerian friend and one of Pope's executors, seems not to have been on very good terms with Warburton. In his letter to Charles Yorke of 8 August [1752], Warburton wrote, 'I should have told you that George Arbuthnot is expected here but he is an easy good natured man, of no consequence to you or me, any further than his excessive love of red mullet' (Eg. 1952, f.4).
    [5] Warburton evidently wanted to include his critique of Bolingbroke in the ninth and last volume of his Pope edition, which contains correspondence to and from Swift, Gay, Allen and Warburton, as well as Pope's will. Warburton's *A View of Lord Bolingbroke's Philosophy* was published by John and Paul Knapton in 1754–5. A second edition came out in 1756 under the imprint of J. and R. Tonson, S. Draper and A. Millar.

Warburton *to* Knapton   19 June 1751
BL: Egerton 1954, f.20   Prior Park

Dear Sir
    I have your favour of the 24 [14] [*sic*] for I find you begin already to
write in the newstile.[1]
    I forgot to have a Book sent in Bords to the Bishop of Lincoln,[2] which I
beg may be done.
    If you please to send me 2 or 3 Copies by the Carrier.[3]
    Poor Mrs Allen continues extremely ill.

                                        I am Dear Sir ever most
                                        affectionately Yours
                                        W. Warburton
                                        P.P. June 19 1751

I beg you would be so good to let Mr Hilyard send to Mrs Hayes as usual
& pay her 10*l.* for which I have sent the inclosed Bill.

Address (f.21): To Mr Knapton Bookseller in Ludgate Street   London

    [1] The Julian calendar officially ended in England on Wednesday, 2 September 1752.
The next day – the first of the new Gregorian calendar – was Thursday, September 14,
thus omitting the eleven days of September 3–13. Apart from being over a year early,
Knapton was evidently a day out: the old style 14 would have been the 'newstile' 25.
    [2] John Thomas (1691–1766) was Bishop of Lincoln from 1744 to 1761.
    [3] Possibly referring to the Pope edition.

Warburton *to* [Anon]   27 June 1751
Boston Public Library: Ch.G.12.56   Prior Park

                                        Prior Park near Bath
                                        June 27 1751
Dear Sir,
    I hope your candor has made you ascribe the deferring my
acknowledgments for your obliging favour of the 20 Apr. last to any
thing rather than to a want of the friendly sense I had, & ought to have,
of it.
    The truth is I found it in my return out of Lincolnshire in Easter term
at my house in London. And, from thence, a sudden & dangerous illness
of Mrs Allen called me immediately home. She has lain ever since, & yet
continues, in so bad a way as keeps us all in great distress. A like
misfortune (which I hope you have long before now happily got over, &
which deprived me some time of the pleasure of hearing from you)

informs you but too sensibly how unfit we are for discharging the common offices of life, while those who are dear to us lye in imminent danger. So that the intent of this is only to assure you of my most cordial esteem.

Your sentiments of Mr Jortin's performance are as just, as the expectations from it were silly. For he himselfe gave no occasion for the idle puffs that went about concerning it, always representing it to his friends for what it is, a discharge of his *common plea*, in many learned & sensible observations occasionally made in his reading that part of antiquity. There are two or three books of other of my friends that I believe will give you more satisfaction, which had I had but a ready conveyance I would have sent you before I left town. The one is an *Essay on the Characteristics*, another, *Notes & Com: on Hor. Ep. to Augustus*; and the third, a *view of the Argum[en]t of the Div. Leg.* with 2 letters between Middleton & me.[1] There is a mastery of reasoning & fine criticism in these books which I dare say will please you. I should detain you a great deal longer upon what is done, or doing, in the literary world was my mind more free & easy than the very dangerous condition of an excellent woman very dear to me will suffer it to be.

I have at length published an Edition of Mr Pope's works, which has been a long time printed, but waited for ornaments & was at last forced to be published without ⟨some of them⟩ some that I intended for it.

> I am Dear Sir your most affectionate & faithfull
> humble Servant   W. Warburton

[1] John Brown, *Essays on the Characteristics of the Earl of Shaftesbury*, (London: printed for C. David, 1751); [Richard Hurd, ed.], *Q. Horatii Flacci, ars poetica. Epistola ad Pisones. With an English commentary and notes* (London: printed by W. Bowyer; and sold by R. Dodsley, and M. Cooper, 1749); the last item is presumably John Towne's *The Argument of the Divine Legation Fairly Stated* (London: C. Davis, 1751).

Warburton *to* [John Nourse?][1]   10 July 1751
Folger Shakespeare Library: Art Vol. a9, p.128   Prior Park

Sir

I have taken the liberty of directing a small box full of Books to you, it comes by Wiltshire [?] the Bath Carrier at an Inn near Fleet Market & will be in town on Fryday or Saturday. I desire you to pay the Carriage from Bath, and that you would scratch out the directions and direct it anew thus

A M. De Silhouette Chancelier de M. La Duc D'Orleans a Paris[2] and be so
good to forward it the best and safest way & as soon as possible to Paris.

Which will much oblige Sir
your faithfull humble
Servt   W. Warburton
Prior Park   July 10 1751

[1] Although Knapton occasionally shipped books to the continent, Warburton does not use the 'Dear Sir' in his opening salutation here as he customarily does in his letters to Knapton; Nourse handled several of Warburton's book orders from France.

[2] Étienne de Silhouette translated *An Essay on Man* into French prose as well as Warburton's *Vindication* (*Correspondence*, 4: 172 n.1, 216 n.1, 219, 484; *TE*, 3.i: xix, xx n.2, xviii). Warburton appended his 'Copie d'une Lettre écrite à Mgr. le Cardinal de Fleury, en lui envoyant les *Dissertations sur l'Union de la Religion, de la Morale, & de la Politique; tirées d'un Ouvrage de Mr. Warburton*' to the Advertisement of *The Alliance between Church and State* in 1766 (*WWW*, 4: 13–18).

Warburton *to* [Knapton]   3 August 1751
BL: Egerton 1954, f.22   [Prior Park]

Dear Sir

I have the favour of yours of the 1st inst. I wish you would send me a set to Correct, for I have never a one.[1]

I believe we shall find our account in having the poem of the *dying Christ*: added to the Essay.[2] I like the project of having the pictures to the small Edn extremely.[3]

I wonder what Bowyer means in not going forward with the Div. Leg:

If one had one's choice one would wish such execrable papers as the Magazines would meddle only with their own trash. But since they do what they please in this blessed Land of Liberty one had better see them impertinent than scurrelous.[4] The Public is a strange machine, which by fits is as easily wound up by the veriest dunce or idiot as by the best Artist, nay shall be set a going so perversely, that it shall not be in the power of human wisdom to reform it. It is the condition of human things that the most insignificant of all animals shall do most unaccountable mischief. The states of holland had like to have been ruined by a single water-rat. In such a case an Author has consolation enough because he knows justice will be done him by Posterity, In the mean time a Bookseller has none who may have contributed as much or more than the Author to oblige the Public.

Mrs. Allen is better but extremely infirm and we are all obliged to you for your kind inquiries.

I am Dear Sir your most affectionate
friend & faithfull servant
W. Warburton
Augt 3 1751

[1] The nine-volume small octavo edition of Pope's *Works* (Griffith 1751*b*), priced at twenty-seven shillings, was advertised in *LM*, 20 (November 1751): 528.

[2] 'The Dying Christian to his Soul' appears immediately before *An Essay on Criticism* in the first volume of 1751*b*, pp.82–3.

[3] 1751*b* contains the same twenty-four engravings as 1751*a*.

[4] Knapton presumably forwarded unfavourable reviews of the Pope edition. By Christmas Warburton had seen John Gilbert Cooper's attack, *Cursory Remarks on Mr. Warburton's New Edition of Mr. Pope's Works*. See Warburton's letter of 9 December 1751, below.

Warburton *to* [Knapton]   13 August 1751
BL: Egerton 1954, f.23   Prior Park

Dear Sir

I have yours of th[e] 10. I forgot in my last, to reply to what you inquired abt in your last but one concerning two of the imitations of the Satires of Horace q[uart]o. with my notes that came to you in the parcel of the two sets. I hardly know what was meant by those qos. but as my Man packed up the books I suppose he put in those as wast paper so desire they may be burnt.[1]

Jortin gave me on several detached pieces of paper a list of errata when he read over the vols. These I gave to Bowyer to extract out of them what was material to print in the list of errata. But for his own credit he was too sparing. I desire you would ask him for those papers & inclose them to me, that I may correct the remainder.

Dear Sir ever most affectionately
yours   W.Warburton
P.P. Augt 13 1751

Address (f.24; incomplete): Free R: Allen   London

[1] Warburton is apparently referring to some quarto sheets of Pope's Horatian imitations (in vol. 4 of the large octavo 1751 *Works*) which were subsequently used in packing books. These may have been printed samples for an abandoned volume intended to accompany quarto editions of *An Essay on Criticism*, *An Essay on Man* and *Epistles to Several Persons*. Knapton evidently asked whether the leaves were of any importance; Warburton assumed they were not.

Warburton *to* [Knapton]   24 August 1751
BL: Egerton 1954, f.25   Prior Park

Dear Sir

I have sent the set of Popes back again corrected.

only at p.231. V. 3. in the notes col. 2d at the bottom abt the court of
Chancery, strike out the correction & let it be as first printed.[1]

Mrs Allen still continues extreme infirm. Mr A. has carried her & the
family to Weymouth. As they stay there some time I thought proper to
retard my going, having time enough to follow them if I take a fancy to
it. In the mean time when you have occasion to write let it be under
cover *To Mr Prinn* at Ralph Allen's Esq. &c otherwise it will go round
about by Weymouth.[2]

                          Dear Sir ever most affectionately yours
                                              W. Warburton
P.P. Augt 24 1751

[1] Pope, *Works*, 3: 230–1: Warburton changed his mind about some alteration in a note
to line 105 of *Moral Essays* III, 'To Bathurst', concerning Sir Robert Sutton's appeal in
the Court of Chancery. Warburton's direction here also draws attention to the change in
layout: in the fourth volume of 1751*a*, Warburton's notes are printed in a single column,
while in the third volume they are given in two columns; notes in the 1752 *Works* appear
in a single column throughout.
[2] Samuel Prynn was Ralph Allen's clerk and a beneficiary of his will in 1764 (Boyce,
p.156).

Warburton *to* Knapton   31 August 1751
BL: Egerton 1954, f.26   Prior Park

                                          P.P. Augt. 31 1751
Dear Sir

I have the favour of yours with the Advertisement inclosed.[1] I think
you do extremely right. But it is enough at any time that I *know* your
opinion in these matters to *approve* of it.

If your second Vol of the illustrious Heads be finished you may send it
hither by the Carrier bound as soon as you can, for Mr Allen.[2]

Mr P. Knapton promised me I should have the little prints before
your transl[ation]. of Rollin's Anc[ient]. Hist[ory]. for my little french
Edn.

Should not I have a sight of the small Edn. of Pope to see there be no
notorious blunders committed for I have never yet seen one sheet of it.[3]
At least somebody should look it over.

Pray when you see Dodsley ask him when it is that he shall want the

Dissertation on the 6th B. of Virgil which I have promised to prepare for him, and if he will let me know I will send it to him, at the time.[4]

I see by Jortin's list that Bowyer had taken in the most considerable of the errata.[5] I wonder whether in the little Edn. the errata are corrected. —— You see in the corrected copy of the large which I sent you back I have made few or no additions or alterations. what I have corrected relates only to the improvement of the stile, or turn of the period, in which I always endeavour to be very exact. and one always finds something or other of this kind to render more perfect.

Dear Sir ever most affectionately yours
W. Warburton

Address, frank and postmark (f.27): To Mr: Knapton Bookseller in Ludgate Street London   Free R: Allen   2/SE

[1] Warburton complained about the Advertisement in his letter of 14 October 1751, below.

[2] Thomas Birch, *The Heads of Illustrious Persons.*

[3] The small octavo edition of Pope's *Works* was published in the autumn.

[4] Warburton's 'Dissertation on the Sixth Book of the Aeneid' was published in Robert Dodsley's Latin-English edition of the *Works* of Virgil on 25 January 1753. See Ralph Straus, *Robert Dodsley: Poet, Publisher & Playwright* (London, 1910; rpt. New York, 1968), p.346.

[5] For Jortin's involvement as a proof-reader of Warburton's Pope edition, see Warburton's letters of 13 August 1751, above, and 9 September 1751, below.

Warburton *to* [Knapton][1]   9 September 1751
BL: Egerton 1954, f.29   Prior Park

P.P. Sepr 9 1751

Dear Sir,

I have the favour of yours of the 7.

I think if Mr Birche or Mr Jortin which you will would just look over the small Edn. it would be perfectly right.[2]

I looked for no other from such a fellow as Osborne.[3] I suppose he was the person that procured Mr York's Opinion.[4] The Rogue I see has been notably handled. But his offering to take 500 of Chambers at the price Baldwin proposes, is such amazing impudence, & detects his whole roguery so barefacedly that nothing was ever equal to it.

I think this is all very well for the present exegency. But while the trade only uses this temporary expedience to stop the mischief from time to time, it will be always breaking out, till at last it will end in a settled confusion & destruction of property. whereas a quarter of that money well employed to solicite justice, either of the Judges, or Legislature, would put an effectual end to the mischief, either by a sentence of the acknowledged property, or by the procuring a new Law.[5]

As for the property I have, if the established Courts of Justice will not secure me in it, I would give my selfe no concern abt it, it is the most indifferent thing to me. But you know I hope, my friendship for you would engage me to serve you every way in my power, for the security of your great property. But let me tell you that you & your Brother are the only persons in the trade for whom I have the least regard in this matter. I have been used in various ways so indifferently by most of the rest, (tho' I think I deserved better of the trade in general, who by their conduct shew, that no gratitude, no obligation, no duty divine or human can bind them where the question is abt getting a penny) I say that was it not on acct of a man of so much worth as your selfe, & whom I so sincerely love, I could, with satisfaction enough, see literary property turned upon the common, to teach those men the baseness of their actions.[6]

You know my fixed opinion is, that the true remedy for any temporary invasion of property is the Court of Chancery.[7] and the only effectual is an application to Parliament. You know my mind at large & my scheme on this subject. I have repeated it often to you. And shall say no more. Only be assured of this I am always at your service and in your own way. For a man that will serve his friend, not in his friend's, but in his own way, serves him only by halves.

I am Dear Sr ever most affectionately
yours   W.Warburton

[1] Cited in part by Evans, pp.141–2.

[2] The small octavo nine-volume edition of Pope's *Works* (Griffith 1751*b*).

[3] Thomas Osborne II (*fl.*1738–67), son of the bookseller of the same name who competed against Curll in the *Dunciad* (*TE*, 5: 303–04), apparently bought sets of Chambers' *Cyclopedia* from Robert Baldwin. The Knaptons and Osborne shared the same imprint on the 1753 two-volume *Supplement to Mr. Chambers's Cyclopedia*. Osborne kept an account with Gosling's Bank; see J. D. Fleeman, 'The revenue of a writer: Samuel Johnson's literary earnings', *Studies in the Book Trade In Honour of Graham Pollard*, OBS, ns vol. 18 (1975), p.224. See *Correspondence*, 4: 222–3; Boswell's *Life of Johnson*, pp.111–12, 115–17; and Plomer.

[4] Philip Yorke, the Lord Chancellor.

[5] For mid-eighteenth-century copyright complexities, see John Feather, 'The Publishers and the Pirates: British Copyright Law in Theory and Practice, 1710–1775', *Publishing History*, 22 (1987): 5–32.

[6] See Eg. 1954, ff.3–4, f.5, and ff.6–7 [November 1755?], below.

[7] In his letter to John Sayer of 28 January 1754*a*, below, Warburton claimed, 'Soon after Mr Pope died I was necessitated to put half a dozen people, who pirated the Essay on Man, into Chancery...'

Warburton *to* Knapton   [September 1751?][1]
BL: Egerton 1954, f.28   [Prior Park]

Dear Sir

I dined with Mr Y.[2] yesterday & he told me that he had the following case laid before him to this effect, not long since,

"That considering the great discouragement of learning by monopolizing the property of Books A. desired to know whether he & B. & C. &c could *safely* print some old Books such as Milton & others when the 2 fourteen years were expired."[3]

He said the case put him in mind of such another, formerly laid before Sr W. Jones; by which he understood that A., under many plausible pretences, had a mind to defraud his Creditors; to which he gave the following Opinion, "If A has a great desire to outwit his Creditors he has nothing to do but to hang himselfe, and, in that case, his goods & chattles will be forfeit to the King." The Opinion Mr Y. gave to these Pirats was, "that they would run themselves into great dangers, & advised them to think of no such thing." And when the Solr came for the case he said this to him, Sr, I know what your Clients would be at, and what has encouraged them to think of this piece of Knavery, it was something that dropt from the Chancellor, tho' he delivered no opinion, in the Scotch cause.[4] But assure them from me that however that cause turns out, they will get nothing by it, for property will be secured by Parliament if it be wanting, and I know many Gentlemen in the house of Commons who will concurr to ⟨secure⟩ remite it.

I thought proper to let you know this,

And am Dear Sr most affectionately
Yours
W. Warburton
⟨Thursday night⟩ Fryday morning

Verso: To Mr J. Knapton

[1] References in Eg. 1954, f.28 and f.29 to Yorke ('Mr Y.') suggest f.28 may have been written later.

[2] Philip Yorke (1690–1764), first Earl of Hardwicke, Lord Chancellor. His second son, Charles Yorke (1722–70), who succeeded him as Lord Chancellor, carried on a long correspondence with Warburton and was to play an important part in the Wilkes affair in 1763. See *DNB.*

[3] The Act for the Encouragement of Learning (i.e. the Copyright Act) of 1710.

[4] In the first test-case over copyright in Scotland, Andrew Millar accused twenty-nine Scottish booksellers, including Gavin Hamilton and Allan Ramsay, of pirating Thomson's *Seasons,* the rights to which he owned. Millar was eventually forced to drop

his suit at the Court of Session in Edinburgh in 1739. He brought another action against twenty booksellers in Edinburgh and against four in Glasgow between 1743 and 1749. The House of Lords overturned perpetual copyright in 1774. See Warren McDougall, 'Gavin Hamilton, Bookseller in Edinburgh', *British Journal for Eighteenth-Century Studies*, 1 (1978): 1–19.

Warburton *to* Robert Dodsley[1]   28 September 1751
Nottinghamshire Archives Office: M9659, f.15   Prior Park

Prior Park Sept. 28 1751
Mr Dodsley

I just now received the inclosed letter from Mr John Gilbert-Cooper junr.[2]

I desire he may have the letter he demands. I am ashamed I was obliged to take notice to you of a thing so much below me as such scurrilous trash. but it concerned the reputation of another honest man.[3] You ⟨will⟩ will readily imagine, that amongst the Dunces who have taken it into their head to be angry, I have a great deal of this miserable ware. But it injuring no body but my selfe, and I very insensible, no body is troubled with it.

Mr Cooper's sentiments of nameless libellers are very commendable. But it would be well if he would consider, whether putting his name to a Libell would excuse his honesty, tho' it might, his honour. I say his honour, for he must certainly have some very peculiar rules of civil commerce, to tell me to my face, or, which is the same thing, under his hand, that *I have used him very ill.* For how stands the fact? He writes a Book, and finds it proper to confute the sentiments of a preceding Writer: which certainly he had a right to do. But as this writer was an utter stranger to him, had never any concerns with him, never mentioned his name or his writings in public or in conversation but with honour, had he a right to use this Author with a scurrility worse than billingsgate; to return to it; to repeat it, and to carry it thro' his whole book? Yet this he has certainly done. And what revenge has the Writer taken? no other than the ⟨slight⟩ casual mention of the Author of the life of Socrates, (without the mention of his name) with a slight joke: which he ought to have taken as a friendly admonition of his folly. Instead of this, he tells me *I have used him very ill.* Is it credible he should venture to say this? Or is there a new system of morality come out for the Wits & Poet's of the time! You are in the midst of them, and can tell. I believe you practice the old; and while you do, I shall always be ready to shew my selfe[4]

Your faithfull
humble Servant
W. Warburton

[1] Reproduced by permission of the Principal Archivist, Nottinghamshire Archives Office. Printed in *Dodsley*, pp.141–2. I am grateful to James Tierney for drawing my attention to this letter.

[2] This enclosure and the letter mentioned in the next line are untraced. John Gilbert Cooper (1723–69) derided Warburton's *Divine Legation of Moses*, accusing the author of plagiarism, in his 1749 *Life of Socrates*, published by Dodsley. Warburton responded by calling the *Life of Socrates* 'a late worthless and now forgotten thing' in a commentary to *An Essay on Criticism* in *Works* (1751), 1: 151, line 92. Cooper's reply to Warburton's letter to Dodsley took the form of the letter-pamphlet, *Cursory Remarks on Mr. Warburton's New Edition of Mr. Pope's Works* (London: Mary Cooper, 1751). In it, Cooper referred to his letter to Warburton: 'Upon this [Warburton's sneer in the 1751 *Works*] I wrote to him, that I thought he had used me very ill, and should take a *proper* notice of him for it in Publick; and in Answer to which he tells a Friend of mine [i.e., Dodsley, in this letter], *That he was surprized I should think myself ill used, for that he never mentioned my Name or Writings in Public, or in Conversation but with Honour, till I had wrote a Book wherein I had treated him thro' the whole with a Scurrility worse than* Billingsgate, *and that he had now taken no other Revenge than the casual Mention of the Author of the Life of* Socrates *(without the mention of my Name) with a slight Joke*' (p.5). This letter-pamphlet is dated 30 October 1751. See Warburton's letter to Knapton of 9 December 1751, below.

[3] Presumably he meant Pope.

[4] Warburton recalled Dodsley's part in John Gilbert Cooper's attacks when the bookseller hoped to acquire Knapton's share of Pope's *Works*. See their exchange between 26 December 1755 and 6 January 1756, below.

Knapton *to* Thomas Birch   1 October 1751
BL: Add. MS. 4312, f.41   [London]

Tuesday Oct. 1st 1751

Revd Sir

I send by the bearer the two Editions of Mr Pope's Works.[1]
The inclosed is a Copy of some Errata Mr W. has sent me in ye Notes——

I am Sr
Yr most humble Servt,
John Knapton

Address (f.42*v.*): To the Revd Mr Birch in Norfolk Street

[1] Knapton presumably sent both the large and small octavo editions (1751*a* and 1751*b*) along with Warburton's list of errata for the inspection of his proof-readers, Birch and Jortin.

Warburton *to* Knapton   14 October 1751
BL: Egerton 1954, f.31   [Prior Park]

Dear Sir

The printer, whoever he be, has had no kind of regard to my directions abt printing the *Advertisement*   For in the begining after the word *Advertisement* I directed it should be said

to the 8° Edn

or something to that purpose. And towards the end tho' I made the alteration which he has printed yet in my last letter to you I told you I had altered my mind & would have it printed verbatim in that place (as well as in all others) according to ye 8° Ed.[1]

Dr Sr ever most affectionately y[ours][2]
W. Warbur[ton]

I propose being in Town the latter end of next week —— Monday Octr. 14 1751

Address, frank and postmark: To Mr: Knapton Bookseller in Ludgate Street London   Free R: Allen   16/OC

[1] Warburton mentioned the Advertisement to the Pope edition in his letter of 31 August 1751 and was angry that Bowyer (or one of his compositors) did not carry out his instructions exactly as requested. The Advertisement to the small octavo edition, 1751*b*, accordingly carried the phrase, 'to the Octavo Edition', referring to the first large octavo, 1751*a*. A note at the end of Warburton's Advertisement in the small octavo reads, 'N.B. This Edition of Mr. Pope's Works is printed verbatim from the large Octavo; with all his Notes, and a select number of the Editor's' (1: xi). Warburton's Advertisement, which gives a volume-by-volume lay-out (for example, it refers to volume 9, the last, containing Pope's letters), was reprinted without modification in the ten-volume edition of 1754 and the six-volume edition of 1770. The printer perhaps felt that Warburton's instructions would confuse readers of later editions in different formats. Warburton evidently intended to refer readers of later editions, some of which would appear in different formats and with different volume numbers, back to the original 1751 *Works*.
[2] Part of the closing salutation and signature has been torn off by the seal.

Warburton *to* [Knapton]   19 October 1751
BL: Egerton 1954, f.32   Prior Park

Dear Sir

I would have the inclosed leaf reprinted and likewise that which I sent you some time ago, which was the first leaf of the Im. of Hor. addressed to Mr Murray.[1] and I am very indifferent whether You reprint any more.

Andr. Millar came up here yesterday to pay me a visit. We talked of matters of his profession. He said several absurd things Which it is not worth while to trouble you with.[2]

I am Dr Sr ever most affectionately
Yours   W. Warburton
P.P. Octr 19 1751

[1] Warburton made a few corrections in *Epistle I. vi*, in the fourth volume of the small octavo edition, 1751*b*.

[2] Andrew Millar had perhaps been trying to persuade Warburton to let him have a share in Pope's works – a goal he achieved by 1755.

Warburton *to* [Knapton]   1 December 1751
BL: Egerton 1954, f.33   Prior Park

Dear Sir

I got well home last night tolerably fatigued. The weather was cold, the roads were dirty, and the post-chaise not hung in air. So that by the time I got hither I was fully satisfied with this amusing exercise. You will not forget your inquiries after what I find will be difficult to get, Narber or pert-mahone Honey.[1]

I beg that three of the 6 sets of Pope[2] may be sent hither & the other three sent to my maid in Bedford Row.

I am with the truest esteem Dear Sir
your most affectionate &
faithfull humble Servt
W. Warburton
P.P. Decr 1 1751

[1] Honey was often named after its place of origin. Sir John Hill published the first book in English on honey and recommended, 'The sort of Honey that is best for a hoarseness, is the true Narbonne kind', *The Virtues of Honey in Preventing many of the Worst Disorders*, 2nd ed. (London: printed for J. Davis; and M. Cooper, 1759), p.9. Richard Hoy advertised 'Narbone Honey' in 1788, Eva Crane, *A Book of Honey* (Oxford, 1980), p.43. The other kind of honey came from Port Mahon, Minorca. Warburton followed up his request for honey in his letter of 22 December 1751, below.

[2] Of the recently published small octavo edition, 1751*b*.

Warburton *to* Knapton   9 December 1751
BL: Egerton 1954, f.34   Prior Park

Dear Sir

I recd your favour of the 6th. I thank God I got well home & continue
tolerably well. I use exercise here which I could not do in town, & hope
to meet you in health, & find you so the latter end of Jany. on my return.

I shall expect the parcel you mention to be sent to the Carrier, in a day
or two. You need not have given your selfe the trouble to send the
Pamphlet of Cooper,[1] for I have never read any of the trash wrote agt me
of several years, any more than I do of anonimous Letters, a method I
learnt of the Bp of London[2] who thinks it an exquisite disappointment,
and, (when they know it) a mortal disappointment to Libellers. I intend
to print a small Vol of Sermons abt 16 or 17.[3] with this title *The Principles
of Religion natural & revealed delivered occasionally in a course of Sermons preachd
before the Hon Soc. of L[incoln's]. I[nn]. &c.*[4] and I would have as small an
impression as can possibly be printed. For I know the difference between
Sermons & plays & novels. But I *would* willingly have it extremely well
printed. nor do I suppose it will get thro' the press before the begining of
next winter.

Another thing I must not forget to mention with regard to the
remainder of the impression of the 2d Vol. of the Div. Leg.[5] I think to
destroy it, paying you back the 25*l*. which I desire you set down to my
account & make me a debtor for. Because I have much improved the 2d
Vol. like the first. and I would have the 1st & 2d of a piece, & fit to be
joined to the last.

I am Dear Sir
Your very
affectionate & faithfull humble Servant
W. Warburton
P.P. Decr 9 1751

Address and frank: To Mr: Knapton Bookseller in Ludgate Street
London   Free R: Allen

---

[1] John Gilbert Cooper's *Cursory Remarks* was published by Mary Cooper in 1751.
[2] Thomas Sherlock (1678–1761), Bishop of London.
[3] He presumably meant sheets.
[4] *The Principles of Natural and Revealed Religion*, 2 vols. London: J. and P. Knapton,
1753–4.
[5] Knapton took his time to do this: see Warburton's letters of 15 October 1752 and 19
December 1752, below.

Warburton *to* Knapton 22 December 1751
BL: Egerton 1954, f.37 Prior Park

Dear Sir

I have the favour of yours of the 19th. You are very good in the affair of the honey and too good an opinion of my pen in that of the sermons. I shall bring or send some copy, & when I return to town we will talk further of the number.[1]

I beg the favour of you to desire Mr Hilliard of York to pay Mrs Hayes ten pounds I suppose he always takes her rect. I beg he would give himselfe the trouble to send to her for I give her no advise. I make you & Mr & Mrs Knapton all the compliments of the approaching season and am

Dear Sir
Your most affectionate & faithfull
humble Servt & friend
W. Warburton
Prior Park Decr 22 1751

I hear Ld Bol. is dead. I believe I have lost an Enemy in his death but I am sure our Country has lost a greater.[2]

[1] Bowyer recorded the printing of 1000 copies of the first volume of Warburton's sermons on 16 December 1752 (Grolier Club archives, 83*v.*).

[2] Henry St. John, Viscount Bolingbroke, died on 12 December 1751.

[Warburton] *to* Knapton[1] [late 1751?]
BL: Egerton 1954, f.36 [Prior Park]

I am by no means satisfied with paying more, for the present books of pope's works, than paper & print; besides binding. The difference between that & the common price is very considerable, in a quantity that comes according to Mr K's acct, to abt 120*l*: and tho' I receive part of the price (above paper & print) back, yet it is not above a half part: therefore I think my selfe very hardly used, as being contrary to the general custom. Nor could the other Proprietors grudge it as I make their property so much better by inserting it into a compleat Edn of the works.

[n.s.]

Verso: To Mr Knapton

¹ This letter is difficult to date. It was evidently meant to be presented by Knapton at a meeting of the other booksellers, Tonson, Lintot, Draper and Bathurst, who were perhaps disturbed by Warburton's controlling share in Pope's *Works*. Warburton received a 51% share – 'above a half part' – of the gross profits (as opposed to the net profits or 'the common price') from the five Pope editions published between 1751 and 1755. See Appendix A.

An opening salution, 'Dear Sir', has been pasted on and appears to have been taken from another letter.

1752

In July, Warburton asked Knapton to send the 'New Ed. of Pope' – the other large octavo edition of Pope's *Works* in nine volumes (the third of five in the series of Warburton-Knapton editions) – to peruse, and later agreed to delay its publication.

Preparations for the small octavo 1753 edition were under way. The arrival of Princess Amelia, who sought a cure for deafness, at Prior Park in August forced Warburton to vacate to Weymouth for a month.

In October he checked the 1752 *Works* for errors. Warburton subscribed early to Hogarth's *Analysis of Beauty*. He supplied notes for Thomas Newton's edition of *Paradise Regain'd*.

Warburton *to* [Thomas Comber]   11 January 1752
Bath Reference Library: A.L. 2314   Prior Park

Dear Sir

I have the favour of yours ⟨of⟩ without date.

I have not seen the pamphlet you mention written agt my Julian, nor shall I ever read a line of it.[1] Every clergyman, not to say every Believer, is equally concerned with me about the truth of that miracle. It is the common cause in which I have performed my share. Besides I have been long in an humour [to] abjure all controversy. Whatever I shall write hereafter will be delivered freely, explained as clearly, & inforced as strongly as I am able. If any one can overthrow it he hath my leave and if any one will support it he hath my thanks: but to trouble my selfe further about the matter, is more, I think, than I ow[e] to the public; is more I am sure than I ow either to truth or my selfe.

Amelia, In my opinion, is neither equal to Tom Jones nor to Jos. Andrews, but is much better than any thing, in this sort of writing, from any other of our countrymen.[2]

The *essay on spirit* is written by Clayton Bp of Clogher.[3] In an English Bishop it would have been called heresy; but in an Irish I suppose it will pass for a blunder. It is in three parts. the middle only is properly his own. The first being little better than an extract from Lock, &c. and the last from Clark. He is of the grosser sort of arians. He holds the holy-ghost to be Gabriel; & Jesus to be Michael, in defiance of the apostle, who says *he took not upon himselfe the nature of Angels*.

—— I apprehend, that ye Bp (who published it against the advise of all his friends) thought it would make a noise. But he is mistaken. The world seems disposed to overlook & to forget it, unless some answerer calls back their attention.

The epigram is a pretty one. I shall be always glad to see any thing that has your approbation.

One Harris, a Gentleman of fortune in Wiltshire, has published a kind of universal or philosophic Grammar, under the title of *Hermes*.[4] It has many good things in it, tho' not comparable to the *Gram. generale & raisonnee* of Port Royal.[5] He is such an idoliser of the Ancients that he is right or wrong as it happens, and as they lead the way.

Byrom of Manchester, a fine genius, but fanatical even to madness, has published a poetical epistle on Enthusiasm: in which he has plentifully abused Middleton & me.[6] He is too devout to cultivate poetry, otherwise he would have excelled in it. He has hit on the true epistolary stile. There are many fine strokes, many negligencies & many obscurities in it.

I am Dear Sir
Your very faithfull & affectionate
humble Servant
W. Warburton
P.P. Jan. 11 1751/2

Endorsed (in another hand): Original Letters from Bishop Warburton to Dr. Thomas Comber
11th Jan. 1751–2 Revd. W. Warburton to Revd. Thos. Comber containing Mr. W.'s opinion on many of the literary productions of the Day. N.B. The above Lr. was printed in the Bath Clu[b] Mus [Misc?]. Vol. 2. p. 257. 258.[7]

[1] Possibly referring to the anonymous confutation, *A Review of the Fiery Eruption which defeated the Emperor Julian's Attempt to Rebuild the Temple of Jerusalem* (1752), which was advertised in *LM*, 20 (1751): 576. At 142 pages, it would seem more substantial than a pamphlet although a current meaning of 'pamphlet' was 'A small book, properly a book sold unbound, and only stitched' (Johnson, *Dict.*).

[2] *Joseph Andrews* (1742), *Tom Jones* (1749) and *Amelia* (1751) were published by Andrew Millar, whose escalating payments – £183, £700, 1000 guineas – prompted Johnson to say, 'I respect Millar, Sir; he has raised the price of literature', Boswell, *Life of Johnson*, pp.205–06.

[3] [Robert Clayton, Bishop of Clogher], *An Essay on Spirit* (London: printed: and sold by J. Noon, G. Woodfall and M. Cooper, 1751; rpt. 1752). He and Warburton were addressed in Richard Moseley's anonymous *A Second Letter to the Right Reverend the Lord Bishop of Clogher... To which is added, a letter to... the Rev. Mr. Warburton* (London: printed for Thomas Payne, 1753).

[4] [James Harris], *Hermes: or, a Philosophical Inquiry concerning Language and Universal Grammar* (London: printed by H. Woodfall, for J. Nourse and P. Vaillant, 1751; 2nd ed., 1765). News of Warburton's approbation of *Hermes* was relayed to the author by his younger brother George William Harris on 23 January 1752. I am grateful to Clive Probyn for sharing his research on Harris. See also Warburton's letter to Harris of 16 February 1765, below.

[5] Claude Lancelot, Antoine Arnauld, *et al.*, *Grammaire générale et raisonnée* (Paris, 1660); trans. as *A General and Rational Grammar* (London, 1753; rpt. 1968). Clive Probyn has pointed out that few scholars in the eighteenth century made a connection between *Hermes* and the Port-Royal *Grammar*. For reference in modern linguistics, see, for example, Noam Chomsky, 'Aspects of the Theory of Syntax', *Readings in the Theory of Grammar from the 17th to the 20th Century*, ed. Diane D. Bornstein (Cambridge, Mass., 1976), pp.218–40; p.221.

[6] John Byrom (1692–1763), born in Broughton, near Manchester, was a fellow of Trinity College, Cambridge. His *Enthusiasm: A Poetical Essay* was published in London: printed for W. Owen, 1752

[7] Untraced.

Warburton *to* [William Hogarth]   28 March 1752
BL: Add. MS. 27995, f.7   Prior Park

Dear Sir

I was pleased to find by the public papers, that you have determined to give us your original & masterly thoughts on the great principles of your Profession.

You ow[e] this to your Country; for you are both an Honour to your Profession, and a Shame to that worthless crew professing Vertu & connoisseurship; to whom, all that grovel in the splendid poverty of wealth & taste are the miserable bubbles.

I beg you would give me leave to contribute my mite towards this work, & permit the inclosed to intitle me to a subscription for two copies.[1]

I am Dear Sir, (with a true sense of your superior talents) your
very affectionate humble Servt
W. Warburton

P.P. March 28 1752

[1] Four days before this letter was written, Hogarth announced his intention of writing the *Analysis of Beauty*. The other copy was probably ordered for Ralph Allen. Subscribers had to wait until the end of 1753 before receiving their copies. See Boyce, pp.203–04; Derek Jarrett, *The Ingenious Mr Hogarth* (London, 1976), pp.154–5; misdated as 1753 in *LA*, 5: 604.

Warburton *to* [Knapton]   17 June 1752
BL: Egerton 1954, f.30   Prior Park

Dear Sir

I got home yesterday in the afternoon, and found the poor Bp of Durham had been dead three or four hours.[1]

I have inclosed five bills for 100*l*. & when I know these have come safe I will send the other halfs to desire you after midsummer to buy me another 100*l*. stock in the same annuities.

I am Dear Sir your most
affectionate friend & faithfull
Servt   W. Warburton
Prior Park   June 17 1752

[1] A long-standing Knapton author, Dr. Joseph Butler (1692–1752), Bishop of Bristol and Durham, published *Several letters to the Reverend Dr. Clarke* with James Knapton in 1716. Warburton recounted the same news in his letter to Thomas Balguy on 21 June 1752 (in *ILH*, 2: 170 and n.). See Warburton's letter of 22 July 1752, below.

Warburton *to* [Knapton]   6 July 1752
BL: Egerton 1954, f.40   Prior Park

P.P. July 6 1752

Dear Sir

I hope you have learnt how to send a small parcel to that Mr *Schmidt* the German, whose directions of address you have.[1] The packet will consist of the following particulars.

The three vols of Div: Leg:
and a small paper packet directed to him.

These two are with my maid in Bedford Row   please to send to her for them. To these I would have added,

The Alliance between Church & State
Julian
and the two parts of the Miscellaneous Remarks &c

And two books to be had of Mr Charles Davis[2]

Inquiry in to the Opinions of the Ancients &c ⎫ By
And the Argument of the Div: Legation &c ⎭ Mr Towne[3]

I begg all the above may be packed up together & directed to Mr *Schmidt* and sent by the properest conveyance.

Dear Sir ever most affectionately yours
W. Warburton

[1] The Lutheran theologian, Johann Christian Schmidt (1706–63), translated Warburton's *Divine Legation of Moses* into German: *Göttliche Gendung Mosis*, 3 parts (Frankfurt and Leipzig, 1751–3). I am grateful to Dr. Hans-Günther Schwarz of Dalhousie for tracking down Schmidt in the *Allgemeine Deutsche Biographie*. Warburton reminded

Knapton of this order of books in his letter of 22 July 1752 and sent him Schmidt's address on 4 March 1754, below.

[2] Bookseller in Holborn (*d.* 1755), see Plomer; *LA*, 8: 461; and George S. Rousseau, 'Science books and their readers in the eighteenth century', *Books and their Readers in Eighteenth-Century England*, ed. Rivers, pp.230–2.

[3] Warburton wrote a preface to John Towne's 1747 *A Critical Inquiry into the Opinions and Practice of the Ancient Philosophers*. See Ryley, pp.5, 96; *LA*, 2: 194; 5: 599, and *passim*; and *DNB*. The second item is Towne's *The Argument of the Divine Legation Fairly Stated* (London: C. Davis, 1751).

Warburton *to* [Knapton] 22 July 1752
BL: Egerton 1954, f.41 Prior Park

Dear Sir

I have heard nothing yet of the set of the new Ed. of Pope which were to be sent to me to look over.[1] I desire there may be sent with them Bp Butler's last Edn. of his Sermons.[2]

Pray, could you contrive to get the books sent into Germany.[3] I am

Dear Sir ever most
affectionately yours
W. Warburton
P. P. July 22 1752

Address and frank (f.42; attached; partly cut): R: Allen London

[1] The 1752 large octavo edition of Pope's *Works*.

[2] Joseph Butler, *Fifteen Sermons preached at the Rolls Chapel* (London: printed by W. Botham, for James and John Knapton, 1726; 4th ed., John and Paul Knapton, 1749; 5th ed., R. Horsfield, 1765).

[3] To Johann Christian Schmidt, as mentioned in his letter of 6 July 1752, above.

Warburton *to* [Knapton] 27 July 1752
BL: Egerton 1954, f.43 Prior Park

Dear Sir

I heartily thank you for yours & for the news it contains. I am glad to hear of Mr C. York's health. I did write to him to congratulate him on his escape.[1]

Is it not an odd thing the Court won't end at once such a piece of roguery as that agt the *Bp* of Win:[2]

I would be obliged to you to get your correspondent at york to pay the little enclosed bill for me.[3] The debt is mine not Mr Allen's.

I am Dear Sir ever
most affectionately Yours
W. Warburton
P.P.   July 27 1752

Address (f.44; detached): To Mr: Knapton Bookseller in Ludgate Street London   Free R: Allen

[1] Charles Yorke perhaps had a mishap on the road.
[2] The controversial latitudinarian Bishop of Bangor, later of Winchester, Dr. Benjamin Hoadly (1676–1761). On 23 May 1753, Hoadly wrote to John Knapton (BL: Eg. 1954, f.109):

Wedn. May. 23.

Mr Knapton
I have now sent you the Confirmation Paper to be printed exactly as I have fixed it to the back of the other. I desire a Proof of it, without fail to morrow morning, in Hill-Street. And when I send it you back, I will give you particular directions how many to print, & how to dispose of them. Dr Pyle is very busy for You, & has made a great progress.

Yr humble servt
B Winchester

[3] John Hildyard, the bookseller in York.

Warburton *to* [Knapton]   3 August 1752
BL: Egerton 1954, f.45   Prior Park

Dear Sir
I thank you for the favour of your last & am much obliged for the contents.
I agree with you that it is better to deferr the publication of the new 8°. till more company comes to Towne.[1]
I think it is right to put the small 8° to the press, to be printed verbatim from the new 8°. with all the Commentaries &c forthwith.[2]
A great woman, now coming to Bath, & hearing that Mr Allen is going to Weymouth, has, in her princely fancy taken a likeing [to] his house, & desired the use of it for 3 weeks or a month.[3] This force[s][4] me to go to Weymouth with the family, m[uch?] agt my will. One would

imagine one was free from the mischiefs of courts when one never goes there.——She comes for a deafness, which the people of Surry pretended to find out and was willing to cure. But I suspect theirs to be a quack-medicine because I saw it advertised in a very scoundrel news-paper.

> I am Dear Sir Your most affectionate
> friend & faithfull Servant
> W. Warburton

P. [P.] Augt 3 1752

Address and frank (f.46; detached): To Mr: John Knapton   Bookseller in Ludgate Street   London   Free R: Allen.

¹ [1] The 1752 large octavo edition of Pope's *Works* in nine volumes.
[2] The account for the first five volumes of the nine-volume 1753 *Works* is dated 6 June 1753 in the Bowyer ledgers (Maslen no. 552; Bowyer no. 114).
[3] The 'great woman' is Princess Amelia (*LLEP*, p.90; 17 August 1752).
[4] A drop of ink has obscured this and a few characters below.

Warburton *to* [Knapton]   19 August 1752
BL: Egerton 1954, f.47   Weymouth

Weymouth Aug. 19 1752

Dear Sir

I don't know whether I told you in my last, that the Goths & Vandals of the Court[1] had driven me from the Muses to the Sea-nymphs of this place; whose favours I court every morning, except Sundays, when like a good Christian Priest I abstain from this profane commerce. I become tolerably reconciled to a place you have heard me exclaim against; but if you ask me when I intend to pay it a second visit, I will answer you as Sir Charles Sidley did his Borough in the hundred of Essex, in which he resided during the great plague. When Sr Charles shall we have the honour of seeing you again?——certainly, my dear friends, against the next plague.[2]

And I will assure you, as Prior Park is now again disburthened of its princely honours I should have returned immediately, but that Mr C. York has just sent me word he is coming to spend a few weeks with me here

Mr Allen desires his best compliments to you, and desires the favour of you to receive the inclosed dr: when it becomes due, and pay it to Mrs

Doddridge's agent, who will come to you for it. It is a charitable present
he makes her in a subscription to her Husband['s] book, for which he
would have only *two copies* sent him when it is published. Be so good to
send the inclosed proofe-sheet to Bowyer and believe me to be my dear
friend

> your most
> affectionate Servt
> W. Warburton

[1] Princess Amelia's entourage.

[2] Sir Charles Sedley or Sidley (1639?–1701) was the model for Lisideius, the defender
of French comedy, in Dryden's *Essay of Dramatic Poesy*.

Warburton *to* [Knapton] 2 September 1752
BL: Egerton 1954, ff.48–9 Weymouth

Weymouth Sepr. 2 1752

Dear Sir

I am gravelled[1] and want your direction to extricate my selfe. I find
on my present plan the sermons will swell to 600 pages. This I suppose is
too much for one vol.   I could make two V[olume]s of it, but I have so
ill an opinion of the sale of this sort of ware that hence arises my
embarras. so that I must be absolutely determined by you, whether I
must contract my scheme & make less than 600 pages, whether 600
pages can be crouded into one vol: or whether we should venture to
divide it in two.

Mr Yorke is here   I shewd him your Letter. he appeared to be
extremely pleased with your remembrance of him, & expressed his great
regard for you. All here desire to be kindly remembered to you and I am

> Dear Sir Your
> very affectionate humble
> Servt
> W. Warburton

Frank and postmark (f.49; top cut away): R: Allen   15/SE

[1] 'To puzzle; to stop; to put to a stand; to embarrass' (Johnson, *Dict.*); 'To set fast,
confound, embarrass, non-plus, perplex, puzzle' (*OED*).

Warburton *to* [Knapton]   8 October 1752
BL: Egerton 1954, ff.50–1   Prior Park

P.P. Octr. 8 1752

Dear Sir

I have recd two marks of your kind concern for my health. I am I hope recovering, – but slowly. And yet keep my room.

I beg you to receive the inclosed & that you will be so good to order the 10*l.* to be paid as usual to Mrs Hayse at York.

I am always with the
most esteem & affection
your most faithfull friend
& Servt
W. Warburton

Frank (f.51): R: Allen

Warburton *to* [John Nourse?]   14 October 1752
Indiana University, Lilly Library   Prior Park

Sir

I have yours of the 12. I would have all the Vols of the Memoires d'Artigny[1] that are now published, which I beg you would get as soon as you can.

In the mean time I desire you would send hither all the Vols of Fontenelle but the two last, which you may remember I bought of you. let them be bound in boards.[2]

—— I suppose you have got the Drakenbourg's Livy[3] bound as I directed and particularly, which is the chief point, that as little as possible of the margin be cut away.

I am Sir your very humble
Servt   W. Warburton
Prior Park   Octr 14 1752

[1] Antoine Gachet d'Artigny, *Nouveaux memoires d'histoire, de critique et de littérature*, 7 vols. (Paris, 1749–56).

[2] Bernard le Bovier de Fontenelle, *Oeuvres. Nouvelle édition augmentée*, 8 vols. (Paris, 1742–51); another new edition began to be published in 1752.

[3] *T. Livii Patavini historiarum ab urbe condita...*, ed. Arnold Drakenborch *et al.*, 3 vols. (Amsterdam and Leiden, 1738–46); 3 vols. (London: John Nourse, 1750; a reissue of the 1747 Paris edition).

Warburton *to* [Knapton]   15 October 1752
BL: Egerton 1954, f.52   Prior Park

Dear Sir
   I continue to recover my health slowly.
   I have not had time any more than to cast my eye over the Edn.

in Vol 5. p. 76.   1 line of Var. for *lines*
                      read *Editions*

   p 167 rem[ark]. on v[erse]. 355   l. 5. for
                            of factions read
                            or factions

in V.4. p. 33. Var. l. 9.   for *thine* read
                              mine

I dare say they are many more if looked into.[1] I leave it to you whether this can be done, & whether each printer should not be required to look over what he printed for this purpose. I have only ordered one leaf to be reprinted which is in the inclosed to Bowyer. So you may publish it as soon as you please.

   I am desirous that all the remaining copies of the 2d V. of the Div. Leg: of which you bought Maude's share may be burnt out of hand only reserving a copy or two which I shall want.[2] I think this the most effectual way of destroying them. For destroyed they must be because I have great improvem[en]ts to make in that Vol.

   I suppose Newton's Edn. of Milton's Poems will now soon be published.[3] If Newton sends me a present of one I beg you would forward it hither.

   Mason has sent word that you sent his acct. and he wants to know of me my sentiments abt your share.[4] I have intimated my mind to him in such a manner as I thought my selfe obliged to do in favour of one who undertook his work as[5] my request & was willing to leave the terms to me & to Mr Mason. I suppose he will act honourably; so as he may have the benefit of your friendship & service for the future. If he does not act right in the affair I beg you would let me know that I may set him right.

                                  Dear Sir ever
                       most affectionately yours
                           W. Warburton
                     P.P.   Oct 15 1752

I understand that Mrs Hayse is not now in york but is out on a visit, but I suppose will return very soon

¹ These errors occur in the 1752 *Works*, 5: 60, 62. Warburton was right in his suspicion that there are more errors: one glaring example appears in volume 4: *297*, where the half-title reads 'EPILOGUE TO THE SATITES'.

² See 9 December 1751 and 19 December 1752. 'Maude' is a corruption of Collet Mawhood, the executor of Warburton's bookseller, Fletcher Gyles (*d.* 1741); see *Correspondence*, 4: 409, 416, *passim*.

³ *Paradise Regain'd*, ed. Thomas Newton (London: J. and R. Tonson, 1752).

⁴ Concerning William Mason's profits on *Elfrida*: see Warburton's letter of 26 October 1752, below, and n.

⁵ Presumably a slip for 'at'.

Warburton *to* [Knapton]   26 October 1752
BL: Egerton 1954, f.53   Prior Park

                                         P.P.   Octr 26 1752

Dear Sir

You are very good in what you say with relation to my friends. In matters that are fit to be done between one man of honour & another in their intercourse of this nature, one cannot prescribe to them in such a manner as perhaps one would think fit to act ones selfe. I did let Mr M.¹ understand that in my opinion one full 3d pt of the clear profits was the last that could possibly be offered. You may easily imagine the import of his letter necessarily led me to go thus low with him. But as he is a very ingenious as well as a very worthy man I hope matters will be settled to your mutual satisfaction.²

I have returned the two leaves corrected   I have inclosed another to be reprinted, and this is all the trouble I shall give you with this Edn.³

                               Dear Sir most faithfully
                                  & entirely yours
                                  W. Warburton

Address and frank (f.54; detached): To Mr: Knapton Bookseller in Ludgate Street London   Free R: Allen

¹ Presumably William Mason rather than Andrew Millar who was also known for being 'very ingenious' when it came to profits.

² See Warburton's letter of 15 October 1752, above. He advised Mason on what percentage of the net profits from *Elfrida* he might expect to receive from Knapton. Mason and Knapton evidently came to favourable terms: *Elfrida* ran to six editions by 1759. Robert Dodsley published Mason's *Musaeus* (1747), *Isis* (1749) and *Four Odes* (1756); the two booksellers later co-published *Caractacus* (London: printed for J. Knapton; and R. and J. Dodsley, 1759; 3rd ed., J. Knapton, R. and J. Dodsley, and R. Horsfield, 1760).

³ If these leaves were for the 1752 edition of Pope's *Works*, Warburton's corrections may have been too late; see his letter of 15 October 1752, above.

Robert Horsfield *to* Thomas Birch 7 November 1752
BL: Add. MS. 4310, f.163 Ludgate Street, London

Ludgate Street Novem: 7. 1752.

Rev: Sir

 Mess: Knapton have an order for The Best Arguments on the Deist Scheme with the best Answers to the amount of about 4*l*. 4*s*. therefore wou'd be oblig'd to You to help them with a list of them

I am. Sr
for Mess: Knapton
Your most humble Servant
R. Horsfield[1]

If you can make out such an Account please to leave it out & it shall be call'd for tomorrow.

Address (*verso*): To The Rev: Mr Birch in Norfolk Street Strand

[1] Horsfield eventually took over the premises in Ludgate Street after Knapton's retirement.

Warburton *to* [Knapton] 4 December 1752
BL: Egerton 1954, f.55 Prior Park

Dear Sir

 I should have left you the inclosed 10*l*. when I saw you last which I think I forgot to do. It is for Mrs Hayes at Yorke, which I beg you would let your correspondent pay her as usual.

 Mr Cole[1] has been with Mr Nesbet below the hill. Mrs Nesbet told my wife he was there. As soon as I heard I sent to desire his company at this place but he was returned. Mr C. York is now with me who sends you & Mr Cole his complim[en]ts.[2]

Dear Sir ever most
affectionately yours
W. Warburton
P.P. Decr 4 1752

[1] Nathaniel Cole, solicitor to the Stationers' Company, who lived in Basinghall Street. Cole served as solicitor to the East India Company and clerk to the Stationers' Company from 1726 up until the year of his death in 1759; *GM*, 29 (December 1759): 606. See Warburton's letter of 4 May 1749 n.7, above. Cole was mentioned by Pope in a letter to Warburton concerning copyright litigation: 'I wish He [William Murray] knew, that the Affidavit & the Book he mentiond, was never sent me, nor have I heard a word from

Mr Cole about it. Pray if you have an Opportunity, just tell him so, with the State of the thing, for certainly if Millar has had redress, I may. and I know tis Mr Murrays Opinion I should prosecute —— ' (*Correspondence*, 4: 425 ([6 Nov. 1742]).
² Part of the second paragraph is torn on the left-hand side.

Warburton *to* [Knapton]   19 December 1752
BL: Egerton 1954, f.56   Prior Park

Dear Sir
    I got well home thro' very bad roads. I wish you would add two more books in bords, one to Dr Forster the late Chap[lain]. to Bp Durham & the present Chap: of the A Bp [Archbishop] but whether yet at lambeth I know not. The other to Dr Heberdine¹ Physician in Cicil Street in ye Strand.
    You remember I repeated my desire that the remaining copies of the 2d V[olume]. D[ivine]. L[egation], except a copy or two for my use, might be burnt directly. I did not mean in an imaginary fire, like that to which the English Catholics devote us heretics at present; but such a one as they sent us to in Q Mary's day. If I cannot prevail in this, I know of no other way than to reprint a leafe or two with some added treason against the omnipotency of a house of Commons, or the omniscience of a first Minister; and then I may get them burnt in pomp, by the hands of the common hangman.

                           Dear Sir ever most affectionately
                                Yours   W. Warburton
                                P.P.   Decr 19 1752

Address and frank (f.57; detached): To Mr: John Knapton Bookseller in Ludgate Street London   Free R: Allen

¹ William Heberden (1710–1801).

Warburton *to* [John Nourse?]¹   [late 1752?]²
Harvard Theatre Collection: TS 937.3.2. (I: 212)   [London]

Dr Sr
    Soon after you left me last night Mr Yorke came & brought me the same apol. of Voltaire with his satire on Maupertieu³ joined with it, which is something longer than the Apology⁴ & much better. He had just recd it from abroad. If you have it not & think proper to translate

the satire likewise I fancy Mr Y. would lend you the use of his copy. if you have any thing to say concerning this matter I shall be at home all this afternoon

Yours very sincerely
W Warburton
Sunday noon

[1] The recipient of this letter was either Nourse or the unknown English translator of Voltaire's two pamphlets, *Défense de Milord Bollingbroke* and *Diatribe du Docteur Akakia.*

[2] Voltaire wrote the anonymous *Diatribe* in November 1752 and became estranged from his patron, Frederick II, as a result of its publication. Some thirty thousand copies were surreptitiously printed against Frederick's wishes. On December 24 Voltaire witnessed the public burning of his pamphlet, which ensured its considerable popularity. Charles Yorke presumably brought a copy from Europe (or had one sent to him) in time for a translation to have been available by February 1753.

[3] Pierre Louis Moreau de Maupertuis, the president of the Berlin Academy, was the victim of Voltaire's *Diatribe.*

[4] Presumably *A Defence of the late Lord Bollingbroke's Letters on the Study and Use of History* which was published with *The Diatriba of Dr. Akakia, the Pope's Physician; the Decree of the Inquisition, and the Report of the Professors of Rome in regard to a pretended President* (Rome, 1753). The translations were advertised in *LM*, 22 (February 1753): 96 (1*s.* each). Warburton's role in the translation of these two pamphlets is worth noting, especially if, by 'Apology', he meant Voltaire's *Défense*. For Voltaire's later attacks in *La Défense de mon oncle* and *À Warburton*, see J. H. Brumfitt, 'Voltaire and Warburton', *Studies on Voltaire and the Eighteenth Century*, ed. Theodore Besterman, 18 (Geneva, 1961): 35–56.

1753

Towards the end of January, Sir John Hill made an unsuccessful attempt to dedicate a two-volume edition of *The Inspector* to Warburton, having already been turned down by Henry Pelham.

In April Warburton was appointed a prebendary of Gloucester Cathedral by Lord Hardwicke, father of his friend Charles Yorke. By June he found 'a Prebendal house or rather two' in Gloucester, which he wanted Knapton to insure with the Sun Fire office.

The second crown octavo edition of Pope's *Works* – the fourth in the series of five Warburton-Knapton editions – was published in nine volumes. Concerned about 'the beauty of the Edn.', Warburton wanted to make a number of changes to the Pope edition, including changing footnotes to endnotes, and putting notes in the same size of font as the text in order to 'swell it out a little more'.

The first volume of Warburton's sermons, *The Principles of Natural and Revealed Religion*, was published. At the end of the year, he was angry with Andrew Millar for undertaking to publish Bolingbroke's *Works*.

Warburton *to* [Sir John Hill][1]   28 January [1753][2]
BL: Stowe MS. 155, f.129   [Prior Park]

Sir

I think my selfe much obliged for the expressions of your good will to me, and am truly sensible of the honour you offer for my acceptance: But I should very much abuse the good opinion you have of me should I suffer you to think of such a thing while there are so many persons eminent for letters in high stations and who are the natural Patrons of learned men.[3] Permit me, in my station, to esteem, & to profess my esteem for your extensive knowledge & great abilities, and to say, you should seek the support & encouragement of them from some great & generous Patron, who knows how to value science, and has a heart to treat it as it deserves. Tis impossible I can be of any other use to you than by exhorting you never to suffer so good talents to be misapplied either on subjects unworthy of you, or by too hasty enquiries into such as are of most importance & which you are so well able to give us new lights in. I hope you will not be displeased with this freedom, any more than for my declining the honour you was so good to intend me. However be assured I have a due sense of it, and shall be always glad of any opportunity of shewing that I am,

Sir, your very faithfull
& most obedient Servant
W. Warburton
Jan. 28

¹ This is the only known letter between Warburton and Hill. For Hill's correspondence and his relations with patrons, see G.S. Rousseau, *The Letters and Papers of Sir John Hill*; and his two supplements: 'Six New Hill Letters', *Medical History*, 28 (1984): 293–302; 'Seven New Hill Letters', *Études Anglaises*, 39 (1986): 174–87 (this gathering stops at Stowe MS. 155, f.127). The above letter has been included in D.W. Nichol, 'A Warburton-Hill Letter: a supplement to Rousseau', *Études Anglaises*, 42 (1989): 185–7. It is significant that Hill regarded Warburton, after the Prime Minister, Henry Pelham, as a potential patron.

² The year is determined by the preceding letter in the folio from Pelham's secretary, John Roberts, to Hill, dated 26 January 1753 (Stowe MS. 155, f.127; printed in Rousseau, 'Seven New Hill Letters').

³ Hill evidently wanted to dedicate his forthcoming two-volume edition of *The Inspector* to Warburton.

Warburton *to* Philip Yorke   19 March 1753
BL: Add. MS. 35592, f.48   [Prior Park]

My Lord

I beg I may be permitted to make your Lordship my warmest acknowledgments for your goodness in mentioning me, so much to my advantage, to the Duke of Newcastle.¹ I have, and it could hardly be otherwise, found the benefit of it: the particulars of which, Mr [Charles] Yorke will acquaint your Lordship with.

I beg to be numbered amongst your most obliged Servants; and that I may be permitted to say, that no one has a higher sense of the obligations of gratitude than,

My Lord, Your Lordship's most
obedient & devoted Servant
W. Warburton
March 19 1753

Endorsed (f.49v.; attached): Mar: 19th, 1753. From the Revd. Mr. Warburton.

¹ Lord Hardwicke evidently nominated Warburton for the prebendary of Gloucester Cathedral.

Warburton *to* [Thomas Pelham-Holles]   21 March 1753
BL: Add. MS. 32731, f.290   [Prior Park]

My Lord

I am bold to make my humblest acknowledgments for the great honour your Grace does me in your regard and protection.

I beg leave to assure your Grace that you have not a Servant who can be more penetrated with gratitude, who has a warmer or deeper sense of your goodness, or is more attached to the duties which result from such obligations.

Permit me, my Lord, with all submission, to subscribe my selfe,
Yours Grace's most obliged
and most devoted Servant
W. Warburton

March 21 1753

Endorsed (f.291*v*.; attached): March 21st. 1753. Mr. Warburton.

Warburton *to* Knapton 25 April 1753
BL: Egerton 1954, f.58 Prior Park

Dear Sir

I got home well, & two or three days after, rec'd the 8° Copy of Pope for the small edn. I have struck out most of the notes & corrected it for that purpose,[1] and have ordered it to be sent back to you by the same conveyance. Concerning which I have only two or three words to add. I beg you would give particular charge for the correct printing. And that the compositors & correctors when they see any manifest erratum in their copy, that they would not let it go on forever but correct it on the spot

My other proposal is That what notes are left be not printed, as in all the other Edns., under each page: but all together at the end of each poem, to which they belong; and the notes of the Dunciad at the end of each Book, as in Mr Pope's q[uart]o edns. both of his Poems & Homer. My reasons are these, first it will be a variety from the other Edns. but principally I think the small chara[c]ter of the notes in the specimen you have, deforms & hurts the beauty of the Edn. it appears to be much more elegant to have nothing but verses in the page or nothing but prose. besides if the notes be thrown together as I propose they will be in the same letter with the text, which will make the Edn. more beautifull, & what is still of more consequence will swell it out a little more, which it will want to be. Again, could I, without trouble, [have][2] a dozen copies printed on a larger paper for presents? I think to go to Gloucester in a few days from whence you sh[all] [h]ear from me. But all letters coming here get to me wherever I am.

Dear Sir ever most affectionately
Yours   W. Warburton
P.P. Apr. 25 1753

Address and frank (verso): To Mr: Knapton Bookseller in Ludgate Street London   Free R: Allen

---

[1] The 1754 ten-volume pot octavo edition carries Pope's notes only. The 1751 frontispiece was re-engraved for this edition. What few notes appeared in the first volume were given at the bottom of the page rather than at the end of the volume. The extra volume was created by spreading *The Dunciad* over two volumes (books I-III in volume 5; book IV in volume 6).

[2] A tear in the page at this point affects some of the following words.

Warburton *to* Knapton   6 May 1753
BL: Egerton 1954, f.59   Prior Park

Dear Sir

I have the favour of your last. A very bad cold has kept me till now at this place. I propose to set out for Gloucester tomorrow. Where a letter simply directed to me at that place will find me.

I beg you would write to your correspondent at yorke to pay for what York newspapers Gilfillan[1] has sent me since I paid the last, and to send me, no more.

I am Dear Sir ever
most affectionately yours
W. Warburton
P. P. May 6 1753

---

[1] John Gilfillan, the printer in York, the bookseller John Hildyard and Knapton shared the imprint on Jaques Sterne, *The danger arising to our civil and religious liberty from the great increase of Papists* (York: printed by John Gilfillan, for John Hildyard and sold by J. and P. Knapton, T. Longman, T. Shewell, and M. Cooper, London, 1747).

Warburton *to* Paul Knapton   30 May 1753
BL: Egerton 1954, f.60   Prior Park

Prior Park   May 30 1753

Dear Sir

By a letter my wife recd from my Servant in London, we find she is just married, so I have a servant to seek. I beg you would give my humble

Service to Mrs Knapton. I was obliged to her for this, who is just gone off, & was a very good Servt. I should be again much obliged to her if it be in her power to recommend me to another. It is possible that some of her Acquaintance may have had people in their Service that they can recommend to her.

> I am Dear Sir Your
> most affectionate & faithfull
> humble Servt.
> W. Warburton

Pray tell Mr J. Knapton I recd his favour at Gloucester & was in hopes of receiving a specimen of the little Edn. of Pope ere now.[1]

Address and frank (f.61; detached): To Mr: Paul Knapton Bookseller in Ludgate Street London   Free R: Allen

[1] The 1754 ten-volume pot octavo edition of Pope's *Works*.

Warburton *to* [John Nourse][1]   [mid-1753?]
Princeton University Library: John Wild Autographs, 3: 113
                                        Bedford Row, London

Sir
    I beg the favour of you to convey for me *Pope's Works*: & another book of mine, which comes along with this to the Baron Montesque and to let him know they come from me to him as a mark of my great esteem & regard for him.[2]

> I am Sir your
> very faithfull humble
> Servt   W. Warburton
> Bedf row. Thursday night

Note (in another hand): Bishop Warburton   Pope's Friend & Editor
Address (separate leaf): Mr. Nourse   Bookseller in the Strand

[1] I am grateful to Jean F. Preston for identifying Nourse as the recipient.
[2] Warburton's unspecified gift to Charles de Secondat, Baron de Montesquieu, might be *Julian*: Charles Yorke transcribed a letter from Montesquieu conveying his admiration of *Julian* in a letter to Warburton on 16 August 1753 (*LLEP*, pp.377–8). In the following year, Warburton told Ii rd that Montesquieu had read the *Divine Legation*.

Warburton *to* [Knapton]   9 June 1753
BL: Egerton 1954, f.62   Prior Park

Dear Sir

I have the favour of yours of the 5th. I heartily thank Mrs Knapton
and shall be much obliged to her.

I am pretty much in the same sentiments as to the notes at the end. But
I entirely submitt it to your better judgment. I thought two advantages
were obvious, the beauty of the Edition, and the thickening it out, which
we thought it would want.

I found at Gloucester a Prebendal house or rather two.   for they are
all divided into two Tenem[en]ts, one is supposed to be resided in, the
other let. I think it proper to ensure them in the sun-fire office at 800*l.*
that is 400*l.* each. They are in the College-green Gloucester Which I beg
you would be so good to do.[1]

I hope to be in Town in a few days and am Dear Sir

Your most faithfull
& affectionate friend &
Servt   W. Warburton

P.P.   June 9 1753

---

[1] In his *Life of Alexander Pope* (London, 1857), p.456, Robert Carruthers mentioned
that Pope had thirty-one shares in the Sun Fire Office valued at £1011 7*s*. Warburton
could also have sought advice about a Sun Fire insurance policy from Ralph Allen,
another of the company's shareholders; see P.G.M. Dickson, *The Sun Insurance Office
1710–1960* (London, 1960), p.291. I am grateful to D. L. Hill of the Sun Alliance
Insurance Group for providing me with a photograph of the entry of Warburton's policy
(no. 136119) which was paid for by John Knapton one week after this letter was posted.
The entry shows that Knapton paid £1 4*s*. on Warburton's behalf for a year's protection
to a maximum of £800. Warburton would have been sent a sun-shaped fire-mark to affix
to his prebendal house and the adjoining structure.

John and Paul Knapton *to* Warburton[1]   10 July 1753
BL: Egerton 1954, f.63 (receipt)   [London]

July. 10. 1753. Recd of the Revd Mr Warburton a Bill drawn by
Tho[mas] Price[2] or Mr John Gorham to John King or order for one
hundred and seven pounds, payable the 5th of Augt for which I promise
to be accountable

John & Paul Knapton

107:0:0

N.B. to buy 100£ NSS Accns.[3] with it

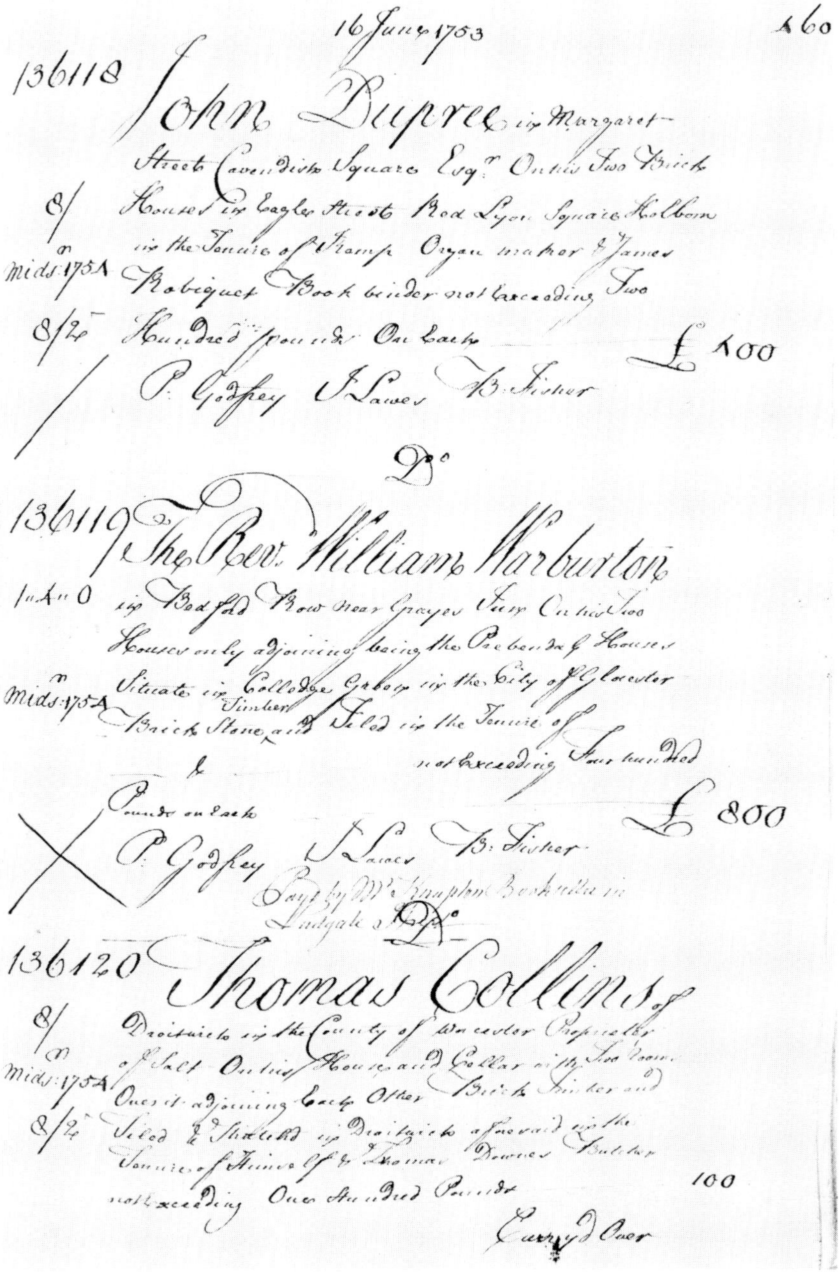

16 June 1753

136118   John Dupree in Margaret
Street Cavendish Square Esqr On his Two Brick
House in Eagle Street Red Lyon Square Holborn
in the Tenure of Tramp Organ maker & James
Mids 1754   Robiquet Book binder not exceeding Two
8/2°   Hundred pounds On Each   £ 100

        P. Godfrey   J. Lawes   B. Fisher

                    Do

136119   The Revd. William Warburton
in Bedford Row near Grays Inn On his Two
Houses only adjoining being the Prebendary Houses
Situate in Colledge Green in the City of Gloucester
Mids 1754   Brick Stone and Timber Tiled in the Tenure of
                not exceeding Four hundred
Pounds on Each   £ 800

    P. Godfrey   J. Lawes   B. Fisher
        Payd by Mr Knapton Bookseller in
            Ludgate S.   Do

136120   Thomas Collins of
Droitwich in the County of Worcester Proprietor
of Salt On his House and Cellar with Two room
Mids 1754   Over it adjoining each Other Brick Timber and
8/2°   Tiled & Thatched in Droitwich aforesaid in the
Tenure of himself & & Thomas Deanes Butcher
not exceeding One Hundred Pounds   100

                    Carryd Over

Plate 4. Warburton's policy with the Sun Insurance Office (16 June 1753).

Verso: 1753 Augt 7. Lent to Mr Warburton 2 Bank Notes

for _ _ _ _ _ _ _ _20£ each_____ £40

Augt 10 _ _ _ _ _ 2 Do_____ 40
                                            ———
                                            80

Remain[der] due to Mr W. Augt 14   27
                                            ———
                                            £107

[1] This receipt, presumably a copy of the original sent back to Warburton, is the only extant manuscript from the Knaptons to Warburton.

[2] Thomas Price was a bookseller in Gloucester (*fl.* 1735–69); the same name appears as a witness to Warburton's will in 1779. John King was a bookseller in Moorfields, London (*c.* 1760); no John Gorham is recorded in Plomer.

[3] Presumably New South Sea Stock.

Warburton *to* Knapton   17 July 1753
BL: Egerton 1954, f.64   Brant Broughton

Dear Sir

I got well hither & propose returning to Prior Park in 4 or 5 days. On examining my finances I find I cannot spare the 107*l*. I desired you to buy stock with, so desire at your leasure when it is paid to send it to me in 3 or 4 bank bills, but only half at a time, that is the bills cut in two.[1]

I hear nothing yet from Bo[w]yer of any proofes, tho' besides the D.L. I have given him copy for the 2d Vol. of Sermons, which I desire you would see may be printed like the first.

I am Dear Sir ever
                                        most affectionately yours
My best respects to   W. Warburton
Mr & Mrs Knapton   B.B.
July 17 1753

[1] It was a customary precaution, dating back to at least 1727, when sending bank bills through the post to cut them in half and mail the halves separately. Printed cheques were introduced in 1781; see Leslie Watkins, *Barclays: a Story of Money and Banking* (London, 1982).

Warburton *to* Knapton   28 July 1753
BL: Egerton 1954, f.65   Prior Park

Dear Sir
   On my getting hither last night I found your two obliging Letters. We have an odd Treasurer[1] who sends us such draughts & then makes us pay for the return. I am much obliged to you for being so brisk with him. If the Bill had been protested it was what they all deserved.
   The inclosed is for Bowyer.

> I am Dr Sr ever most affectionately
> Yours
> W. Warburton
> P.P.   July 28 1753

Address and frank (f.65*v*.; partly cut away): Mr: John Kn[apton] Bookseller in L[udgate Street]   Free R: Allen.

[1] Untraced.

Warburton *to* Knapton   9 August 1753
BL: Egerton 1954, f.66   Prior Park

Dear Sir
   I recd two halves of 2 20*l*. notes   when you have sent the other 2 halves be pleased to omit the remainder of the money till I write for it.
   There is at the end of the 2d part of the 2d Vol of D.L. in those copies which I would have destroyed an *Appendix* intitled an *Appendix containing some remarks* 2d Edn. I wish you would have those sheets which contain 76 pages taken out of all the Copies & sent to my house at Bedford Row.
   I see there is a new Edn. of Gibson's Cambden's Britania just published.[1] If the maps be good, I would have that Edition.
   Mr Allen, who is a subscriber to your Dictionary of Commerce desires you would send him the 1st Vol. in Boards.[2]

> I am Dear Sir ever most
> Affectionately Yours
> W. Warburton
> P.P. Augt 9 1753

[1] *Britannia: or, a Chorographical Description of Great Britain and Ireland, Together with the Adjacent Islands. Written in Latin by William Camden ... and Translated into English, with Additions and Improvements*, rev. Edmund Gibson, 3rd ed., 2 vols. (London: R. Ware,

J. and P. Knapton, T. Longman, C. Hitch, D. Browne, H. Lintot, C. Davis, J. Hodges, A. Millar, W. Bowyer, J. Whiston, J. and J. Rivington, and J. Ware, 1753). Edmund Gibson, D.D. (1669–1748), was Bishop of Lincoln (1716) and Bishop of London (1723). This folio edition was advertised in *LM*, 22 (November 1753): 534.

[2] *The Universal Dictionary of Trade and Commerce*, trans. Malachy Postlethwayt, 2 vols. (London: J. and P. Knapton, 1751–5). This is based on the *Dictionnaire universel* by Jacques Savary de Bruslon (Paris, 1723–30). The Knaptons issued *A Dissertation on the Plan... of the Universal Dictionary* in 1749; the subscription notice is dated 30 May 1752. See John Feather, *Book Prospectuses before 1801 in the John Johnson Collection* (Oxford, 1976).

Warburton *to* Knapton   3 September 1753*a*
BL: Egerton 1954, f.67   Prior Park

Dear Sir
    Mr Allen desires the favour of you to receive the inclosed Dr. for 37*l*: 19*s*. when due and to pay

	l.	*s*	*d*
To Vile & Com.	15	15	0.
To Briscoe	13.	13:	0
To Andrews	3:	0:	0:
	32:	8:	0

The bills are inclosed. You will see that to Andrews is only 1*l*. 10*s*. but you are desired to order him to send hither 2 doz. more of Pyrment water[1] which will be 1*l*: 10*s*. more & so pay him the 3*l*:

	l.	*s*	*d*
The remainder is	5	11	0.

which with the 27*l*. in hand I desire you to change into a note & send me down hither.
    Mr Allen was very diffident in venturing to give you all this trouble But I assured him you would with great pleasure order one of your servants to do all this.

                                        I am Dear Sir ever most
                                        Affectionately Yours
          P.P.   Sept. 3 1753   W. Warburton

Address, frank and postmark (f.68*v*.): Mr: J. Knapton   Bookseller in Ludgate Street London   Free R: Allen. 5/SE

[1] Related to 'pyrrey', an obsolete form of 'perry' or pear cider (*OED*). Andrews, Briscoe and Vile were presumably merchants or suppliers.

Warburton *to* James Leake[1]   3 September 1753*b*
Princeton University Library: Robert H. Taylor Collection
                                                    Prior Park

                                                    Sept 9. 1753[2]
Mr Leake
  As soon as the D. of Grafton comes to Bath I should be obliged to you
to let me know, because I have a message to him from Mr Allen, which I
shall send to him by Prinn.[3]
  Pray tell Mr Richardson that I have read over the two Vols of Sr C. G.
which he left here, and that they excell his Clarissa.[4]

                                      Your very humble Servt
                                           W. Warburton
                                      P.P.   Sepr 3 1753

Addendum (in Leake's hand): Mr Pierce[5] tells me Mr Warburton is vastly
pleasd with Sr Ch. Gr. I saw Mr Allen the morning he set out for
Weymouth. he enquird how I left You & returns his Thanks for the
Perusal of the 2 Vols. My Obligations for Your late & Numberless
former Favours to me & mine are too many ever to be forgot, the
Remembrance of 'em will ever remain Strong in my Memory   Pray
God bless You & Yours, which wish[?] my Thanks & Services to You all
is from

                                      Yr most obliged &
                                Humble Servt &c   J. Leake

Miss Bell Chauncy of Kensington[6] Sent a Messenger to Enquire how Mr
& Mrs Richardson & Daughtrs were. I suppose You[7]

  [1] This letter is listed in Eaves and Kimpel, *Samuel Richardson: a Biography*, p.668.
Richardson was married to Leake's sister, Elizabeth. This letter suggests a reconciliation
following Richardson's cancellation of Warburton's 1748 'Editor to the Reader' in the
fourth volume of *Clarissa* and Warburton's retaliation by recycling it – with Richardson's name replaced by Fielding's – in *Works* (1751), 4: 166–9 n.
  [2] This date appears not to be in Warburton's hand (as the one given below his
signature clearly is); it is perhaps the date Leake forwarded this letter with his own
added message for Richardson.
  [3] Augustus Henry Fitzroy (1735–1811), 3rd Duke of Grafton; Samuel Prynn was
Allen's servant.
  [4] Richardson's *Sir Charles Grandison* was published in 1753–4.
  [5] Presumably Dr. Zachary Pearce, who performed the Allens' marriage service in
1737 and became Dean of Westminster Abbey in 1756, rather than the surgeon
Jeremiah Peirce who was named in Allen's will.
  [6] Possibly related to Dr. Charles Chauncy, who owned a crayon portrait of Clarissa
and was asked (as Leake was) to render advice on *Sir Charles Grandison* (Eaves and
Kimpel, *Samuel Richardson: A Biography*, pp.228, 594).
  [7] The rest of this line has been pasted over.

Warburton *to* Knapton   24 September 1753
BL: Egerton 1954, f.69   Prior Park

Dear Sir

I recd the Bills, for which Mr Allen returns you many thanks. I have the Banknote likewise for 32*l*. 11*s*.

I hope you continue well and all the Family. And that Mr Paul's Regimen has by this time perfectly reinstated him in his health.[1] I think with pleasure on the day we all spent at Marshgate[2] and in Richmond Gardens. Where I suppose you have had many a walk since.

I am Dr Sr ever most
Affectionately Yours
W. Warburton
P.P.   Sepr 24 1753

[1] An intimation of Paul Knapton's flagging health two years before death.
[2] Knapton's residence, see Mack, *Collected*, pp.519–20 n.3.

Warburton *to* [Knapton]   17 October 1753
BL: Egerton 1954, f.70   Prior Park

Dear Sir

Bowyer, I hope, by this time has finished the two parts of the First Vol of Div. Leg.

I beg you will order him to let your binder have a copy with all the reprinted leaves. His Compositor made sad blunders in paging two sheets, so He wrote me word he would reprint them at his own expence. I mention this that you may keep him to his word.

I desire that this copy m[a]y be stitched in bords. It is for the Arch *Bp*.[1] but a letter must go with it which I will send by my next.

I am Dear Sir ever
most affect. yours
W. Warburton
Prior Park   Octr. 17 1753

Note (possibly Knapton's hand): (abt Mr Hildyard[2])

[1] Thomas Herring (1693–1757), Archbishop of York and Canterbury; elevated to Canterbury in 1747 upon the death of John Potter. He bought a copy of Pope's *Works*, vol. 2, in 1735 (Mack, *Collected*, p.653).
[2] John Hildyard, the bookseller in York.

Warburton *to* [Knapton]   22 October 1753
BL: Egerton 1954, f.71   [Prior Park]

Dear Sir
    I thank you for your favour. I had quite forgot Mrs Haye's money. I
beg you would write immediatly on the rect of this to Mr Hildyard to
desire he would pay the 10*l.* as usual, and to make my compliments and
excuses to her for the neglect. I have inclosed a ten pound note; and am

Dear Sir Your most Affectionate
Servt   W. Warburton
Octr 22 1753.

In the copy[1] to the A[rch]. B[ishop]. be so good at p.304 2d part. l. 16. to
strike out the word *inscriptions* with a pen.
    I hope to be in town abt the begining of next week

[1] *Divine Legation*, II. ii.

Warburton *to* [Knapton]   30 December 1753
BL: Egerton 1954, f.72   [Prior Park]

Dear Sir
    I thank you for the trouble I give you. As to the oath[1] if it be soon
ready to be taken by commission, & the commission be not much
expence I can take it here.

I am Dear Sir ever
most affectionately yours
W. Warburton
Decr 30 1753

[1] See Warburton's letter of 7 January 1754, below.

[Warburton] *to* [Andrew Millar]   [late December 1753]
BL: Egerton 1959, f.16*v.* (transcript)[1]

Answr to Mr M.'s first Letter.

—— As to what you say concerning the publication of B[olingbroke]'s
works my answer is this, That, in a plain question of right & wrong, an
honest man has nothing to do but consult his own breast. It appears to
me that he who for gain contributes, in any way, to the spreading of a

work which, in his own conscience, he believes injurious to society, is just as honest a man as he who for a reward undertakes to scatter poison in to all the Wells & Cisterns of his Neighbourhood.[2]

[n.s.]

[1] In Warburton's hand.

[2] Millar's first letter and the reply sent by Warburton are untraced. Warburton enclosed the above transcript of his reply with his letter to Knapton of 7 January 1754, below. Millar evidently attempted to placate Warburton about his role in the publication of Bolingbroke's *Works* without success. The following two letters (1 and 3 January 1754) reflect the entrenched attitudes of the shrewd bookseller and the stern clergyman.

1754

This was to be a troublesome year for Warburton. It began with Millar's defence of his involvement in the publishing of Bolingbroke's *Works*. However, Mallet's edition of Bolingbroke's *Works* gave Warburton grounds to attack Pope's old mentor in *A View of Lord Bolingbroke's Philosophy, Letters First and Second*. An anonymous acquaintance chastised Warburton for stirring up old ashes.

By the end of January, Warburton had to contend with John Sayer's request to print Pope's original text from the *Essay on Man* alongside his Latin translation. Warburton felt proprietorial, concerned that others might borrow Pope's literary property in a similar fashion without his express permission. With Knapton's advice, he finally agreed to allow Sayer to print an edition of five hundred copies.

Another legally complex demand came from Robert Foulis who wanted to make Pope's works more accessible and affordable to a Scottish readership. With Murray's help he retained lawyers in London and Edinburgh to look into the matter of copyright in relation to Pope's will. Foulis made a compelling case for the encouragement of learning.

Warburton was appointed Chaplain to King George II and was made Doctor of Divinity by the Archbishop of Canterbury. He also published the second volume of *The Principles of Natural and Revealed Religion*. The last of the five Warburton-Knapton editions of Pope's *Works* – the pot octavo – was published in ten volumes; many of Warburton's notes were cut at his own suggestion.

Andrew Millar *to* [Warburton]   1 January 1754
BL: Egerton 1959, f.15   London

London 1 Jany 1753
Revnd Sir

I recd the favr of your's, and thank you for it. You Observe very justly, that in a Plain Question of right and wrong, an honest man need only consult his own breast, and express yourself very strongly wt regard to one's contributing in any degree towards spreading Poisoning opinions. So far as this relates to Ld B ——— s works I cannot help thinking that whatever his Lo[rdship] advances against Christianity will be so far from being of any prejudice to its Interests, that I am fully convinced it will be of advantage to them on the whole, by engaging persons of real abilities and just discernment to place the Evidences of our Religion in a stronger & clearer light. I need not tell you Sir that the Evidences of Xtianity has never been so well understood as since Diests have written wt such freedom agt it ——— as to my Putting my name to them, I have consulted Two D[octor]s. of Divinity of ye Church of England, a Bishop, some of ye most eminent of ye Dissenting Ministry & several Lay People of Candor & reputation distinguished in ye World and not unknown to you, who are all upon this Point clear and advise me to it, as Mallet puts his name as Published by him and Printed for The Editor —— and my name is only one amongst others of my Trade.[1]

There is scarce any however on whom Judgement in any Matter of Difficult determination, I would sooner rely on than on yours or to whom I would be more desirous of approving my self; and I am persuaded when you have duly considered the Matter you will not think I have counteracted The Dictates of a good heart by doing a Thing of this nature, or That Christianity can suffer any thing essential to its best Interest by any thing Ld B —— is capable of advancing. I am Revnd Sir Yr Most oblidged & Obedt Sert

And: Millar

Endorsed (*verso*): Millar's Letter abt Bolingbr[oke]

[1] Millar's name headed the list of the 1754 imprint in the first volume of Bolingbroke's *Works*: London: Printed for the Editor; and sold by A. Millar, in the Strand; G. Hawkins, near Temple-bar; R. Dodsley, in Pall Mall; and S. Bladon, in Pater-noster-row. MDCCLIV.

Warburton *to* Andrew Millar   3 January 1754
BL: Egerton 1959, f.16 (transcript)[1]   Prior Park

P.P.   Jan. 3 1754

Answer to Mr M[illar].'s 2d letter

Sir

I never thought my opinion of much weight where better judges were of a different; on the other hand, I would not see an honest man deceive himself, If I could set him right.

I believe with you, that these execrable writings[2] will be the occasion of putting Truth in a more irresistable light. I believe too, that providence produces a deal of good out of every species of natural and moral evil. But this, I think, will not justify any one in deliberately contributing to the propogation of that *Evil*. And whatever benefit to Religion may arise from the learned confutation of B[olingbroke'].s impieties, it will be but a poor reperation for the vast mischief they will do amongst the weak heads and bad hearts of *a People*

Few wou'd receive more contentment in Seeing, or more pleasure in answering these writings than my Self: Yet God forbid, I should ever preferr my private Satisfaction to the peace and happiness of Society.

At the same time I make no question but you Satisfy your own judgment when you act on different Sentiments: and then nobody has any reason to be disatisfied with you: at least, not I, to whom you pay a compliment,[3] which I had no pretentions to expect, when you are pleas'd to account to me for your conduct. I am &c

[n.s.]

[1] The heading and date are in Warburton's hand; the rest is by an amanuensis.

[2] Bolingbroke's *Works*. Warburton had already prepared an attack on Bolingbroke which he decided to omit from the 1751 Pope edition. See his letters of 3 June 1751, above, and 19 June 1754, below.

[3] Referring to Millar's attempt to mollify Warburton in his letter of 1 January 1754, above.

Warburton *to* [Knapton]   7 January 1754
BL: Egerton 1954, f.73   [Prior Park]

Jan 7 1754
Dear Sir

I recd the Comn. for the Oaths from Mr Herring and have returned it to him by this post. He asked me whom he should deliver the Degree to when compleated   I said to You who would pay him all fees a bill of which he sent me which I here inclose. I wish you could know whether any thing more is to be given him or given to servants. I believe Birch can inform you best. I wish you would take an opportunity to ask him. but it will be time enough when the instrument is compleated. I have sent you inclosed 2 halfs of two twenty pound notes to pay the secretary. Pray open the paper for the other half parts.

The other papers which I inclose are just for your brother and you to laugh over in great secret.[1] Millar has determined after all to be concerned in the publication of Bol[ingbroke']s. Works, and had a mind to make a dupe of me to approve his conduct. On which acct writing to me to borrow a book which he could not get elsewhere He told me as a Piece of news that B.'s works would be publ[ished]. in Feb. and as Mallet put his name to them; so some of my friends (hinting at the Sol[icito?]r) thought he need have no scruple to put his. This occasion'd the answer to his first letter.[2] He replied: which reply I have sent with a copy of my answer to that, as well as to the first.—— You will smile; and your brother will call him a R —— [asca]l. I know what I think him However I should not have given my selfe the trouble but that I was resolved he should have no pretence of putting me amongst his *approbation-Doctors*. But all this inter nos. Dear Sir my complimts of the season to all the family. believe me

Ever most affectionately yours
W. Warburton

[1] Warburton evidently enclosed the preceding three letters ([late December 1753], 1 and 3 January 1754).

[2] See Warburton's unsigned transcript [late December 1753], and n.2, above.

Warburton *to* [Knapton]   19 January 1754
BL: Egerton 1954, f.74   Prior Park

                                   Prior Park   Jan 19 1754
Dear Sir

I return you my hearty thanks for the trouble I have given you in this affair. You have done every thing mighty right. I would desire you to keep the patent till I come to Town, which will not be till Easter Term   I have been so very indifferent ever since I left you of my cold, & have since got another that I do not care to venture on a winter journey so far, especially as in the middle of next month I must go to Gloucester.

I think it would be very proper now to get a complete copy (which is now entirely finish'd) of the two parts of the first Vol. of D.L. for Birch in order to finish the index. For as Bollingbroke is just comming out I think it will be very proper soon to publish either with animadversions on him or without as I see occasion.

                              I am Dear Sir ever most affectionately
                                   yours   W. Warburton

I beg the favour that you would send somebody to Mr T. Pain's the Book-seller[1] at the Mews Gate to desire him to tell Mr Hethcote (my assistant at Lincoln's Inn[2] that I shall not be in London this term, that he may take care of the Chappel – I don't know where Mr Hethcote lives – Mr Paine does.

[1] Thomas Payne (1719–99); see Plomer.

[2] No closing bracket. Ralph Heathcote (Ryley, p.5; *LA*, 5: 536).

John Sayer *to* Warburton   26 January 1754
BL: Egerton 1954, ff.76–7   Panton Street, London

Sir,

Intending to proceed with the publication of Mr: Pope's Essay on Man translated (wch: I had for some time laid aside) and being in Town with this View before Xtmas I called on Mr: Knapton (who at the time of printing the third Epistle wrote me a Letter on account of my having subjoined the English to the Translation) and was informed by him that

it was by your Direction, and that the Property was in You;[1] He likewise
told me that You was not in Town, but said he wou'd write to You for
your Permission, and shd. have your Answer in about ten Days, but
upon sending a Gentleman to enquire, I found that he did not write,
giving for the reason that You wou'd be in Town in a little time. On
Thursday last I called at your House again, and was sorry to hear of the
Occasion of your Detention in the Country, which makes it necessary for
me to write instead of waiting on you for your Leave to print the
Original with the Translation. The reason of my not solliciting the
favour of you before was really, as Mr: Knapton supposes in his letter,
my Unacquaintance with the Nature of literary Property, but the
acknowledging this joined with my request I am persuaded will be
sufficient with you to grant me the Liberty, as I apprehend that the
printing a small Number by Subscription, or even a large number can be
of little or no Prejudice to your Editions, and as I am satisfied of your
known Attachment to Mr: Pope's writings and Desire to have them
published as generally as may be with any Propriety. From this
Assurance it is that from asking this Favour I proceed to ask another,
Your Encouragement of the Translation by such a Number of
Subscriptions as You can easily obtain among the Gentlemen of your
Acquaintance, which I hope for from Mr: Pope's great Desire to have
the Essay translated into Latin,[2] and your approbation of the Specimen
I sent You before Publication, which I hope the Whole of the Third
Epistle equally merited, and the Others will. I have been at considerable
Expence already, but by your favour (which I cannot but naturally look
for) and that of some People of Note, whose Compliments I had upon
the Translation, and that of Alexander's Feast, I am in some expectation
that if I am no Gainer, I may not be a Loser   I am with Respect; Sir,

Your Humble Servt.

Jan. 26th. 1754   John Sayer

Panton Street near the Haymarket
at Mr: Green's a Mercer; Sign the Sun.

Address (f.77): For the Revd. Dr: Warburton These

[1] Proposals for printing John Sayer's Latin translation of the *Essay on Man* by
subscription were issued in Oxford on 19 November 1750. See Harry Carter, *A History of
the Oxford University Press*, 1 (Oxford, 1975): 539. A notice also appeared in *LM*, 21
(March–April 1752): 195: 'Mr. Pope's third Essay on Man: Translated into Latin Verse.
By J. Sayer, M.A. pr. 2s. 6d. Rivingtons.' In his 1752 Latin translation of the third epistle
of *An Essay on Man*, Sayer 'borrowed' Pope's original text (which is printed in double
columns at the foot of each page) without seeking Warburton's permission. Thus Sayer's
request to use part of Warburton's literary property came after the fact. Since Sayer
planned to continue with his English-Latin translation, he followed Knapton's advice to

go through proper channels. See *De Homine. Poema Alexandri Popii. Quatuor Epistolis Conscriptum*, a Johanne Sayer, A.M. Latine Redditum. Oxonii, Typographeo Clarendoniano, Impensis Jacobi Fletcher Bibliopolae. Prostant apud J. & J. Rivington, M. Cooper, & W. Owen, *London*. MDCCLII. See also *Alexandri Popii, sive Universi Generis Humani Supplicatio*. Latine Reddita a Johanne Sayer, A.M. Londini: Impensis W. Owen, ad Insigne Capitis Homeri, in vico vocato Fleet-Street. 1756. The text of Pope's *Universal Prayer* appears on the left-hand side, with the Latin translation on the right.

[2] In his letter of 6 November [1743], Pope had hoped Christopher Smart might translate the last epistle of *An Essay on Man* into Latin (*Correspondence*, 4: 483–4).

Warburton *to* John Sayer   28 January 1754*a*
BL: Egerton 1954, f.78   Prior Park

Sir

I have yours of the 26. It is true the letter you speak of, as written to you by Mr Knapton, was written by my direction. Soon after Mr Pope died I was necessitated to put half a dozen people, who pirated the Essay on Man, into Chancery since which I have been but little injured in my property of it: which is now divided between Messrs. Knapton & me. They are the best judges whether giving you permission to print it with your translation will injure the sale of that, which at a considerable expense, they have always in trade. You may be assured if they imagine it will be the least injury to it they will refuse their permission. And you cannot wonder at it: For tho' printing books be their trade they never asked, nor used without asking, such a liberty.

I am sorry you have been, I won't say at *considerable*, but at any expense on this project. However I have the satisfaction to reflect that I neither put you upon it, nor encouraged you in it.

As you seem to make too slight of property, so you infinitely overrate my power of serving you in the subscription. I indeed have none at all, further than subscribing to it my selfe. This I am willing to do, for as many copies as you think reasonable, tho' I am an entire stranger to you. When I say subscribe, I mean to your translation. For as to the liberty of printing the original with it, as I said before, I have it not to give; part of the property being Messrs Knapton. And I am (as it is very fit I should be) governed in this matter entirely by what they think proper to do. They will injure no man, and are ready to do civilities even to strangers in all reasonable matters. but sure it is not reasonable to expect they should give away their property.

I am, Sir, Your very humble Servt
W. Warburton
P.P.   Jan. 28 1754

Address (f.78*v*.): To The Revd Mr J. Sayer   Panton Street near the Hay-market   At Mr Green's a Mercer, Sign of the Sun

Warburton *to* Knapton   28 January 1754*b*
BL: Egerton 1954, f.75   [Prior Park]

Dear Sir

The inclosed speak themselves.[1] If you think my Answer fit to be sent I wish a copy may be taken of it. For the man's an entire stranger to me.

I have looked into Bolingbroke. If one of the damned was to be made, in a poetical description, exclaiming against Moses & Paul he could not do it with more rage and blasphemous language than is done by this noble Lord. And this, that good Man A Millar helps forwards into the world for the pure sake of Religion & the public good.

I am Dear Sir en[t]irely
Yours W. Warburton
Jan. 28 1754

Address and frank (f.75*v*.): Mr Warburton   To Mr: John Knapton Bookseller in Ludgate Street London   Free R: Allen

[1] Referring to Sayer's letter of 26 January 1754 and Warburton's reply of 28 January 1754*a*, above, which Warburton enclosed for Knapton's reading.

Warburton *to* Knapton   7 February 1754
BL: Egerton 1954, f.79   Prior Park

Dear Sir

Pray thank Mrs Knapton for the favour of her letter & for her kindness in indeavouring to procure me a good Servant.

I hope the index is going forward.[1] I have got Bolingbroke's works by favour of Millar. 'Tis rage & madness it selfe. I shall have occasion to take him to task in every Vol. I publish of the Div. Leg. In his 1st Vol. which I would have published next winter I propose to have a Preface in the first part and an appendix in the second, to divide the Vols more equally. If I can include what I have to say in the preface in a 100 pages it will do. I say the same of the Appendix. Would not this be a better way than publishing what I have to say on the subject of the 1st Vol. in a separate book, published along with the two parts? You know best. This severe weather has made me deferr my Gloucester journey a few days longer.

I am Dear Sir most
affectionately yours
P. P.   Feb. 7 1754   W. Warburton

P.S Dear Sir after I had written the above and forgot to send it away, I recd your favour of the same date. I agree entirely to all you say of that silly affair of Sayer's; and desire you would absolutely do what you think proper. If you find any reason to allow him to print any number of the original in Q[uart]o. we perhaps may have this advantage of binding him under his hand Never to print any more of this nor any other of Mr Pope's works without leave obtained in writing —— But nothing can be replied to the fitness of all you say. —— I hate to write letters over again so if you will be so good to scratch out for so many copies as he shall think fit leaving only my promise of subscribing, and pray let it be sent to him.[2]

There is another inconvenience of suffering one man to print the original, that it may put it into the head of another to do the like, so we shall have some fool or other allways upon our hands. Perhaps you will think this of weight absolutely to refuse him —— for here comes in the cautionary rule *venienti occurrite*.[3] Bollingbroke's works will put many a good man in mind of these Lines of Pope

"Not Danté, dreaming o'er th'infernal State,
E'er saw such Scenes of rage, despair, & hate.[4]

Verso: To Mr Knapton

[1] Birch's index of *The Divine Legation*, I, parts i-ii, as mentioned in Warburton's letter of 19 January 1754, above.
[2] Knapton apparently suggested modifications to Warburton's reply to John Sayer (28 January 1754*a*). Warburton offered to subscribe to Sayer's Latin translation 'for as many copies as you think reasonable'. Knapton perhaps thought this might be too much of an encouragement to Sayer who hoped to print more than the 500 copies Knapton was willing to allow.
[3] 'Run up to meet the one who is coming', Julius Caesar, *De bello civili*, 3: 79. 7.
[4] 'Not *Dante* dreaming all th'Infernal State,/Beheld such Scenes of *Envy, Sin*, and *Hate*', 'Donne IV', ll. 192–3 (*TE*, 4: 43).

Warburton *to* Knapton   11 February 1754
BL: Egerton 1954, f.80   Prior Park

Dear Sir
   In my last I mentioned my setting forward to Gloucester as this day. The weather has made me deferr it till this day sev'night.
   I beg when this dr[aft]. becomes due you will receive it for me.
Be so good to let me know it is come safe.
   Concerning what I said in my last abt the Preface & postscript would

it be right to print any more than for the 1s[t] Vol. of D.L. and sell them seperately? I fancy not.

Dear Sir ever most affectionately
Yours   W. Warburton
Prior Park Feb. 11 1754

Address and frank (f.81; attached, partly cut and pasted on): To Mr: Knapton   Bookseller in Ludgate Street London   Free R: Allen

Warburton *to* Knapton   16 February 1754
BL: Egerton 1954, f.82   Prior Park

Dear Sir

I have your favour of the 14th. and am much indebted to you for your two kind presents & desire the honey may be sent to my house in Town to be keep [*sic*] in a cool place till I give further orders abt it.

Dr Birch is in the right. I would have a large index.

This morning I recd a letter from A. Millar. who is at length come about again, and his final resolution is not to have his name to Bols. works, nor to have any thing to do with them. The first good thing in this world is a steady honest man, the next is a sincere penitent.[1] But I would not willingly profess to any but of the first kind, what I do with pleasure to you, that I am

Dear Sir your very affectionate
Friend   W. Warburton
P.P.   Feb 16 1754

Address, frank and postmark (f.83): To Mr: J Knapton   Bookseller in Ludgate Street London   Free R: Allen   18/FE

[1] Millar's 'penitent' phase did not last long. See his letter of 1 January 1754 and n., above; and Warburton's letter to Millar of 20 March 1754, below.

John Sayer *to* Warburton   22 February 1754
BL: Egerton 1954, ff.85–6   Panton Street, London

Sir,

Tho I was in hopes of having a Letter from You in Answer to mine of January last,[1] yet hearing by Mr: Knapton I return you my Thanks for your Leave to subjoin Mr: Pope's Essay on Man to am [*sic*] Impression of 500 Copies of my Translation of that Work into Latin; This favour much obliges me, and I shall observe the Directions you prescribe about the size and manner of printing the thing, viz: in Quarto, and with the Original under the Translation, in the same form that, without your Permission thro my unacquaintance with the Nature of Literary Property, the Third Epistle was published.[2] I dont know whether I shall print even so many as 500, but if I s[houl]d. find it necessary to do off a few more I dare say You will not be against my Request, as the printing the Original in this form and size will certainly be of very little detriment to you, and I may hope from you (exclusive of the reasons mentioned in my last) as an Encourager of any branch of Literature, that a Thing which I beleive to be the most difficult of any Work in our Language to be translated, and has cost me so much labour and pains (tho I hope the elaborateness will not appear more than it ought in the Version) may be attended with some Advantage. Reckoning my own extraordinary expences in attending the thing in Town, I shall not get a Shilling by 300 or 400 Subscriptions. I do not intend (tho I wanted your Answer much with regard to my Proposals) publishing the Translation till about this time twelvemonth, and therefore I had scarce till now turned my thoughts to the execution of the typographical part any farther than to write to you for the Liberty and Permission You are pleased to grant him, who is with thanks and respect,

Sir,

Feb. 22d. 1754	Your Obliged
Panton Street near the Haymarket	Humble Servant
at Mr: Green's a Mercer, Sign the Sun.	John Sayer.

Verso (f.86): Mr Sayer's Letter

[1] Warburton's reply (28 January 1754a) to Sayer's first letter of January 26, above, which was sent to Knapton for approval and copying, apparently was not posted. Either Knapton sent his own letter, specifying the number of copies to be printed (which Warburton left open), or Sayer pre-empted such a reply by visiting Knapton's bookshop.

[2] In 1752.

Warburton *to* [Knapton]	4 March 1754a
BL: Egerton 1954, f.84	Gloucester

Dear Sir

I am perfectly well satisfied with all you have done with Mr Sayer. I have inclosed his letter to me with my answer which, if you approve, I desire may be sealed & sent by the penny-post.[1]

I can depend so much I suppose on Dr Birch's care & discretion that se[e]ing the sheets of the index (to correct if I find need) before they are worked off will be sufficient. Besides, I can hardly read his hand.

You may remember you once sent for me a packet (which went very safe) directed according to the following address

A Monsr
Mr Schmidt[2] le Conseiller du Consistoire Ecclesiastique et le Predicateur de la Cour de son Altesse Sme. Le Marggraf regnant de Brandenbourg-Coulmbach   par Rotterdam
                                          Cologne
                                          Nurnberg
                                          à Bayreuth

I desire that a set of pope small 8°. with all my notes & Com[mentaries]. bound, and the sermons in boards & this new Edn. of the 1st Vol of Div. Leg. in boards may be forthwith packed up and directed as on the other side.[3] and be so good to get it rightly forwarded. I have written to Mr Schmidt two or three posts ago that I had ordered them.

This morning brought me your favour with the half of the 30*l*. note inclosed, of which I have the other half.

I am Dear Sir Your
most affectionate & faithfull
Servant   W. Warburton

Gloucester March 4 1754.

I propose to stay here all this Month, & shall be glad to hear of your health. A letter directed for me only at Gloucester will find me.

[1] See Sayer's letter of 22 February 1754, above, and Warburton's reply to Sayer, 4 March 1754*b*, below.

[2] For Schmidt, see Warburton's letter of 6 July 1752, above.

[3] Warburton wanted Knapton to send Schmidt the 1751 (if still in stock) or 1753 crown octavo edition of Pope's *Works* as well as *The Principles of Natural and Revealed Religion*, 2 vols. (London: printed for J. and P. Knapton, 1753–4) and a copy of the yet-to-be-published first volume (parts 1 and 2, containing books I–III) of *The Divine Legation of Moses*, 4th ed., corr. and enlarged, 5 vols. (London: printed for J. and P. Knapton, 1755–65).

Warburton *to* John Sayer   4 March 1754*b*
BL: Egerton 1954, f.87 (copy)[1]   Gloucester

Copy of Dr Warburton's Letter to the Revd Mr J. Sayer answer to[2]

Sir

I have yours of the 22d past. My unwillingness to hinder a project that you have judged for your advantage induced me to consent that you might print 500 Copies of your Translation of the Essay on Man, with the Original. But I must desire you to give notice in your Book, that it is done by my express permission; otherwise th[os]e seeing the Original with your Translation might encourage some or other to pirate it. I cannot take it well when I have been so ready to comply thus far, that you should press me to consent to any greater number; which I can by no means do. I am sorry both for your pains & expence: you have repeated this Consideration in your Letters; which would make a Stranger to us both imagine, that I had conceived some way or other, to set you upon this project, or encouraged you in it. I know the hazard of literary Projects too well to encourage even my friends and acquaintance in them, much less one to whom I am entirely unknown. Nor Do I think Mr P.'s fame, which I should be always desirous of promoting, at all concerned in ye matter. If you translate his Poem well, the reputation will be yours; if it be without Success, he loses nothing by ye miscarriage. My Civility is paid to you not him. I was unwilling to be thought hardly of by a Stranger (for amongst those who know me I run no danger) though I thought the request not very reasonable. But I perceived by the turn of your Letters, you was disposed to see the thing in a different light from what I do: and I was willing to comply as far as in prudence I ought, to what I thought your prejudices——

I have told you my mind without reserve, & am—— Sr

Yr very humble Sert

Gloucester   WW
Mar. 4. 1754

Endorsed: Copy of Dr Warburton's Letter to the Revd Mr J Sayer

[1] Knapton transcribed this letter, as Warburton requested in the above letter of the same date. The hand is the same as that of the receipt dated 10 July 1753, above.

[2] These two words are not in Knapton's hand.

Warburton *to* Andrew Millar   20 March 1754
BL: Add. MS. 4320, f.183 (transcript)[1]   Gloucester

Dr. Warburton to Mr. And. Millar

Sr.****

I find in the papers accusations to stir up the public Resentment agst. the Editor of Lord Bolingbroke's Works. This I think ridiculous & unfair. He is not accountable to any particulars in what concerns his own conscience only: & it is perfectly ridiculous to suppose, that Lord Bol. left him the property of his Writings with design they should be suppressed. The very contrary purpose is evident to the common Sense of Mankind. But there is a contradiction between this & the Declaration in the prefatory Letter to Mr. Pope? Why? his whole Book is full of Contradictions, as well as weak reasonings of pernicious principles. I perhaps may have occasion in due time to shew all this. But what is this to the Editor? Let the Author answer for it; & he will have a hundred Writers, I make no doubt, to call him to account. But if the Editor grows jealous in [sic] he did, in the Case of the Publication of the Patriot King, of one, who neither thought nor said a Word of him, but address'd all he had to say to Lord Bolingbroke, & yet was villainously abus'd as somebody or other in that account he will find himself business. The worst I wish him is the best his Friends can wish, that if he have not publish'd these Works with a perfectly satisfied conscience, he may make his peace, not with particulars or the public, which are nothing, but with him, who only can heal a wounded conscience, or inlighten an erroneous one.

I am, Sr
Your assured & faithfull
Friend & humble Servant
W. Warburton

Gloucester March 20 1754

¹ This transcript is not in Warburton's hand.

Warburton *to* [Knapton]   1 June 1754
BL: Egerton 1954, f.88   Prior Park

Dear Sir

I beg the inclosed may be composed with expedition.[1] You will tell Bowyer that I make a secret of my name. I got down well & think I am better.

ever most Affectionately yours,
W. Warburton

P.P. June 1st. 1754

¹ Warburton presumably enclosed material for his anonymous *A View of Lord Bolingbroke's Philosophy.*

Warburton *to* [Knapton] 19 June 1754
BL: Egerton 1954, f.89 Prior Park

Dear Sir

I have here inclosed a little more copy of the *Letter*. Be so good to pay the above ten pounds to Mrs Hayse this midsummer.

Pray send me in Leake's parcel one of my *Alliances*,[1] and one of those *letters to Bol*: which was printed for the large Pope, & suppressed.[2]

I am Dear Sir
yours most affectionately
W. Warburton
P.P. June 19 1754

Endorsed (in Knapton's hand): Recd pages 21 to 36 incl. sent to Boyers June 21.[3]

[1] *The Alliance between Church and State* (London: Fletcher Gyles, 1736; 3rd ed., corr. and enlarged, J. and P. Knapton, 1748).
[2] Intended for the large octavo 1751 *Works*; see his letter of 3 June 1751*b*, above.
[3] Proof-sheets for *A View of Lord Bolingbroke's Philosophy. Letters First and Second* to be published later on in the year.

Warburton *to* [Knapton] 23 June 1754
BL: Egerton 1954, f.90 Prior Park

Dear Sir

If you think it better to print my *View of Bolingbroke['s] Philosophy* in 8°. I submit to your better judgm[en]t & agree to it, only on this condition that you make a *very beautifull book* of it.

I am Dear Sir ever
most affectionately yours
W. Warburton
P.P. June 23 1754

Frank and postmark (f.91; attached): Free R: Allen London 25/JU

Warburton *to* Knapton 2 July 1754
BL: Egerton 1954, f.92 Prior Park

Dear Sir

I hope you recd my last abt the 4° or 8°, in which I left the matter entirely to your discretion. I have inclosed the conclusion of the first letter & the begining of the second. For I propose to have this view in *four Letters*. I would not have the end of one and the begining of another both on the same *leaf*; neither would I have an entire blank *page*. I suppose the printer can contrive to prevent either inconvenience.

Dear Sir ever
most affectionately yours
W. Warburton

P.P.   July 2 1754

Endorsed (in Knapton's hand): from p. 41. to 56 sent to Bowyer
Address, frank and postmark (*verso*): To Mr: J: Knapton   Bookseller in Ludgate Street London   Free R: Allen   4/[JU]

Warburton *to* Knapton   28 July 1754
BL: Egerton 1954, f.93   Prior Park

Dear Sir
    I am favoured with yours of the 24   You may be assured that Mr Allen's & my regard for you will never make us forgetfull of your interest. It vext us both that we were entirely unknowing in this thing till it was too late to make our good intentions of service. As to my selfe I beg you would never be backward & reserved in whatever you think my friends[hi]p for you may be of use to you.[1]
    I think you said you recd for my use 60*l.* from Mr J. Wright.[2] Pray at your leasure remit it to me in a b.b.[3] cut in two.

Dear Sir ever most
affectionately yours,
P.P.   July 28 1754   W. Warburton

Address and frank (f.94): To Mr. J. Knapton Bookseller in Ludgate Street 30/JU

[1] Without knowing the contents of Knapton's letter, it is impossible to divine from Warburton's words what 'this thing' is. It may be an intimation of Knapton's increasing financial problems.
[2] Possibly from the estate of John Wright whose burial on 9 July 1754 was noted by J. McLaverty in *Pope's Printer, John Wright* (p.8). In his later years, Wright printed the Pope-Swift *Miscellanies* (vol. 1, 1744; vols. 2-3, 1747).
[3] Presumably a bank bill.

Warburton *to* [Knapton]   20 August 1754
BL: Egerton 1954, f.97   Prior Park

Dear Sir
    You will receive two dr[aft]s. inclosed, on Mr Shelvock,[1] for 120*l*. Be
so good to receive them when due: and let one of your people pay the
inclosed bill to James the Linnen draper. and keep back ten pounds to be
sent to Mrs Hayes next Michaelmas, and let me have the remainder
returned to me hither, in bank notes as usual.

                                        I am Dear Sir ever
                                  most affectionately yours
                                           W. Warburton
                                  P.P.   Augt 20 1754

[1] George Shelvocke, the Secretary to the Postmaster-General, whom Ralph Allen
'used as a kind of banker' (Boyce, p.170).

Warburton *to* Knapton   25 August 1754
BL: Egerton 1954, ff.95–6   Prior Park

Dear Sir
    I received your favour of yesterday. One of the Letters of the *view* is
now printed, it takes up almost four sheets.[1] I beg you would send for
them, and when you have cut away the leaf which begins the second
Letter, tack the first Letter together, and send it with the inclosed in a
sealed packet to the Arch Bishop. which will oblige,

                                  Dear Sir, Your most faithfull
                                        & affect. Servt
                                           W Warburton
                                  P.P.   Augt 25 1754

Address, frank and postmark (f.96): To Mr: Knapton   Bookseller in
Ludgate Street London   Free R: Allen   27/AV   BATH

[1] The first two letters, comprising 175 pages in octavo, of Warburton's *A View of Lord
Bolingbroke's Philosophy* were published by John and Paul Knapton in 1754. The
remaining two letters were published separately in 1755. See Warburton's letter of 18
January 1755, below.

Warburton *to* [Knapton]   1 September 1754
BL: Egerton 1954, f.98   Prior Park

Dear Sir

I have considered and found that the two first Letters of the 4 of the
view of Bol. Philosophy will make abt 12 sheets, on this account, and on
another which I will tell you presently, I would have the 2 first Letters
published seperately from the other two as soon as ever they are printed,
and therefore I desire you would oblige Bowyer to print two sheets a
week (as now he prints but one) otherwise the second Letter will not be
printed off by Michaelmas which I would by all means have done.

My principal reason is this, the Observations in the two first Letters
are most obvious and therefore I would not have any body be before
hand with me. For then they would lose the grace & advantage of
novelty. On which account I would have the 2 first Letters published
together as soon as ever they can be printed off. At the same time I
propose to go on at the press with the 3 & 4th Letter which will be abt 2
months more er'e they be printed off.

Dr Sr ever most affectionately Yours
W. Warburton

P.P.   Sepr 1. 1754
(How goes the Index on).

Endorsed (in Knapton's hand): (Copy. p. 113. to 132   5 Sheets sent to
Bowyer Sept 3d)

Warburton *to* Knapton   7 September 1754
BL: Egerton 1954, f.99   Prior Park

Dear Sir

I have recd the other three halves of the 20*l*. notes as likewise 2 halves
of a 20*l*. & a 30*l*. note.

I beg you would give the inclosed to the Printer and when it is worked
off to send it to me.

Dear Sir ever most
affectionately yours,

P.P.   Sepr 7. 1754   W. Warburton

Your friend Mr Waple & the Attorney Gen[era]l[1] dined with me here yesterday, where I am at present alone. He told me he had the pleasure with Mr C. Yorke of dining with you not long since at Marsh Gate.

I have sent Bowyer all the remaining copy of the 2d Letter.

Address and frank (*verso*): To Mr Knapton Bookseller in Ludgate Street London   Free R: Allen

¹ William Murray; and John Waple (*d.* 1763), Treasurer of Gray's Inn and Accountant-General in Chancery; *GM*, 33 (March 1763): 146.

Warburton *to* [Knapton]   14 September 1754
BL: Egerton 1954, f.100   Prior Park

Dear Sir

I have recd the remainder of the half bank notes.

The inclosed is the title of the *View*, together with the first leaf to be reprinted with it.

I think you may advertise it whenever you please.

I desire you would take of the Printer, the three sheets F. G. H. which together with the last leaf of sheet E. which begins the second Letter   I desire you would tack together for the Arch Bp.

And then take of the Printer all the sheets that are printed off of the second Vol. of Sermons. in these you will find one Sermon on the *last Supper* and another on the *Marriage union*. I desire you would take these out, and stitch them seperately, and then be so good to send these two, and the three sheets of the view, in one packet to the Arch Bishop.

The remaining sheets of the 2d Vol of sermons be so good to send to me in Leak's Parcel.

Dear Sir ever most affectionately
yours   W. Warburton

Date (f.101*v*.): P.P. Sepr 14 1754
Endorsed (f.101*v*.; in Knapton's hand): Sent leaf of E. & Sheets of F G H and the 2 Sermons to the Arch Bishop   Sept 19

[William Murray?] *to* [Warburton]¹   [late 1754?]
BL: Egerton 1959, ff.31–4   [London?]

There is not a Person in the World who Loves you more, than He from whom this Intimation comes; He gives it, because He Truly & Warmly wishes well, to your Person, your Advancement, & your Fame. He is grieved to the Heart to find the Reception your two Letters meet with from the World. you not only have never shewn them to any Friend, but in all Probability have never read them twice over yourself: & yet the Subject made the work very Interesting, & Matter of great Importance to you; Especially at your Entrance upon a new & higher Scene of Life.[2]

It Vexes me to hear so many Positively deciding that the Author must be —— by the Scurrility & Abuse: The Letters are universally read, & it is almost universally agreed, that Ld Bolingbroke deserved any Treatment from you, both as a Man personally ill used by him, & as a Clergyman, a Member of that order which he had Treated in the like manner. But it may dishonour a Gentleman & a Clergyman to give him that treatment he deserved, especially after his Death; it is falling into the very Fault so Justly objected to him. Every body would have applauded your selecting those Instances of his Railing Arrogance, & Abuse; had not you followed his example. You reprove him, Just as if a Man with Oaths should reprove an-other for Swearing.

The letters *purport* to be a View of his *Philosophy*, they *are* a View of his Life, Morals, Politics & Conversation. It may be True, & Just, but that is not the Question. Whether he made a good treaty, or wrote the Craftsman, neither concludes for or against the Divinity of the Christian Religion.[3]

You had so fair an Opportunity of acting with becoming Dignity, by saying, that as he treated you with Personal Scurrility, as well as all the great assertors, Ancient, & Modern, of Christianity, the Public Indignation with which that part was recieved, was the properest Reply; but besides, he was Dead: therefore you would say nothing of the Author &c:, but your warmth & Resentment has run away from your Judgement.

Lord Bolingbroke is so Universally & so Justly Obnoxious to all sorts, & Ranks of People, that from regard to him no body cares how he is treated: but be assured that your Manner has destroyed the Merit of the Work.

Besides you have let many Strange Similes, Allusions, & expressions, fall from your Pen, & most astonishingly conclude the whole in a Piss Pot.

Lord Bolingbroke deserved every thing of you, but who are these Friends & Admirers of his whom you represent as Applauding all he wrote, whom you bring in Unnecessarily upon many occasions? I dare to say they are very few, you had better have Named them.

Bond is one but Harpax is a Score.[4] Take my word for it, His illustrious Friend Sr George Lyttelton never will forgive the mention you make of him, tho' flattering, & honourable, as long as he lives.[5]

But what grieves & hurts your Freinds the most is still behind; Poor

Pope did not diserve to be treated by you, with so much Cruelty, Contemp[t], & Injustice; & in my Conscience I believe you do not mean it, & have wrote with so much haste, as not to have weighed the force of your own words, & manner.

In a work where Lord Bolingbroke is represented as a Monster, hated both of God, & Man; why is Pope always & Unnecessarily brought in, only as his Friend & admirer? why as approving of, & Privy to, all that was addressed to him? why should he, who had many great Talents, & Amiable Qualities, be described only by the Slighting Epithets of *Tunefull* & *Poetical*?

What say you of him in the Second letter Fol 63 & 75 is so ridiculous that it is impossible to be true;[6] if ever he said any such thing at all, it must have been in a Joke, & yet you averr it to have been in good Earnest.

But whether true, or false, why mention it to expose his Memory? But you even throw reflexion upon yourself; your Excellent Commentary upon The Essay on Man Maintained, & ably shewed the System to be Orthodox. here you say that Pope announced the glad Tidings of all these things to the World; in what work can he be said to have done it except in his Essay on Man? Besides the very Expression of *announcing the glad Tidings* marks him out, as not only the Forerunner, & Di[s]ciple, but the Applauder, & Teacher, of this abominable Philosophy, & yet you have Pledged your Veracity to the World for the Contrary; that he neither approved nor Taught it. Had you pursued the advantage which you have ingeniously taken, from an expression in one of Pope's letters, to have shewn that Pope differed from Lord Bolingbroke where he was in the wrong, that he not only Condemned, but despised the Futility of his Reasoning against Revelation, that where he was right, Pope improved but never Servilely followed, or copied his Ideas, you would have done honour to your Friend, & yourself. you would have served the Cause of Religion, you would have discredited Lord Bolingbroke more by the Contrast.

I have Scored some few of the exceptionable passages & expressions in th' inclosed letters for your reconsideration. Ask some honourable Friend, ask Mr Yorke, ask the Attorney General. ask Sr John Legonier,[7] I dont say his Opinion but what he hears in every Company, where the letters happen to be Mentioned. Ask any of the Bishops, or any of your learned Friends of either University, they must tell you, how much a work well meant, & with Merit in the Argumentative Part, has suffered, by being Liable to Objections of the Sort above mentioned.

Indeed it has furnished your Enemies with a Handle to do you infinite Mischief. your *Cold* Friends lament, & make the worst sort of excuse, by imputing it to a Temper contracted from the long Habit of drawing

Blood in Controversy. Your *warm* Friends are out of Countenance & forced to be Silent, or Turn the discourse. This intimation is given you with a View, that so far as your own Judgment, or information from others, shews it to be Just, you may retrieve the Mischief, as far as is possible, before you put your Name to the work, or suffer it to pass thro' a new Edition. You never will know from whom it comes, & if you are convinced it comes from one of your Sincere Friends, it Matters not from which of them.

[n.s.][8]

[1] This unsigned letter appears to be a transcript. As the closing states, this is intended to be taken as constructive, yet anonymous, criticism. It did not prevent Warburton from publishing the last two letters of *A View of Lord Bolingbroke's Philosophy* early in 1755. Lord Mansfield is identified in an anonymous addendum; he is mentioned indirectly in the letter as the Attorney-General.

[2] Warburton was made Chaplain to King George II in 1754; and in March of the following year, with the help of Murray, was made a prebendary at Durham worth £500 (*DNB*).

[3] Warburton was seeking to diminish Bolingbroke's record of achievements in the Treaty of Utrecht (1713) and contributions to the *Craftsman* (*c.* 1730–4) as well as his professed deism.

[4] *Satire II. i*, line 44, (*TE*, 4: 9).

[5] As one who had been close to both Bolingbroke and Pope, Lyttelton now preferred to have his name kept out of Mallet's and Warburton's works; see his letters of 2 September 1745, above, and 20 January 1768, below.

[6] In *A View of Lord Bolingbroke's Philosophy*.

[7] Jean Louis Ligonier (1680–1770), M.P. for Bath from 1748 and friend of Ralph Allen (see Boyce).

[8] f.34*v*. (in a different hand) reads: '*Anonymous Letter* on the Bishop's Treatment of Ld Bolingbroke & *Pope* in his View of Bolingbroke. N.B. From Lord Mansfield. 1756.' 1756 is unlikely as Warburton's *A View of Lord Bolingbroke's Philosophy*, *Letters First and Second* appeared in 1754; the third and fourth *Letters* (not mentioned here) were published early in 1755.

[Warburton] *to* [Knapton]   [November 1754]
BL: Egerton 1959, f.25 (transcript)   [Prior Park]

I have spoken to the A[ttorney General].[1] He has Sent for one Ross[2] a Sol[icito]r to come to him. To him he will give his Orders to write to Scotland to retain Solrs. & Council —— and to begin the pros[ecution]: immediately in the court of Sessions —— But for nothing but what is within the Act of Q. Anne —— That the Ld Advocate should be retained —— and him he will speak with when he comes to Town. —— All this I foresaw. But as it was thought necessary to have the A G's advise: there was a necessity of submitting to it in all things —— As for my part as far as threatening & commencing a prosecution goes I am for it. But no farther. Neither my property nor my inclination will make it worth my while to be engaged in a tedious Law suit To all which I have an utter aversion —— It is a different case with men who have great property. —— If the principal Booksellers will consider it as a common cause & join in it with their contributions well & good.

[n.s.]

¹ William Murray, the Attorney-General. This transcript is undated and unsigned, although it predates 28 November 1754, below.
² Murray retained George Ross, a solicitor in Conduit Street, who then retained Ronald Crawfurd in Edinburgh; see 28 November 1754, below.

Robert Foulis *to* [Warburton]   27 November 1754
BL: Egerton 1959, f.17   Glasgow

Reverend Sir,
    What I have to say in answer to yours, I have done myself the honour to address to the Attorney-General.¹

                                                   I am
                                                   Sir
                          Your most Obdt: Humble Servt:
                                           Robert Foulis

Glasgow   ⎫
27th Novr 1754   ⎭

¹ Warburton's letter to Foulis is untraced. Scottish reprints of Pope's works had recently proliferated. No Glasgow editions of Pope's works appeared until 1750 when the Foulis press published the first edition of *An Essay on Man* and Robert Urie printed *Four Ethic Epistles* for Daniel Baxter. Foulis advertised the 1751 edition of *An Essay on Man*, priced at sixpence, in the *Scots Magazine*, 22 (February 1751): 112. William Duncan junior of Glasgow came out with *Moral Essays* and James Reid of Leith published *Rape of the Lock, An Essay on Man* and *Moral Essays* in 1751. Foulis continued with *Poems on Several Occasions* in 1752. In 1753, Hamilton and Balfour of Edinburgh published *A Supplement to Dr. Swift's Works* with Pope's additions. In 1754, the Foulis press reprinted *An Essay on Man*; Robert Urie published *An Essay on Criticism, An Essay on Man* and *Moral Essays*; and Yair, Fleming and Hunter appeared in the imprint of Pope's *Essays, Epistles, and Odes* at Edinburgh. Aberdeen entered the lists in 1754 with Pope's *Epistles to which is subjoined, The Messiah. . . .* printed and sold by F. Douglas and W. Murray.

Ronald Crawfurd *to* George Ross   28 November 1754
BL: Egerton 1959, ff.23–4 (transcript)   Edinburgh

(Copy)   Edinburgh 28 Novr *1754*

Dr Sir

I wrote you last post that I was in hopes to get an appointment made with Lord Advocate & Mr Lockhart,[1] to have known how we are to proceed in Dr Warburton's Affairs; but I will not be able to obtain the Meeting for a day or two. I wrote you that it was proper the Probate of Mr Pope's Will should be sent down, with a Certificate that the Books were entered in Stationers' Hall, the Universities &c. Agreeable to the Act of the 8th of the Queen, for Encouragement of Learning;[2] but on considering a little more on this affair, I find myself without Sufficient Materials, for carrying on this Prosecution.

Mr Pope by his Will only gives the Doctor, such Books as he hath written, or shall write Commentaries upon, which he has not otherwise disposed of or alienated.[3] This seems to imply as if Mr Pope had alienated the property of some of his Works. It will be necessary therefore, that a particular List or Schedule of such part of the Works as Dr Warburton apprehends to be his property, and to fall under the Will, be sent me, with the Probate and Certificate, so as the Action or Complaint be properly laid —— It becomes the more necessary that care be taken, the Lybell be properly laid, for in looking to the foresaid Act of the 8th of the Queen, I observe that the Author of all Books composed after the 1710, has ye sole privilege of printing &c for 14 years after publication of the Book; And after the Expiry of 14 years, if the Author shall be then alive, the Sole Right & Privilege of printing shall return to him for another Term of 14 years.—— Now if any of Mr Pope's Works were published preceding the 1710 (which I beleive was the case as to some of his early Writings, his puerilities as he terms them) or if in any of his later Works, the first Term of 14 years from the Publication was not expired at the time of his death, then I apprehend the exclusive Privilege determined on the Lapse of the first Term, and even as to the 2d Term of 14 years, tho' the Act gives the Author if Living, the priviledge for a 2d term of 14 years; yet I have a doubt If on his Death, such Privilege is assignable for what part of the 2d term may be then to run. It seems to be only personal, to the Author himself, but not to his Executors or Assigns; and it would be proper that Dr Warburton make out a distinct memorial of this matter, with a condescendance of ye particular Books, he apprehends to be his property, the dates of their publication to shew whether the Terms were expired, or not, at Mr Pope's death, or if they are expired since. And also that he will distinguish what part of Mr Pope's Works were alienated before his death. I beleive the Entry in Stationers' Hall is not material Except we were sueing for the Penalties, which I apprehend is not the Case, but for Damages, and to stop the printing.[4]

We are very much Strangers here to the particulars of the Laws in relation to the property of Books. It came to be lookt into a little in the Action you mention, that Andrew Millar and the Booksellers of London brought against the Booksellers of Edinburgh,[5] But as it must be well understood in England, where it is so much a matter of property, and where many Actions must have been brought, I think it would be right that Dr Warburton laid his Case before the Attorney General, for opinion, and that he transmit such opinion for our Government and direction, together with such Title (if he has established it) as entitles him to the Property of the Works, Certificate of Entry in Stationers' Hall, with a particular condescendance of the Books pirated, of which he claims the property, the date of publication &c, In Short Such Evidence as would found & support him, were the Action to be brought and tried in Westminster Hall, for 'till I have such Materials, it is not practicable to make a proper Lybell, far less can it forw[ar]d us in applying for a Prohibition or Injunction to stop the others from Printing. And indeed I wish I had delayed making an appointment with our Lawyers, till I heard further from you or from ye Doctor, as it is putting us to an unnecessary Expence at present, 'till I can lay more of the matter before them.

You will communicate to Dr Warburton what I now write, and assure him of my best Offices and Endeavours to serve him, to which his Merit and Labours for the Publick entitle him, Besides its' being accompanied with a Recommendation from Mr Attorney General, which will always have the greatest weight with me

I am Dr Sr
Your most obliged
& obedt Servt
(Signed)   Ronald Crawfurd

Address: To George Ross Esq on Conduit Street
Endorsed: Mr Crawfurd's letter Nov. 28.

[1] Robert Dundas of Arniston was the Lord Advocate in Scotland from 16 August 1754; Lockhart was possibly Alexander Lockhart, Lord Covington.

[2] The 1710 Copyright Act.

[3] Warburton included Pope's will, with the clauses Crawfurd is citing, at the end of volume 9 of the 1751 *Works* and in subsequent editions.

[4] i.e. by Robert Foulis.

[5] Millar launched the first test-case over copyright in Scotland in December 1738 when he had twenty-nine Scottish booksellers summonsed. He claimed he had a

common law right to Thomson's *Seasons* and wanted £100 from each of the booksellers. He dropped his suit in 1739, but renewed his charges in 1743 backed by sixteen other London booksellers (including the Knaptons, Thomas Longman and John Rivington). This long-drawn-out legal battle ended unsuccessfully in the Edinburgh Court of Session in 1749.

In his unpublished Edinburgh University Ph.D. thesis (1974), 'Gavin Hamilton, John Balfour and Patrick Neill: a study of publishing in Edinburgh in the 18th century', Warren McDougall wrote, 'William Warburton, claiming the copyright of the *Works* of Alexander Pope, objected when Robert Foulis was printing Pope's *Letters* in 1754, but on Foulis's writing to Attorney-General William Murray, Warburton was advised to come to a financial settlement' (pp.101–02). See his chapter IV (pp.85–102), for more on Millar's suits.

Warburton *to* [Knapton]   6 December 1754
BL: Egerton 1954, f.102   Prior Park

                                         P. P. Decr 6 1754
Dear Sir

I beg you will be so good to receive the inclosed bill for 90*l*: and that you will pay 60*l* of it to Mr Garth my Landlord, (who was not in town when I was there) for half a year's rent due at Michmas last. 10*l*. I desire you would send this Christmas to Mrs Hayse at Yorke, and desire you would send the remaining 20*l* to me in a bank note.

I inclose two Letters from the two Scotch Booksellers to me.[1] with my answer to one of them, by which you will see my sentiments of both. when you have read my Letter and taken a copy of it, I beg you would seal & send it by the Post.

I desire our friend Mr Mason may have a copy of the Div. Legation in boards, and the *Bp* of Chester[2] the same.

                                 I am Dear Sir your
                            most affectionate & faithfull
                                 friend   W. Warburton

You will not forget the parcel into Germany.[3]

Verso: Since the writing what is within I have not only recd yours with the two Letters from Ross & Crawfurd, but like wise two from the Attorney-General. Fowlis' letter to him & a Copy of his Answer, —— altogether, with the rigour & alertness of the prosecution if they persist will I hope soon end this affair —— All must be left to your discretion in which I repose my selfe and authorize all you think proper —— One thing only I would recommend as they are willing to desist one would make the terms of submission as easy to them as we can. —— I am sure you will rejoice in the attorney's Letter as it is relative to all property and as he seems to make it a point to establish it for the good of Letters.

¹ One letter is probably the brief note of 27 November 1754, above; the other is unknown. Robert and Andrew Foulis perhaps wrote to Warburton earlier to ask for permission to print Pope's works. For their editions of Pope's *Poetical Works* (1768, 1773, 1785) and other titles, see Philip Gaskell, *A Bibliography of the Foulis Press*, 2nd ed. (Winchester, 1986).

² Edmund Keene (1714–81), Bishop of Chester.

³ Presumably to Mr Schmidt (see Warburton's letters of 6 and 22 July 1752 and 4 March 1754, above).

Robert Foulis *to* [William Murray]   20 December 1754
BL: Egerton 1959, f.20   Glasgow

Honourable Sir,

I had the honour and favour of yours and ask pardon for presuming to give you this further trouble, at a season of the year, when you cannot have much time to spare for matters of so small a consequence.

I am not altogether unacquainted with the history of Monopolies granted by Princes to authors, Editors, Printers and Booksellers: I have had likewise occasion to examine the new doctrine by which authors are supposed to be vested with a property, not only antecedent to all acts of parliaments, but even such an one as claims indefeasibility, and refuses to be limited by the highest national authority.

I will not offer to trouble you with this subject at present, but shall be extremely glad at a Season when you are more at leisure to do it fully and freely, not with a view to hurt but to serve Learning. I shall only beg leave to take notice, that no Bookseller ever purchases the work of an author, without hopes of being indemnifyed by the first edition.

Milton, or any English author, could not only have been printed in Scotland until the Union of the Kingdoms, but even to the last Act of Queen Anne: And at present they have a right to print what ever they are not forbid by that Act. As in Ireland they can print all without exception, I dont find that the best men among them make any scruple to encourage it; and I know the most Learned and worthy men in this country, think we do public service in reprinting, whatever we can according to Law, that is any way calculated to do good.

Tho' I have taken this Liberty, that you may see I act from principle, yet I must own it gives me a great deal of pain, that any action of mine should have given you so much trouble; nothing could have been more contrary to my intentions, wherever the blame may lye; all that I can now do to repair it, is with your permission to lay aside the design. Private profit is what I have too much undervalued in my other undertakings, to regard it in the present circumstances.

As I did not doubt the truth of the message, I readily presumed you had obtained Dr Warburton's consent, and was afraid that I should rather have given offence, by being too remiss than too forward. No part of Mr Pope's works are as yet printed but his Miscellanies, except half the first Volume of his Letters, which I know by experience I can sell to young Students & others who cannot afford to buy the works.

As I am entirely to be directed by you, if you order I will go on with the edition, which consists of a thousand copies, and oblige myself to give Dr Warburton what proportion of the impression you approve, for his consent, but however you determine, I beg it may be without any regard to my interest. What I put a value upon, and a high one, is your kind intention. I ask pardon for the freedom and length of this, and beg leave to subscribe myself with the most respectful submission and gratitude,

> Honourable Sir,
> Your most Obliged
> & most Obedient Servt:
> Robert Foulis

Glasgow }
20. Decr 1754 }

P.S. I have been long known to Lord Selkirk, and Lord Cathcart,[1] both as to my way of thinking and acting, to whom I refer if you choose to take the trouble of enquiring. RF

[1] Dunbar Hamilton Douglas, 4th Earl of Selkirk, and Charles Schaw of Sauchie, Lord Cathcart.

William Murray *to* [Warburton]   28 December 1754
BL: Egerton 1959, f.18   Kenwood

Kenwood 28th Decr 1754

Dear Sir

I have just received the inclosed[1] to which I have returned a very civil Answer & applauded his Behaviour but thrown out some Objections to his general Reasoning. I have sd I wou'd immediately send his Letter to you & desire you to write to him.

I shou'd be very sorry to have the Question agitated first in Scotland; besides the great Expence it may involve you in & therefore I think you shou'd consider his Behaviour as handsome & close with him upon generous Terms for the Edition of 1000, taking an Engagement that He will print no more. & the Title Page must show it to be an Edition authorized by you. My best compliments to Mr Allen & many thanks for the Guinea Hens He was so good as to send me. I am Dr Sr.

Ever & most affly Yrs &c
W: Murray

[1] i.e. Foulis' letter of 20 December 1754, above, concerning the printing and publishing of Pope's works in Scotland. In the light of Andrew Millar's long and costly experience at the Edinburgh Court of Session, from 1738-9 and later from 1743-9, Murray was advising Warburton against taking any legal action.

Warburton *to* [Knapton]   30 December 1754
BL: Egerton 1954, f.104 (fragment)   Prior Park

I need not explain the nature of the two inclosed.[1] If the Attorney insists on those terms from Foulis we must I think comply. You, perhaps, have properer to urge. I have writ to the Attorney to this effect that he knows you have part of the property with me. That you manage the affairs. That you are as ready to take his: ⟨the Attorney's⟩ directions, as I am. And that you will wait on him.

Dear Sir
ever most affectionately
Yours
W. Warburton

P.P. Decr 30 1754

It runs in my head it will be better to let Fowlis print a *part* of Pope's works upon terms than the *whole* and since this seems to satisfy him, if the Attorney will be satisfied too it would be best. But he must be satisfied

[1] The two letters Warburton enclosed were presumably Foulis' letter to Murray (20 December 1754) and Murray's letter to Warburton (December 28).

1755

Warburton was appointed to the prebend at Durham in March with help from Murray, then Attorney-General. Warburton completed *A View of Lord Bolingbroke's Philosophy* with his third and fourth Letters.

The last of the Knapton small octavo editions of *An Essay on Man* with Pope's frontispiece and Warburton's notes was published.

The Knapton debt to William Bowyer rose sharply in the first half of the year. Paul Knapton's death on June 12 seems to have precipitated a financial crisis. Total collapse of the Knapton bookselling business seemed imminent. On June 14, twenty-five members of the book trade paid various sums amounting to £475 4s. into the Knapton account at Gosling's bank. A trusteeship was formed to administer Knapton's financial affairs. Bowyer declined to act as a trustee.

A large part of Knapton's stock and copyrights was auctioned off on September 25. Warburton told Hurd that his good will towards Knapton saved the bookseller from ending up in the list of bankruptcies. On October 18, twenty-six members of the book trade paid £1386 13s. 4d. into the Knapton trustee account at Gosling's bank. Andrew Millar bought out the Knapton share in Pope's *Works* much to Robert Dodsley's chagrin. Henry Lintot considered reviving his claim to the *Dunciad*; Warburton countered with a threat to publish an edition of Pope's Homer with his notes.

Warburton delivered a sermon on the Lisbon earthquake.

Warburton *to* Knapton   12 January 1755
BL: Egerton 1954, ff.105–06   Prior Park

Dear Sir

I recd your last two Letters. I am glad to understand that your cold is almost gone.

The affair with Fowlis goes on very well, & you have writ him a very proper Letter.

To tell you truth I neither like Law litigations, nor soliciting my friends to secure my property of this kind, besides I could do this with a better grace as well as more readiness for another than for my selfe. All this considered I have thoughts when we have settled all matters abt Pope to dispose of my property in it, of which you may be sure you shall have the refusal: nor shall I ever be the less warm to assist you at all times to the best of my power to the better security of your property. But I shall be determined, in this intention, by your advise.

I propose being in town the week after next. I wish you would send me the 3d part of *Alexander the corrector* just published.[1]

I am Dear Sir Most affectionately
Yours   W. Warburton

P.P. Jan. 12 1755

Verso (f.106): The 3d pt of Alexander the Corrector need not be sent. *Endorsed* (not in Knapton's hand): Dr. Warburton's Letter of Jan 12 abt Pope & JK's answer 15th.

[1] Alexander Cruden, *The Adventures of Alexander the Corrector* (part 1, London: printed for the author: and sold by Richard Baldwin, 1754; part 3, printed for the author and sold by M. Cooper, 1755).

Warburton *to* [Knapton]   18 January 1755
BL: Egerton 1954, f.107   Prior Park

Dear Sir

I would have this 3d Letter of the View out as soon as it can.[1] I have sent Bowyer all the copy, and have all the copy written for the preface which will make between 2 & 3 sheets which with abt 7 of the Letter will make such a pamphlet as the other.

I have your answer to my Last and I shall always do every thing that may be most conducive to the security of your very considerable property.[2]

                                         I am Dear Sir ever
                                        most Affectionately yours
                                             W. Warburton
P.P. Jan 18. 1755

Frank and postmark (f.108): Free Allen   London   20/IA

[1] The third letter of *A View of Lord Bolingbroke's Philosophy*. The fourth letter appeared later in 1755.
[2] The letter Warburton mentions here and Knapton's reply are untraced. Warburton's assurance in this postscript is perhaps a response to worries expressed by Knapton over copyright, Millar's overtures concerning Pope's works or cash-flow problems, in which case this may have been a foreshadowing of the crisis in the summer.

[Anon] *to* [Anon]   [early 1755?]
BL: Egerton 1959, f.22 (transcript)   Edinburgh

Transcript from a Letter from Edinburgh to a Gentleman in London

Mr Dalton of Glasgow came to Town last night, and tells me that He and Fowlis are printing Pope's Works compleat, and that they have got a Letter from a Patron of Mr Warburton's,[1] encouraging them to it, and an Edition is likewise printing in Edinburgh, and that both are advanced some volumes.[2]

Edinburgh at Murray & Cochrane and in Fleming's printing house, upon the Risk of Donaldson and young Fleming——— [3]

[n.s.]

[1] William Murray.

[2] Possibly delayed until 1764 when two editions of Pope's *Works* were published, one in duodecimo, 6 vols. Edinburgh: printed for J. Balfour, 1764; another also in duodecimo, 4 vols. Edinburgh: printed in the year 1764 (no printer or bookseller given).

[3] Dalton is untraced; Murray and Cochrane as well as Alexander Donaldson and Robert Fleming are cited in Philip Gaskell, *Foulis Press*. See also Warren McDougall, 'Gavin Hamilton, Bookseller in Edinburgh'.

Warburton *to* [John Nourse]   11 August 1755
Yale University, Beinecke Library: Osborn Files f c 76/2   Prior Park

Dear Sir

I recd yours ——— and the Chef d'Oeuvre; which might as well have been sent by Leak's parcel. The Memoirs of Mad[emoise]lle daughter of Gaston Duke of Orleans Brother to Lewis XIII: I saw & turned over in your shop, it is in 6 or 7 small vols.[1] I had read it long before & therefore cannot be mistaken ——— order them to look amongst the small books & it will be found. With this I would have sent me Gedonius's fr[ench]. trans. of Quintilian. it is in 2 or 3 vols 12° or 8° 2d Edn.[2]

I shall be very desirous of those pieces of Tacitus translated by Blaterie which you have sent for.[3] if in the mean time you can get the book of Valliant I shall be much obliged to you[4]

A letter to me under Mr Allen's Cover always comes safe & free.

I am Sir ever most faithfully
Yours   W. Warburton

Prior Park
Augt 11 1755

[1] Anne Marie Louise Henriette d'Orléans (1627–93), Duchesse de Montpensier, *Mémoires*, 7 vols. (London [Paris], 1746); in duodecimo.

[2] *Quintilien de l'institution de l'orateur*, trans. M. l'Abbé Gedoyn, 4 vols. (Paris, 1752); in duodecimo. A quarto edition was published at Paris in 1718.

[3] *Traduction de quelques ouvrages de Tacite*, trans. M. l'Abbé de la Bléterie, 2 vols. (Paris, 1755); this is a Latin-French edition in duodecimo.

[4] Warburton's order from Paul Vaillant is untraced.

William Bowyer *to* Knapton   20 September 1755
Nichols, *Literary Anecdotes*, 2: 278–9   [London]

Sept. 20, 1755.

I was last night informed that it was reported I had advised taking out a statute against you. As no one, I am persuaded, hath a deeper sense of obligations to you, or feels more for your present troubles, I was shocked at this charge of ingratitude and inhumanity. I knew, with the rest of the world, that your good-nature only had brought you into your present difficulties, and that your affliction under them arose more from the inconveniencies you brought on others than on yourself. It must add not a little to your disquiet, to think you have a monster among your creditors:[1] but I owe it both to you and them to testify that you can have but *one*; for I never heard any of them propose taking a step which might ill suit your inclinations; or, what was more tender, your credit. If a statute was ever mentioned, it was feared only from the intricacy of your affairs, not suggested from the malevolence of any heart. I say this, to clear others, not myself; for it is too much for me to think that such an imputation should live, and be carried to your ear. My heart, Sir, will ever wish you happiness; but for fear it should fall under any misconstruction of it after so bad a representation of it, I must beg you will give me leave to renounce the office of being one of your trustees,[2] in which it will be impossible for me after this to act with freedom, though I intend ever so uprightly. I know not whether another trustee must be chosen in my place; but, if there must, whatever additional expence that may occasion, I will thankfully defray. I would further beg, that no enquiry may be made who propagated the story of me; for as I suspect no one person, so I would continue to harbour no ill thoughts of any particular; and I will rest satisfied in the persuasion you will ever retain your good ones, of, Sir,

Your sincere friend and most humble servant, W. B.

I would have waited on you with the inclosed renunciation, but that I am hastening into the country.

[1] The Knaptons held an account with the Bowyers from 1725 to 1764. It shows a steady accumulation of unpaid bills in the 1750s. By 9 June 1755, the Knaptons owed £1470 6s. Paul Knapton's death three days later seems to have precipitated near bankruptcy. Bowyer was paid in full within three years of the Knaptons' liquidity crisis. I am grateful to Keith Maslen for supplying me with this and other detailed information from the Bowyer ledgers. The Knaptons also lagged behind on their payments to Strahan for the printing of Johnson's *Dictionary* throughout the early 1750s. See J.A. Cochrane, *Dr. Johnson's Printer*, pp.26–7.

[2] Gosling's bank ledgers name the following trustees: T. and T. Longman, Charles Hitch, Andrew Millar, Robert Dodsley and John Knapton himself.

Warburton *to* Richard Hurd[1]   24 September 1755
Folger Shakespeare Library: Y.c.1451 (4)   Bedford Row, London

My dearest Friend

I received your most tender letter & sympathize with you most heartily.—— Let me have better news.

A very disagreeable affair has brought me to Town a month before my usual time. Mr Knapton, whom every body, & I particularly, thought the richest Bookseller in Town, has failed. His debts are 20,000*l.* and his stock is valued at 30,000*l.* but this value is subject to many abating contingencies: and you never at first hear the whole debt. It is hoped there will be enough to pay every one.[2] I don't know what to say to it. It is a business of years. He owes me a great Sum. I am his Principal Creditor. And as such I have had it in my power, at a meeting of his Creditors, to dispose them favourably to him and to get him treated with great humanity & compassion. I have brought them to agree unanimously to take a resignation of his Effects, to be managed by trustees, and in the mean time, till the effects can be disposed of to the best advantage, which will be some years in the doing, to allow him a very handsome subsistence. For I think him an honest man, tho' he has done extreme ill by me, and, as such, love him. He falls with the pity & compassion of every body. His fault was extreme indolence. I was never more satisfied in any action of my life than in my service of Mr Knapton on this occasion, and the preventing (which I hope I have done) his being torn in pieces. Yet you must not be surprised, I am sure I should not, if you hear (so great is this world's love of truth & of me) that *my* severity to him destroyed his credit, and would have pushed him to extremity. I will assure you you have heard many things of me full as true: which tho at present Apocryphal, may, by my never contradicting them, in time become holy-writ, as the Poet says.[3] God bless you and believe me to be, &c My Dearest Friend with humblest affection

Bedford row, Sepr. 24 1755   Yours   W. Warburton

Address (verso): To The Revd Mr R Hurd at Shifnal in Shropshire or Staffordshire[4]

---

[1] The opening salutation has been crossed out with a single line and above it has been added 'Letter LXXXIII', presumably by Hurd in preparation for *LLEP*, pp.143–4.

[2] Most of the Knapton stock and copyrights were sold on the following day, Thursday, 25 September 1755, at the Queen's Head Tavern in Paternoster Row. See Appendix B for the catalogue.

[3] Possibly an allusion to 'Trifles light as air/Are to the jealous confirmations strong/As proofs of holy writ' (*Othello*, 3.iii.326–8), *The Complete Oxford Shakespeare*, general ed. Stanley Wells and Gary Taylor (Oxford, 1987).

[4] Shifnal is in Shropshire.

Warburton *to* [Henry Lintot?][1]   31 October 1755
BL: Egerton 1959, f.27

                    Octr. 31 1755

I have only two things to say to Mr Lintot that if he thinks he has any claim to any part of the property of the Dunciad he must prosecute it by Law; his claim of the present profits must be made on Mr Knapton & his trustees and I shall give them a bond of indemnity.

If he attempts to print the Dunciad or any part of it at any time I shall immediate[ly] print the Homer to which I likewise have a dormant claim, with improvements ⟨both⟩ in the version & additions to the notes, both of which I have ready.[2]

                                                    W.W.

[1] This is either a note to himself or for Lintot, possibly sent via Knapton (cited in *Dodsley*, p.214 n.6).

[2] Henry Lintot, one of the booksellers of the 1751 *Works*, bought the full copyright of the *Dunciad* on 15 December 1740 against Pope's wishes. Pope lodged a complaint in Chancery on 16 February 1743 (PRO: C11/549/39). See *Correspondence*, 4: 240, 333 n.1, 394, 425 n.5, 455 and n.4.; 5: xxxiv-v. Warburton published an edition of the *Dunciad* (London: printed for J. and P. Knapton, 1749 [1750]); Foxon P800. Lintot's attempts to do the same were quashed by Warburton's threat to revive his claim to Pope's translations of the *Iliad* and *Odyssey* by publishing an annotated edition.

Warburton *to* Joseph Atwell   9 December 1755
BL: Egerton 1955, f.34   Prior Park

Dear Sir,

When I came back hither from London I understood you came to Bath soon after I had left the Country; being summoned to Town a month before my usual time on a very disagreable occasion, the failing of my Bookseller, who was indebted to me in a large sum of money. He is a very honest Man: and I had then the satisfaction of recommending him very effectually to the favour of his Creditors, when the prospect of his affairs presented a very ill face. Matters have since born a better aspect, and he is likely to have a considerable surplusage.

I understand the Referrees of your Church-differences have determined in your favour; & it could hardly be otherwise. But in favour of the old man, it seems, they have softened one part, & have made the illegal acts he did, while governing alone, valid.

What a sad calamity has befallen Lisbon![1] Time was, when the imaginary displeasures of Heaven, in a Comet or an Eclipse, have disarmed warring nations when their swords were already lifted up for mutual slaughter. But I don't hear that these marks of divine displeasure on a sinfull people are likely to abate our & our Neighbour's animosities against one another. It is indeed a dreadfull thing to suppose these disasters the vengeance of our offended Master; but it is ten times more terrible to believe we have our precarious being in a forlorn & fatherless World. In the first case we have it in our power to avert our destruction by the amendment of our manners: in the latter, we are exposed without hopes of refuge to the free rage of matter & motion in a ferment.[2]

Be so good to give me the satisfaction of knowing the state of your health, there being no one who is more sincerely or warmly,

Dear Sir, your most
affectionate & faithfull friend
& Servant
W. Warburton

Prior Park
Decr 9 1755

Verso (in another hand): Dr Atwell
Address, frank and date: To the Revd. Doctr: Attwell at Gloucester   Free
R: Allen
Decr. 9th. 1755.

[1] The Lisbon earthquake occurred on the morning of All Saints' Day, 1 November 1755, while thousands of pious Roman Catholics were attending mass. Within moments, a thousand homes and thirty churches were destroyed, and 15,000 people were killed. Another 15,000 died as a result of injuries or the tidal wave and great fire that followed. Warburton published a sermon entitled *Natural and Civil Events the Instruments of God's Moral Government. Preached at Lincoln's-Inn-Chapel, on the first public fast-day after the calamity of Lisbon, 1755*, in which he stated, 'The general calamities, arising from natural causes, to God's displeasure against sin, displays his glory in the fairest colours, and establishes man's peace and happiness on the most solid foundations' (*WWW*, 5: 285–98; p.292).

[2] This paragraph is cited in *SUP*, pp.257–8.

Warburton *to* [Knapton][1]   [December 1755?]
BL: Egerton 1954, ff.3–4   [London][2]

Dear Sir

I have altered my mind as to the books bought of Pope's Exec[uto]rs.[3] I think proper to have half with Mr Draper & Mr Millar.[4] You must deduct what you have received by the sale of part, from the sum you paid for them. and then put half the remainder on the Cred[ito]r side of my acc[oun]t. They I suppose will make no scruple to take, & pay for, the other half. This is my determination and I will be beholden to no body. I have endeavoured to consult other people's ease & profit & conveniency, & will for the future consult my own. You will remember only, that those which I sent from prior park are my own sole property.

Dear Sir your very
affectionate Friend,
W. Warburton

Monday evening

Verso (post-mark on f.4): PENY POST PAYD Stevenson

[1] This letter and its two companions below (Eg. 1954, f.5 and ff.6–7) are difficult to date. Warburton may be referring to the near-failing of the Knapton business in 1755, shortly after Paul Knapton's death. The Abstract of Accounts (Eg. 1959, f.30; see Appendix A), giving each bookseller's profits, was drawn up for the five editions of Pope's *Works* published between 1751 and 1754. For an estimate of the 1751 figures, see Appendix A, and D. W. Nichol '"So proper for that constant pocket use": Posthumous Editions of Pope's *Works* (1751–1754)', *Man and Nature*, vol. 6, ed. Kenneth Graham and Neal Johnson (Edmonton, 1987), pp.81–92; p.87. Most of the remaining Knapton stock and copyrights were put up for auction on 25 September 1755.

[2] In Eg. 1954, ff.6–7 below (which forms a part of this series of three letters), Warburton mentioned 'I have but a very few days to stay in Town'. While Warburton was at Prior Park on December 9 and 28, he may have had to make a short trip to London to wind up his business with Knapton and come to an agreement with his new principal bookseller, Andrew Millar, and Somerset Draper.

[3] It would appear that Warburton was attempting to settle unsold copies of Pope's works (bought from his executors, Bolingbroke and Marchmont), transferring part-ownership from Knapton to Millar and Draper. This old stock may have been difficult to sell in the light of more recent editions. '[Sherburn] has seen letters from Murray to Martha Blount, which show that about 1748 all the unsold copies of Pope's poems were sold by the executors to Warburton, and he thinks that the Knaptons' edition [of *Four Ethic Epistles* which was suppressed until 1748] may be connected with this transaction' (*TE*, 3.ii: xiii n.3).

[4] Warburton mentioned taking his business to Millar and Draper and selling 'what I did sell to them' in his letter to Dodsley of December 26, below.

Warburton *to* [Knapton]   [December 1755?]
BL: Egerton 1954, f.5   [London]

Dear Sir

say nothing of the contents to the bearer. I have sold what I proposed this Morning to Messrs Millar & Drayper.[1] But have bit my selfe. I agreed as I thought to sell them in proportion as they bought of you & they understood me, in proportion as I had sold to you. I was extreme vexed: but my honour was concerned so I have got 250*l* instead of 425*l*. All the satisfaction I have in this ugly affair is that you have got a better

price. For they say they would never have given what they have to you
but for the reason above, their understanding me in a sense I never
thought of.

                              Dr Sr always affectionately yours
                                          W. Warburton
Saturday morning

¹ Somerset Draper's name appeared in the imprints of Pope's *Works* from 1751 to
1756; he and Andrew Millar shared the same imprint in the 1756 edition. Millar's name
recurred on another six Warburton editions (1757*a*; 1757*b*; 1760; 1764*a*; 1764*b*; 1766).

Warburton *to* [Knapton]   [December 1755?]
BL: Egerton 1954, ff.6–7   [London]

Dear Sir
     I wrote to you on saturday morning¹ to let you know, how finely I was
bit by my own folly. I understood I was to have in proportion as they
bought of you, & they understood I was to have in proportion as I had
sold to you. I don't blame them, for, I dare say, we misunderstood one
another. I only blame my selfe, for not coming to a better explanation
with them before. However I submitted to take all the loss of the mistake
on my selfe; and for this reason; they might have said, I pretended this
other meaning, different from theirs, when I found how much you had
advanced upon them; and I had it not in my power to shew the contrary,
because it was a matter that passed only in my own mind. And I should
not care to be even suspected of so bad a thing for a much larger sum: so I
executed the Deed. Not that I had intended ever to draw them up to the
extent of your price, had it been left to me.—— But the thing is now
done & past, & I have only to look forward.
     I beg you would finish my account of Pope;² and draw out what I am
debter to you, in that account.
     As to the Books you bought of the Execrs. you & Mr. M[illar]. &
D[raper]. must adjust the disposal of them as you think fit. I think it but
reasonable that I at least should have nothing to do in them. They are
part of the management of the affair which you & they undertake.
     I beg I may now have this acct without delay, because I have but a
very few days to stay in Town.
     The other acct will be then distinct, which I hope I shall have settled
too, a few days after. In the mean time they propose to take into this
warehouse ⟨as to those copies of the 2d Vol. of D.L. which you bought
the half of, of Mahaud and which I ordered to be rendered imperfect,

they will give them room too; and you will set down on the D[ebto]r side
of my acct of Pope, what you paid to Mahaud for them.$\rangle^3$ all the Copies
of my Writings which you & I have a joint interest in. Because this is the
time of year for advertising.[4] I told them the terms they were to print for
me were to be the same that I gave you. They print them at their hazard,
& are to have Half the clear profits. which they think very good &
generous.

I suppose you will have little difficulty in adjusting with them the
price of the claim you have in those copies: and you can have no
difficulty or imbarras[5] in drawing out my account concerning them. I
find a necessity of being thus explicit, least I have any other ugly
mistake in my transactions with them concerning my meaning. And this
would have vexed me much more than it does, but that I conclude both
from the nature of the thing, and what they assured me, that the price
they understood I intended to let them have the share for, which I sold
them, induced them to rise so high in the purchase of yours. For nobody
can wish you better than I do, nor rejoice more in the good prospect of
the issue of your affairs. And I hope you are sensible of it.

> I am Dr Sr your very assured
> & affectionate friend & humble
> Servt   W. Warburton

Monday morning

P.S. I was looking over your Note of 500*l.* which, on acct of the
Statute, you renewed in time. I find it bears the Date Decr 15 1744 and
bears interest, as it is expressed, after the rate of 4 p[er] cent. I mention
this because perhaps you might be at a loss for the precise date.[6]

---

[1] i.e. the preceding letter (Eg. 1954, f.5).

[2] Some time after the Knapton liquidity crisis of June 1755 and perhaps not long after
this letter was sent, Somerset Draper drew up an Abstract of Accounts for Pope's *Works*
from 1751 to 1754 (see Eg. 1959, f.30 in Appendix A).

[3] This interpolation is marked with an x and given as a footnote.

[4] Warburton may well have had the Christmas season in mind, although a survey of
lists in *GM* and *LM* shows that the high season for book notices could last from December
through to May.

[5] This variant from the French word for 'embarrassment' dates from Pepys in 1664;
the Abbé d'Allainval title, *L'embarras des richesses*, was known from 1726 (*OED*).

[6] On Monday evening, Warburton mentioned changing his mind 'as to the books
bought of Pope's Execrs': Bolingbroke, Marchmont and himself. He decided to split his
share (presumably of Pope books) with Somerset Draper and Andrew Millar.
Warburton's tone was adamant: 'This is my determination and I will be beholden to no
body.' Warburton's reminder to Knapton about the annual interest on his loan may
help date this letter to December.
The next letter explains how Warburton misunderstood the intricacies of the
transaction and lost £175 in the exchange. Now he sounds embarrassed and secretive,
beginning with 'Say nothing of the contents to the bearer'. Warburton's loss, however,

seems to have been Knapton's gain. The £250 Warburton received may help date the
letter, as a deposit of £250 was made to Warburton's account at Gosling's Bank on 22
November 1755. Warburton had wished to have the remainder of the second volume of
The Divine Legation destroyed (9 December 1751 and 15 October 1752), although
Knapton may have persuaded him to sell imperfect copies.

Warburton *to* Robert Dodsley[1]   26 December 1755
Edinburgh University Library: La.II.153   [Prior Park]

Mr Dodsley

let us not be misunderstood. When you came to me in Town, I told
you, *whenever I sold my whole property in Pope I would contrive if possible you
should have some share*. And I remember very well, as I found you disposed
to understand this as a promise to let you have some share whenever I
sold *any*, I set you right, & repeated to you again that my meaning was
when I *parted with the whole*. For at that time, I had determined with my
selfe to employ Mr Millar & Mr Draper in my concerns. I had my
reasons on account of my knowledge of them, & affairs I have had with
them. They had always done every thing to my satisfaction. And I must
have things done my own way. On which account I sold, what I did sell
to them, much cheaper than they bought of Mr Knapton.[2]

You will ask me then how I came to say I would contrive, if possible,
that you should have some share when I sold the whole? It was partly on
your importunity; partly out of regard I have for your Brother here;[3] &
partly because Mr Pope had a regard for you: tho', as I told you, I
thought you had not been very regardful of the memory of a man to
whom you was so much obliged.

But as you m[ention][4] Mr Millar in a complaining way, I must tell
you, you do him much injury to think you had any right to any part of
that he bought of me or Mr Knapton. I chose him preferably to another:
I chose him because I would have to do with no other, but of my own
appointment; and had he, (because you had told him of your willingness
to be concerned with him in purchasing some share of Pope) let you have
any which he purchased, without my knowledge & consent he had
broke his word with me & violated his reputation. I am not a person to
be bought & sold. Mr Knapton, who is an honest & a virtuous & a
gratefull man, would have suffered me to be as much master of the sale of
his part of this property as if it had been my own. And it is with men of
that Character only, that I hope I shall ever be concerned.

You will do Mr Millar & me but justice, (a justice which I must expect
of you) to communicate the contents of this to him: and that if you have

said any thing contrary to these contents (which in every part is exactly true) that you would own your selfe mistaken.[5]

I am your very humble Servt.
W. Warburton

Decr. 26 1755

[1] Printed in *Dodsley*, pp.212–14.
[2] See Eg. 1954, ff.3–7 above.
[3] Isaac Dodsley (*d.* 1781?) was Ralph Allen's gardener (*Dodsley*, p.4).
[4] There is a tear in the MS. at this point.
[5] See Dodsley's fragment (*c.* 6 January [1756]) and letter of 6 January [1756], below.

Warburton *to* [Anon][1]   28 December 1755
Folger Shakespeare Library: Y.c.1451 (9)   Prior Park

I shall be in Town the latter end of January, and on your return I hope you will not leave London without letting me know of your being there.[2]

I am my dear Sir with the
truest esteem   Your most
Affectionate & faithfull humble
Servant
W. Warburton

Prior Park
Decr 28 1755

Note (stamped number): 137
Note (in another hand): Bishop Warburton

[1] Lot 1011 in the sale of the Thacher Library at the Anderson Auction Co., 10 January 1916.
[2] While there is nothing to suggest the identity of the recipient, it is worth noting Warburton's planned itinerary at this time.

1756–1759

Dodsley complained of Warburton's neglect in transferring his business (including the Pope copyrights) from Knapton to Millar. Warburton evidently still bore some ill will towards Dodsley for publishing John Gilbert Cooper's *Life of Socrates* (1749), followed by *Cursory Remarks* (1751) under Mary Cooper's name. Dodsley pointed out that Millar, now chosen to publish both Pope and Warburton, was also responsible for the works of Bolingbroke. His controversy with Robert Lowth flared up in 1756.

By 3 June 1756, Bowyer was paid 75% of the amount outstanding by Knapton. Within three years of Paul's death, the financial crisis seems to have passed; John Knapton continued to do business with Bowyer.

The Warburtons had a son, named after his grand-uncle, Ralph Allen, early in May 1756. In 1756, Warburton published a sermon, *Natural and Civil Events the Instruments of God's Moral Government* and was appointed Dean of Bristol in September 1757 by Pitt. In the same year, Hurd published his *Remarks on Mr. David Hume's Essay on the Natural History of Religion*.

A Supplement to the Works of Alexander Pope (1757), printed for Mary Cooper, contained poems (like 'Sober Advice from Horace') and letters not included in the Warburton edition. Warburton changed his London residence from Bedford Row to Grosvenor Square, which he maintained until his death. On 24 July 1759, he obtained a royal licence for the sole right to print and publish Pope's *Works* for fourteen years.

Robert Dodsley *to* [Warburton][1]   [*c.* 6 January 1756]
Hyde Collection, Somerville, New Jersey   [Pall Mall, London]

Sir

I recd your two letters,[2] & should have answer'd them sooner but that I was going out of Town. I must confess your strange treatment of me lays me under some difficulty how to behave.[3] To be silent under such severe Imputations, would be injustice to my self; and I am afraid it will ⟨be difficult⟩ not be easy for me to say what ⟨I ought⟩ most modest Resentment would dictate, without giving You offence, which ⟨I⟩ ⟨would willingly avoid⟩ ⟨am anxious to avoid⟩ ⟨am really anxious to avoid⟩ ⟨to [?] avoid⟩ ⟨to wholly avoid⟩ ⟨to⟩ ⟨I am Sensible however that I am but a Bookseller, I will endeavour not to forget that Modesty and Respect which I owe to your superior Character as a Clergyman⟩ not withstanding all you have said, I would willingly avoid; I know I am but a Bookseller, and you a Divine ⟨but when⟩ tho' pounc'd by an Eagle: but even a wren will complain. I ⟨will⟩ must therefore proceed.

---

[1] I am grateful to Viscountess Eccles for supplying me with a photocopy of this draft (reflecting Dodsley's agitation with Warburton) and the following letter of 6 January 1756; and to James Tierney for directing my attention to this. See *Dodsley*, pp.214–15.

[2] See Warburton's letter of 26 December 1755, above; the other letter is unknown (*Dodsley*, p.553).

[3] Dodsley, who had been set up in the bookselling business with the poet's help, observed Pope's first meeting with Warburton in Lord Radnor's garden late in April 1740. According to Joseph Warton, Dodsley was 'astonished at the high compliments paid [to Warburton] by Pope' (Pope, *Works*, ed. Joseph Warton, 9 vols. (1797), 9: 342). Perhaps the would-be editor detected some resentment in the upwardly-mobile bookseller. While Dodsley played a part in some works that were bound to offend Warburton, he also took an interest in keeping Pope's memory alive by publishing such works as Mason's *Musaeus* (1747).

Robert Dodsley *to* [Warburton][1]   6 January [1756]
Hyde Collection, Somerville, New Jersey   Pall Mall, London

                                        Pall mall Jany. 6th. [1756]
Sir
                     vide the back of ye Paper

⟨I was favour'd with two letters from you, one on Monday, the other on Tuesday last,[2] which I shou[ld] have answer'd sooner but that I was then going o[ut] of town.⟩ In the first of your letters I am charg'd (tho' without proof and I hope without foundation) with a want of regard to the Memory of Mr Pope,[3] in suffering little scribb[lers] to defame him thro' my press:[4] and this is given as t[he] reason why you did not chuse to treat with me for [a] share in his works. In the second this charge is d[ropped?] and I am tax'd with ⟨no want of Insensibility⟩ a want of Sensibility, in applyi[ng] to you for favours, after having, seven years ago, prin[ted] a book in which the Author (who put his name to hi[s] work) had treated You ⟨with disrespect⟩ with ill manners. I am also charg'd with not resenting properly, a forg'd Letter se[nt] to You in my name:[5] which last, as I was entirely ignora[nt] of it, and You then did me the Justice to acquit me, have now even forgot on what occasion it was writte[n]. As to the first charge, my want of respect to the Memo[ry] of Mr Pope; as it is my pride that he was my friend, so it is my consolation under the misfortune of your censure, that I cannot charge my self with the least forgetfulness of what I owe him. But ⟨You will pardon my remarking by the way, that your respect to his Memory did not hinder You from employing⟩ ⟨did your respect to his Memory not hinder You from employing⟩ ⟨I suppose it was this respect paid to his Memory that led you to employ⟩ suppose [I h]ad been somewhat remiss in this respect had not you employ'd as the Printer of his works, ⟨him⟩ the person who publish'd the most virulent Libel that has yet appear'd against ⟨your Friend, and who is also a Proprietor in the works of your greatest Enemy, And as⟩ him? ⟨I mean a Preface to ye Patriot Ki[ng.]⟩[6] As to my having printed a book in which you was disrespectfully treated ⸺ I would beg leave to ask, what You would have said to Mr. Knapton had he ⟨objected against printing the many invectives which You have thrown out against some of your opponents.⟩ refused to print some of your ⟨Works?⟩ Pieces? ⟨And had not he, long⟩ Did you ⟨make it any objection to him⟩ object to him, that he had, before You employ'd him, printed Dr. Sykes's book,[7] professedly written agst. You? It does not appear that you did. I do not mention these Instances as charging either Mr. Knapton or Mr. Millar with the least crime, but only to shew, that what You have thought proper to make an objection against *me*, was not thought so in regard to *them*. ⟨The next⟩ Another charge ⟨against⟩ upon me is, my want of Sensibility in applying to You for favours. I must own I was not conscious that I had ever given you any just cause of Offence: neither can I look upon my ⟨application to You to purchase at any valuable Consideration, or at any reasonable price,⟩ offer to You of purchasing at reasonable price, a share of that Property, part of which you had already dispos'd of to others, as ⟨applying⟩ an application for any singular favour. +⟨An[d] as to giving⟩ But I give my self the air you say, of one who had some mer[it] with you⟨,⟩ ⸺ I do not believe, on a perusal of my letter, tha[t] You will find me guilty of any such Presumption: but I did so ⟨assume⟩ presume, how strangely was I mistaken! for by your uncharitable ⟨slur⟩ sneer on the morals of a Bookseller, a[nd] from the very hard conclusion of your last Letter, it ⟨seems⟩ appears ⟨if⟩ that You ⟨could scarce⟩ cannot allow me even the merit of comm[on] Honesty; ⟨since you there⟩ ⟨and⟩ but treat me as one with whom Yo[u] would by no means chuse to have any dealings. This las[t] ⟨charge⟩ stroke I must own would have given me some pain, were I no[t] in hopes that the opinions of all who best know me, and of the public in general, are somewhat different from that which I am so unfortunate as to find is yours of

Sir
Your very humble Servant
R Dodsley

P.S. +However, grant it was a favour, I never ask'd but once, & never recd a denial till now; & the[re]fore your reproaches of Importunity, of not bein[g] content with a simple denial, but forcing You [to] tell me all your mind, I think might have been sha[meless?]

---

[1] *Dodsley*, pp.215–17.

[2] The location of Warburton's letter of 27 December 1755 is unknown. According to Dodsley's reply, Warburton, who was perhaps trying to clarify his reasons, altered the emphasis of his reason for rejecting Dodsley's request for a share in Pope's works.

[3] Dodsley is echoing a phrase used by Warburton in his letter of 26 December 1755,

above. Warburton may have construed John Gilbert Cooper's attack on the 1751 *Works* as an attack on Pope rather than on his editing.

[4] Both seem to have John Gilbert Cooper in mind.

[5] This forged letter is unknown, but was evidently designed to turn Warburton against Dodsley.

[6] Dodsley is pointing out the apparent contradiction in Warburton's reasons for choosing Millar over himself. If Warburton had been indisposed to take his business to Dodsley because he had published works critical of Warburton, then Millar, who had published Bolingbroke's *Patriot King*, together with Mallet's stinging Advertisement, should have been the last person Pope's editor would have chosen.

[7] John and Paul Knapton published both sides of the *Divine Legation* debate: Arthur Ashley Sykes' *An Examination of Mr. Warburton's Account of the Conduct of the Antient Legislators* (1744), Warburton's *Remarks on several occasional reflections: in answer to the Reverend Doctors Stebbing and Sykes* (1745) and Sykes' *A Defence of the Examination of Mr. Warburton's Account of the Theocracy of the Jews* (1746).

Warburton *to* John Nourse[1]　　　　　　　　　　15 March 1756
University of Michigan, University Library　　　　　Prior Park

Dear Sir

I am extremely sorry that so infamous a Cheat has escaped so well.[2]

I wish you would get me the Third Volume of Doddridge's Family expositor 4°.[3] I want it to compleat my set. And when the Comte de Calus 2d V[o]l. comes, to send them both hither.[4]

If the french Comedy of the Pedant be Marivaux's I have it already, having the small Edn of his plays which you mention[5]

　　　　　　　　　　　　　　　　I am Dear Sir, with
　　　　　　　　　　　　　　much esteem your very faith-
　　　　　　　　　　　　　　　　-full humble Servt
Prior Park　　　　　　　　　　　　W. Warburton
March 15 1756

Address (detached): To Mr: Nourse　　Bookseller in the Strand London
Free R: Allen

[1] This letter has been mounted on a leaf in Cornelius Brown's *Lives of Nottinghamshire Worthies* (London, 1882), vol. 2. Originally owned by Percy J. Cropper, who added portraits, autographs and prints, this set was purchased from Bernard Quaritch in 1965.

[2] Untraced.

[3] Philip Doddridge, *The Family Expositor: or, a Paraphrase and Version of the New Testament*, 6 vols. (London, 1739–56).

[4] Untraced.

[5] Possibly a confusion of Marivaux's *Le Père prudent et équitable* in *Oeuvres de théâtre*, 5 vols. (Paris and Geneva, 1755?); or Cyrano de Bergerac, *Le pédant joué*, in *Oeuvres*, 3 vols. (Amsterdam, 1741).

Warburton *to* [John Nourse?]   5 May 1756
Yale University, Beinecke Library: Osborn Files   Prior Park

Dear Sir
    I have recd your Catalogue[1] pray put by for me

√   p. 6.   No. 93   Vignola[2]
√   p. ead.   No. 106. Dati vite de Pittori[3]
√   p 7.   No. 119   Dolce dial: sur la Peint:[4]
√   p. ead.   No. 125   Apuleius[5]
√   p. 14.   No. 309   Strebæus.[6]
√   p. 19   No. 433. Terenzio It. & lat.[7]
sold/ p. ead.   No. 443. Barbaro dell' Eloq:[8]
√   p 24   No. 553. Ariosto tutte le opere.[9] &c if the comedies be
                               amongst them
√   p. 42.   No. 971   Davila[10]
√   p. 52.   No. 1118 Aretæus lat.[11]

These you may please to send to my house in Bedford Row. The Bible
may stay in your custody and the Bib: come by Leak's parcel hither.

                                          I am Sir your very faithfull
                                                humble Servant
Prior Park   W. Warburton
May 5 1756

Note (verso): Dr. Wm Warburton died Bishop of Gloucester 11 [*sic*] June
1779

[1] Without the catalogue (untraced), one can only guess at some of the following items.
The check marks in the left-hand margin were probably made by the bookseller who
noted one item as being sold.
[2] Possibly the architect and contemporary of Palladio, Giacomo Barozzi (called Il
Vignola), *Regole delli cinque ordini d'architettura* (1562); or *Regole della prospettiva prattica*
(Venice, 1743).
[3] Carlo Roberto Dati, *Vite de pittori antichi* (Florence, 1667).
[4] Lodovico Dolce, *Dialogo della pitura... dialogue sur la peinture*, trans. Paul Vleughels
(Florence, 1735).
[5] Printed works of Apuleius date back to *Metamorphoseos* (Rome, 1469) and *Opera*
(Venice, 1493), a two-volume edition of which was published at Paris, 1688.
[6] Jacobus Ludovicus Strebæus, Renaissance commentator on classical rhetoric.
[7] *Il Terentio Latino* (Venice, 1548–80); *Comoediae*, ed. N. Fortiguerra (Urbino, 1736).
[8] Daniello Barbaro, *Della eloquenza* (Venice, 1557).
[9] Ariosto, *Opere*, ed. G. A. Barotti, 4 vols. (Venice, 1741).
[10] Enrico Caterino Davila, *The History of the Civil Wars of France* (London, 1678; rpt.
trans. Ellis Farnesworth, 2 vols., 1758).
[11] Aretæus, *Aretæi libri septem*, trans, J. P. Crassus (Venice, 1552); *De causis et signis
acutorum morborum* (Oxford, 1723).

Warburton *to* [Mercy Doddridge]   6 May 1756
Pierpont Morgan Library   Prior Park

Good Madm

I think my selfe much honour'd by the favour of your obliging Letter of the 19 past, which I received this morning. Mr Allen joins with me in returning you our best thanks for the valuable present of our Friend Dr Doddridge's Hymns.

We have received the last Volumes of the *Family expositor*,[1] and have turned them over with great pleasure. They are full of all that piety, moderation, & good sense which so eminently distinguished the Character of our Friend.

We hope the subscription answered the uses of the Family, in some measure correspondent to the service this excellent work will do the public.

Mr Allen & I desire you to believe that we shall always be glad of any opportunity of service, which may manifest our real regard to your & to your Family's interests. I am Madm, with the best wishes for your health & happiness,

Your most obedient & faithfull
humble Servant
W. Warburton

Prior Park
May 6 1756

P.S My Wife & Mrs Allen desire their best respects

[1] Philip Doddridge, *The Family Expositor*, 6 vols. (London, 1739–56). See Warburton's letter to John Nourse of 15 March 1756, above.

Robert and Andrew Foulis *to* Andrew Millar   25 September 1756
Edinburgh University Library: Dc.4.102   Glasgow

N5833S   22/25 Sept
£20 Sterling   Glasgow Septr. 1756

Sir,

Please pay to James Dychman[1] & company twenty days after date ye sum of twenty pounds Sterl: value in paper furnished for printing Pope's Works as advised by, Sir,[2]

Your most humble Servts
Robert & Andrew Foulis

To Mr Andrew Millar
Bookseller in London

Verso: [Bear] the Contents to Mess[rs] Kennedy & Bell on order
James Dichman & Co.
Kennedy & Bell
Peter Johnson
Thos. Browne
To Jn Smith
The Bond Reced
Witness John Allison
For Wm Gibson

[1] James Dechman is listed in a group of merchants in the imprint of the 1737 Glasgow edition of the works of Isaac Ambrose (David Murray, *Robert & Andrew Foulis and the Glasgow Press* (Glasgow, 1913), pp.15–16).

[2] The Foulis brothers evidently arranged for the sale of paper stock to Millar for the printing of Pope's works.

Warburton *to* Andrew Millar   7 February 1757
SUP, pp.309–10   [Prior Park?]

Copy of a Letter from Bishop Warburton to Mr. Millar

Feb. 7th, 1757.

Sir,

I supposed you would be glad to know what sort of book it is which you are about to publish with Hume's name and yours to it.[1] The design of the first essay is the very same with all Lord Bolingbroke's, to establish *naturalism*, a species of atheism, instead of religion; and he employs one of Bolingbroke's capital arguments for it. All the difference is, it is without Bolingbroke's abusive language.

All the good his mutilation and fitting it up for the public has done, is only to add to its other follies that of contradiction. He is establishing atheism; and in one single line of a long essay professes to believe Christianity. All this I shall show in a very few words on a proper occasion.[2]

In the mean time, if you think you have not money enough, and can satisfy your conscience, you will do well to publish it; for there is no doubt of the sale among a people so feverish, that to-day they burn with superstition, and to-morrow freeze with atheism. But the day of the publication and the *fast day* will be an admirable contrast to one another.[3]

I dare say you knew nothing of the contents; but the caution of poor Mr. K. was admirable on the like occasion with this very man, Hume. He wrote to Mr. K. to offer him a copy, that had nothing to do with religion, as he said.[4] Mr. K. replied, that might be; but as he had given great offence, and he (Mr. K.) was himself no judge of these matters, he desired to be excused.

You have often told me of this man's moral virtues. He may have many, for aught I know; but let me observe to you, there are vices of the *mind* as well as of the *body*: and I think a wickeder mind, and more obstinately bent on public mischief, I never knew.

W.W.

[1] Millar perhaps sent Warburton an early specimen of Hume's *Four Dissertations* (London: A. Millar, 1757); this included *The Natural History of Religion*. As in the case of Bolingbroke's *Works* (1754) and Warburton's *A View of Lord Bolingbroke's Philosophy*, 2nd ed. (London, 1756), Millar's name appeared in the imprints of both sides of the controversy.

[2] Warburton's intentions were evidently fulfilled by Hurd's *Remarks on Mr. David Hume's Essay on the Natural History of Religion: Addressed to the Rev. Dr. Warburton* (London: M. Cooper, 1757).

[3] Millar and Knapton had already co-published Hume's *Essays Moral and Political* (London: J. and P. Knapton, C. Hitch and A. Millar, 1741; 3rd ed. 1748). According to Ernest C. Mossner, Hume's biographer and editor, 'by 1757, the name of David Hume was known throughout Great Britain and on the Continent as Britain's most famous (and infamous) man of letters,' David Hume, *A Treatise of Human Nature*, ed. Ernest C. Mossner (Harmondsworth, 1985), p.24. Warburton saw some irony in publishing *Four Dissertations* shortly before Easter.

[4] Letter untraced.

Warburton *to* John Nourse   9 September 1758
Bath Reference Library: A.L. 2312   Prior Park

Prior Park Sepr 9 1758

Dear Sir

I have recd the two packets of Books. I just looked into Gillet's transl. of Josephus.[1] The part I read was his VIth. remark on the XVIII book of Antiquities in the 3d Tom. it is a dissertation (equal to a moderate sized pamphlet) of the famous testimony (so much the subject of Critical debate) of Josephus, concerning J. C. He has exhausted the subject, and in so incomperable a manner, both as to learning reasoning & candour, that he has fairly ended the controversy. Was an important and serious question of Criticism & Theology any longer desirving the attention of the public I should think a translation of it would do very well. But a bawdy ⟨*pope*⟩² poem, a frivolous Romance, or a state-Libel only now deserve our notice.

I desire you to send me hither Aboulfeda Annales Moslemici 4°³ and L'Origine des loix, des Art[s] —— 3 Vs 4°. by the same conveyance with the other⁴

> I am your very faithfull
> & obedient Servt
> W. Warburton

Envelope and postmark: To Mr: Nourse Bookseller in the Strand London Free R: Allen 11/SE

---

¹ Flavius Josephus, *Nouvelle traduction de l'historien Joseph, fait sur le grec: avec des notes...* *par le R. P. Gillet*, 4 vols. (Paris, 1756–67).

² Possibly Warburton began to write 'paper'.

³ Ismail-Ibn-Ali Abu Al-Fida or Abulfeda (1273–1331), the Moslem prince and historian, was mentioned by George Perry in a letter to John Nichols, from Calcutta on 1 October 1783: 'The titles may be met with in Catalogues, especially as I would wish a retrospect of about ten years, recollecting to have seen a thick quarto volume of Abulfeda, translated in Holland or Germany, and marked 1*l*. 1*s*. (*LA*, 6: 638).

⁴ A.Y. Goguet, *De l'origine des loix, des arts, et des sciences*, 3 vols. (Paris, 1758).

Warburton *to* John Nourse   14 December 1758
Yale University, Beinecke Library: Osborn Files   Prior Park

Dear Sr

I see by the advertis[e]ments, Mr Church's Spencer goes forward.¹ I always intended to subscribe & therefore desire you will subscribe for me.

Pray let me know how those Epistles in dogrel verse, that we looked into together, at your shop, are received; and whither the Author is known.² I would not have it mentioned that I enquire abt them.

> I am your very faithfull
> friend & humble Servt
P.P. Decr 14 1758   W. Warburton

Endorsed: Prior Park Decr. 14. 1758 Dr Warburton [in Nourse's hand?] *Address and postmark* (*verso*): 16[?]/DE   To Mr: Nourse   Bookseller in the Strand   London   Free R: Allen   BATH

---

¹ Edmund Spenser, *The Faerie Queene*, ed. Ralph Church, 4 vols. (London: William Faden, 1758–9). John Upton's edition of Spenser was reprinted, in 2 vols., folio, by J. and R. Tonson in 1758.

[2] These might refer to John Gilbert Cooper's anonymous *Epistles to the Great, from Aristippus in Retirement* (London: R. and J. Dodsley, 1757), an extract from which appeared in *LM*, 26 (Nov. 1757): 527-8. *The Call of Aristippus*, dedicated to Mark Akenside, was added as a fourth epistle, also published by the Dodsleys, in the following year (*GM*, 28 (March 1758): 130).

Warburton *to* [Mercy Doddridge]   8 March 1759
Historical Society of Pennsylvania: Grosvenor Square, London
Dreer Collection

                                Grosvenor Square   8 March 1759
Madm,

I have the honour of your Letter of the 26 past, which was sent me from Prior Park to this place.

You have explained your case very well, and I will give you my thoughts upon it—— A royal patent or License may be obtained on very easy terms, and without wasting your interest to obtain it.[1] You may have it for asking, and at the moderate expense of 10 *l*. But I know of no service it is, to the protection of any Author's property. If the work was written within fourteen years, the property is secured by Act of Parliament; when that time is elapsed, it is then claimed by common Law. In this latter case the right has been broke into, by rascally booksellers, from time to time; and so has the right in the former; but both one and the other is, upon the whole, tolerably well preserved. They fright you with stories of the invasion of literary property, in order, I suppose, to get yours the cheaper. But whether the property be within, or without, the fourteen years, the Patent gives the proprietor no additional security. The *use* of a Patent is for new inventions in medicine or mechanics, which gives the inventor an exclusive right to make and vend his inventions or improvements for fourteen years. But with regard to books, it is of no real or material use. You will ask then how it comes to pass that you see every newspaper full of advertisements of Books printed & printing, recommended by the King's patent to all his good Subjects? This is another of the Booksellers' roguerys, whereby they impose upon the Common people, who seeing the King's patent, think, in good earnest, that he is solicitous to recommend the book which he thus honours, to their special notice; and they have no conception that he would thus recommend any thing that was not very good in its kind.

So far as to the present state of your property in Dr Doddridge's Works. As to the stating and finishing your accounts with Mr Waugh,[2] in this, I think you have done perfectly right. Your intention of disposing of the printed copies at once, is surely no less prudent, and will save you a world of trouble in bringing the Booksellers to account with you from time to time in order to be cheated at last. If for these and the right of reprinting 500 of the 4 last V:s of the family expositor the Bookseller would give you 500 *l*. I think it would be a better bargain than 650 *l*. for all the printed Copies & the whole copy right together. As Dr Doddridge's works are chiefly practical, the copy right must be worth something considerable. I am sensible indeed you could not so well preserve it from invasion as the booksellers can. Where each abstains from plundering another, because that other has it in his power to plunder him again, by way of reprisal. On the whole therefore if you could get a reasonable price for the copies and the property together, I should be apt to advise you to close with a purchaser.

With regard to spreading the Drs works amongst the public, to be sure the very best way is to sell the property of them to a Bookseller. for they spare no pains in getting of their own ware.

As the Dr expressed a desire that his Lectures should be published, I make no doubt they are very worthy of the public. And I think, by what he shewed me of his Scheme, he had taken pains about them. Yet I much suspect (considering the didactic and severe nature of such kind of compositions) that if you published them at your own expence you would hardly be a saver; if a Bookseller would undertake it at his, you would scarce be a gainer. I should therefore propose, if you think you lye under obligations to give them to the public, that they be printed by subscription. If on proposing a subscription you meet with reasonable encouragement, you gain your end, which is the discharging this act of piety to the deceased. If you have not encouragement, at least you have done your part.

> I am Madm, with the truest regard & esteem,
> your very faithfull and obedient humble
> Servant   W. Warburton

[1] See Warburton's memorandum of 18 May 1759, n.1, below.
[2] The bookseller James Waugh.

Warburton *to* David Garrick[1]   [*c.* 2 April 1759]
Folger Shakespeare Library: W.b.114   [Prior Park?]

Dear Sir

Upon a supposition there may be a chance, like that in a state Lottery, of se[e]ing you here, if you have an hour to drink tea, we have ventured to tell you that Mr Blackbourne & Dr Browne[2] are with us and the pleasure your company would give us.

ever most affectionately yours
W. Warburton

P.S. Tho the above you will treat as it deserves. what follows is more serious. our Child a day or two ⟨ago⟩ was inoculated, & I don't know whether Mrs Garrick & you have had the small-pox.[3]
Fryday afternoon

Note: (in another hand in red ink): *William Warburton*
Address (*verso*): To David Garrick Esqr.   Southampton Street   Covent Garden

[1] Not in *LDG*, which is comprised of letters written *by* Garrick. This was lot 1445 in the Sotheby's catalogue of William Wright's books, 19 June 1899.
[2] Probably Francis Blackburne and Isaac Hawkins Browne. In 1758, Ralph Allen Warburton 'was enamoured by Dr. Browne's fiddle-stick' (Boyce, p.250; *LLEP*, p.199).
[3] Ralph Allen Warburton (1756–75) was inoculated for smallpox in the spring of 1759 and recovered by April 28. Warburton mentioned his son's health in two letters to Thomas Balguy, dated 2 April and 28 April 1759 (University of Texas at Austin; Boyce, p.251).

Warburton (memorandum)   18 May 1759
BL: Egerton 1959, f.29*v*.

An acct of the profits of Pope while I had 2 3rds of his work.[1]

May 18 1759   Since I made up my accts with Mr Knapton, and his selling his share (which was the 3d pt of Pope) to Messrs Tonson & Millar, and my selling to them one 6th more, so that my share in Pope is now one half, Messrs Tonson and Millar have printed two Edns. one in crown 8° and another in pot octo. and are now abt to print a third in large octo. which when sold will produce for my share of the clear profits of these three Edns.

940*l*.[2]

according to the accts in these papers.[3]

Besides the profits of the Edns. of the Essay on Man which continue selling separately.

[1] 'A royal licence gave Warburton sole right for 14 years from 24 July 1759 to print, publish and vend the Works which he had annotated', *The New Cambridge Bibliography of English Literature*, ed. George Watson, vol. 2, 1660–1800 (Cambridge, 1971), col. 501.

[2] This sum has been inked over.

[3] Pope, *Works*, 9 vols. (London: printed for H. Lintot, A. Millar, J. and R. Tonson, S. Draper, and C. Bathurst, 1756)

——, 9 vols. (London: printed for A. Millar, J. and R. Tonson, H. Lintot, and C. Bathurst, 1757*a*)

——, 10 vols. (London: printed for A. Millar, J. and R. Tonson, H. Lintot, and C. Bathurst, 1757*b*)

——, 9 vols. (London: printed for H. Lintot, A. Millar, J. and R. Tonson, C. Bathurst, R. Baldwin, W. Johnston [and 6 others in London], 1760).

1760–1765

Pope continued to be popular: in 1760 alone, editions of *An Essay on Man* were published in London, Glasgow and Belfast; translations came out in Berne (1760), Lausanne (1762) and – a polyglot, in five languages – Amsterdam (1762). 1764 saw eight editions of Pope's *Works*: three were published by Millar *et al.* in London, three in Edinburgh and two in Dublin. Fredrick Nicolai's ten-volume Berlin edition of Pope's *Works* was published in 1762–4. A monument was erected to Pope's memory in St. Mary the Virgin, the Twickenham parish church, in 1761, bearing his editor's name.

Warburton was consecrated Bishop of Gloucester on 20 January 1760 and ten days later he delivered a sermon before the Lords in the Abbey Church, Westminster. He published *A Rational Account of the Nature and End of the Sacrament of the Lord's Supper* (1761), *A People's Prayer for Peace* (1761) and *The Doctrine of Grace* (1763).

Warburton's latter years as Pope's editor were far from placid. A rumour circulated that Laurence Sterne was intending to model Tristram Shandy's pedantic tutor on Warburton; the novelist responded satirically to this in a letter to Garrick. In 1763 Philip Nichols renewed the quarrel with Hanmer in *The Castrated Sheet*. In November 1763, parts of the obscene parody, *An Essay on Woman*, with notes attributed to Warburton, were read aloud in the House of Lords by the Earl of Sandwich; Warburton gave a speech against John Wilkes and conveyed the excitement of the moment in his letters to Ralph Allen. Wilkes' friend Charles Churchill satirized Warburton in *The Duellist* (1764). Wilkes' anonymous 'Notes on the Fragment of a Dedication to the Bishop of Gloucester', appended to Churchill's posthumous *Sermons* (1765), claimed that the son of the Archbishop of Canterbury, Thomas Potter (1718–59), had sired Warburton's only son. Ralph Allen died on 27 June 1764; the death of his widow two years later left Prior Park in the Warburtons' care.

Warburton *to* [Samuel Richardson?][1]   26 January 1760
Folger Shakespeare Library: W.b.474   Grosvenor Square, London

Dear Sir
    I thank you heartily for your kind congratulations. I know they come from the honestest heart that ever was.
    I will take the first opportunity of enquiring in Salisbury Court after your health
                        and am your very affectionate & faithfull humble Servt
                                                    W. Warburton
Gros. Sq.
Jan. 26 1760

[1] The FSL *Catalog of Manuscripts* has listed the recipient as: '[Henry? Woodfall?] of Salisbury Court'. The Woodfalls were long connected with the printing and publishing of Pope's works. For Henry Woodfall's account with Bernard Lintot for the printing of Pope's *Works*, see P.T.P. 'Pope and Woodfall', *N&Q*, 1st ser., 11 (19 May 1855): 377–8. Woodfall ornaments appear on at least nine editions of Pope's works in 1736–7. Henry Woodfall is named as the printer of two of Warburton's sermons ([1755], 1767) and as a bookseller on six imprints of Pope's *Works* (1764–80). However, according to George

Walter Thornbury in *Old and New London*, 6 vols. (London, 1873–8), the Woodfalls lived in Salisbury Square, while Richardson lived in Salisbury Court (1: 140). Warburton's letter to James Leake (3 September 1753*b*, above), extending his compliments to the author of *Sir Charles Grandison*, suggests any estrangement had subsided. While Woodfall had good reason to compliment Warburton, the 'honestest heart' suggests the recipient was Richardson.

Warburton *to* David Garrick[1]   7 March 1760
Private Correspondence of David Garrick,   Grosvenor Square, London
1: 115–16

                                          March 7, 1760, Grosvenor-square
My dear Sir,

You told me no news when you mentioned a circumstance of zeal for your friends; but you gave me much pleasure by it and the inclosed, to have an impertinent story confuted the first moment I heard of it; for I cannot but be pleased to find I have no reason to change my opinion of so agreeable and so original a writer as Mr. Sterne; I mean my opinion of his moral character, of which I had received from several of my acquaintance so very advantageous an account. And I cannot see how I could have held it, had the lying tale been true, that he intended to injure one personally and entirely unknown to him. I own it would have grieved me, (and so, I believe, it would him too, when he had known me and my enemies a little better,) to have found himself in company with a crew of the most egregious blockheads that ever abused the blessing of pen and ink.

However, I pride myself in having warmly recommended "Tristram Shandy" to all the best company in town, except that at Arthur's.[2] I was charged in a very grave assembly, as Dr. Newton can tell him, for a particular patronizer of the work; and how I acquitted myself of the imputation, the said Doctor can tell him. I say all this to show how ready I was to *do justice* to a stranger. This is all I expect from a stranger. From my friends, indeed, I expect, because I stand in need of, much *indulgence*. To them, (being without reserve,) I show my weaknesses. To strangers I have the discretion not to show them; at least, those *writing* strangers, I mentioned before, have not yet had the wit to find them out.

If Mr. Sterne will take me with all my infirmities, I shall be glad of the honour of being better known to him; and he has the additional recommendation of being your friend.

                                                  I am, dear Sir,
                    Your most affectionate and faithful humble servant,
                                                    W. Gloucester.

[1] Also in *LLS*, p.95.
[2] Robert Arthur's Chocolate House in St. James's Street, London.

Laurence Sterne *to* Warburton   9 June 1760
Letters of Laurence Sterne, p.112   York

York, June 9, 1760

My Lord,

Not knowing where to send two sets of my Sermons, I could think of
no better expedient, than to order them into Mr. Berrenger's hands,[1]
who has promised me that he will wait upon your Lordship with them,
the first moment he hears you are in town. The truest and humblest
thanks I return to your Lordship for the generosity of your protection,
and advice to me; by making a good use of the one, I will hope to deserve
the other; I wish your Lordship all the health and happiness in this
world, for I am

Your Lordship's
Most obliged and Most grateful Servant,
L. Sterne

P.S. I am just sitting down to go on with Tristram, &c. —— the
scribblers use me ill, but they have used my betters much worse, for
which may God forgive them.

[1] Richard Berenger (1720–82) was a friend of Warburton and Gentleman of the Horse
to George III (*LLS*, p.100).

Warburton *to* [Laurence Sterne][1]   15 June 1760
Folger Shakespeare Library: W.b.481, p.149 (copy)   Prior Park

Prior Park June 15th: 1760.

Revd. Sir,

I have your favour of the 9th. inst:[2] and am glad to understand, you
are got safe home, and employ'd again in your proper Studies &
amusements. you have it in your Power to make that which is an
amusement to yourself & others, useful to both: at least, you should
above all things, beware of its becoming hurtfull to either, by any
violations of decency & good manners: but I have already taken such
repeated Liberties of advising you on that head, that to say more would
be needless, or perhaps unacceptable.

Whoever is, in any way, well received by the Public is sure to be
annoyed by that Pest of the Public, profligate Scribblers. This is the
common lot of successfull Adventures. But such have often a worse evil to
struggle with, I mean the over officiousness of their indiscre[e]t friends.

There are two Odes, as they are called, printed by Dodsley.[3] Whoever was the Author, he appears to be a monster of impiety & lewdness. Yet such is the mall[i]gnity of the Scribblers, some have given them to your friend, Hall: and others, which is still more impossible, to yourself: Tho' the first Ode has the insolence to place you, both in a mean, & a ridiculous light. But this might arise from a tale equally groundless & malignant, that you had shew[n] them to your Acquaintance in MS. before they were given to the Public. Nor was their being printed by Dodsley the likelyest means of discrediting the Calumny.

About this time, another, under the mask of friendship, pretended to draw your Character; which was first published in a *female Magazine*[4] (for Dulness, who often has as great a hand as the Devil in deforming God's works of Creation, has *made them*, it seems, *male and female*) and from thence it was transferred into a *Chronicle*. Pray have you read it, or do you know its Author?

But of all these things, I dare say, Mr: Garrick, whose prudence is equal to his honesty or his talents, has remonstrated to you with the freedom of a friend. He knows the inconstancy of what is called the Public, towards all, even the best intentioned, of those who contribute to its pleasure or Amusement. He (as every Man of honour & discretion would) has availed himself of the public favour, to regulate the taste, and, in his proper Station, to reform the manners of the fashionable World, while by a well-judged Oeconomy, he has provided against the temptation of a mean & Servile dependency on the follies & Vices of the Great.

In a word, be assured, there is no one more sincerely Wishes your Welfare & happiness than,

Revd Sr, &c

W.G.

Endorsed (by David Garrick): Dr Warburton to Sterne with Sterne's Answr.

[1] This transcript is not in Warburton's hand; it differs slightly from the text found in *LLS*, pp.112–14.

[2] See *LLS*, p.112.

[3] John Hall-Stevenson, *Two Lyric Epistles: one to my cousin Shandy, on his coming to town* (London: R. and J. Dodsley, 1760). Warburton might have paid particular attention to the fact that this work was published by Dodsley.

[4] The *Royal Female Magazine* published a racy account of Sterne in its April 1760 issue, which was quickly circulated (*LLS*, p.111 n.2).

Warburton *to* David Garrick[1]   16 June 1760
Private Correspondence of David Garrick, 1: 117   Prior Park

Prior Park, June 16, 1760

Dear Sir,

I must not forget to thank you for the hints I received from you by Mr.
Berenger, concerning our heteroclite Parson. I heard enough of his
conduct in town since I left it, to make me think he would soon lose the
fruits of all the advantage he had gained by a successful effort, and
would disable me from appearing as his friend or well-wisher.

Since he got back from York, I had the inclosed letter from him, which
afforded me an opportunity I was not sorry for, to tell him my mind with
all frankness, as you will see by the copy of what I wrote to him. If it have
the effect I wish, it will be well for him; if it have not, it will be at least
well for me, in the satisfaction I shall receive by the attempt to do him
service.

[1] Also in *LLS*, p.114.

Laurence Sterne *to* Warburton   19 June 1760
Letters of Laurence Sterne, pp.115–16   Coxwold

Coxwould, June 19, 1760

My Lord, ——

This post brought me the honour of your letter, for which, and for
your kind and most friendly advice, I return your lordship all I am able,
my best thanks. Be assured, my lord, that willingly and knowingly I will
give no offence to any mortal by anything which I think can look like the
least violation either of decency or good manners; and yet, with all the
caution of a heart void of offence or intention of giving it, I may find it
very hard, in writing such a book as 'Tristram Shandy', to mutilate
everything in it down to the prudish humour of every particular. I will,
however, do my best; though laugh, my lord, I will, and as loud as I can
too.

With regard to the 'Lyrick Odes', all I know of them is this: that the
first ode, which places me and the author in a ridiculous light, was sent
to me in a cover without a name, which, after striking out some parts, as
a whimsical performance, I showed to some acquaintance; and as Mr
Garrick had told me, some time before, he would write me an ode, for a

day or two I supposed it came from him. I found afterwards it was sent me from Mr. Hall; for from a nineteen years' total interruption of all correspondence with him, I had forgot his hand, which at last when I recollected, I sent it back.[1] The second ode, which abounds with indecencies, is, I suppose, his too; as they are published together, there can be little doubt. He must answer for them; having nothing myself to answer for with regard to them but my extreme concern, and that a man of such great talents as my acquaintance Mr. Hall is, should give the world so much offence. He has it greatly in his power to make amends; and, if I have any penetration, and can depend upon the many assurances he gives me, your lordship will, I hope, live to see it. He is worth reclaiming, being one of those whom nature has enabled to do much hurt or much good.

Of all the vile things wrote against me, the Letter your Lordship mentions in the female magazeen, is the most inimicitious, & gave me, for that reason, the most concern, under which I had no better relief, than denying the facts, & crying out against the hardship done me, by such a contexture of Lies tack'd together not to serve me, but to overthrow me——God knows, too often such profligate Wretches gain their End.——every mortal in Town says it was wrote by a Dr Hill who wrote the Inspectors, & who, they tell me has the property & management of that Magazeen——Garrick tells me the same story & with reasons to confirm it. These strokes in the Dark, with the many Kicks, Cuffs & Bastinados I openly get on all sides of me, are begining to make me sick of this foolish humour of mine of sallying forth into this wide & wicked world to redress wrongs, &c. of wch I shall repent as sorely as ever Sancha Panca did of his in following his evil genius of a Don Quixote thro thick & thin——but as the poor fellow apologised for it,——so must I. *"it was my vile* fortune & my *Errantry & that's all that can be said* on't. Otherwise I wish from my heart, I had never set pen to paper, but continued hid in the quiet obscurity in which I had so long lived: I was quiet, for I was below Envy——& yet above Want; & indeed so very far above it, that the idea of it never once enterd my head, in writing;——& as I am now 200*ll* a year further from the Danger of it, than I was then, I think it never will; for I declare I have all I wish or want in this world, being in my calculation of Money, all out as rich as my friend Garrick, whose goodness of heart & honest Cowardice in keeping *so far* out of the way of Temptation, I nevertheless esteem & admire.

The Bishop of Carlisle did me the Honour yesterday of a Call; of whom I had the satisfaction of enquiring after yr Lordships health, & particularly how far the Waters had relieved you under the pain & indigestion you complain of——he hoped yr Lordship was better.

I wish your lordship all the most grateful man can wish——happiness in this world and in the next.

I am, my Lord,
with all Esteem & Duty
Yr Affte Servant   Laur: Sterne

[1] Warburton's letters may have prompted the resumption of Sterne's correspondence with John Hall–Stevenson; see *LLS*.

Warburton *to* Laurence Sterne   26 June 1760
Letters of Laurence Sterne, pp.118–19   Prior Park

Prior Park, June 26, 1760.
Rev. Sir,

I have the favour of your obliging letter of the 19th. It gives me real pleasure (and I could not but trouble you with these two or three lines to tell you so) that you are resolved to do justice to your genius, and to borrow no aids to support it, but what are of the party of honour, virtue, and religion.

You say you will continue to laugh aloud. In good time. But one who was no more than even a man of spirit would wish to laugh in good company, where priests and virgins may be present...

Do not expect your friends to pity you for the trash and ribaldry scribbled against you; they will apter to congratulate you upon it.

Notwithstanding all your wishes for your former obscurity, which your present chagrin excites, yet a wise man cannot but choose the sunshine before the shade; indeed, he would not wish to dwell in the malignant heat of the dog-days, not for the teasing and momentary annoyance of the numberless tribes of insects abroad at that time, but for the more fatal aspect of the superior bodies.

I would recommend a maxim to you which Bishop Sherlock formerly told me Dr. Bentley recommended to him, that a man was never writ out of the reputation he had once fairly won, but by himself.

I am, &c.,
W. G.

Warburton *to* [John Nourse]   2 October 1760
Folger Shakespeare Library: Art Vol. a10, p.250   Prior Park

Dr Sr

I recd the journals. I would have the following books, & what of them you have by you, I would have sent hither in boards.

4th Vol of Gillet's trans: of Josephus publ. at Paris last November.[1]
Le Beau's Hist. du Bas Empire – the 3d & 4th Tomes 8°.[2]
Oeuv[r]es de Fontanelle the 9 & 10 Tomes 8°.[3]
Longus past. of Daph[n]is & Chloe, Greek & Lat: 4°. with the original plates of Audrand.[4]
Lettres de Mad. La Marquise de Villars 12°.[5]
Histoire des Mathem[atiques]: par Montucla 2 Vs. 4° Paris.[6]

Your faithfull humble
Servt W. Gloucester

Prior Park
Octr 2 1760

Endorsed (in an unknown hand; cut away): Prior Park. Octr 2. 1760
Note (in another hand, at top): (Bishop Warburton)
Note (in another hand, in pencil): To Mr Nourse   Bookseller, Strand

[1] Warburton mentioned receiving part of R. P. Gillet's translation of Josephus (1756–67) in his letter of 9 September 1758, above (see also n.1).

[2] Charles Le Beau, *Histoire du Bas-Empire, en commençant à Constantin-le-Grand*, 29 vols. (Paris, 1757–1817). Twenty volumes (1757–76) remain in the Hurd Library.

[3] *Oeuvres de Monsieur Fontenelle*, new ed. (Paris, 1758–61).

[4] *Longi pastorialium, de Daphnide et Chloë, libri quatuor, Graece et Latine... distincta viginti novem figuris aeri incisis à B. Audran*, ed. J. S. Bernard (Paris [Amsterdam], 1754).

[5] *Lettres de Madame la Marquise de Villars* (Amsterdam, 1760).

[6] Jean Étienne Montucla, *Histoire des mathématiques*, 2 vols. (Paris, 1758).

Warburton *to* [A bookseller][1]   29 January 1761
European Magazine, 24 (October 1793): 246–7[2]

Sir Thomas Hanmer's Letter from Mildenhall to Oxford, Oct. 24, 1742, is one continued falshood from beginning to end.[3]

It is false that my acquaintance began upon an application from me to him; it began on an application of the present Bishop of London[4] to me in behalf of Sir T. Hanmer; and, as I understood, at Sir T. Hanmer's desire. The thing speaks itself. It was publicly known that I had written notes on Shakespeare, because part of them were printed; few people knew that Sir T. Hanmer had. I certainly did not know; nor indeed, whether he was living or dead.

The falshood is still viler (because it sculks only under an insinuation), that I made a journey to Mildenhall without invitation; whereas it was at his earnest and repeated request, as appears by his letters, which I have still by me.[5]

It is false, that the views of interest began to shew themselves in me to this *disinterested Gentleman*. My resentment at Sir T. H.'s behaviour began on the following occasion: —— A Bookseller in London,[6] of the best reputation, had wrote me word, that Sir Thomas Hanmer had been with him, to propose his printing an edition of Shakespeare on the following conditions: Of its being pompously printed with Cuts (as it was afterwards at Oxford), at the expence of the said Bookseller, who, besides, should pay one hundred guineas, or some such sum, to a friend of his (Sir T. H.'s), who had transcribed the Glossary for him. But the Bookseller, understanding that he made use of many of my Notes, and that I knew nothing of the project, thought fit to send me this account. On which I wrote to Sir T. Hanmer, upbraiding him with his behaviour, and demanding out of his hands all the Letters I had written to him on the subject; which he unwillingly complied with, after cavilling about the right of property in those letters, for which he had (he said) paid the postage.

When the Bookseller would not deal with him on these terms, he applied to the University of Oxford, and was at the expence of his purse in procuring Cuts for his Edition, and at the expence of his reputation in employing a Number of my Emendations on the Text, without my knowledge or consent: and this behaviour was what occasioned Mr. Pope's perpetuating the memory of the Oxford Edition of Shakespeare in the *Dunciad*.[7]

This is a true and exact account of the whole affair, which I never thought worth while afterwards to complain of but to the Bishop of London, at whose desire I lent Sir Thomas Hanmer my assistance: nor should I ever have revived it, but for the publication of this scandalous letter *sent from Oxford to this Philip Nichols*, to be inserted in the Biographia Britannica.[8]

W. G.

Jan. 29*th*, 1761.[9]

[1] Warburton addressed this letter to one of the booksellers of *Biographia Britannica*, possibly J. and R. Tonson or Charles Bathurst, who also had a share in Pope's *Works* at the time.

[2] This letter is prefaced by another explaining the origin of the quarrel:

To the EDITOR of the EUROPEAN MAGAZINE.

SIR, *Oct.* 13, 1793.

I Was not a little surprized to see in your last Magazine, p. 183 [below], a Letter of the late Sir THOMAS HANMER to Dr. SMITH, of Oxford, and which it were to be wished, for the Honour of some of the Persons concerned, had been consigned to that Oblivion which it so justly merits. As, however, this matter is revived, and likely, from the celebrity of your Publication, to be read by many, and continued to another Age, I depend upon your known Impartiality and Regard to Literature, to insert the following plain Narrative in Answer to this Extraordinary Letter.

I am, Yours, &c.
C. K.

PHILIP NICHOLS, one of the Writers (and, as he stiles himself, one of the Proprietors) of the Biographia Britannica, had got into his hands three Letters, which, for aught appears, are originals of the late Sir Thomas Hanmer. One of them is the Letter in question, which you have published in your September Magazine, and which certainly conveys a more than indirect charge against the Bishop of Gloucester, as if his Lordship had robbed the spital – that is, that Mr. Warburton had paid a sly, designing visit to Sir Thomas Hanmer, and had so far abused that Gentleman's hospitality, as, from the inspection of the Baronet's papers, to purloin from them whatever he thought proper for an edition of the Plays of Shakespeare which he was then preparing to publish. This Letter was communicated by Nichols to the Bishop, January 29, 1761, who sent it the same day with his observations on it, to one of the principal Proprietors of the Biographia. His Lordship's strictures appeared so full and satisfactory, that even Nichols agreed to omit Sir T. Hanmer's Letter; and the propriety of this omission must be evident to every man of sense and candour who reads it. Nichols, by having this Letter in his possession, and being at liberty to publish it or not, as he should think proper, perhaps expected some great consideration from the Bishop, to whom he applied several times, but who would have nothing to do with him. Finding himself disappointed, he published, in 1763, the Castrated Sheet, accompanied with the most malicious insinuations of the Bishop's conduct.

It now remains to let the Reader judge for himself, by laying before him the Bishop's strictures on this charge, and which were designed to have been printed in the Biographia, if the sheet had not been cancelled (p.246).

This is the article, referred to by 'C. K.' above, from *European Magazine*, 24 (September 1793): 183–4:

BISHOP WARBURTON

Sheet 41 Q, pages 3743, 3744, in the first part of the sixth Volume of the first edition of the Biographia Britannica, was originally castrated at the desire of this learned Prelate: it was, however, reprinted after Sir Thomas Hanmer's Article in the Appendix to the Biographia, and so paged as to be inserted in its original place. The sheet which gave offence to the Bishop contained a letter of Sir Thomas Hanmer's to Dr. Smith, dated October 28, 1742, Milden-Hall; in which, amongst other things, he says, "I am satisfied that there is no edition of Shakespeare *coming* or *likely* to come from Warburton, but it is a report raised to serve some little purpose or other, of which I see that there are many on foot. I have reason to know that Gentleman is very angry with me for a cause of which I think I have no reason to be ashamed, or he to be proud. My acquaintance with him began upon an application from himself, and at his request. The Bishop of Salisbury (Dr. Sherlock) introduced him to me for this purpose only, as was then declared, that as he had many observations upon Shakespeare then lying by him, over and above those printed in Theobald's Book, he much desired to communicate them to me, that I might judge whether any of them were worthy to be added to those emendations which he understood I had been long making upon that author. I received his offer with all the civility I could; upon which a long correspondence began by letters, in which he explained his sense upon many passages, which *sometimes* I thought just, but mostly *wild and out of the way.* Afterwards he made a journey hither, on purpose to see my books: he staid about a week with me, and had the inspection of them, and in all this while I had no other suspicion of any other design, in all the pains he took, but to perfect a correct Text of Shakespeare, of which he seemed very fond. But not long after the views of interest began to shew themselves, several hints were dropped, of the advantage he might receive from publishing the work thus corrected; but as I had no thoughts at all of making it public, so I was more averse to yield to it in such a manner as was likely to produce a paltry edition, by making it the means only of getting a greater sum of money by it. Upon this he flew into a great rage, and there is an end of the story; with which I have thought it best to make you acquainted, that as you mention the working of his friends, you may judge the better of what you see and hear from them, and may make what use you please of the truth of facts which I now have laid before you.

[3] Sir Thomas Hanmer (1677–1746) of Mildenhall, Suffolk, was a speaker of the House of Commons. See *The Correspondence of Sir Thomas Hanmer*, ed. H. Bunbury (London, 1838); and for an account of the printing cost of Hanmer's Shakespeare edition in six volumes quarto, see Harry Carter, *A History of the Oxford University Press*, p.304. According to Dibdin, 'In the year 1747, when Warburton's edition was selling off at 18*s.* a copy (the original price having been 2*l.* 8*s.*), Hanmer's edition, which was published at 3*l.* 3*s.*, rose to 9*l.* 9*s.*, and continued at that price until its reprint in 1771' (*DNB*, Hanmer). However, according to marginalia on the 1755 'Catalogue of Books in Quires' (Appendix B), Andrew Millar bought 35 sets of Warburton's Shakespeare edition for £1 7*s.* per set.

Leslie Stephen outlined the origins of the quarrel: Warburton told Birch in 1737 of his intention to edit Shakespeare; he exchanged notes with Hanmer; both men were initially unaware of the other's intentions; Warburton grew angry at not getting his notes back from Hanmer in 1739; Hanmer wrote to Joseph Smith of Queen's College, Oxford, in 1742 offering his edition and explaining the conflict with Warburton; Philip Nichols, who wanted to print this letter in the entry on Smith in *Biographia Britannica*, showed the proof-sheet to Warburton who then wrote the above letter explaining his side of the dispute; Nichols disclosed the contents of Hanmer's letter in *The Castrated Sheet of Sir Thomas Hanmer* in 1763 (*DNB*, Warburton).

[4] Thomas Sherlock (noted in text).

[5] The present location of Hanmer's letters is unknown although Gertrude Warburton's inventory includes letters to 'Sr. Thos. Hanmer & Theobald —— a large Bundle' (3 May 1780, below).

[6] Possibly John Knapton who co-published reprints of Hanmer's edition of Shakespeare 'printed from the Oxford edition in quarto' in 1745, 1747, 1748 and 1750–1.

[7] 'There mov'd Montalto with superior air;/His stretch'd-out arm display'd a Volume fair' (*Dunciad*, 4 lines 105–06; *TE*, 5: 351).

[8] *Biographia Britannica: or, the lives of the most eminent persons*, vol. 1, London: Printed for W. Innys, W. Meadows, J. Walthoe, T. Cox, A. Ward, J. and P. Knapton, T. Osborne, S. Birt, D. Browne, T. Longman and T. Shewell, H. Whitridge, R. Hett, C. Hitch, T. Astley, S. Austen, C. Davis, R. Manby and H.S. Cox, C. Bathurst, J. and R. Tonson and S. Draper, J. Robinson, J. Hinton, J. and J. Rivington, and M. Cooper, 1747. The imprint of volume 6, part i (which contains the biography of Smith), reads: London: Printed for J. Walthoe, T. Osborne, H. Whitridge, C. Hitch and L. Hawes, R. Manby, J.

and R. Tonson, H. Woodfall, J. Rivington, C. Bathurst, L. Davis and C. Reymers, R. Baldwin, W. Johnston, G. Keith, J. Richardson, T. Longman, B. Law and Co., G. Kearsley, and J. Hinxman, 1763. The biographical account of Hanmer which begins the 'Appendix to the Supplement' of the 1766 *Biographia Britannica*, vol. 6, part ii, alludes to the Warburton-Hanmer dispute and Nichols' *Castrated Sheet*: 'To this pamphlet was annexed the castrated sheet, reprinted with additions obtained after it was first printed in the *Biographia Britannica*, in order to restore it to its proper place...' (p.223 and n.).

[9] The contributor appended the following note to Warburton's letter: 'To this very manly and satisfactory vindication, upon an attack equally malicious and unsupported, it may be necessary just to add, that Sir Thomas Hanmer's letter is addressed to a person who was not very likely to have given the Bishop an opportunity to have vindicated himself, and who very possibly did not believe one single word of the allegations it contained' (p.247).

Warburton's version of events would appear to be borne out in a letter he sent to Hanmer from Newark in May 1739 (in the Pierpont Morgan Library):

Newarke 21 May 1739

Sir,

Having been informed that you was in treaty with a Bookseller about a new Edition of Shakespear, I beg leave to remind you of all that has pass'd between us; not with any intention to complain; for that is below me; but in order to shew the justice of the request I am going to make to you; and which occasions you this trouble.

About three Years ago my Lord of Salisbury, whose favours to me necessarily give him an absolute power over me, desired I would communicate to you what remarks I had made upon Shakespear: which command I so readily complied with, that I immediately put into your hands a paper I chanced to have then in Town; and, as soon as I got down into the Country, began a weekly correspondence on my part, which continued for above a twelvemonth; In which I transcribed a great number of notes, remarks, & emendations &c sufficient to furnish out a new Edition. And all this without the least reserve.

When this was done, you was pleased to invite me, the following Summer, to Mildenhall, to look over your book. I went. I looked it over: and, before I left you, made you the offer of taking upon my selfe the drudgery of a new Edition, where the text should be settled according to your own pleasure. You appeared not to be averse to it: but gave me to understand, that as you intended no profit to your selfe from the Edition, so I was not to look for any. I took the liberty of telling you that such intention became your quality: but that that conduct which was suitable to your fortune & Station would be a ridiculous affectation in mine. There the matter rested till my return; and then I repeated, in a letter to you, the substance of my offer; and endeavoured to shew the reasonableness of it. To this you returned me for answer, that you believed it could not be made worth my while to undertake a new edition. Notwithstanding all this discouragement, amidst all my endeavours to oblige you, I still, Sir, you know, went on in communicating to you, with my usual frankness, my Observations on Shakespear, and in returning the best answer I could to your Queries.

Last Spring you was pleased to inform me you should be in London abt Easter, & expressed an inclination of seeing me there. I wrote you word I should be there. I was so & paid my respects to you. I then expected you had considered fully of the matter, & would communicate your thoughts freely to me. To engage you to declare your selfe I told you, as was true, that I had been asked by some of the

Society for the encouragement of learning to print an Edition of Shakespear with them. And, at the same time to assure you that I was disposed to do nothing but in concert with you. I told you, you might expect to be troubled with some more of my remarks on Shakespear. Yet all this drew nothing from you. And you forced me to leave you in an Opinion that you was resolved I should have no concern in the Edition. And it now appears I was not mistaken. After all this I thought my selfe at liberty to declare publicly that I would give an Edition of Shakespear my selfe. Which was only returning to the resolution in which my Lord Bishop of Sarum [i.e. Salisbury] found me when he first asked me to communicate my remarks to you. And to shew the Public I am in earnest, I have given a specimen & Plan of a New Edition to the Authors of the Universal Dictionary to be inserted into the Article of Shakespear.

This, Sir, I am sure you will do me the Justice to own is a true state of the Case. You hold your selfe disengaged. I complain not. All I mean is to shew the reasonableness of my request. Which is only this that you would be so good as to return me all my letters of remarks & papers: and, as the contents of them are as much my property as any thing can be any Man's, that you would be pleased to dispense with doing me the Honour of using or inserting any of the emendations or Remarks into your Edition. A place where I should have the greatest honour to appear in, but that I shall, my selfe, have occasion for these materials. This request is perhaps in part needless. For I remember you told me you intended to have no notes, but that your emendations should support themselves. But as the complying with it is a matter of great Consequence to me tho' of little or none to you, you will be so good to excuse my having made it, & for now again repeating it. Be pleased to send the letters & papers sealed up, to Mr Gyles's Bookseller in Holborne who will convey them to me. Your Compliance with this will engage me to profess my selfe

Hond. Sr. Your most
humble Servant
W. Warburton

Address and postmark: To the Honourable Sr Thomas Hanmer in Grovenor-Street   London   21/MA
Endorsed: May 21. 1739   Mr Warburton with a copy of my answer

---

Warburton *to* John Nourse   8 June 1761
Historical Society of Pennsylvania: Dreer Collection   Prior Park

Prior Park   June 8 1761

Sir

I see in your Advertisem[en]t Histoire de l'Universite de Paris par Crevier[1] & Suite de la Collection complette de Voltaire[2]

I desire you would send me these in boards. But if you do not send them to me by a Machine which comes to Bath the latter end of this week they will come too late for I shall have left the place the begin[n]ing of next week on my Visitation.

Your very faithfull Friend
& humble Servt
W. Gloucester

if there be any more of my journals come you will send them with the above.

Envelope and postmark: To Mr Nourse Bookseller in the Strand London W. *Gloucester*. Free   [1?]0/JV BATH

[1] Jean Baptiste Louis Crevier, *Histoire de l'université de Paris*, 7 vols. (Paris, 1761).
[2] *Collection complette des oeuvres de Mr. de Voltaire*, 17 vols. ([Geneva], 1757 [1756]).

Warburton *to* Richard Hurd   27 December 1761
LLEP, pp. 246–7 (Letter CLIV)   Prior Park

Prior Park, December 27th, 1761.

LET me wish you (as we all do) all the happiness that goodness can derive from this season.

The honour this country derives from the Duke of York's visit can hardly compensate the bad news of a Spanish war, which puts the city of London in a consternation. This event does honour to Mr. Pitt's sagacity, and the wisdom of his advice upon it. Whether this war, which was forseen by no body to be inevitable but by him, can be successfully managed by any body but him, time must shew; for I would not pretend to be wiser than our teachers, I mean, the *news-writers*, who refer all doubtful cases, as the Treasury does all desperate payments, to time. The best thing which time (since I wrote last) has brought to pass, is the advancement of Mr. Yorke to be Attorney-General. I would have you, by all means, write him your compliments upon it, for, with a high value, he has a great friendship for you. What you say of Hume is true: and (what either I said in my last, or intended to say), you have taught him to write so much better, that he has thoroughly confirmed your system.

I have been both too ill and too lazy to finish my discourse on the Holy Spirit. Not above half of it is yet printed.

I have been extremely entertained with the wars of Fingal.[1] It can be no cheat, for I think the enthusiasm of this specifical sublime could hardly be counterfeit. A modern writer would have been less simple and uniform.—— Thus far had I written when your letter of Christmas-day came to hand; as you will easily understand by my submitting to take shame upon me, and assuring you that I am full convinced of my false opinion delivered just above concerning Fingal. I did not consider the matter as I ought. Your reasons for the forgery are unanswerable. And of all these reasons, but one occurred to me, the *want of external evidence*, and this I own did shock me. But you have waked me from a very pleasing dream; and made me hate the impostor, which is the most uneasy sentiment of our waking thoughts.

I am much pleased with what you tell me of a set of sermons ad populum, I mean to people of condition. For nature formed you for, and providence will bring you to, another Theatre. Your judgment of Clarke is like your other judgements of men, perfectly exact and true.

I received a letter from Mason of the 14th, and he tells me news —— that your letters on Chivalry are in the press, and he desires when they come out, I would send them to him in covers.

Sterne has published his fifth and sixth Volumes of Tristram. They are wrote pretty much like the first and second, but whether they will restore his reputation as a writer with the public, is another question. —— The fellow himself is an irrecoverable scoundrel.

My discourse on the Holy Spirit, grows upon me, especially in the latter part about the Mothodists [*sic*], which is the part I could have wished would have grown the least. But a wen grows faster than sound flesh. I have yet printed off but 72 pages.

I think the Booksellers have an intention of employing Baskerville to print Pope in 4to. so they sent me the last 8vo. to look over. I have added the inclosed to the long note in the beginning of the *Rape of the Lock*, in answer to an impertinence of Joseph Warton. When you have perused it, you will send it back.[2]

I have sometimes thought of collecting my scattered anecdotes and critical observations together, for the foundation of a life of Pope, which the booksellers teaze me for. If I do that, all of that kind must be struck out of the notes of that edition. You could help me nobly to fill up the canvas.[3]

[1] James Macpherson's *Ossian*.

[2] This addition was evidently not printed: Warburton's long note on Rosicrucianism at the opening of *Rape of the Lock* (canto 1, line 20) underwent a number of minor changes in wording in the 1766 and 1769 *Works*, vol. 1, but there was nothing to irritate a future editor of Pope. Hurd perhaps advised discretion.

[3] Hurd declined this invitation to assist Warburton with his literary projects at this time, which paved the way for Owen Ruffhead's 1769 *Life of Pope*.

Warburton *to* [Thomas Newton]   17 April 1762
Pierpont Morgan Library   Prior Park

My dear Lord,
    Your notice of his Grace's entertainment is very kind. My Wife's ill state of health prevents me from getting to Town.

I intrust it to you to make my best compliments to his Grace, & how glad I should have been of doing my selfe the honour to pay my duty to him on this occasion.

You was very welcome to have taken a copy of the *Letters to Kennicot*.[1] I remember you asked to see one of my circular Letters abt Confirmation. I had no printed copy. But I found by accident the press-copy which had been sent me back. The great success of it will be sufficient to shew you, that when you have fixed upon a Confirmation you cannot do better than to be very serious with your Clergy & write them something that will shew them they are not words of course. —— My Discourse on the holy Spirit grows upon me towards the latter end, but I hope to have it out before Whitsontide.

I have seen *Hogarth's* print of the *Ghost*.[2] It is a horrid composition of lewd Obscenity & blasphemous prophaneness for which I detest the artist & have lost all esteem for the man. The best is, that the worst parts of it have a good chance of not being understood by the people.

My dear Lord your most
affectionate & faithfull Friend
W. Gloucester

Prior Park
Apr. 17. 1762.

Note (in another hand): To Bp Newton

[1] Thomas Rutherforth, *A Letter to the Reverend Mr. Kennicott, in which his defence of the Samaritan Pentateuch is examined* (Cambridge: printed by J. Bentham for Messrs. Thurlbourn and Woodyer; and sold by J. Richardson and J. Beecroft, A. Millar, and C. Bathurst, London, 1761); and, with the same imprint, *A Second Letter to the Reverend Dr. Kennicott* (1762).

[2] There is no print by this name in Ronald Paulson's *Hogarth's Graphic Works: first complete edition*, 2 vols. (New Haven and London, 1965). Warburton had probably seen a copy of Hogarth's *Credulity, Superstition, and Fanaticism* which was published in April 1762. Included in this print is the notorious Cock Lane Ghost 'who is referred to specifically at the top of the congregation's thermometer, where she holds a mallet for knocking in one hand and a candelabra in the other' (1: 243). Fanny Lynes, the Cock Lane Ghost, also appeared as 'Ms Fanny' standing in the pillory (again holding her mallet, used for ghostly knocking) beside John Wilkes (who had attacked Hogarth in *North Briton*, no.17) in *The Times, Plate II*, although Hogarth suppressed this print. Warburton had another reason to be angry with Hogarth at this time: the Bishop's head was supposedly used to model the first hair-piece in the row of the Episcopal order (from the coronation of George III on 22 September 1761) in *The Five Orders of Periwigs* (November 1761; see Paulson no.208). Charles Churchill's *The Ghost* made capital of the Cock Lane Ghost story, attacking Lord Mansfield and Dr. Johnson, who took part in the investigation. Books 1 and 2 of *The Ghost* were published in March 1762; book 3 appeared in October 1763 with book 4 following in November.

Warburton *to* Thomas Becket   9 May 1762
Historical Society of Pennsylvania: Gratz Collection   Prior Park

Mr Becket

I beg you would direct the inclosed to Mr Dalrimple who it seems is now Sr David Dalrimple.[1] but as I neither know his titles nor address, I have left the direction to you and have franked it, because I suppose it is to go by the post

Your assured freind & Servt
W. Gloucester

P.P. May 9 1762

[1] David Dalrymple (1726–92) was the eldest son of Sir James Dalrymple (*d.* 1750); raised to the bench of the Court of Session as Lord Hailes in 1766. The National Library of Scotland holds 26 letters from Warburton to Lord Hailes between 1762 and 1776 (MS. 25295, ff.120–69).

Warburton *to* [John Nourse]   28 July 1762
Yale University, Beinecke Library: Osborn Files   Gloucester

Gloucester —— July 28 1762

Dr Sr

I recd (as you intimated) two copies of the maid in Orleans: one of which I shall bring back to you.[1] I have likewise yours of the 24 with an acct. of your sending Rousseau of Education,[2] which I shall take care to have sent to me hither. Any thing that comes to you worth my having will always be acceptable to me

Being your assured
friend & faithfull humble
Servt
W. Gloucester

[1] Voltaire's burlesque poem on Joan of Arc, *La pucelle d'Orléans, poeme heroi-comique* (London [Amsterdam], 1756). *The Maid in Orleans* was advertised in *LM*, 27 (1758): 485 (2 vols., 6*s.* each). Pye, the bookseller listed, is not in Plomer.
[2] Jean Jacques Rousseau, *Émile, ou l'education* (1762).

Warburton *to* [Sir Edward Littleton][1]   15 May 1763
Folger Shakespeare Library: W.a.57 (3)   Prior Park

Dear Sir

I have the honour of your favour of the 4. And the satisfaction I should have had in an application to the C[h]amberlain, was much exceeded in the pleasure I have had, in seeing my honourable Friend express so noble a disdain of vice, corruption & profligacy of manners. Go on, Dear Sir, in vindicating that most respectable of Characters, *An honest Country Gentleman of Quality*, by an open detestation of the Spawn of Arthur's, whether of Whigg or Tory complexion, as alike fatal to all public & private virtue: And encourage in your selfe *that strong antipathy of Good to Bad*,[2] as the only security from an almost universal infection.

I have the honour to be Dear Sir
Your very affectionate & Obedient
humble Servant
W. Gloucester

Prior Park
May 15 1763

Endorsed: Bishop of Gloucester 15: May: 1763:

[1] Other letters in this group of manuscripts are addressed to Sir Edward Littleton, Bart., in Staffordshire.
[2] An allusion to Pope: 'Ask you what Provocation I have had?/The strong Antipathy of Good to Bad', 'Dialogue II', lines 197–8 (*TE*, 4: 324).

Warburton *to* Ralph Allen   16 November 1763
SUP, pp.224–7   Grosvenor Square, London

Grosvenor Square, Nov. 16, 1763.
Honoured Sir,
    I have sat down to write you an account of what passed yesterday in the House of Lords, on the opening of the session. But, before I begin, I must premise how I came to have that share in it which I had.
    On my coming to town, I found a letter from Lord Halifax, intimating that it was desired that I should be in town at the opening of the Parliament. In about a week after Lord Sandwich came to me from the same authority, with the most execrable papers in his hand that I believe ever polluted the light. They were parodies in print of the *Essay on Man* and the *Universal Prayer* by Pope, and of the *Veni Creator* in the "office of making Priests and Bishops." The *Essay on Man* is called an *Essay on Woman*, "with Notes and Commentary by Dr. Warburton." He desired to know whether I was willing to have him prosecuted for breach of privilege. I said, that though I was so diabolically treated as to have my name put to such a heap of diabolic lewdness and blasphemy, and other insults in the book, yet I despised the man as so infinitely beneath me, that I was in no disposition to prosecute him, unless the King desired it

as for his service. He said it was much so; and I consented that he (Lord Sandwich) should move it, and I would speak what I thought fit on the occasion.

When I had wrote thus far I was called to the House; else it had been my intention to give you a minute history of the whole of yesterday's transaction. But I must defer it to my next, and shall only tell you at present, that the crime was received by the House with the utmost astonishment and detestation. It was fully proved, and he was voted guilty of it. But before punishment he was to be heard, as to-morrow; but this morning Wilkes fought a duel with Martin, and had two bullets lodged in his body, which Hawkins extracted, and declares he may live.[1] So that this action of madness and despair will retard the continuance of his prosecution, both in our House and in the House of Commons; for the same day a message came to the King from that House, complaining of the North Briton, No. 45, which has proved to be his by the same evidence that proved his diabolic parodies in ours. The House voted it scandalous, infamous, and tending to a *treasonable* insurrection. Mr. Pitt objected to the word *treasonable*, and divided with a minority of 111 against 270; C. Townshend with the minority, but spoke nothing. If he lives he will be expelled that House, and pilloried, fined, and imprisoned, I suppose, by ours.

I would not lose this early post, just to give you the sum of things. I reserve the particulars to my next.

> I am, honoured Sir,
> Your most dutiful nephew
> and faithful servant,
> W. Warburton.

P.S. You cannot conceive the horrors of this crime. I shall send you a copy of my speech: I exaggerate nothing, and by that you may judge.[2]

I told you some time ago that I was sure the opposition would degenerate into a *faction*. It has done so. The people see it; and they are likely to be ruined.

---

[1] 'Mr. Graves extracted the ball'; and on December 16, the House of Commons sent Wilkes an order 'That doctor Heberden, physician, and Mr. Caesar Hawkins, one of his majesty's serjeant-surgeons, be desired to attend John Wilkes, esq. from time to time, at proper intervals, to observe the progress of his cure', *The Correspondence of the late John Wilkes*, introd. John Almon, 5 vols. (London, 1804; rpt. New York, 1970), 2: 17–18.

[2] For Warburton's speech, see *SUP*, pp.277–83.

Warburton *to* Ralph Allen   17 November 1763
SUP, pp.227–31   Grosvenor Square, London

Grosvenor Square, Nov. 17, 1763.

Honoured Sir,

In my letter of yesterday I was forced to break off my narrative, where I told you I consented, for the King's service, to prosecute Wilkes. The whole proceeding was well planned, digested, and executed; and the secret so well kept, that when Lord Sandwich opened it, there were only two or three of the Cabinet Council that knew any thing of the matter. But it being immediately on the King's retiring after his speech, the House, I think, was fuller tha[n] ever I knew, and a great crowd of the foreign ministers just before me; but when Sir Sept.[1] found I intended to speak, he very dexterously removed them all to another part of the House.

Lord Sandwich began with all the expressions of horror to open the affair. He read many parts that he supposed were not too shocking; and it was necessary to support the charge, that some should be read. In the midst, Lord Lyttelton affected to be so much shocked, that he rose up, and desired no more might be read; but the House said, Go on. When he had gone through those parts which it was possible to be heard read, he was then to proceed to examine witnesses to prove Wilkes to be the author. When he had done his speech, and before the witnesses were examined, I rose up, and made a speech to the House, a copy of which I here enclose, that you may judge of this diabolic enormity; for nothing is aggravated.

When I had done, Lord Sandwich proceeded to the examination of witnesses; the sum of which was, that Wilkes gave them to be printed to the evidence, corrected them himself, owned that he was the author, and that it cost him great pains and labour; that thirteen copies were printed, and no more. By the way, Lord Sandwich told me that, before the Parliament met, Wilkes, who had dispersed these copies to his friends, called them all in for fear that any one should escape into the enemy's hands; and then thought himself secure.

In the course of the examination, it appeared that some letters which were produced of Wilkes, to show he was the author, had been seized by the Secretary of State's warrant. On which Temple rose up, and said he had as great an abhorrence of the *Parodies* as any Lord in the House (when it is generally reported and believed, that he had them in his possession, shewed them to others, and was much delighted with them); but that the legality of the method by which they were obtained ought to be inquired into; that the liberty of the subject was concerned in it; and a great deal of nonsense to that purpose. He spoke wretchedly ill, as usual, and was as wretchedly seconded by Lord Sandys, who is gone over to the opposition. They were answered by the Duke of Bedford, Lord Halifax, Lord Sandwich, and by the Chancellor[2] with his usual heat. Still Temple hung upon it, and I believe rose up half a dozen different times, till Lord Mansfield, finding there would be no end, rose up, and, as he always does, ended the dispute at once. He said he knew nothing of this prosecution till he came into the House (which was true, for I first told him of it at his coming into the House). He said nothing was more absurd than the objection. The coming by evidence illegally does not make that evidence illegal in the trial of a criminal. That frequently criminals have been taken up by such as had no authority to do so; but that hinders not their being brought to justice. In short, he exposed and ridiculed the objection so effectually, that the House called out to *go on*. So that the wretch was fully convicted, and the House proceeded to the severest vote against the criminal. But here again Lord Mansfield interposed, and said he had his doubts whether it was regular to come to that vote till Wilkes had been heard. On which Lord Sandwich said, if he had such doubts, he would defer the vote to this day. While this was doing in the House of Lords, they were prosecuting the effect of the King's Message against Wilkes in the House of Commons. When the wretch heard the news of what was done in our House, he was supposed to be so thunderstruck as to become desperate; and yesterday morning he sent a challenge, with most opprobrious language, to Martin, to meet him immediately in the field. Martin did so, and lodged a brace of bullets in his body; so that we are much afraid he will escape the pillory, and a thousand actions besides. If he recovers, and the House of Commons expel him immediately, then Sir Sept. takes him up. If his expulsion hangs, then there must be a conference between the two Houses before we can get him...

I break off at present to go to the House, being summoned on Wilkes's affair. When I come back I propose to finish my letter.

I have just come from the House, where they have passed two more votes against Wilkes. The one is, that (besides the offence against me, which is to be punished by the House,) the House shall address the King, that he will be pleased to give order to the Attorney-General to prosecute Wilkes, his aiders and abettors, for blasphemy, in his courts of justice. Of these aiders and abettors *Churchill* is supposed to be one; and some think there are others of higher rank.

The other vote is, that, considering Wilkes's inability, by reason of his wound, to appear to-day, that this affair be resumed next Tuesday; and that nothing shall excuse his attendance but the oaths of his physicians and surgeons, that he is incapable of attending.

Yesterday the House of Commons voted their address upon the King's speech, without a division.

Wilkes is supposed to be out of danger of every thing but the gallows.

I am, honoured Sir,
Your most dutiful nephew
and devoted servant,
W. Warburton.

[1] Sir Septimus Robinson was Gentleman Usher of the Black Rod, responsible for maintaining order in the House of Lords, from 16 April 1761 until his death on 5 September 1765. I am grateful to D. J. Johnson, Deputy Clerk of the Records, Record Office, House of Lords, for this information.

[2] Robert Henley was Lord Chancellor from 1761 to 1766.

Warburton *to* Ralph Allen[1]   26 November 1763
Bath Reference Library: A.L. 367   Grosvenor Square, London

Grosvenor Square, Nov. 26, 1763.

Honoured Sir

On thursday night the House of commons sat till two a clock in the Morning, and came to these two resolutions

1.   that the North Briton, No. 45 is an insolent & scandalous & false abuse on the person of the King & the two houses of Parliament tending to raise traytorous and seditious disturbances to the overthrow of the Constitution & that it shall be burnt by the hand of the common hangman. [The lawyers say it is every thing short of Treason.]

2.   That privilege of parliament does not extend to crimes & misdemeanours of this Nature.

Mr York never distinguished himself to so much advantage on the court side of the question, and against the party he is gone over to, as on this occasion. He was universally applauded. And Mr Pitt appeared to be so much nettled, that he abused the Lawyers in general, who that day were all against him. However he said that "as to that impious Man, who occasioned the dispute, and had blasphemed God & the King, he ought to be thrust out of the House" and then thrust out his crouch [crutch] in the action of a man driving a noxious animal from him.

The next day the Commons sent to desire a conference with us. And the two Houses met in the painted chamber, when the commons desired our concurrence to their two votes. So we parted, & returned to our several Houses. When we came to ours, & made our report, it was agreed to immediately, nomine contradicente, that we should concurr with them in their first vote. The Ld Temple desired it might be put off till the Lords had been summoned to attend on this occasion. D[uke]. of Bedford bad him look round & see whether he had ever known a fuller house. And if they were already there, what occasion for a summons? As to the 2d resolution, it was agreed that we should take it into consideration next tuesday. Wilks continues to be yet in danger. The monster is so singularly circumstanced that his greatest enemies wish his life, to bring him to punishment, and his greatest Friends wish his death, to shake off that load upon them, and perhaps to prevent some discoveries. Poor Lord Hardwick is supposed to be going off.

My duty & love to all.
Honoured Sir your most dutifull
Nephew & faithfull Servt
W. Warburton

Gr Sq
Novr 26 1763

[1] Printed in *SUP*, pp.231–3, with stylistic changes and without the last sentence.

Warburton *to* Ralph Allen   1 December 1763
Yale University, Beinecke Library: Grosvenor Square, London
Osborn Files

Grosvenor Square, Dec. 1, 1763.

Honoured Sir,

What passed to-day in the House was, several conferences with the Commons to adjust the ceremony of agreeing with them in the votes against the North Briton, the having it burnt by the common hangman on Saturday, and the two Houses addressing the King on the occasion next Monday.

To-day sixteen Lords in the minority protested against what passed on Tuesday, of no privilege of Parliament for seditious libels. The protest is, it seems, a very long and a very furious one. The Duke of Devon was in the number, but not the Duke of Newcastle.

I am, honoured Sir,
Your most dutiful nephew,
and faithful servant,
W. Gloucester.

Warburton *to* [James Harris][1]   16 February 1765
Yale University, Beinecke Library: Grosvenor Square, London
Osborn Files

Grosvenor Square Feb. 16 1765
Worthy Sir
   I have my best thanks to return you for the valuable Present of your
noble work on Grammar.[2] A work much wanted, and which a number
of imperfect attempts did but weakly supply. You are very candid &
modest in your account of some who have gone before you in this
carreer, who might, thereby, become able to mislead, did not your fuller
& juster Rules prevent that inconvenience.

I am with great esteem,
Sir, your very Obedient
& faithfull humble Servant
W. Gloucester

[1] Clive Probyn has searched extensively through Harris's correspondence for *The
Sociable Humanist: the life and works of James Harris 1709–1780* (Oxford, 1991) and found no
letters to Warburton. See also his article, 'James Harris to Parson Adams in Germany:
some light on Fielding's Salisbury set', *Philological Quarterly*, 64 (1985): 130–9, for
Harris's support of Upton's *Critical Observations on Shakespeare* (p.134).
[2] James Harris, *Hermes*. See Warburton's letter of 11 January 1752, above.

Warburton *to* John Nourse   25 May 1765
BL: Add. MS. 12113, ff.12–13   Prior Park

P.P. May 25 1765

Dr Sr
   I have yours of the 23   I would have Wolfius[1] bound in the french
way but very carefully & well & with as large a margin as is possible. I
suppose the french Materia medica of G.[2] is bound by this time   I
would have it sent by the Machine. Pray send me by Leak's parcell
2.   Mably's Observ. sur l'H. d F.[3]
22   Lucette 2 parties 12°
100 Le success d'un Fat.[4]
pray let Wolfius be sent hither as soon as done.
   I heartily wish you a good Journey to Par. see if you can get me there a
book I mentioned to you some time ago   it was published a year or two
ago at Turin by an ecclesiastic   it is a commentary on a Bas relief that
he pretends was a representation of the Elusinian Mysteries. —— There
was an old *litteral* translation of Don Quixote in french[5] published soon

after the writing the book   if you could pick up a good copy of that for me I should be obliged to you   And if you can meet with the following
Fasciculus prim. nova librorum variorum collectienes Magdsburg 1709 8°.[6]
De odio humani generie Christianis objecto 8°. by J. Fred. Gruner[7]
Candelaio Comedia del Bruno Nolaio.[8] Par. 1582 12°.
Salvian de Gubernatione Dei Baluze[9] Par. 1669 8°.
Alphensi de Vargas[10] – Delatio de Stratagemalis & sophismatis politicis Societ. Jesu Gen. 1642⟨12°⟩
Jacobi Gothofroius[11] opuscula varia. Geneva 1654. 2°
Borri[12] – Chiave del cabinetto di cav. Rossi Gen. 1681. 12°

Faithfully yours
W. Gloucester

Note (f.12v.; in another hand): Prior Park May 25. 1765 Bishop of Gloucester
Endorsed (f.12v.): Prior Park May 25. 1765 The Bishop of Gloucester
Note (in yet another hand): presented to Mr. Upcott 17 June 1832
Address, frank and stamp (f.12): To Mr J. Nourse the King's Bookseller in the Strand London W. Gloucester. Free. 27/MA FREE BATH

[1] Possibly C. F. von Wolff, *Jus naturæ*, 8 vols. (1742–8); *Jus gentium* (1749); or *Philosophia moralis*, 5 vols. (1750–3).

[2] Possibly William Carter, *Generale materiæ medicæ compendium ... autore G. C. Coll. Med. Lond.* [1707].

[3] Gabriel Bonnot de Mably, *Observations sur l'histoire de France*, 2 vols. (Geneva, 1765). This set is still in the Hurd Library.

[4] Untraced.

[5] Possibly Cesar Ovdin's translation, *L'ingenieux don Quixote* (Paris, 1614).

[6] Untraced.

[7] Johann Friedrich Gruner, *De odio humani generis Christianis olim a Romanis objecto* (Coburgi, 1755).

[8] By Giordano Bruno.

[9] Salvianus Massiliensis and Vincentius Lirinensis, *Opera*, ed. S. Baluzius (Paris, 1669).

[10] Alphensus de Vargas (Caspar Schoppe), *A. de V.... relatio ad reges et principes christianos de stratagematis et sophismatis politicis societatis Jesu* ([Padua?], 1636; [Cologne?], 1641; [Genoa?, 1642?]).

[11] Jacques Godefroy, *J. Gothofredi opuscula varia, juridica, politica, historica, critica*, 7 pts. (Geneva, 1654–68).

[12] Joseph Francis Borri (1627–95). According to Hugh James Rose in *A New General Dictionary* (London, 1850), 'Some works, printed at Geneva, in 1681, are attributed to him.'

1766–1780

Warburton continued to write sermons: *A Sermon... for the Propagation of the Gospel in Foreign Parts* (1766); and *Sermons and Discourses on Various Subjects and Occasions* (1767). The quarto edition of Pope's *Works* was finally published in 1769 with Ruffhead's *Life of Pope* in lieu of Warburton's biography. Wilkes' story of Gertrude Warburton's alleged affair with Thomas Potter was included in *The New Foundling Hospital for Wit* (3: 89–105) in 1769. Gertrude auctioned off many of her late uncle's effects and leased out Prior Park in October 1769.

Ralph Allen Warburton, the Bishop's only son, died early in the summer of 1775 from a consumption. Warburton never completely recovered from the shock. Plans for continuing with the third volume of *The Divine Legation* were abandoned. John Knapton died in 1770. His executors, George Knapton, John Partridge and Robert Horsfield, signed Gosling's ledger which showed a final balance of £331 10s. 5½d. on 4 October 1770. In his will he left £4000 to be invested and some £1400 in bequests.

The case of *Millar* v. *Taylor* over perpetual copyright ended in 1769 in favour of Millar (who had died the year before), but the decision was overturned in 1774 in *Donaldson* v. *Becket*, thus ushering in a new era of publishing. Warburton died on 7 June 1779 and was buried in Gloucester Cathedral. His will was proved on July 6 (PRO: Prob.11.328). A copy of his will, witnessed by William Griffith and Thomas Price on 30 May 1777, is kept in the Gloucestershire Record Office.

In May 1780, Gertrude Warburton sent an inventory of her late husband's papers to Hurd. His widow sold his library, including books bequeathed by Pope, to Hurd who placed them in his new library in Hartlebury Castle. Hurd assembled Warburton's writings for the 1788 edition of his *Works*, the expenses for which were met by his widow. Gertrude eventually married her late husband's chaplain, Martin Stafford Smith, who inherited Warburton's papers when she died in 1796.

Warburton *to* [John Nourse]   1 May 1766
Yale University, Beinecke Library: Grosvenor Square, London
Osborn Files

Sir

    I shall keep the little novel of Mad. Beaumond and like it so well that I desire to see her other larger novel.[1] Valliant has published a little posthumous thing of Fathr. Harduin's.[2] I desire you to get it for me & send it with the other, and what else you think worth sending

always faithfully yours
W. Gloucester

Grosvr Square May 1st 1766.

Endorsed: The Bishop Gloucester May 1. 1766

---

[1] Anne Louise Élie de Beaumont, *The History of a Young Lady of Distinction*, 2 vols.

(London, 1754); *The History of the Marquis de Rochelle*, 2 vols. (London, 1765; 2nd ed., 1766).

[2] Jean Hardouin, *Joannis Harduini, Jesuitae, ad censuram scriptorum veterum prolegomena* (London: P. Vaillant, 1766).

Jonathan Toup *to* John Nourse[1]   24 October 1766
Edinburgh University Library: St. Martin's-by-Looe, Cornwall
La.II.646, 255

St Martins 24 Oct.

Sir,

I had a letter yesterday from Mr Bowyer. he says he cannot undertake my *Crit. Epistle* for want of able compositors. he is angry, I find, about my late Inscription to the Bp of Gloucester. But what has Mr Bowyer to do with the squabbles of Bp. W. & his antagonists? I have wrote him again by this post, & desired he would undertake this, as well as the former. I would have you talk with him about it, & let me know. I could send the copy up immediately. If he will not, we must look out for some other hand; but would much rather have him. I hope when his passion subsides, he will come again to himself.

I am your most obedt Servt.

Jo. Toup.

I find Mr Reiske has publishd his *Animadvers. on Diogenes Laertius*, & I see by ye paper you have *Gregorius de [D]ialectis*.[2] I should be glad of both. you may send them to Mr Woodley of Norfolk Street, who will send me a Box soon——

Address (*verso*): To Mr John Nourse Opposite Catharine Street in the Strand London
Endorsement: [St] Martin 24 Octr 1766 The Revd Mr Toup answerd Novr 22
Postmark: [24?]/OC

[1] Jonathan Toup (1713–85) was a philologist and editor of classical texts. His tutor at Exeter College, Oxford, was John Upton, author of *Critical Observations on Shakespeare* (London, 1746), the second edition (1748) of which criticized Warburton's 1747 edition of Shakespeare. Toup's *Epistola critica* (London: J. Nourse, 1767) was dedicated to Warburton (*DNB*; *LA*, 2: 339–45); a copy remains in the Hurd Library. See John Feather, 'John Nourse and his Authors', *Studies in Bibliography*, 34 (1981): 205–26.

[2] Johann Jacob Reiske, *Animadversionum ad Græcos auctores*, 5 vols. (Leipzig, 1757–66); and Gregorius [Pardus], Archbishop of Corinth, *Gregorius, Corinthi metropolita, de dialectis* (Leyden, 1766).

Warburton *to* [John Nourse]   16 December 1766
Yale University, Beinecke Library: Osborn Files   Prior Park

                                        Prior Park Dec 16 1766
Sir
    I believe that Mr James Hutton[1] will, next week, leave a book for me
with you. I would have it sent to me together with the Physical
directions of that Swiss Physician in two little vols in french. I had one of
them, of you, before, but have given it away —— and Recherches sur
l'Origine des Decouvertes attribuees aux Modernes &c advertised by
Vaillant[2]
    I desire the favour of you to send as usual a double Barrell of the best
Colchester oysters by the next Carrier directed *To Mrs Warburton at
Brant Broughton near Newarke*

                                        Your faithfull friend
                                            & Servant
                                        W. Gloucester.
Frank (pasted on): W. Gloucester Free

[1] More likely the Moravian James Hutton (1715–95), whose wife was Swiss, than the
Edinburgh geologist of the same name.
[2] Louis Dutens, *Récherches sur l'origine des découvertes attribuées aux modernes* (Paris, 1766).

Warburton *to* [John Nourse]   30 November 1767
Historical Society of Pennsylvania: Gratz Collection   Prior Park

Dear Sir
    If any books for me be come I desire you would send them hither such
as the remaining Vols in 4° of Gillet's new Translation of Josephus in
french,[1] any more vols of the Mem. of belles Let. 4°[2] —— any more vols
of the Hist. of the lower Empire[3] and of the Histoire de France by
Villeret. &c[4]

                                        I am always faithfully
                                            Yours
                                        W. Gloucester
Prior Park
Novr 30 1767

[1] Warburton ordered Gillet's translation of Josephus in his letters to Nourse of 9
September 1758 and 2 October 1760, above.
[2] Académie des Inscriptions et Belles-Lettres, *Histoire de l'Académie... avec les mémoires de
litterature*, 50 vols. (Paris, 1717–1809 [1808]); in quarto. In 1742 the Knaptons, Francis

Cogan and John Nourse published an abridged translation by John Martyn and Ephraim Chambers, *The Philosophical History and Memoirs of the Royal Academy of Sciences at Paris*, 5 vols.

[3] Charles le Beau's 29-volume *Histoire du bas-empire*; see Warburton's letter to Nourse of 2 October 1760, above.

[4] Paul François Velly, *Histoire de France depuis l'établissement de la monarchie jusqu'au regne de Louis XIV*, 22 vols. (Paris, 1761–71). The Hurd Library holds vols. 1–8; vols. 8–17 (ed. C. Villaret); and vols. 17–22 (ed. J. J. Garnier). Hurd's annotations appear in vols. 1–14.

George Lyttelton *to* Warburton   20 January 1768
Lewis Walpole Library, Yale University   London

                                                 London Jan: 20. 1768
My Lord
   I shall take the liberty to send your Lordship, by the next Bath Coach, the second Edition of my History of K. H. II. which is much more correct than the first.[1] It would have been sent to you sooner, if I had not expected to have the pleasure of seeing you soon in town, which some of your Friends now inform me I shall not have this whole Winter. Be pleased therefore to accept of this small Present, in return for much better books, which you have formerly given me, and as a Mark of that Homage which is due to your Lordship from every member of the Republick of Letters. I have the honour to be with great respect

                                                          My Lord
                                              Yours Lordship's
                                                   most obedient
                                              & most humble servant
Endorsed: (To Bp. Warburton)   Lyttelton
Verso: Jan. 20. 1768.

[1] Warburton helped Lyttelton for many years with his *History of the Life of King Henry the Second*, the first and second editions of which were published by W. Sandby and J. Dodsley in four volumes in 1767–71.

Warburton *to* [Isaac Hawkins Browne][1]   7 February 1768
Cambridge, Trinity College Library: MS R.4.57[27]   Prior Park

                                            Prior Park Feby 7 1768
Sir
   I have the honour and favour of receiving from you the very valuable present of your Father's Works: Whose great Parts & knowle[d]ge, in more arts & sciences than one, few men had the pleasing opportunity of

knowing more than I had.[2] His happy vein in Poetry made him stand amongst the foremost of the art, in his life time, and he will be amongst the last that Barbarity and Ignorance (fast returning upon us) shall be able to obliterate. This mark of your filial Piety to so distinguished a Person will do you lasting honour, and give much pleasure to the Friends of his family, in which number I desire to be reckoned, being

Sir, your obliged and obedient
humble Servant
W. Gloucester

[1] This letter is in a volume assembled by Isaac Hawkins Browne, the younger (1745–1818). I am grateful to David McKitterick, Librarian of Trinity College, Cambridge, for bringing this letter to my attention.

[2] Isaac Hawkins Browne, the elder (1705–60), *Poems Upon Various Subjects* (London, 1768). This collection is in Latin and English; Warburton would also have taken an interest in *Fragmentum Isaaci Hawkins Browne Arm. sive, Anti-Bolingbrokius* (London, 1768; part 2, 1769).

Warburton *to* John Nourse   24 May 1768
Pierpont Morgan Library   Prior Park

Prior Park 24 May 1768

Dr Sir

I hope this letter will find you perfectly recovered, and yet I had my doubts considering I had not heard from you. I desire you to send me, in boards, Petrarch's life[1] in 3 Vs. 2°. and what else you have for me particularly the Acad. of Inscriptions &c.[2]

I am your faithfull
friend & Servt
W. Gloucester

Address, frank and stamp: To Mr Nourse Bookseller in the Strand London   W. Gloucester Free.   BATH FREE 26/MA
Endorsed: Prior Park May 24. 1768 The Bishop of Gloucester answerd May 29. 1768

[1] Jacques François Aldonçe de Sade, *Mémoires pour la vie de François Pétrarque*, 3 vols. (Amsterdam [printed in Avignon], 1764–7); in quarto. This set remains in the Hurd Library, with Hurd's annotations in volume 2.

[2] For the Académie des Inscriptions et Belles-Lettres, see Warburton's letter to Nourse, 30 November 1767, above.

Warburton *to* [Charles Bathurst?]¹   22 December 1768
Pierpont Morgan Library   Prior Park

Prior Park Decr 22 1768.

Sir

I received yours of the 15.

Lord Bathurst, for whom I have a very great regard, in a visit he was so good to make me, here, told me that he had something to ask of me in your favour, in the Bookseller's way, he did not know, or did not recollect the particulars of it, but perhaps I might know what you wanted. I was as much at a loss as himselfe; but said, that any favour which I had in my power to grant I should be ready, on his Lordship's account, to oblige you in.

If I had had the least conc[ep]tion, that you wanted to purchase Mr Millar's share of Pope, I could have given him a more explicite Answer: For not many days after Mr Millar's death I engaged my selfe to two Persons to use all my interest with the Execrs in their behalfe, concerning the Purchase

I am, Sir, your humble Servant
W. Gloucester

P.S. But to give all the satisfaction I am able to Ld Bathurst in this affair, as you say you have written to Dr Millar now at Bath (whom I have not seen) If he & the rest of the Trustees or Execrs. are disposed to treat with you ⟨and⟩ abt the Purchase, I shall interfere no further abt it, having, as I told you already, on Mr Millar's death solicited them in behalfe of the two persons I mentioned

---

¹ The writer was evidently a bookseller, although attempts at identifying his handwriting have been inclusive. As he seems to have been successful in obtaining Millar's share (or part of it), his name would have appeared on either the 1769 or 1770 imprint. The last edition of Pope to come out before Millar's death in 1768 was the 1766 *Works* in 9 volumes octavo printed for A. Millar, J. and R. Tonson, C. Bathurst, H. Woodfall, R. Baldwin, W. Johnston, B. Law, T. Longman, T. Caslon, Johnson and Davenport, and M. Richardson. The 1769 edition in 5 volumes quarto (with Owen Ruffhead's 'Life') was printed for C. Bathurst, H. Woodfall, W. Strahan, J. and F. Rivington, W. Johnston, B. White, T. Caslon, T. Longman, B. Law, Johnson and Payne, S. Bladon, T. Cadell, and executors of A. Millar (a sixth volume was added in 1807). The 1770 edition in 9 volumes octavo was printed for C. Bathurst, W. Strahan, J. and F. Rivington, R. Baldwin, W. Johnston, T. Caslon, T. Longman, B. Law, Johnson and Davenport, T. Davies, T. Cadell, and W. and J. Richardson (there was another 1770 edition in six volumes duodecimo with the same booksellers listed in the imprint). There was another London edition in 8 volumes octodecimo printed for S. Crowder, C. Ware, and T. Payne (Payne appeared in the 1769 imprint).

The new names in the 1769 edition were W. Strahan, J. and F. Rivington, B. White, Payne, S. Bladon, T. Cadell and the executors of A. Millar. Payne's name appeared in a different 1770 edition with S. Crowder and C. Ware. The names of Davenport and R. Baldwin (in 1766) were not given in the 1769 *Works*, but reappeared in the 1770 edition. The new names in the 1770 edition were T. Davies and W. and J. Richardson. Cadell can be discounted as the writer as he was one of Millar's executors (along with his widow, Jane Millar, and his brother, Dr. William Millar, of Antigua) as can John Richardson, who is named in the memorandum.

[Charles Bathurst?] (memorandum)[1]   *c.* 22 December 1768
Pierpont Morgan Library   [Prior Park]

Upon the Death of Mr Andrew Millar, his Brother & Executor Dr. Millar told me, that the Bishop of Gloucester, from whom Mr Millar derived his Share in the Copy Right of Pope's Works, had reserved to himself the Liberty to nominate the person or persons, who were to be the purchasers upon any Alienation, & that it was to be valued by Mr. John Rivington. —— Mr. Millars Death happened about the Middle of the Summer 1768,[2] and in the Course of it I applied to my good Friend Lord B. then in the Country to recommend me to the Bishop, that I might be admitted purchaser. I acquainted Dr M. that I had done so, who replied that it would be very agreable to him. My Lord was so kind to recommend me; the Bishop['s] L[ette]r. to me on the Occasion is annexed.* At the beginning of Winter, when my Lord came to Parliamt.

[1] See the preceding letter from Warburton of 22 December 1768, n.1.
[2] Millar died on 8 June 1768. His widow remarried Sir Archibald Grant of Monymusk, Aberdeenshire. The business was carried on by Thomas Cadell who had begun his apprenticeship under Millar in 1758 and maintained the business well into the nineteenth century.

Warburton *to* [Richard Hurd][1]   23 September 1769
Folger Shakespeare Library: Y.c.1451 (5)   Gloucester

Gloucester Sepr 23 1769
My dearest Friend,
I have your two letters of the 15 & 19 instant to acknowle[d]ge. and am extremely obliged to you for satisfying Ld Mansfield's kind enquiries. Almost every letter one receives, which tells or enquires after news even of the present, is sufficient to convince us of the Pyrr⟨h⟩onism of History.
I am much concerned to find that you do not receive the benefit, you

would wish, from your Succedaneum.[2] For to tell you the truth I regard
⟨the present⟩ rage for sea-bathing as only a fashionable folly. Our
modern Pagans seem to have adopted the Maxim of their predecessors,
that the Sea is a cure for all mortal ills.

Garrick's *portentous* ode, as you truly call it, has but one line of *truth* in
it, which is where he calls Shakespear *the God of our Idolatry*: for *sense* I will
not allow it: for that which is so highly satirical, he makes the topic of his
Hero's encomium.[3] The Ode it selfe is below any of Cibbers. Cibber's
nonsense was something like sense; but this man's sense whenever he
deviates into it, is much more like nonsense.

We too have had our Jubile[e]; but held in the old Jewish manner,
when it was a season for reliefe of the distressed; which was truly *singing to
God with the voice of melody.* We too, and with a vengeance, *exalted our
singing voice,* in the language of Old Hopkins & Sternhold,[4] the Cibber
and the Garrick of their time for ode-making. But here we forsook our
Jewish model. You know that the *hire of a Whore & the price of a Dog* were
forbid to be offered up to the God of purity. But we presumed to offer up
to him, the *hire of two Whores.* You may judge by what I am going to say,
what it is that passes under the name of Charity amongst us. We have got
for the distressed Clergy of the three Dioceses, some 340*l.* And to procure
this, we have levied upon the Country 684: 6: 10. for their entertainment
in Fidlers & Singers; of which sum 100*l.* is contributed by me & my
Coadjutor.

I am now to give you an account of what you had more at heart, my
Michaelmas Ordination. Tho I gave notice of it, according to your
direction in the Gloucester Journal; yet had it not been for a little Welch-
Deacon, who flew hither from his native Mountains by accident, like a
Woodcock in a mist, it had been a *Maiden Ordination,* and I must like the
Judges, ⟨have⟩ given gloves to my Officers: For an examination is a kind
execution.

My own Mr Hurd! ever yours.
W. Gloucester.

---

[1] Lot 346 in Sotheby's catalogue, 8 June 1903. The opening salutation has been scored
out for printing as Letter CCXIX in *LLEP*, pp.327–8.

[2] 'A cure, a holiday' (*OED*).

[3] David Garrick, *An Ode upon Dedicating a Building, and erecting a statue, to Shakespeare*
(London: T. Becket and P. A. de Hondt, 1769).

[4] John Hopkins (*d.* 1570) and Thomas Sternhold (*d.* 1549) assisted in the translation of
the metrical version of the Psalms.

Warburton *to* [Jeremiah Milles?]   9 July 1770
Lewis Walpole Library, Yale University   Gloucester

                                              Gloucester July 9 1770
Dear Sir

 I return you my best thanks for your very agreable Present, read to the
Antiqn. Society, concerning the Wardrobe acct under Richd 3. which
Bp Littleton¹ mistook & misled Mr Walpole. You have cleared up the
matter very satisfactorily; and shewn that the *record* leaves the common
historical acct of the murder of the 2 infant Princes just where it found it.
I presage that, under your prudent direction, this Society will do honour
to the literary State of our Country.

                          I am with true esteem, Sr your
                          very faithfull & obedient humble
                                                  Servant
                                            W. Gloucester

Verso: Bp Glouc July 9th 1770

¹ Charles Lyttelton (1714–68), antiquary and Bishop of Carlisle.

Warburton *to* [Thomas Cadell?]¹   24 October 1770
Gloucestershire Record Office: D1361/2   Gloucester

                                              Gloucester Octr 24 1770
Sir
 I have recd the acct, and doubt not but it is very right, since it has
passed your review. But I do not understand it at all. When Messrs
Tonson & Millar drew out thei[r accounts?]² I understood it all, and, for
the exactness of it, depended (as I had reason) on them. They paid me
(by a dr[aft]. on Gosling) what was due to me, and I gave them a
discharge. I have the same confidence in you. and therefore desire you
will pay to Messrs Gosling & Clive what is due to me and their rect shall
be a discharge, and when I come to town I shall give any other that is
requisite.
 Nothing can be exacter than your bill. only I returned, for you to sell
for me, Capells Shakespea[re]³ & I think Dow's In[?]tan⁴; but of this
latter book I am not sure. And you have given me no credit for these, as
you have rightly done for Haw[ke]sworth's Telemachus.⁵ when this is
settled, I will give you a Dr on Messrs Gloucester

                          I am your faithfull Friend & Servt
                                          W. Gl[oucester]⁶

¹ Cadell became Warburton's main bookseller after the death of Andrew Millar in 1768.

² There is a tear in the manuscript at this point.

³ Shakespeare, *Works*, ed. Edward Capell, 10 vols. (London: J. and R. Tonson, 1768). Warburton evidently sent his set back for resale. In the 1770 edition of Pope's *Works*, Warburton added Capell's name to a venomous note on his detractors, Edwards, Upton and Theophilus Cibber (*Epistle to Arbuthnot*, 1.169).

⁴ This title is partly blotted out: Alexander Dow, *The History of Hindostan* (London: T. Becket and P. A. de Hondt, 1768); or Dow, *Tales, Translated from the Persian of Inatulla of Delhi* (London, 1768).

⁵ François de Salignac de la Mothe Fénelon, *The Adventures of Telemachus*, trans. John Hawkesworth (London: W. and W. Strahan, 1768).

⁶ The bottom of this page has been worn away.

Warburton *to* William Mason¹   24 January 1771
Folger Shakespeare Library: Y.c.1451 (6)   [Gloucester]

To Mr Mason
Dear Sir
    you know how highly I deem of Elfrida and Caractacus. Yet *argentile* & Curan will be my favorite (for cause) when you have put your last hand to it.² To say more or otherwise would be unjust and unkind both to you & my selfe in our union of warm & honest friendship

                       Adieu
                 W. Gloucester
Jany 24 1771

Endorsed: Warburton, bishop of Gloucester

¹ Item 695 in Halliday catalogue no. 56 (1921).
² *Elfrida* (1752); *Caractacus* (1759); *Argentile and Curran* is in *Poems*, 3 vols. (York, 1796–7).

Warburton *to* Thomas Cadell¹   1772
Folger Shakespeare Library: Y.c.1451 (1)   Gloucester

                   Glouceste[r]² 6 1772
Dr Sr
    You m[ay] [re]member that a few months ago, I order'd one [of] Dr Hurd's lecture sermons to be sent to the Gentleman in Holland as here

directed in this inclosed Letter.[3] I neglected to advertise him of it till now. So I must desire you to put the inclosed Letter into the general Post. But as I do not know what postage is to be paid I desire you would take care of that & put it to my account.

> Your faithfull friend
> & Servant
> W. Gloucester

Address, frank and stamp (*verso*): To Mr T. Cadell Bookseller in the Strand London *W. Gloucester Free* FREE GLOUCESTER GLOUCES-TE[R] [stamp showing day and month is incomplete] *Note* (in another hand): Warburton

[1] Item. 391 in Simmons and Waters catalogue no. 218 (1908).
[2] Leaf torn through month and part of top two lines of letter.
[3] Richard Hurd, *An Introduction to the Study of the Prophecies concerning the Christian Church... in twelve sermons* (London: T. Cadell, 1772). The enclosed letter is untraced, as is the 'Gentleman in Holland'.

Warburton *to* Gosling & Clive   22 December 1772
National Library of Scotland: MS. 968, f.74   Gloucester

                              Gloucester Decr 22 1772
                                          18 Jan.[1]
To Messrs Gosling and Clive[2]

Sirs
    be pleased to pay to John Pitt Esq. on order three days after sight the sum of one hundred and sixty two pounds and place it to my account.[3]

Warburton
£162

Endorsed (in another, possibly Gosling's, hand): Accttd 12 Jany GG   D12

[1] In another hand.
[2] See Frank Melton, 'Robert and Sir Francis Gosling: Eighteenth-Century Bankers and Stationers', *Economics of the British Booktrade 1605–1939*, ed. Robin Myers and Michael Harris (Cambridge, 1985), pp.60–77.
[3] John Pitt, favourite cousin of the Prime Minister, frequented Prior Park. Warburton's wife, Gertrude, visited Mrs Pitt in Dorset in August 1754 (Boyce, p.222).

David Garrick *to* Warburton[1]   21 April 1774
Folger Shakespeare Library: Y.c.2600 (181)   Hampton

Hampton
April 21 —— 1774

Will your Lordship permit me to recommend to your perusal the inclosed plan for a pronouncing Dictionary; it is written by a most Worthy, ingenious Friend of mine who has studied his subject deeply, and I hope to the purpose —— my regard for his Worth as a man, may make me partial to him as an author.[2] I shall truly know what advice I should give him, if your Lordship would honour me with your sentiments —— Let me assure you, that he is not one of the genus irritabile, and that he will be as grateful for your Lordships Objections as he will be proud of your approbation —— the fear of interrupting your Studies, or being admitted when you have better Company, has often restrain'd my inclination of paying my respects to your Lordship, but I intend doing myself that honour in a few days. It is with great pleasure I have heard, that the Drs Hurd, Robertson, Beattie & other respectable names have written Letters in favour of literary property —— it will be of the greatest service to the Cause.[3] Mrs Garrick presents her respects with Mine to your Lordship & Mrs Warburton, I am

my Lord & c
D. G

[1] Printed in *LDG*, 3: 928–9.

[2] John Walker, *A General Idea of a Pronouncing Dictionary of the English Language on a Plan Entirely New* (London, 1774). This was dedicated to Garrick. The *Pronouncing Dictionary* was finally published in 1791.

[3] The 'cause' of perpetual copyright, which Warburton had upheld in his 1747 *Letter... Concerning Literary Property* and Andrew Millar won (posthumously) in 1769, was finally lost in the House of Lords on 26 February 1774. The landmark case of *Donaldson* v. *Becket* was decided in favour of the Scottish printer-bookseller, Alexander Donaldson, and against the copyright owner of Thomson's *Seasons*, Thomas Becket. 'An attempt to reverse the verdict by legislation was lost in 1774 on its second reading in the House of Commons', John Feather, *A History of British Publishing*, p.83.

Warburton *to* [A bookseller]   23 January 1775
OB: MS. Montagu d. 10, f.282   Gloucester

Jany. 23 1775
Gloucester

Dear Sir
    I have recd your[s] of the 20 inst: with your acct of our affairs and the ballance for your care & exactness of which I am much obliged to you

and greatly bound. You will be so good to send me my bill of what I am indebted to you for the books I ordered to be sent to me from your shop

I am Sir your very obliged
and faithfull humble Servant
W. Gloucester

You will be pleased to pay to Mr Cadell for my use payable, as you desire, two months after sight what is due to me. So there will be no occasion for me to draw on you

Warburton *to* Catherine Malet (memorandum) 23 July 1777
BL: Egerton 1960, ff.11–12   [Gloucester]

23 July 1777

For Miss Cath: Malet[1] to be given to my Wife by her, when she sees proper. As I am bishop of Gloucester it is not improper to have me buried in the Collegiate Church there, with as little expence as possible. But this with the certain approbation & good likeing of my wife, and principally to save her the expence of having me carried to the Burial place at Claverton near Bath.

W. Gloucester

Verso: To Miss Malet.[2]

[1] Catherine Malet's correspondence with the Warburtons dates from 1769.

[2] f.12 (detached; different paper stock) reads: 'This is the last will & testament of Mr. William Warburton.' Possibly from a later date, this attempt at writing dwindles into a scrawl.

Gertrude Warburton *to* [Richard Hurd]   3 May 1780
Hartlebury Castle: Hurd MS. 16, ff.10–11   Prior Park

Prior Park May 3rd: 1780.

My Lord

 I have made use of all the leisure I could get amidst my own business to look into the Bishop's Papers, and have taken an acct: of the whole wch: your Lordship will find enclos'd.[1] The printed fragment of the D. Leg: is not to be found, nor any M.S. of it; they are, I suppose, in Cadel's hands who informed me long since that he had a great many Copies printed off. There is also an acct: with Mr Cadel, in my favour, wch: I wish to settle as soon as possible.

Your Lordship will favour me by letting me know what part of the Papers you wish to see, & what part of them you wd. advise me to burn.[2] The poor Bishop himself destroyd numbers of Letters & other papers before his Death. It may be right to return Lord Mansfields Letters, the only one of his Correspondents now alive, except Dalrymple.[3]

I find several sheets of paper written by Mr Arnold chiefly copies of Letters from the late A. Bp. to his Father.[4] What wd. you have me do with them?

I am very glad your Lordship has bought the Books & hope they will fully answer your expectations. Your attention to my present difficulty in regard to a Bailiff is extreamly kind & Friendly.[5] If your Brother should succeed in getting a Person to my mind he will in a great measure restore to me that tranquillity wch: Chapman's infirmities & foibles have long destroyd.[6]

Dr Balguy looks pale, but he can eat a good Dinner and he promises to repeat it very often at P.P. Miss Drake is in high beauty.[7]

I am with all sincerity & respect
Yours Lordships most Obedeint and
obliged Humble Servant
Ger^{de}: Warburton

Enclosed: f.11: inventory

Contents of the large Box of Papers.[8] ——
Bishop's MSS ——

2 Foul Copies of Discourse on *Fate* —— Ditto of *Julian*, transcribed for the Press, Text & Remarks. —— (1st. printed Copy of Julian. —— part of a printed Vol: of Sermons) Paper agst. Voltaire.[9] —— *Sermons*, about 20, a few of wch. are printed. —— Speech in House of Lords on Marriage Contract.[10] —— 2 or 3 Charges to Clergy. —— Directions (to Mr. W) for the Study of Theology. —— Hints for the Jewish part of the 3d. Vol: of D. L. collected under their several Heads. —— Foul Copy of Remarks & Introduction to last Vol: of D. L. Papers agst. Bolingbroke. —— 2 Discourses on Sacrifice, foul Copies. —— Apothegms. —— 3 or 4 old Almanacks with little Notes & Remarks on Blank Leaves & Margins. —— Several other small promiscuous Papers, wch. seem of no Consequence. —— —— —— 1st. Copies of Review of Bol: and Doctrine of Grace.[11] —— 2 foul Copies of parts of D. L. ——

—— —— ——
Letters fm. the Bishop to Sir Thos. Hanmer, a large *Bundle*.[12] To Dr. Middleton, abt. 20 —— To Dr. Lowth, 1 Letter.[13] —— To Mr.

Cleveland 2 Letters, with some printed Verses and other Trifles. ——
To Dr. Atwell, a considerable number.

  Letters to the Bishop from Bp. of Salisbury abt. a dozen. —— Ld.
Mansfield 2 or 3 dozen. One fm. Mr. Hunter on Ld. Bolingbroke. ——
Ld. Lyttleton 10 or 12 —— Dr. Middleton 20 or 30. —— Mr. Pitt 12 or
15. Montesquieu[14] —— 2. Fr[ench]: —— Mr. Pope 2 large Parcels.
—— Sr. Thos. Hanmer & Theobald —— a large Bundle —— ——
Jane —— 1, & Bps. Ansr. Jortin 1 —— & Bps. Ansr. —— Birch 8 or
10 —— Mr. Hooke 10 or 12 —— Ld. Chesterfield 6 or 8 —— Mr.
Towne on Theological Subjects,[15] a large Parcel. —— Dalrymple,
relating to his Work, the Annals of Scotland.[16] —— Bp. Hare[17] 10 or
12 —— Mr. C. Yorke, a large Bundle. Mr. Joseph Charles,[18] on
Scripture. ——Lawrence Sterne 4 or 5. Dr. Lowth, several. —— ——

—— ——

Other Papers, MSS.

A Dissertation on 2 of Agur's Wonders;[19] Drinking of the Brook in the
Way; with a Letter to the Bp. dated at Newton, fm. T. Comber, who
seems to be the Author of the whole. —— Literary Remarks fm. Mr.
Towne. —— Papers fm. Mr. Knapton's Executors & Millar's
Account. —— Large Bundle of Letters & other Papers concerning
Pope. Specimen of a Lat: Translation of Pope's Essay on Man by John
Sayer. —— Lat: Verses, a Dialogue inter mercatorem & Civem de
Pace. —— Remarks on a Tour abroad. —— Passages fm. *Gr*[eek]. Lat.
& Eng: Authors, parallel with some in the Essay on Criticism; 1 sheet it
seems to be in Pope's Hand. —— A short Answer to Ld. Bolingbroke
sign'd *Philolethes*.[20] —— Florus to Silvia, a Poem, with a Letter fm. T.
Comber Junr. —— Ethick Epistles —— Remarks on Pope's Poems.
—— Lat: & Eng: Poems —— Saml. Langley written on the
out[side] —— 3 Letters of Mr. Locke to Dr. Dennis Grenville, after-
wards Dean of Durham, fm. the originals in the possession of R.
Rawlinson, L.L.D. —— An Acct. of the 2d. Vol. of D.L. by Dr.
Dodridge. A few other Papers relating to Durham Family Matters, &
other Things of little Consequence. ——

  [1] Gertrude Warburton's inventory is on f.11.
  [2] The extent of Warburton's destruction of his own manuscripts is unknown, as is any
subsequent burning. None of the papers listed in Gertrude Warburton's inventory is
known to survive at Prior Park or Hartlebury Castle.
  [3] William Murray, Lord Mansfield, whose library was destroyed in the Gordon Riots of
June 1780, died in 1793. Sir David Dalrymple, Lord Hailes, survived until 1792. For
Warburton's letters to Dalrymple, see 9 May 1762 n.1, above; Dalrymple's letters to
Warburton are untraced.
  [4] Possibly Thomas Secker, Archbishop of Canterbury (*d.* 1768).

[5] Gertrude Warburton had taken legal action against her cousins, Ralph, Philip and Mary Allen, in 1779 (Boyce, p.297).

[6] Probably John Chapman, surviving executor of Ralph Allen's will (Boyce, pp.291, 297).

[7] Thomas Balguy read a sermon at Hurd's consecration in 1775 and later declined Warburton's vacant bishopric on the grounds of failing health. Miss Drake was perhaps the daughter of Balguy's son-in-law and editor, Dr. Drake, mentioned in Francis Kilvert's *Memoirs of... Richard Hurd*, pp.40, 122.

[8] Whether the following papers were sent from Prior Park to Hartlebury Castle is uncertain. Possibly some of the items mentioned were destroyed, while others survive. One wonders, for example, whether the unspecified contents – 'Mr. Pope 2 large Parcels', 'Papers fm. Mr. Knapton's Executors & Millar's Account', 'Large Bundle of Letters & other Papers concerning Pope', 'Passages fm. *Gr*[eek]. Lat. & Eng: Authors, parallel with some in the Essay on Criticism; 1 sheet it seems to be in Pope's Hand' – survive in the British Library Egerton MSS. Also worth noting in connection with the letters of 28 January–4 March 1754, above, is the 'Specimen of a Lat: Translation of Pope's Essay on Man by John Sayer'.

[9] Warburton considered publishing a refutation of Voltaire, but Hurd persuaded him that he should not try to 'break a butterfly upon a wheel' (*DNB; WWW*, 1: 105).

[10] *On the Nature of the Marriage Union* (1775).

[11] Warburton, *Doctrine of Grace* (London: A. Millar and J. and R. Tonson, 1763).

[12] As he had done with Theobald, Warburton carried on a lengthy correspondence concerning Shakespearean criticism with Sir Thomas Hanmer in 1735 before he realized that they both were intending to publish their own editions. Philip Nichols published a pamphlet on the ensuing quarrel entitled *The Castrated Sheet of Sir Thomas Hanmer* in 1763.

[13] See Brian Hepworth, *Robert Lowth* (Boston, 1978). It was Lowth who complained that Warburton used the footnotes to the *Dunciad* and the *Divine Legation of Moses* as his 'ordinary places of literary executions' (*DNB*).

[14] Warburton began a brief correspondence with Montesquieu after sending him *A View of Lord Bolingbroke's Philosophy* in 1755.

[15] John Towne supported the *Divine Legation* in 1751 and continued to defend Warburton in *Remarks on Dr. Lowth's Letter to the Bishop of Gloucester* (London: L. Davies and C. Reymers, 1766).

[16] David Dalrymple, *Annals of Scotland*, 2 vols. (1776–9).

[17] Francis Hare, Bishop of Chichester, had recommended Warburton to Queen Caroline shortly after the publication of *The Alliance between Church and State*, but shortly before her death in 1737.

[18] Vicar of Wighton and author of *The Dispersion of the Men at Babel Considered* (London: J. Whiston and B. White, 1755; rpt. 1769).

[19] Possibly referring to a collection of fourteen sermons by William Agar, rector of South Kelsey, *Military Devotion* (London, [1758]).

[20] Perhaps written in the wake of the *Patriot King* controversy; or this might be an unpublished reaction to a pamphlet such as Cantabrigiensis Philologus, *The Freethinker's Criteria Exemplified, in a vindication of the characters of M. T. Cicero and the Duke of Marlborough against the censure of Lord Bolingbroke* (1755).

APPENDICES

APPENDIX A

ACCOUNTS OF POPE'S *WORKS* (1751–4)

In the latter half of the eighteenth century, the copyright to Pope's *Works* was worth more to booksellers than the combined copyrights to the works of Milton and Shakespeare.[1] The division of profits shared by Warburton and his booksellers may be determined from the extant accounts of Pope's *Works*.[2] Shares were calculated on the number of sheets assigned. In modern reckoning, Warburton had just over 50·5%; the Knaptons 25·2%; Tonson & Co. (including Draper) 6·7%; Lintot 12·9%; and Bathurst 4·7%. Warburton thus had a controlling share, invested in the Knapton business and received a considerable return.[3] Pope's *Works* went through many reprintings in various formats throughout the latter half of the eighteenth century, running to twenty London editions by the time of Warburton's death in 1779. By 1800, multi-volume editions had been published in Dublin, Edinburgh, Glasgow and Berlin. Translations of Pope's works were published in Oxford, Cambridge, Paris, Halle, Altenburg and Berne. The Warburton edition was not entirely superseded by the editions of Gilbert Wakefield in 1794 or Joseph Warton in 1797.

The accounts for the first five Warburton editions indicate that 10,750 sets of Pope's *Works* were produced between 1751 and 1754 at a net profit of £5203. 18s. 6½d. Even by today's standards, a return of more than £100,000 for 10,750 nine- or ten-volume sets of poetry over a four-year period is remarkable. Warburton had considerable financial incentive to publish the edition. The first account (BL: Eg. 1959, f.29) gives a breakdown of the production costs and profits for the large octavo 1752 edition; the second account (BL: Eg. 1959, f.30) gives an overview of the first five Warburton editions (including the 1752 edition). The main production costs would have gone towards paper stock and printing charges; the designers and engravers of the two dozen illustrations would presumably have been paid their commissions in advance. The 1500 sets of the nine-volume large octavo 1751*a* edition yielded 13,500 single volumes; 3000 sets of 1751*b* yielded 27,000; 750 sets of 1752 yielded 6,750; 2500 sets of 1753 yielded 22,500; 3000 sets of the ten-volume pot octavo edition of 1754 yielded 30,000. The total production of 10,750 sets amounted to 99,750 single volumes.

Over the four-year period, the proportion of cheaper editions (in crown and pot octavo) to large octavo editions was three to one: 7000 sets in crown and pot octavo compared to 2250 large octavo. The projected number of buyers of the more expensive edition fell: the availability of the cheaper 1751 crown edition or sluggish sales of the first large octavo edition of 1751 may have caused the booksellers to halve the 1752 print run. Many of Warburton's notes and commentaries were omitted from the cheaper editions (with his permission) which reduced the number of printed sheets and helped cut costs. The increased print-run of the 1754 pot octavo edition, stretched out to ten volumes, again with Warburton's permission, suggests that, in general, sales were by no means expected to decline.

The booksellers would have had to anticipate demand and order accordingly from their printers, William Bowyer, the younger, for the large octavo 1751 *Works* and William Strahan for at least some of the 1752 sheets. An over-optimistic prediction could mean a long-term backlog in the warehouse. The Knaptons and their associates would have felt fairly confident about the turnover of Pope's *Works*. If, for example, sales of the first small octavo edition of 1751 had been disappointing, then the Knaptons surely would not have ordered 2500 sets in the same format for the 1753 edition. Most sets would have been absorbed by the London market, the majority of them being sold at the Knaptons' shop in Ludgate Street (and the premises of the other shareholders) to other booksellers and their own customers. However, consignments would have been sent to provincial booksellers. The Bath bookseller James Leake had an arrangement with the Knaptons – 'Leak's parcel' – so that when a customer like Ralph Allen wanted an item, his order could be delivered within a week by coach.

Assuming all the sets of Pope's *Works* eventually found a home, the booksellers seemed to be guaranteed substantial profits from the sale of Pope's *Works*. Yet there is a cautionary note: in 1755 the main proprietors of Pope's *Works*, John and Paul Knapton, verged on bankruptcy. Paul Knapton died, leaving his brother to put most of their stock and copyrights up for auction. Their share in Pope's *Works* was bought privately by Somerset Draper, who already had a small share with the Tonsons, and by Andrew Millar. Millar's name appeared second in the list of booksellers on the 1756 imprint and headed half a dozen other editions up until 1766, after which the Pope copyright was swallowed up by larger congers.

The number of editions published after Pope's death attests to his continuing influence throughout the latter half of the eighteenth century. The controversy over the 1751 edition and Warburton's fluctuating reputation helped boost sales and sustain Pope's fame well into the nineteenth century when Byron locked horns with William Lisle Bowles over his judgement of the poet's deficiencies in the 1806 edition of Pope's *Works*. Not only Gibbon and Byron were inspired by Pope to varying heights of poetry and prose, but so too in countless different ways were the largely unknown buyers of Pope editions who propped up the book trade.

Bowyer's ledgers list the various printing charges from 1751 to 1753 and give a rough indication of Warburton's cancels. The account of the five Warburton editions of Pope's *Works* was drawn up by Somerset Draper, who evidently had a talent for figures and negotiations: he was one of two mediators selected in 1754 to settle the dispute between David Mallet and the bookseller Richard Francklin over the publication of Bolingbroke's works reported in *An Act before the First Act of Elvira* (London: R. Francklin [1754?]). Draper's account may have been drawn up as part of the settling of Knapton's financial affairs, although Warburton had also thought about disposing of his share in his letter of 12 January 1755. Warburton made a rough memorandum of his profits on 18 May 1759.

ABSTRACT OF ACCOUNTS FOR THE 1752 EDITION OF POPE'S *WORKS* IN LARGE OCTAVO (9 VOLUMES)

BL: Egerton 1959, f.29   17 January 1753

Popes Works   large 8vo   2d. Edit: 9vs: No. 750

Jan: 17. 1753

	[Volume]	[No. of sets]	[Printing costs]	[Selling price]	[Net]
	Shts:Pages	Produce	Cost of 14s. 2¼	Sold at 33s.	Profit
		Books	£. s. d.	£. s. d.	£. s. d.
Dr. Warburton & Mr. Knapt.	147. 7.	570⅔	404.16. 4	941.12.	536.15. 8⅔
Messrs. Tonson & Co.*	12.11.	49.	34.15. 2½	80.17.	46. 1. 9½
Mr. Lintot	24.10.	95⅓	67.12. 6½	157. 6.	89.13. 5½
Mr. Bathurst†	9. .	35.	24.16. 9⅔	57.15.	32.18. 3⅔
[Total]	193.12.	750.	532. .10⅔	1237.10.	705. 9. 2⅔
			[Printing costs:]		532.—10.
			[Total Sales:]		1237.10.—

* Somerset Draper's share was included in the Tonsons' profits.

† Charles Bathurst was not named in the imprint of the 1751 edition, although he received a share of the profits.

DRAPER'S ABSTRACT OF ACCOUNTS FOR
POPE'S *WORKS* 1751–4

BL: Egerton 1959, f.30:

Abstract of Accounts Popes Works 5 Editions

[Year]		[Format/No. of volumes]		[No. of Sets]	£. s. d.
[1751a]	No.1	Large octavo 9 Vols Total Profit on		1500	1380. 9. 5.
[1751b]	2	Crown [9 vols] Edition	D°	3000	1334. 7. 5½
[1752]	3	Large octavo [9 vols] 2d Edition	D°	750	705. 9. 2.
[1753]	4	Crown octavo [9 vols] 2d Edition	D°	2500	986.15. 0.
[1754]	5	Pot octavo 10 Vols.	D°	3000	796.17. 6.
				10750	5203.18. 6½

Dr. Warburton & Mr. Knaptons share—

		£. s. d.
[1751a]	in No. 1	1050.11.11.
[1751b]	No. 2	1000. 4. 6.
[1752]	No. 3	536.15. 8.
[1753]	No. 4	759. 7. 6.
[1754]	No. 5	592. 1. 6¾
		£3939. 1. 1¾

Tonson & Co share

	£. s. d.
in No. 1	90. 7. 2.
No. 2	93.10. 4.
No. 3	46. 1. 9½
No. 4	63.15. 0.
No. 5	56. 0.11¼
	£349.15. 2¾

Mr. Lintots share—

[1751a]	No. 1	175. 8. 3.
[1751b]	No. 2	177.13.10½
[1752]	No. 3	89.13. 5½
[1753]	No. 4	121. 0. 0.
[1754]	No. 5	107. 8.11.
		£671. 4. 6.

Mr Bathursts share

No. 1	64. 2. 1.
No. 2	62.18. 9.
No. 3	32.18. 3.
No. 4	42.12. 6.
No. 5	41. 6. 1.
	£243.17. 8.

		[% of share]
Dr. Warburtons ⅔ ⎫ of 3939. 1. 1¾	2626. 0. 9.	[50·5%]
Mr Knapton ⅓ ⎭	1313. 0. 4½	[25·2%]
Mr Tonson & Co	349.15. 3.	[6·7%]
Mr Lintot	671. 4. 6.	[12·9%]
Mr Bathurst	243.17. 8.	[4·7%]
	£5203.18. 6½	100%

Verso: Mr Draper's Acct of Pope

The detailed information provided by the account for the five Warburton editions (1751–4), collated with the data in the account for the 1752 large octavo edition makes it possible to reconstruct the account for the 1751 large octavo edition. This first edition contains the same number of sheets as the 1752 edition, so figures were more or less double. On a proportional basis, printing costs of the 1752 edition were slightly less (the difference would have been £29 had the 1752 print-run been the same). The 1752 account gives the unit cost of production (14s. 2¼d.) and the wholesale price (33s.), which the retailer then sold for £2 2s., thereby making a profit of 9 shillings per set (approximately 21%). The Knaptons and their partners would have made a profit of 27s. 9¾d. per set (approximately 66%). The 1751 and 1752 large octavo editions had the same wholesale price.

PROJECTED ABSTRACT OF ACCOUNTS FOR THE 1751 *WORKS* IN LARGE OCTAVO (based on BL: Egerton 1959, ff.29–30)

	Shts: Pages	No. of sets	Printing costs	Selling price	Profit
			£. s. d.	£. s. d.	£. s. d.
Warburton & Knapton	147. 7	1141⅓	832.12. 1.	1883. 4. .	1050.11.11.
Tonson & Co.	12.11	98.	71. 6.10.	161.14. .	90. 7. 2.
Lintot	24.10	190⅔	139. 3. 9.	314.12.	175. 8. 3.
Bathurst	9.	70.	51. 7.11.	115.10.	64. 2. 1.
Total	193.12	1500.	1094.10. 7.	2475. .	1380. 9. 5
					1094.10. 7.
					£2475.00.00.

While the above accounts provide figures of the exact number of Pope's *Works* printed, they do not indicate how long each edition took to sell out. Since the Knaptons often promoted their stock through the books they sold, advertisements may give a rough indication of how long an edition took to sell out. No advertisements appeared in the first three Warburton editions of Pope's *Works*, however a list of 'BOOKS printed for John and Paul Knapton, in *Ludgate-Street*' was placed at the end of the third volume of the 1753 *Works*. This advertisement gives some indication of the Pope stock then in hand. First on the list was the large octavo *Works* of 1751 or 1752. Next came the *Essay on Man* priced at 1s. 6d. which could refer to any one of five editions of the *Essay* published by the Knaptons after Pope's death; one edition carried a price of eighteen pence on its title-page.[4] Copies of the 1743/4 quarto editions of the *Essay on Criticism* and the *Essay on Man* were still available at three shillings. Two editions of the *Dunciad* with Warburton's notes were also available – the 1743 quarto at four shillings and the 1749/50 octavo at two shillings. The Knaptons still had copies of 'Four Ethic Epistles' – the 1744 'death-bed' *Epistles to Several Persons* in quarto, which was suppressed until 1748 – in stock, although their 1747 octavo edition of *Ethic Epistles* (containing the *Essay on Man* and what Warburton later called the *Moral Essays*) does not appear on the 1753 list. Folio and quarto editions of Pope's *Letters* in two volumes, dating back to 1737, were still for sale. Pope's translation of the *Odyssey* was advertised in the quarto five-volume series (volumes four and five could be bought separately in the same format). There were still copies for sale of the folio edition of Pope's *Works II*, some eighteen years after it was published by Lawton Gilliver. The last Pope item on the 1753 list was a two-volume translation in duodecimo, *Selecta Poemata Italorum* for six shillings. The 1753 advertisement continued with a selection of Warburton's writings, including *Julian*, the *Divine Legation* and his 1742 *A Critical and Philosophical Commentary on Mr. Pope's Essay on Man*, the expanded version of his *Vindication*.

A similar list of books appeared at the back of the fourth volume of the ten-volume edition of Pope's *Works* in 1754. The only additional item in the Pope catalogue was the 1751 small octavo edition which sold for twenty-seven shillings. Like its larger counterpart, this edition was advertised as having Warburton's notes (although the title-page reads 'With Occasional Notes'; many were dropped from the first edition) and the same twenty-four copper-plates. That the same dozen Pope titles were advertised from one year to the next suggests a sluggishness in trade. Buyers of Warburton editions would have little incentive to add, for example, the 1735 *Works II* to their already 'complete' set. Mid-century buyers moved away from the old, extravagant folio and quarto editions. The Knaptons attempted to adapt to the market by producing cheaper editions, such as the 1754 pot octavo.

Another source for gaining a perspective on the problems booksellers faced with crowded stockrooms is *A List of Books printed by the Booksellers of London and Westminster, in different sizes; by which it will appear that cheap editions of all useful books, that are capable of being reduced into a small size, have been published by the said booksellers: with the number of years an impression of each is selling.* This undated pamphlet, produced by the trade in making its case in support of common law right of ownership in 1774, gave statistical information on the long-term investment by booksellers in their wares. It offers a number of examples of the list price and length of time editions of Pope's *Works* took to sell out:

	£. s. d.	Years in selling
Pope's Works 5 vols 4° printed 1769	5. 5. 0.	– –
– – – – 9 vols Medium, 8vo	2.14. 0.	7
– – – – 9 vols Crown, 8vo.	1. 7. 0.	7
– – – – 10 vols pott 8vo.	1. 1. 0.	18
– – – – 6 vols 12mo. printed 1771	.18. 0	– –

If '10 vols pott 8vo.' is the 1754 edition, then the booksellers had to wait almost two decades before the last set was sold. However, the picture is incomplete and perhaps slanted in the booksellers' favour: the figures, for example, do not say whether 95% of the sets sold out within the first five years or whether a few stray sets might have been found years later in a stockroom.

[1] Terry Belanger, 'Booksellers' Trade Sales, 1718–1768', *The Library*, 5th ser., 30 (1975): 281–302; 295–6.

[2] For accounts of Pope's 1717 *Works*, see J. D. Fleeman, '18th-century Printing Ledgers', *TLS* (19 Dec. 1963), p. 1056; and for *Works* (1735–7), P. T. P., 'Pope and Woodfall', *N&Q*, 1st ser., 11 (19 May 1855): 377–8.

[3] In more recent times, Philip Larkin struck a similarly lucrative deal with one of his publishers: 'So publication of *The Less Deceived* went ahead, with a contract . . . which entitled Larkin to 50 per cent of all profits – one of the most generous in the history of publishing – and an eighteenth-century subscription scheme which meant him furnishing the Hartleys [his publishers] with the names of potential buyers: what he called his "sucker list"', Blake Morrison, 'Self-portrait with poet', *TLS* (7–13 July 1989), p.740 (review of Jean Hartley's *Philip Larkin, the Marvell Press and Me*).

[4] Maslen; Foxon P868; Griffith 607.

APPENDIX B

THE KNAPTON TRADE-SALE CATALOGUE
(25 SEPTEMBER 1755)

BL: C.170.aa.1(67)

John Knapton was forced to put part of his stock and copyrights up for auction in order to settle his debts with Warburton (who told Hurd he was Knapton's biggest creditor), Bowyer and various other members of the book trade.[1] His share in Pope's *Works* (not listed here) was sold privately to Andrew Millar. Thirty-five sets of Warburton's eight-volume, octavo edition of Shakespeare were bought by Millar at £1 7*s.* per set.

Knapton was forced to part with such prized copyrights as Anson's *Voyages* and Rapin's *History* (which fetched £1190). The trade sale realized over £4600. The ultimate purpose of the trade sale – to pay off his debts – was eventually accomplished: Knapton was able to pay off his creditors by November 1758. Knapton disposed of more of his stock at the sale of Knapton, Rivington, Johnston, and Law on 29 September 1761.

Copyrights changed hands frequently, and whole shares were broken into complex fractions. Item 164 – a $\frac{1}{24}$ share of the octavo edition of Basil Kennett's, *Romae Antiquae Notitia: or, the Antiquities of Rome* (8th ed., London: printed for D. Brown, J. Knapton, R. Knaplock, J. Sprint, D. Midwinter [and 5 others], London, 1726; 12th ed. corr. and improved, London: printed for W. Innys, J. & P. Knapton, S. Birt, D. Browne, T. and T. Longman, 1754) – was bought by Andrew Millar for £5 5*s.* 3*d.* It turned up in a sale of 'the property of the late Mr. Charles Bathurst': a $\frac{1}{32}$ share sold for 10*s.* 6*d.* (BL: Add. MS. 38730, ff.16*v.*–17; 19 December 1786). Between 1755 and 1786, the value of the whole property would appear to have fallen from £126 6*s.* to £16 16*s.*

There are two known copies of the trade-sale catalogue, both in the British Library: the one reproduced here is the more fully annotated of the two.

---

[1] I am grateful to Dr J. A. Edwards of the University of Reading Library for supplying me with photocopies of the Knapton trade-sale catalogue (Longman nos. 67–8). See Terry Belanger, 'Booksellers' Trade Sales, 1718–1768', for the standard study of trade-sale catalogues and the complexity of copyright shares.

A
CATALOGUE

OF

BOOKS in QUIRES, and COPIES,

Part of the STOCK of Mr JOHN KNAPTON,

To be SOLD at the

QUEEN's-HEAD Tavern, in PATER-NOSTER-ROW,
on *Thursday*, September 25, 1755.

Three Months Credit for Ten Pounds; Six Months for Twenty
Pounds; Two Six Months for One Hundred Pounds; Three Six
Months for One Hundred and Fifty Pounds; and Four Six Months
for Two Hundred Pounds; or for any Sum above Three Hundred
Pounds, Six Six Months, figning Notes dated from the Sixteenth
Day after the Delivery.

Any Purchafer may difcount his own Notes at the Rate of Five per Cent. per Annum.

The Numbers of feveral Books will be put up in Lots, or together, as the
Company choofe. No Books to be made perfect, unlefs the Imperfections are demanded in Fourteen Days after Delivery.

*The Sale will begin punctually at 12 o'Clock, and Dinner will be on the
Table at Two.*

178	A	Infworth's Dictionary, 4to.		90	Bladen's Cæfar, 8vo.	
50		Ditto Folio.		20	Bengelii Teftamentum Græcum Oxoniæ.	
72		Anfon's Voyage, 4to. Large Paper.		66	Burkit on the New Teftament, Folio.	
240		Ditto 8vo.		8	Biographia Britannica, 3 vols. Folio.	
10		Albinus's Anatomical Tables, and Syftem of the Blood-Veffels and Nerves, Folio, with Explanations, 4to.		200	Boyer's Grammar.	
				6	Bacon's Works, 3 vols. Folio.	
				4	Barlow's Juftice.	
10		Ditto with Explanations, Folio.		217	Dr Clarke's Works, 4 vols. Folio.	
3		Atlas Maritimus, Folio.		36	——— Ditto Large Paper.	
3		—— General, Folio.		246	——— Ditto Vol. 3d and 4th, Folio.	
40		Amelia, 4 vols.		40	——— 18 Sermons, 8vo.	
16		Abernethy's Pofthumous Works, Vol. 3d, and 4th.		988	——— Sermons, 11 vols. Eighteens.	
8		Bedford's Chronology, Folio.		297	——— Sermons on the Attributes, 8vo.	
600		Beveridge's Chronology, Lat. 8vo.		160	——— Paraphrafe on the Evangelifts, 2 vols. 8vo.	
120		Bifhop Butler's Sermons, 8vo.		150	——— on the Trinity, 8vo.	
80		——— Analogy, 8vo.		360	——— Letters to Dodwell, 8vo.	
250		Boyer's French Dictionary, 8vo.		720	——— On the Ch. Catechifm, 12mo.	
20		Ditto in Quarto.		900	——— Effays, 12mo.	
10		Barnet on the Articles, Folio.		380	——— Homer, 4 vols 4to. Ill. & Od.	
8		Bowen's Compleat Atlas, Folio.		750	——— Ditto Illiad, 2 vols. 8vo.	
50		Bennet on the Common Prayer, 8vo.		280	——— Grotius.	
20		Beveridge's Thoughts, 2 vols. 8vo.		175	Dr John Clarke's Sermons at Boyle's Lectures, 2 vols. 8vo.	
240		Ditto in 12mo.		240	——— Rohault's Phyfics, 2 vols. 8vo.	
24		Boyle's Lecture Sermons, 3 vols. Folio.		760	——— Demonftrations of Sir Ifaac Newton's Principles of Philofophy, 8vo.	
225		Bland's Military Difcipline, 8vo.		280	Cudworth of Morality, 8vo.	
34		Bates's Works, Folio.		50	Cruden's Concordance, 4to.	
15		Bentley's Terence, 4to.		4	Calmet's Dictionary, 3 vols. Folio.	
9		Ditto Large Paper.		200	Calamy's Sermons, 8vo.	
500		Blackmore of the Dropfy.		16	Chambers's Dictionary, 2 vols. Folio.	
12		Britifh Compendium, 3 vols.		44	——— Supplement, 2 vols, Folio.	
360		Bailey's Dictionary, 8vo.		80	Clare	

50 Clare on Fluids, 8vo.
50 Chillingworth's Works, Folio.
500 Bp Chandler's Defence of Christianity, &c. 3 vols. 8vo.
20 Collins's Supplement to the Peerage, 2 vols, 8vo.
15 Camden's Britannia, 2 vols. Folio.
350 Clergyman's Companion, 8vo.
100 Ciceronis Orationes Delph. 8vo.
78 Cicero per Davis, Cantab. 6 vols. 8vo.
40 —— de Natura Deorum, per Davis, 8vo.
360 —— de Finibus, 8vo.
150 —— de Divinatione, 8vo.
300 —— Academica, 8vo.
300 Common-Prayer best Companion, 8vo.
16a Cantemir's (Prince) Othman Hist. Folio.
150 Cellarius's 33 Maps of Ant. Geography.
550 Geographia Antiqua, suited to Cellarius's Maps, 4to.
3? Collier's Supplement, Folio.
43 Chess made easy, 12mo.
24 Crouche's Rates, Vol. I.
660 Crevier's Lives of Roman Emperors, Vol. 1st, 2d, and 3d.
N.B. The 4th, 5th, and other Volumes are printed, and the Purchaser of Vol. 1st, 2d, and 3d, is to have them, paying the Expence of Paper and Print.
200 Coles's Dictionary, 8vo.
22 Congreve's Works, 3 vols. 12mo.
9 Card, 2 vols. 12mo.
450 Ditton of Fluxions, 8vo.
720 Dougharty's Gauging, 12mo.
20 Description of Holland, 8vo.
12 David Simple's Letters, 2 vols. 8vo.
664 Devil of a Wife, 12mo.
17 Dennis's Fables, 8vo.
England's Gazetteer, 3 vols. 12mo.
250 Echard's Gazetteer, 8vo.
60 Ecton's Thesaurus, 4to.
50 Fleetwood's Relative Duties, 8vo.
106 Ford de 39 Articulis Ecclesiæ Ang. 8vo.
18 Fiddes's Life of Cardinal Wolsey, Folio.
96 Fleetwood's Works, Folio.
17 Franklin's Phalaris.
34 Fielding's Journal, 12mo.
13 Fuller's Family Dispensatory, 8vo.
8 Foster's Discourses, 2 vols. 4to.
24 Gay's Fables, Vol. 2d. 4to. Fine Paper.
150 Gibbs's Rules for Drawing, Folio.
56 —— Designs of Architecture, Folio.
126 Garretson's Exercises, 12mo.
50 Gay's Fables, Vol. 1st. 8vo.
250 Ditto, Vol. 2d. 8vo.
120 Gordon's Grammar, 8vo.
90 Gentleman Instructed, 2 vols. 12mo.
18 Garth's Ovid, 2 vols. 12mo.
20 Grey's Remarks on Shakespear, 2 vols.
23 Gil Blas, 4 vols. Eighteens.
10 Houbraken's Heads of Illustrious Persons, with Birch's Lives, 2 vols. Folio, Imperial Paper.
100 Ditto 2 vols. Folio, Small Paper.
80 Howell's Medulla Historiæ Anglicanæ, 8vo.
160 Hawney's Measurer, 12mo.
325 Hales of Eaton's Tracts, 12mo.
276 History of Charles XII. 3 vols. 8vo.
22 Henry on the Bible, 5 vols. Folio.
16 Heath's Account of Scilly, 8vo.
25 Hawney's Trigonometry, 8vo.
48 Howell's Hist. of the Bible, 3 vols. 8vo.
25 Horace Delphini, 8vo.
1 Harris's Lexicon, 2 vols. Folio.
18 Heister's Anatomy, 8vo.

16 Hatton's Comes.
75 Howell's Letters.
156 Hedericus's Lexicon.
21 Hervey's Meditations, 2 vols. large 8vo.
36 Hudibras, Eighteens.
750 History of China, 8vo.
50 Juvenal Delphini.
590 Jackson on the Lord's Prayer, 12mo.
100 Jenkins on the Christ. Relig. 2 vols. 8vo.
70 Jameson on the Pentateuch, Folio.
19 Keil on the Animal Œconomy, 8vo.
4 Kettlewell's Works, 2 vols. Folio.
128 Kennet on the Creed.
50 ——'s Antiquities.
120 Laurence's Surveying, 12mo.
104 Littleton's Dictionary, 4to.
40 L'Estrange's Æsop, 2 vols. 8vo.
60 Ditto Vol. 2d.
22 Littlebury's Herodotus, 2 vols. 8vo.
44 Lowthorp and Jones's Abridg. 5 vols. 4to.
19 Leng's Sermons, 8vo.
34 Laurence's Christian Morals, 8vo.
50 —— Christian Prudence, 8vo.
8 Lowth's Commentary, Folio.
3 L'Estrange's Josephus, Folio.
300 Life of Prideaux, 8vo.
24 Langham's Duties, 12mo.
7 Life of Bolingbroke, large 8vo.
20 Ditto, small 8vo.
58 Leusden's Compendium.
12 Miscellanea Curiosa, 3 vols. 8vo.
184 Marshall on Daniel's Weeks, 8vo.
225 Military Memoirs of Marshal Turenne, &c. 8vo.
30 Motteux's Don Quixote, Eighteens.
470 Manners of the Romans, 8vo.
24 Montfaucon's Regal Antiquities of France, with 300 Copper Plates, 2 vols. Folio.
240 Mihles's Surgery, 8vo.
100 Methodists Compared, 2 vols. 8vo.
100 —— 2d volume.
800 —— 2 vols. 12mo.
5? Miller's Kalendar, 8vo.
8 Ogle's Chaucer, 3 vols. 8vo.
29 Ovid's Epistles, 12mo.
40 —— Art of Love, 12mo.
5 Puffendorf's Law of Nature, Folio.
84 Pearson on the Creed, Folio.
45 Potter's Antiquities, 2 vols. 8vo.
450 Pope's Poemata Italorum, 2 vols. 8vo.
100 Patrick's Christian Sacrifice, 12mo.
40 Plato's Works, 2 vols. 12mo.
25 Puffendorf's Introduction, 2 vols. 8vo.
80 Pyle on the Epistles, 2 vols 8vo.
18 Persian Tales, 3 vols. 12mo.
33 Patrick's Commentary, 2 vols. Folio.
15 Plutarch's Lives, 9 vols. Eighteens.
46 Rapin's Hist. of England, with the Heads and Monuments, 15 vols. Folio.
320 Ditto Cuts to be work'd off.
58 Rapin's Hist. of England, with the Heads and Monuments, 15 vols. 8vo.
28 —— Continuation, 2 vols. Folio.
264 —— Abridgment, 2 vols. 8vo.
280 Richardson's Remarks on Milton, 8vo.
105 Religion of Nature, 8vo.
1390 Rollin's Ancient Hist. 12 vols. Eighteens.
570 Ditto, 10 vols. 8vo.
33 —— Roman Hist. 16 vols. 8vo.
110 —— Arts and Sciences, 4 vols. 8vo.
400 Revenues of the Romans, 8vo.
23 Rowe's Lucan, 2 vols. 12mo.
91 System of Geography, 2 vols. Folio.
290 Stephens's Sermons against Popery, 8vo.
350 Salmon's Gazetteer, 12mo.

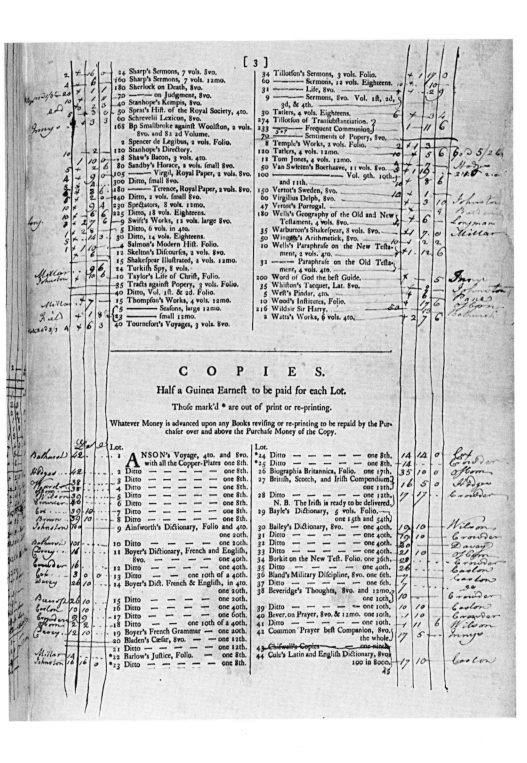

24 Sharp's Sermons, 7 vols. 8vo.
160 Sharp's Sermons, 7 vols. 12mo.
180 Sherlock on Death, 8vo.
70 ——— on Judgment, 8vo.
40 Stanhope's Kempis, 8vo.
50 Sprat's Hift. of the Royal Society, 4to.
60 Schrevelii Lexicon, 8vo.
168 Bp Smallbroke againft Woolfton, 2 vols. 8vo. and 82 2d Volume.
2 Spencer de Legibus, 2 vols. Folio.
120 Stanhope's Directory.
8 Shaw's Bacon, 3 vols. 4to.
80 Sandby's Horace, 2 vols. fmall 8vo.
105 ——— Virgil, Royal Paper, 2 vols. 8vo.
300 Ditto, fmall 8vo.
180 ——— Terence, Royal Paper, 2 vols. 8vo.
240 Ditto, 2 vols. fmall 8vo.
230 Spectators, 8 vols. 12mo.
225 Ditto, 18 vols. Eighteens.
9 Swift's Works, 12 vols. large 8vo.
5 Ditto, 6 vols. in 4to.
30 Ditto, 14 vols. Eighteens.
4 Salmon's Modern Hift. Folio.
12 Skelton's Difcourfes, 2 vols. 8vo.
15 Shakefpear Illuftrated, 2 vols. 12mo.
24 Turkifh Spy, 4 vols.
10 Taylor's Life of Chrift, Folio.
35 Tracts againft Popery, 3 vols. Folio.
40 Ditto, Vol. 1ft. & 2d. Folio.
15 Thompfon's Works, 4 vols. 12mo.
5 ——— Seafons, large 12mo.
23 ——— fmall 12mo.
40 Tournefort's Voyages, 3 vols. 8vo.

34 Tillotfon's Sermons, 3 vols. Folio.
60 ——— Sermons, 12 vols. Eighteens.
31 ——— Life, 8vo.
9 ——— Sermons, 8vo. Vol. 1ft, 2d, 3d, & 4th.
30 Tatlers, 4 vols. Eighteens.
274 Tillotfon of Tranfubftantiation.
233 ——— Frequent Communion.
70 ——— Sentiments of Popery, 8vo.
8 Temple's Works, 2 vols. Folio.
120 Tatlers, 4 vols. 12mo.
12 Tom Jones, 4 vols. 12mo.
50 Van Swieten's Boerhaave, 11 vols. 8vo.
100 ——— Vol. 9th. 10th. and 11th.
150 Vertot's Sweden, 8vo.
60 Virgilius Delph. 8vo.
47 Vertot's Portugal.
180 Wells's Geography of the Old and New Teftament, 4 vols. 8vo.
35 Warburton's Shakefpear, 8 vols. 8vo.
50 Wingate's Arithmetick, 8vo.
10 Wells's Paraphrafe on the New Teftament, 2 vols. 8vo.
32 ——— Paraphrafe on the Old Teftament, 2 vols. 4to.
200 Word of God the beft Guide.
35 Whiston's Tacquet, Lat. 8vo.
5 Weft's Pindar, 4to.
10 Wood's Inftitutes, Folio.
216 Wildair Sir Harry.
2 Watts's Works, 6 vols. 4to.

C O P I E S.

Half a Guinea Earneft to be paid for each Lot.

Those mark'd * are out of print or re-printing.

Whatever Money is advanced upon any Books revifing or re-printing to be repaid by the Pur-chafer over and above the Purchafe Money of the Copy.

Lot.
1 ANSON's Voyage, 4to. and 8vo. with all the Copper-Plates one 8th.
2 Ditto ——— — — one 8th.
3 Ditto ——— — — one 8th.
4 Ditto ——— — — one 8th.
5 Ditto ——— — — one 8th.
6 Ditto ——— — — one 8th.
7 Ditto ——— — — one 8th.
8 Ditto ——— — — one 8th.
9 Ainsworth's Dictionary, Folio and 4to. one 20th.
10 Ditto ——— — — one 20th.
11 Boyer's Dictionary, French and Englifh, 8vo. ——— — — one 40th.
12 Ditto ——— — — one 40th.
13 Ditto ——— — one 10th of a 40th.
14 Boyer's Dict. French & Englifh, in 4to. one 20th.
15 Ditto ——— — — one 40th.
16 Ditto ——— — — one 40th.
17 Ditto ——— — — one 60th.
18 Ditto ——— — one 10th of a 40th.
19 Boyer's French Grammar ——— — one 12th.
20 Bladen's Cæfar, 8vo. ——— — one 12th.
21 Ditto ——— — — one 12th.
*22 Barlow's Juftice, Folio. ——— — one 8th.
*23 Ditto ——— — — one 8th.

*24 Ditto ——— — — — one 8th.
*25 Ditto ——— — — — one 8th.
26 Biographia Britannica, Folio. one 17th.
27 Britifh, Scotch, and Irifh Compendium one 12th.
28 Ditto ——— — — one 12th.
N. B. The Irifh is ready to be delivered.
29 Bayle's Dictionary, 5 vols. Folio, one 15th and 54th.
30 Bailey's Dictionary, 8vo. ——— one 40th.
31 Ditto ——— — — one 40th.
32 Ditto ——— — — one 40th.
33 Ditto ——— — — one 40th.
34 Burkit on the New Teft. Folio. one 36th.
35 Ditto ——— — — one 40th.
36 Bland's Military Difcipline, 8vo. one 6th.
37 Ditto ——— — — one 6th.
38 Beveridge's Thoughts, 8vo. and 12mo. one 10th.
39 Ditto ——— — — one 10th.
40 Bever. on Prayer, 8vo. & 12mo. one 10th.
41 Ditto ——— — — one 10th.
42 Common Prayer beft Companion, 8vo. the whole.
43 Chifwell's Copies ——— one ninth.
44 Cole's Latin and Englifh Dictionary, 8vo. 190 in 8000.

Lot.

45 Cole's Latin and English Dictionary, 8vo. 100 in 8000. — *Osborn 18 0 0*
46 Ditto — 66 in 8000 — *Robinson 11 11*
47 Ciceronis Orat. Delph. 8vo. one 15th. — *Crowder 8 10*
48 Ditto — one 15th. — *Hodges 9 15*
49 Ditto — 41 in 2000. — *Co 9 4*
50 Chambers's Dictionary and Supplement, 4 vols. — one 64th. — *Crowder 55*
51 Ditto — one 64th. — *Easton 51 10*
52 Ditto — one 64th. — *Hodges 51 10*
53 Ditto — one 64th. — *Coll 52 10*
54 Cooke's Reports, 7 vols. 8vo. one 16th.
55 Ditto — one 16th.
56 Cheyne's Diseases of Body and Mind, 8vo. one half. — *Millar 56*
— Regimen, 8vo. — one half.
57 Clarke's Sermons, in 10 vols, 8vo, one 8th. — *Do 56*
58 Ditto — one 8th. — *65 5*
59 Ditto — one 8th. — *Baldwin 84*
60 Ditto — one 8th. — *Millar 65*
61 Ditto — one 8th. — *Co 67*
62 Ditto — one 8th. — *70*
63 Ditto — one 8th. — *Baldwin 76*
64 Ditto — one 8th. — *Richardson 8*
65 Clarke on the Attributes, 8vo. — one 8th. — *Co 8*
66 Ditto — one 8th. — *8*
67 Ditto — one 8th.
68 Ditto — one 8th. — *Baldwin 8 8 0*
69 Ditto — one 8th. — *Ward 8 8 0*
70 Ditto — one 8th. — *Hodges 8 15 0*
71 Ditto — one 8th. — *Innys 8*
72 Ditto — one 8th. — *Millar 5 12 6*
73 Clarke's 18 Sermons, 8vo. one 8th. — *5 12 6*
74 Ditto — one 8th. — *Do 5 12 6*
75 Ditto — one 8th. — *Do 5 12 6*
76 Ditto — one 8th. — *Do 5 12 6*
77 Ditto — one 8th. — *Do 5 12 6*
78 Ditto — one 8th. — *Do 5 12 6*
79 Ditto — one 8th. — *Do 5 12 6*
80 Ditto — one 8th. — *Johnston 17 17*
81 Clarke's Paraphrase, 2 vols. 8vo. one 8th. — *17 17*
82 Ditto — one 8th.
83 Ditto — one 8th. — *Bathurst 19*
84 Ditto — one 8th. — *Hodges 17 17*
85 Ditto — one 8th. — *Johnston 17*
86 Ditto — one 8th. — *Baldwin 18 5*
87 Ditto — one 8th. — *Easton 18 5 0*
88 Ditto — one 8th. — *3 8 0*
89 Clarke's 3 Essays, 12mo. & 8vo. half. — *Johnston 3 10 6*
90 Ditto — half. — *Millar 8*
91 Clarke one the Catechism, 12mo. half. — *Johnston 12 15*
92 Ditto — half.
93 Clarke's Letters to Dodwell.
— Leibnitz's Papers.
— Scripture Doctrine of the Trinity.
— Letter to Dr Wells.
— Reply to Mr Nelson.
— Observations on Waterland's second Defence.
— Modest Plea continued.
— Letter to R. M.
— Letter to the Author of true Scripture Doctrine.
— 3 Letters, with the Doctor's Answers.
— Apology for Dr Clarke.
— Letter to Mr B. Hoadly. the whole.
94 Clarke's Grotius, English, 8vo. — half. — *Rivington 2 15*
95 Ditto — half. — *Do 2 15*
96 Clarke Homeri Ilias, 2 vols. 4to. & 8vo. one 8th. — *Baldwin 20*
97 Ditto — one 8th. — *Rivington 21*
98 Ditto — one 8th. — *Crowder 22*
99 Ditto — one 8th. — *Rivington 21*
100 Ditto — one 8th. — *Casey 27*

Lot.

101 Ditto — one 8th. — 21
102 Ditto — one 8th. — 21
103 Ditto — one 8th. — 22 5
104 Clarke Homeri Odyssea, 2 vols. 4to. and 8vo. — 6 6
105 Ditto — one 8th. — 5 5
106 Ditto — one 8th. — 5 5
107 Ditto — one 8th. — 5 5
108 Ditto — one 8th. — 5 5
109 Ditto — one 8th. — 6 6
110 Ditto — one 8th. — 6 6
111 Ditto — one 8th. — 6 6
112 Clergyman's Companion, 8vo. one 10th. — 2 2 0
113 Ditto — one 10th. — 4
114 Collins's Peerage — one 12th. — 23 15
115 Ditto — one 12th. — 27 5
116 Clare on Fluids, 8vo. — one 10th.
117 Dampier's Voyages, 4 vols. 8vo. with all the Cuts one 4th. — 6 6
118 Ditto — one 4th.
119 Ditto — one 4th.
120 Ditto — one 4th.
121 Dougharty's Gauging, 12mo. one 4th. — 2 12 6
122 Ditto — one 4th. — 2 12 6
123 Ditto — one 4th. — 2 12 6
124 Ditto — one 4th. — 3 3
125 Echard's Gazetteer, Part I. — one 6th.
     Ditto Part II. — one 6th.
126 Ditto Part I. — one 96th.
     Ditto Part II. — one 36th.
127 Echard's Terence — one 21st.
121 Farquhar's Plays, Sir Harry Wildair, the whole, — 12
     The Inconstant — one 3d.
129 Ecton's Thesaurus, 4to. — one 9th. — 5 5
130 Garretson's Exercise, 12mo. — one 32d. — 3 15
131 Gordon's Grammar, 8vo — one 24th. — 5 15
132 Grotius on War and Peace, folio. one 8th. — 10
133 Gay's Fables, 2d Vol. — one 4th. — 27
134 Ditto — one 4th. — 27 10 0
135 Gibbs's Rules for Drawing, with the Plates — one 6th.
136 Ditto — one 6th.
137 Gibbs's Architecture — one 6th.
138 Ditto — one 6th.
139 Geographia Classica, 29 Maps — one half.
140 Ditto — one half.
141 Hill's Arithmetic, 8vo. 100 in 2100. — 13 10
142 Horseman's Conveyancing, 3 vols folio one 8th. — 63
143 Ditto — one 8th. — 63
144 Ditto — one 8th. — 58
145 Ditto — one 8th. — 56
146 Ditto — one 8th. — 55 10
147 Ditto — one 8th. — 55 10
148 Ditto — one 8th. — 55 10
149 Ditto — one 8th. — 56
150 Horace Delphini, 8vo. — one 18th. — 18 18 0
151 Jacob's Law Dictionary, folio one 40th. — 23
152 Ditto — one 40th. — 23
153 Ditto — one 40th. — 23
154 Ditto — one 40th. — 23 10 0
155 Hutchenson on the Passions, 8vo. one 8th. — 3 15
156 Ditto — one 40th. — 4
157 Hudibras, 12mo. and 18mo. 60 in 4000. — 7 10 0
158 Hatton's Comes Commercii one 56th. — 13 5
159 Ditto — one 40th. — 5
160 Hederici Lexicon, Greek and Latin, 4to, 125 in 3000. — 16 16 0
161 Ditto — 125 in 3000. — 16 16 0
162 Ditto — 125 in 3000. — 17
163 Keay's Measuring — one 8th. — 16 0 0
164 Kennet's Antiquities, 8vo. — one 24th. — 5 5
165 Lawrence's Surveying, 12mo. the whole — 4 10
     — Land Steward, 8vo. one 3d.
166 Leusden's Compendium — one 12th. — 1 10 0
*167

Hodges	4	10	0

Lot.

*167 Latin Common-Prayer, 12mo. one 12th.
168 Medulla Historiæ Anglicanæ Howell's
    one 16th.
169 Ditto ——— ——— one 16th.
170 Motteux's Don Quixot, 4 vols. 12mo.
    and Eighteens ——— one 24th.
171 Meredith's Copies ——— one 16th.
172 Ovid Metam. Delphini ——— one 24th.
173 ——— Epistles Delphini ——— one 18th.
174 Potter's Antiquities, 2 Vols 8vo. one 12th.
175 Ditto ——— ——— one 48th.
*176 Puffendorf's Introduction, 2 vols one 8th.
*177 Ditto ——— ——— one 8th.
*178 Reflections on Learning, 8vo. ——— half.
*179 Ditto ——— ——— half.
180 Religion of Nature delin. 8vo. one 4th.
180 Ditto ——— ——— one 4th.
181 Ditto ——— ——— one 4th.
181 Ditto ——— ——— one 4th.
182 Stanhope's St Austin, 8vo. ——— one 10th.
183 Ditto ——— ——— one 10th.
184 Sherlock on Death, Judgment, Provi-
    dence, Future State, Sermons, 2 vols
    Popery ——— one 8th.
185 Scarron's Works, 2 Vols 12mo. one 6th.
186 Sharp's Works, 7 Vols 8vo. and 12mo.
    one 5th.
187 Shakespeare, 9 vols Eighteens
188 Stanhope's Kempis, 8vo. one 8th of a
    4th and a 7th of a 3d.
189 Stanhope's Directory, 8vo. two 15ths.
190 Stanhope's Epistles, 8vo. 4 vols. one
    12th and one 72d.
192 Terence Delphini, 8vo. one 32d and one
    240th.
193 Tillotson's Works, folio, 8vo. and
    eighteens ——— one 40th.
194 Ditto ——— ——— one 40th.
195 Temple's Works, 2 vols folio 38 and
    two thirds in 500.
196 Tatler, 4 vols 12mo, ——— one 20th.

Lot.

197 Virgil Delphini, 8vo. ——— one 18th.
198 Ditto ——— ——— one 30th.
199 Salmon's Gazetteer, 12mo, ——— one 10th.
200 Wingate's Arithmetic, 8vo. ——— one 8th.
201 Ditto ——— ——— one 8th.
202 Ditto ——— ——— one 8th.
203 Ditto ——— ——— one 8th.
204 Weeks Preparation, Keeble's, 1st part
    one 8th.
205 Ditto 2d part ——— one 8th.
206 Wells's Dionysius, 8vo. ——— one 8th.
207 ——— Geography to the Maps, 8vo.
    one 3d of 220.
208 Rapin's History of England, with the
    Heads and Monuments, Genealogical
    Tables, &c. on 77 Copper-Plates 2
    Vols folio. And Rapin's Hist. 15 vols,
    8vo. with Heads, Monuments, &c.
    one 8th.
209 Ditto ——— ——— one 8th.
210 Ditto ——— ——— one 8th.
211 Ditto ——— ——— one 8th.
212 Ditto ——— ——— one 8th.
213 Ditto ——— ——— one 8th.
214 Ditto ——— ——— one 8th.
215 Ditto ——— ——— one 8th.
216 Tindal's Continuation, Summary and Me-
    dallic Hist. 3 vols. Folio, containing
    12 Heads engraven by Houbraken,
    37 Plates of Medals,
    72 Plans, Maps, and Charts. And,
    Tindal's Continuation, 13 vols. 8vo.
    one 8th.
217 Ditto ——— ——— one 8th.
218 Ditto ——— ——— one 8th.
219 Ditto ——— ——— one 8th.
220 Ditto ——— ——— one 8th.
221 Ditto ——— ——— one 8th.
222 Ditto ——— ——— one 8th.
223 Ditto ——— ——— one 8th.

APPENDIX C

POPE-KNAPTON AND WARBURTON-KNAPTON IMPRINTS

(a) Pope-Knapton Imprints

(Pope items edited by Warburton from 1745; ESTC search conducted 31 May 1990; all items in octavo unless otherwise noted.)

1728.1   *The works of Mr. William Shakespear . . . Publish'd by Mr. Pope and Dr. Sewell,* 10 vols. London: printed for J. and J. Knapton, J. Darby, A. Bettesworth, J. Tonson, F. Fayram, W. Mears, J. Pemberton, J. Osborn and T. Longman, B. Motte, C. Rivington, F. Clay, J. Batley, Ri., Ja. and B. Wellington, 1728. James and John Knapton head the list of booksellers in the imprints of vol. 1 (general title-page) and vol. 10 only; vols. 1–9 are reissues of the 1728 Tonson edition. ESTC t138590; Griffith 210.

1737.1   *Letters of Mr. Alexander Pope, and several of his friends.* London: printed by J. Wright for J. Knapton, L. Gilliver, J. Brindley, and R. Dodsley, 1737. ESTC t005513; Griffith 454; quarto.

1737.2   *Letters of Mr. Alexander Pope, and several of his friends.* London: printed by J. Wright for J. Knapton, L. Gilliver, J. Brindley, and R. Dodsley, 1737. 'Like Variant *a* [1737.1] in all respects but one: the sig. B sheet was reprinted from a new setting of type . . . a larger font was used for the footnotes' (Griffith). [Not in ESTC]; Griffith 455; quarto.

1737.3   *Letters of Mr. Alexander Pope, and several of his friends.* London: printed by J. Wright for J. Knapton, L. Gilliver, J. Brindley, and R. Dodsley, 1737. ESTC t005514; Griffith 456; folio.

1737.4   *Letters of Mr. Alexander Pope, and several of his friends.* London: printed by J. Wright for J. Knapton, L. Gilliver, J. Brindley, and R. Dodsley, 1737. ESTC t005515; Griffith 457; folio.

1738.1   Jonathan Swift, *An imitation of the sixth satire of the second book of Horace. . . . The first part done in the year 1714, by Dr. Swift. The latter part now first added, and never before printed.* London: printed for B. Motte and C. Bathurst, and J. and P. Knapton, 1738. Most of the additions are by Pope. ESTC t005776; Foxon S860; Griffith 479; folio.

1739.1   *Poems, and imitations of Horace. By Mr. Pope. Now first collected together.* London: printed for J. and P. Knapton, L. Gilliver, J. Brindley, and R. Dodsley, 1738 [1739]. ESTC t005484; Griffith 504; quarto.

1741.1   *The works of Mr. Alexander Pope, in prose. Vol. II.* London: J. & P. Knapton, C. Bathurst, R. Dodsley, 1741. John Wright ornaments. [Not in ESTC]; Griffith 529; small folio.

1741.2   *The works of Mr. Alexander Pope, in prose. Vol. II.* London: printed for J. and P. Knapton, C. Bathurst, and R. Dodsley, 1741. John Wright ornaments. ESTC t005467; Griffith 530; large paper folio.

1741.3   *The works of Mr. Alexander Pope, in prose. Vol. II.* London: printed for J. and P. Knapton, C. Bathurst, and R. Dodsley, 1741. John Wright ornaments. ESTC t005468; Griffith 531; quarto.

1742.1   *The works of Mr. Alexander Pope: containing his epistles and satires: with some never before printed.* London: printed by J. Wright for J. Knapton, L. Gilliver, J. Brindley, and R. Dodesley [*sic*], 1737 [1742]. ESTC t116579; Griffith 474; folio and quarto (made-up volume).

1744.1   *Epistles to several persons.* [London, 1744]. William Bowyer ornaments (see 1748.3, below). ESTC t005485; Griffith 591; quarto.

1745.1   *An essay on man: by Alexander Pope esq. enlarged and improved by the author. With notes by William Warburton, M.A.* London: printed for John and Paul Knapton, 1745. William Bowyer ornaments. ESTC t005613; Foxon P867; Maslen 1745*a*; not in Griffith.

1745.2   *An essay on man: by Alexander Pope Esq. enlarged and improved by the author. With notes by William Warburton, M.A.* London: printed for John and Paul Knapton, 1745. William Bowyer ornaments. ESTC t005614; Foxon P868; Maslen 1745*b*; Griffith 607.

1745.3   *An essay on man: by Alexander Pope, Esq. enlarged and improved by the author. With notes by William Warburton, M.A.* London: printed for John and Paul Knapton, 1745. William Bowyer ornaments. ESTC n009745; Foxon P869; Maslen 1745*c*; Griffith 608.

1746.1   *An essay on man: by Alexander Pope Esq. enlarged and improved by the author. With notes by Mr. Warburton.* London: printed for John and Paul Knapton, 1746. William Bowyer ornaments. ESTC t005616; Foxon P871; Maslen 1746; Griffith 620.

1747.1   *Ethic epistles: by Alexander Pope Esq;.* London: printed for J. and P. Knapton, 1747. ESTC n007289; not in Griffith.

1747.2   *The Works of Shakespear* [see Warburton-Knapton 1747c, below].

1748.1   *An essay on man: by Alexander Pope Esq. enlarged and improved by the author. With notes by Mr. Warburton.* London: printed for John and Paul Knapton, 1748. William Bowyer ornaments. ESTC t005617; Foxon P872; Maslen 1748*a*; not in Griffith.

1748.2　*An essay on man: by Alexander Pope Esq. enlarged and improved by the author. With the commentary and notes of Mr. Warburton.* London: printed for J. and P. Knapton, 1748. William Bowyer ornaments. ESTC t005618; Foxon P873; Maslen 1748*b*; Griffith 631.

1748.3　*Four ethic epistles by Alexander Pope, Esq. With the commentary and notes of Mr. Warburton.* London: printed for J. and P. Knapton, 1748. ESTC n031903; quarto (see 1744.1, above).

1749.1　*An essay on man: being the first book of ethic epistles to H. St. John L. Bolingbroke. With the commentary and notes of Mr. Warburton.* London: printed for J. and P. Knapton, 1743 [1749?]. ESTC t005620; quarto (see Foxon P865 n.).

1750.1　*The Dunciad: complete in four books, according to Mr. Pope's last improvements. With several additions now first printed. . . . Published by Mr. Warburton.* London: printed for J. and P. Knapton, 1749 [1750]. William Bowyer ornaments. ESTC t005563; Foxon P800; Griffith 638.

1751.1　*An essay on man: by Alexander Pope Esq. enlarged and improved by the author. With the notes of Mr. Warburton.* London: printed for J. and P. Knapton, 1751. William Bowyer ornaments. ESTC t005622; Griffith 656.

1751.2　*The works of Alexander Pope Esq. in nine volumes complete. With his last corrections, additions, and improvements; . . . Together with the commentaries and notes of Mr. Warburton,* 9 vols. London: printed for J. and P. Knapton, H. Lintot, J. and R. Tonson, and S. Draper, 1751. William Bowyer ornaments. ESTC t005432; Griffith 643–651.

1751.3　*The works of Alexander Pope Esq. in nine volumes complete. With his last corrections, additions, and improvements. Published by Mr. Warburton,* 9 vols. London: printed for J. and P. Knapton, H. Lintot, J. and R. Tonson, and S. Draper, 1751. William Bowyer ornaments. ESTC t005433; Griffith 653; small octavo.

1752.1　*The works of Alexander Pope Esq. in nine volumes complete. With his last corrections, additions, and improvements; . . . Together with the commentary and notes of Mr. Warburton,* 9 vols. London: printed for J. and P. Knapton, H. Lintot, J. and R. Tonson and S. Draper, and C. Bathurst, 1752. William Bowyer and William Strahan ornaments. ESTC t152369.

1753.1　*An essay on man: by Alexander Pope Esq. enlarged and improved by the author. Together with his MS. additions and variations, as in the last edition of his works. With the notes of Mr. Warburton.* London: printed for J. and P. Knapton, 1753. William Bowyer ornaments. ESTC t005625.

1753.2　*The works of Alexander Pope Esq. in nine volumes, complete. With his last corrections, additions, and improvements; . . . Together with the commentary and notes of Mr. Warburton,* 9 vols. London: printed for J. and P. Knapton, H. Lintot, J. and R. Tonson and S. Draper, and C. Bathurst, 1753. ESTC t005434.

1754.1   *The works of Alexander Pope, Esq. in ten volumes complete. With his last corrections, additions, and improvements; . . . printed verbatim from the octavo edition of Mr. Warburton,* 10 vols. London: printed for J. and P. Knapton, H. Lintot, J. and R. Tonson and S. Draper, and C. Bathurst, 1754. William Bowyer ornaments. ESTC t005435.

1755.1   *An essay on man: by Alexander Pope, Esq. enlarged and improved by the author. Together with his MS. additions and variations, as in the last edition of his works. With the notes of Mr. Warburton.* London: printed for J. and P. Knapton, 1755. William Bowyer ornaments. ESTC n009349.

1755.2   *Histoire de Martinus Scriblérus, de ses ouvrages & de ses decouvertes; traduite de l'anglois de monsieur Pope.* Londres: chez Paul Knapton, 1755. False imprint; possibly printed in Paris. ESTC t005687; duodecimo.

1755.3   *Histoire de Martinus Scriblerus, de ses ouvrages & de ses decouvertes; traduite de l'anglois de Monsieur Pope.* Londres: chez Paul Knapton, 1755. False imprint; possibly printed in Paris. The introduction ends on p.xxii in this issue. ESTC n001134; duodecimo.

(b) Warburton-Knapton Imprints

(All items below in octavo.)

1742a   *A critical and philosophical commentary on Mr Pope's Essay on man: in which is contain'd a vindication of the said Essay from the misrepresentations of Mr. de Resnel, the French translator, and of Mr. de Crousaz.* London: printed for John and Paul Knapton, 1742. ESTC t132396.

1742b   *A sermon preached at the Abbey-church at Bath: for promoting the charity and subscription towards the General Hospital or Infirmary in that city; on Sunday, October 24. 1742 . . . To which is added, a short account of the nature, rise, and progress, of the General Infirmary at Bath.* London: printed for J. Leake, at Bath; and sold by J. and P. Knapton, 1742. ESTC t047572.

1744a   *Remarks on several occasional reflections: in answer to . . . Dr. Middleton, Dr. Pococke, . . . Serving to explain and justify divers passages, in The divine legation, objected to by those learned writers. To which is added, a general review of the argument of The divine legation. . . . Together with an appendix in answer to a late pamphlet entitled, An examination of Mr. W—s second proposition.* London: printed for John and Paul Knapton, 1744. ESTC t112821.

1745a   *A faithful portrait of Popery: by which it is seen to be the reverse of Christianity; as it is the destruction of morality, piety, and civil liberty.* London: printed for J. and P. Knapton, 1745. ESTC t035240.

1745b   *Remarks on several occasional reflections: in answer to the Reverend Doctors Stebbing and Sykes. Serving to explain and justify the two dissertations in the divine legation, concerning the command to Abraham to offer up his son; and the nature of the Jewish theocracy.* . . . *Part II. and last.* London: printed for John and Paul Knapton, 1745. ESTC t132886.

1745c   *A sermon occasioned by the present unnatural rebellion.* . . . *Preached in Mr. Allen's chapel at Prior-park near Bath.* London: printed for J. and P. Knapton, 1745. ESTC t045853.

1746a   *An apologetical dedication to the Reverend Dr. Henry Stebbing, in answer to his censure and misrepresentations of the sermon preached on the general fast day, appointed to be observed December 18, 1745.* London: printed for J. and P. Knapton, 1746. ESTC t022209.

1746b   *The nature of national offences truly stated.* . . . *A sermon preached on the general fast day, appointed to be observed December 18, 1745.* London: printed for J. and P. Knapton, 1746. ESTC t039702.

1746c   *A sermon occasioned by the present unnatural rebellion*, 2nd ed. London: printed for J. and P. Knapton, 1746. ESTC t172801.

1746d   *A sermon preach'd on the thanksgiving appointed to be observed the ninth of October: for the suppression of the late unnatural rebellion* . . . London: printed for J. and P. Knapton, 1746. ESTC t004534.

1747a   *A letter from an author, to a Member of Parliament, concerning literary property.* London: printed for John and Paul Knapton, 1747. Anonymous. ESTC t037853.

1747b   [Catharine Cockburn] *Remarks upon the principles and reasonings of Dr. Rutherforth's Essay on the nature and obligations of virtue: in vindication of the contrary principles . . . inforced in the writings of the late Dr. Samuel Clarke. Published by Mr. Warburton with a preface.* London: printed for J. and P. Knapton, 1747. Anonymous: by Catharine Cockburn. William Bowyer ornament. ESTC t001538.

1747c   *The works of Shakespear in eight volumes. The genuine text (collated with all the former editions, and then corrected and emended) is here settled: being restored from the blunders of the first editors, and the interpolations of the two last: with a comment and notes, critical and explanatory*, ed. Alexander Pope and William Warburton, 8 vols. London: J. and P. Knapton, S. Birt, T. Longman and T. Shewell, H. Lintott, C. Hitch, J. Brindley, J. and R. Tonson and S. Draper, R. Wellington, E. New, and B. Dod, 1747. ESTC t138851; Griffith 621.

1748a   *The alliance between church and state: or, the necessity and equity of an established religion and a test law demonstrated*, 3rd ed., corrected and enlarged. London: printed for J. and P. Knapton, 1748. ESTC t021263.

1750a   *Julian: or a discourse concerning the earthquake and fiery eruption, which defeated that Emperor's attempt to rebuild the temple at Jerusalem.* London: printed for J. and P. Knapton, 1750. ESTC t132391.

1751a   *Julian: or a discourse concerning the earthquake and firey [sic] eruption, which defeated that Emperor's attempt to rebuild the temple at Jerusalem,* 2nd ed., with additions. London: printed for J. and P. Knapton, 1751. ESTC t132390.

1753a   *The principles of natural and revealed religion occasionally opened and explained: in a course of sermons preached before the Honourable Society of Lincoln's Inn.* 2 vols. London: printed for J. and P. Knapton, 1753–4. ESTC t132873.

1754b   *A view of Lord Bolingbroke's philosophy: in four letters to a friend. Letters first and second.* London: printed for John and Paul Knapton, 1754. Anonymous. ESTC t113197.

1755a   *The divine legation of Moses: in nine books. The fourth edition, corrected and enlarged.* London: printed for J. and P. Knapton, 1755. Vol. 1, parts 1 and 2 (books I–III). Vols. 3[2]-5 (books IV–VI) published by A. Millar, and J. and R. Tonson, 1765. Books VII–VIII were never published; book IX was published as a supplement in 1788. ESTC t127851.

1755b   *A view of Lord Bolingbroke's philosophy: in four letters to a friend. Letter the third.* London: printed for John and Paul Knapton, 1755. Anonymous. Also issued as part of *A view of Lord Bolingbroke's philosophy, compleat in four letters to a friend,* London, 2nd ed., 1756. ESTC t113195.

1755c   *A view of Lord Bolingbroke's philosophy: in four letters to a friend. Letter the fourth and last.* London: printed for John and Paul Knapton, 1755. Anonymous. Also issued as part of *A view of Lord Bolingbroke's philosophy, compleat in four letters to a friend,* London, 2nd ed., 1756. ESTC t113196.

APPENDIX D

WARBURTON'S 1747 *SHAKESPEAR* COPYRIGHT ASSIGNMENT AND 1759 ROYAL PATENT FOR POPE'S *WORKS*

In *The Birth of Shakespeare Studies*, Arthur Sherbo declared, 'Warburton's is surely one of the worst editions of Shakespeare ever published'.[1] The booksellers of the day evidently thought otherwise, hoping that a 'melting down' of Pope's 1725 edition with Warburton's acumen would prove popular. Pope's *Shakespear* inspired a long correspondence between Warburton and Theobald (BL: Eg. 1956, 38 letters; FSL, 68 letters; *ILH*, 2: 204–626). Warburton later corresponded with Sir Thomas Hanmer (Eg. 1957, 23 letters), but he fell out with both editors, concerned that his ideas might be plundered. From Oxford, Pope wrote to assure Warburton that Hanmer had not plagiarized his notes (4: 438–9).

Nichols listed the amounts editors of Shakespeare and their assistants were paid for their labours: Rowe (£36 10*s*. 0*d*.); Hughes (£28 7*s*. 0*d*.); Pope (£217 12*s*. 0*d*.); Fenton (£30 14*s*. 0*d*.); Gay (£35 17*s*. 6*d*.); Whalley (£12 0*s*. 0*d*.); Theobald (£652 10*s*. 0*d*.); Warburton (£500 0*s*. 0*d*.); Capell (£300 0*s*. 0*d*.); Johnson (1st ed. £375 0*s*. 0*d*.; 2nd ed. £100 0*s*. 0*d*.), for a total of £2,288 10*s*. 6*d*. (*LA*, 5: 597). While his edition attracted a considerable amount of negative criticism and fared poorly in the market-place, Warburton commanded a high fee for his edition. The 1753 Edinburgh edition was based on Warburton's edition.[2]

After the fourteen-year term, provided for in the 1710 Copyright Act, expired, Warburton obtained an additional term by Royal Patent in 1759.

---

[1] (East Lansing, 1986), p. 12.
[2] See Warren McDougall's identification of John Reid as editor in 'Copyright Litigation in the Court of Session, 1738–1749, and the Rise of the Scottish Book Trade', *Edinburgh Bibliographical Society Transactions*, 5th part, 5 (1988): 2–31, p. 14.

(a) WARBURTON'S COPYRIGHT ASSIGNMENT WITH JACOB TONSON FOR THE 1747 *SHAKESPEAR* EDITION

Warburton *to* Jacob Tonson[1]   24 January 1747
Folger Shakespeare Library: S.a.165 (F9.17.41)   [London]

Know all Men by these presents, That I William Warburton Master of Arts, Rector of Brant Broughton in Lincolnshire, for and in consideration of the sum of Five hundred Pounds of lawful money of Great Britain to me in hand paid by Jacob Tonson Citizen & Stationer of London for himself and the other Proprietors of the Copy right of Shakespears Plays, the receipt whereof, I do hereby confess and acknowledge; Have granted, bargained, sold, assigned, transferred and set over, and by these presents do Grant, bargain, sell, assign, transfer and set over, unto the said Jacob Tonson, his Executors, Administrators and Assigns, all the full and sole right and title of in and to the Copy of the Notes, Corrections, emendations, Preface and other additions, which I have made to the Plays of the said Shakespear, and all my Copy-right, Interest and Claim of, in or to the same and every part thereof, To have and to hold the same and every part thereof unto the said Jacob Tonson his Executors, Administrators and Assigns, for the benefit of himself, and the other Proprietors of the copy-right of the said Shakespears Plays, as his and their own proper Goods and Chattels for ever. In Witness whereof I have hereunto set my hand and seal this twenty fourth day of January in the twentieth year of the Reign of our Sovereign Lord George the Second, and in the Year of our Lord One Thousand seven hundred and forty-six.

Signed, sealed and delivered

(being first duly stamped)

in the presence of

W. Warburton

[witnessed by:] Betty Athy[?] Thomas Taylor

Endorsement: Mr Warburtons Assignment for his Edition of Shakespear £500 T.22. 30

[1] For the full imprint of Warburton's Shakespeare edition, see Appendix C. This copyright assignment was acquired by the FSL from Dobell in 1941 (catalogue 66, item 43): 'WARBURTON (William) THE ORIGINAL ASSIGNMENT BY WM. WARBURTON TO JACOB TONSON AND THE OTHER PROPRIETORS OF THE COPYRIGHT OF HIS EDITION OF SHAKESPEAR'S PLAYS. . . . one page, folio, *With three sixpenny embossed stamps*, £25 ($100)'.

(b) WARBURTON'S ROYAL PATENT TO PUBLISH POPE'S WORKS[1]
(24 JULY 1759)

GEORGE R.

GEORGE the Second, by the Grace of God, King of Great Britain, France and Ireland, Defender of the Faith, etc. To all to whom these Presents shall come, Greeting: WHEREAS Our trusty and well-beloved William Warburton, Doctor in Divinity, Dean of our Cathedral Church of Bristol, hath, by his Petition, humbly represented unto Us, that the late Alexander Pope, Esq; having by his Will bequeathed unto him, the Petitioner, the Property of all such of his Works already printed, as he the said Petitioner hath written, or shall write, Commentaries, or Notes, upon; and all the Profits which should arise, after his Death, from such Editions as he, the said Petitioner, should publish, without future Alterations;[2] and that being desirous of reaping the Fruits of his Labour, which he cannot enjoy without Our Royal Licence and Protection, he hath therefore most humbly besought Us to grant him Our Royal Privilege and Licence for the sole Printing, Publishing and Vending the said Works, for the Term of Fourteen Years; We being graciously pleased to gratify him in his said Request, do, by these Presents, agreeable to the Statute in that Behalf made and provided, for Us, Our Heirs and Successors, give and grant unto the said Doctor William Warburton, Dean of Bristol, his Executors, Administrators, and Assigns, Our Royal Privilege and Licence for the sole Printing and Publishing the said Works, for and during the Term of Fourteen Years; to be computed from the Day of the Date hereof; strictly forbidding and prohibiting all Our Subjects within our Kingdoms of Great Britain and Ireland, and other Our Dominions, to reprint or abridge the same, either in the like, or any other Volume or Volumes whatsoever, or to import, buy, vend, utter or distribute any Copies of the same, or any Part thereof, reprinted, beyond the Seas, within the said Term of Fourteen Years, without the Consent or Approbation of the said Doctor William Warburton, Dean of Bristol, his Heirs, Executors, and Assigns, by Writing under his or their Hands and Seals first had and obtained, as they and every of them, offending herein, will answer the contrary at their Perils; whereof the Master, Wardens, and Company of Stationers of Our City of London, the Commissioners and other Officers of Our Customs, and all other Our Officers and Ministers whom it may concern, are to take Notice that due Obedience be given to Our Pleasure herein signified. Given at Our Court at Kensington, the Twenty-fourth Day of July 1759, in the Thirty-third Year of Our Reign.

By His Majesty's Command,
HOLDERNESSE.

[1] Warburton's term of ownership of any Pope copyright would have expired by 1758. This Royal Patent, extending Warburton's copyright by an additional fourteen years (to 24 July 1773), appeared opposite the general title-page of subsequent editions of Pope's *Works*. The text here has been taken from the 1770 large octavo edition (EUL copy: V* 21.39).

[2] A number of the preceding phrases have been taken verbatim from the clause in Pope's will relating to Warburton's legacy.

APPENDIX E

BIOGRAPHICAL APPENDIX

For main sources of information, see Short Forms and Abbreviations or List of Works Cited, *Alumni Oxonienses (1715–1886)*, ed. Joseph Foster (Oxford, 1888) and *Musgrave's Obituary*, ed. Sir George J. Armytage (London, 1900). For references (other than in Plomer) to booksellers outside London, see John Feather, *The Provincial Book Trade in Eighteenth-Century England* (Cambridge, 1985); and Robert Hay Carnie and Ronald Paterson Doig, 'Scottish printers and booksellers 1668–1775'. Letter-writers, recipients and important or frequently mentioned persons are listed, as well as those involved with the publishing of Pope's works. Some persons mentioned remain unidentified. Letter-writers and recipients are given in capitals.

Key: AP = Alexander Pope; JK = John Knapton; WW = William Warburton.

ALLEN, Ralph (1694–1764). Patron of Fielding, AP and WW. WW married his niece Gertrude Tucker in 1746, and they lived with the Allens at Prior Park. Through his influential connections, WW found new preferment. The driving force behind the improved postal system, Allen franked many of WW's letters. WW ordered books for Allen through JK. In his will he bequeathed £5000 to WW as well as his library which included the books left to him by AP. He married his second wife, Elizabeth, née Holder (1698?–1766), in 1737. WW mentioned her flagging health during the 1750s.

Arbuthnot, George (1703?–76). The second son of AP's Scriblerian friend, he served as AP's counsel in his copyright case against Henry Lintot. AP asked him to act as WW's attorney in his case against Mawhood in 1742. He was one of the executors of AP's will in which he was left AP's portrait of Bolingbroke, the watch given to him by the King of Sardinia and £200. WW evidently thought little of him after AP's death.

ATWELL, Dr. Joseph (*fl.* 1733–55). Rector of Exeter College, Oxford, 1733–7; M.A. (1718); B.D. (1728); D.D. (1733). WW wrote to him of JK's near-failing in 1755.

Balguy, Thomas (1716–95). A Warburtonian, educated at St. John's College, Cambridge (B.A. 1737); lectured on moral philosophy; favoured for preferment by Hoadly. He declined WW's vacant bishopric in 1781.

BATHURST, Charles (1709–86). Bookseller; reputedly a baronet; successor to Benjamin Motte (who published the AP-Swift *Miscellanies* and *Gulliver's Travels*). Ten of AP's letters to him survive. He had hoped to become WW's publisher on Gyles' death. He is connected with AP-JK books from 1738.

Although his name does not appear in the 1751 imprint of AP's *Works*, he received a 4.7% share of the profits.

BECKET, Thomas (*fl.* 1760–75). Bookseller who lost the landmark copyright case of *Donaldson* v. *Becket* in 1774; a go-between for WW and Dalrymple.

BIRCH, Thomas (1705–66). Proof-read (along with John Jortin) the 1751 *Works*. He supplied biographies to accompany the Vertue and Houbraken engravings in the large folio two-vol. *Heads of Illustrious Persons* (1743–51) published by the Knaptons. His correspondence with JK and others is in the BL. (Gunther).

BOLINGBROKE, Henry St. John (1678–1751), Viscount. AP's 'guide, philosopher and friend' and WW's rival, Bolingbroke perhaps swayed the poet more towards deism than AP knew. As one of the executors of AP's unpublished manuscripts, Bolingbroke came into conflict with WW in the *Patriot King* controversy. Bolingbroke died a bitter man, feeling betrayed 'by the Injustice and Treachery of Persons nearest to me; by the Negligence of Friends; and by the Infidelity of Servants'. His fortune was valued at less than £1000 (BL: Official Publications 357.D.9–12). In 1754, WW attacked Mallet's edition of Bolingbroke's *Works* (1753–4) published by Millar. (Dickinson).

BOWYER, William, the younger (1699–1777). The 'learned' printer; in 1737 he succeeded his father who had printed AP's *Works* in 1717; he printed the 1751 edition of AP's *Works* and much of the 1752 edition (along with William Strahan); WW's repeated demands led to a heated correspondence and long-standing antipathy. His ledgers reflect the Knaptons' spiralling debt in the early 1750s. He declined to act as one of JK's trustees in 1755. (Fleeman, '18th-century Printing Ledgers').

BROWN, John (1715–66). His poem, *An Essay on Satire: Occasion'd by the death of Mr. Pope*, was published by Dodsley in 1745 and attracted WW's attention. After glowing lines were added about AP's editor, WW inserted *An Essay on Satire* before *An Essay on Man* in vol. 3 of the 1751 *Works*, and it was retained in subsequent editions. (Templeman).

BROWNE, Isaac Hawkins, the younger (1745–1818). Son of Isaac Hawkins Browne, the elder, (1705–60) whose *Poems Upon Various Subjects* appeared in 1768, the same year as *Fragmentum Isaaci Hawkins Browne Arm. sive, Anti-Bolingbrokius*.

CADELL, Thomas (1742–1802). Bookseller who began his apprenticeship under Andrew Millar in 1758 and became a partner in 1765. He succeeded to the business on Millar's death in 1768. His name appeared at the end of the imprint of the 1769 quarto edition of AP's *Works*; and, with William Strahan, he published three editions of *An Essay on Man* in 1771, 1774 and 1777. He also published WW's works (1767–88) and Hurd's 7-vol. edition of WW's *Works* (1788).

Chesterfield, Philip Dormer Stanhope (1694–1773), 4th Earl of. Friend of AP who mentioned him in *Dialogue II* and *1740*. Dr. Johnson's least favourite patron, he offered to take WW to Ireland in 1745 as his private chaplain. WW politely declined and dedicated the 1748 edition of *Alliance between Church and State* to him. He was mentioned as a mutual friend of WW and Bolingbroke who would be concerned about WW's planned biography of AP. He defended the introduction of the Gregorian calendar in the House of Lords during the 1751 debate over the Calendar Reform Bill.

Cibber, Colley (1671–1757). In response to his substitution for Theobald in the revised *Dunciad*, he attacked AP in *Another Occasional Letter* and publicized WW's former alliance with Theobald.

Cibber, Theophilus (1703–58). Ridiculed WW as AP's editor in 'A Serio-Comic Apology', appended to his edition of *Romeo and Juliet* (C. Corbett & G. Woodfall [1748?]), and at greater length in *A Familiar Epistle to Mr. Warburton from Theophilus Cibber* (1753).

COCKBURN, Catharine, née Trotter (1679–1749). Shortly after AP's death, she approached WW, asking about *The Divine Legation*. He then presented her with copies of AP's two *Essays* and the *Dunciad*. WW supplied a preface for her refutation of Rutherforth's *Essay on Virtue* and told JK he did not think that her book had been sufficiently publicized. Bowyer printed 1000 proposals for her *Works* on 1 April 1749 (Ledger 478*v*; Maslen 74*v*). Her *Works* were published in two vols. by the Knaptons in 1751.

Cole, Nathaniel (*d.* 1759). Solicitor to the East India Company; elected Clerk of the Stationers' Company on 1 October 1723; freed by redemption on 3 February 1736. He advised AP and Dodsley on how to deal with Watson's piracy of the *Letters* in 1737 and Corbett's edition in 1741. He was acquainted with JK and Charles Yorke. (Nichol, 'Pope, Warburton, Knapton, and Cole').

COMBER, Thomas (*fl.* 1750–2). Rector of Morborne and Buckworth; presumably related to Thomas Comber, Dean of Durham (1645–99), whose *Companion to the Altar* (6th ed.) was published by James Knapton *et al.* in 1721.

Cooper, John Gilbert (1723–69). A contributor to Dodsley's *Museum* from 1746, he instigated a quarrel with WW in *The Life of Socrates* (R. Dodsley, 1749) by reflecting disparagingly on *The Divine Legation of Moses*. WW replied in kind in the footnotes to *An Essay on Criticism* in *Works* (1751), 1: 151, thereby inviting Cooper's *Cursory Remarks on Mr. Warburton's new Edition of Mr. Pope's Works*. (London: M. Cooper, 1751).

Cooper, Mary (*fl.* 1731–61). Trade publisher; married Thomas Cooper (*d.* 9 Feb. 1743) on 2 May 1731, who published some of AP's works (Griffith 472, 473, 511, 512 and, with R. Dodsley, 505, 523, 524, 583, 584). Her name appears in imprints to John G. Cooper (q.v.), AP's 1743 *Dunciad* (Foxon P796) and the 1757 *Supplement* to AP's *Works*. (Treadwell).

CRAWFURD (Crawford, Crauford), Ronald (*d.* 1762). Edinburgh solicitor, admitted Writer to the Signet in 1732; Commissary Clerk of Peebles in 1742.

His letter of 28 November 1754 to George Ross probably persuaded WW not to pursue legal action against Foulis in Scotland.

Dalrymple, Sir David (1726–92), Lord Hailes. Admitted to the Faculty of Advocates in 1748; raised to the Bench as Lord Hailes in 1766; appointed a Lord of the Justiciary in 1776; Scottish historian, judge, editor of Sir Adam Gordon's *Edom of Gordon* (1755) and author of *Memorials and Letters Relating to the History of Britain in the Reign of James I* (1762); *An Account of the preservation of King Charles II, with his Letters* (1766); *Memorials and Letters Relating to the History of Britain in the Reign of Charles I* (1766); *Annals of Scotland from Malcolm Canmore to Robert I* (1776); *Disquisitions concerning the antiquities of the Christian church* (1783). WW corresponded with him from 1762 to 1776.

DODDRIDGE, Philip (1702–51). Nonconformist minister who published 6 vols. of *The Family Expositor* (1739–56) and corresponded frequently with WW. (Nuttall, *Calendar*).

DODDRIDGE, Mercy, née Maris (1709–90). WW offered her advice on copyright and her late husband Philip's literary property. (Nuttall, *Handlist*).

DODSLEY, Robert (1703–64). AP helped to set him up as a bookseller with a loan; published Mason's *Musaeus* and Brown's *An Essay on Satire* (which was revised and later included by WW in the 1751 *Works*). Dodsley's hopes of acquiring a share in AP's works were dashed by WW after JK's set-back in 1755 because he had published John Gilbert Cooper's *Life of Socrates* in 1749. (Straus; Tierney).

Draper, Somerset (1706–56). Bookseller; partner of Jacob and Richard Tonson and close friend of Garrick (fourteen letters from 1744 to 1751 from Garrick to Draper survive in *LDG*). He was expected to deliver the corrected copy of WW's 1747 Shakespeare edition. His name appears on the imprints of AP's *Works* from 1751 to 1756. He drew up the abstract of accounts for the five editions of AP's *Works* from 1751 to 1754; his share was included under 'Mr Tonson & Co' (BL: Eg. 1959, f.30). WW mentions him in association with Millar after Knapton's collapse in 1755. His brother-in-law, James Clutterbuck, was mentioned by Gertrude Warburton in a letter to Yorke (Eg. 1952, f.234). (Boswell, *Life*; Garrick).

Edwards, Thomas (1699–1757). Barrister, critic and F.S.A. who corresponded with AP about his grotto and sent minerals for it from Bristol. He later crossed swords with WW. His satiric attack on WW's edition of Shakespeare earned him a place in the footnotes to the 1749 *Dunciad* and the 1751 *Works* alongside Theophilus Cibber and John Upton (*Works*, 4: 23; 'Arbuthnot', 1. 169 n.; *TE*, 5: 398). *A Supplement to Mr. Warburton's Edition of Shakespear* was first published by Mary Cooper in 1747. From the third edition (1750), its publisher was Charles Bathurst, who concurrently held a share in the WW edition of AP's *Works*. Later under the title, *The Canons of Criticism*, it swelled and proved popular, with a seventh edition published in 1765. Samuel Johnson compared the literary contest to a fly pestering a horse, 'but yet the

horse is the nobler animal', although Joseph Warton tended to agree with
Edwards.

ETOUGH, Henry (1677–1757). Rector of Therfield, Hants., who shared a
common interest with Birch and WW in the publication of Cockburn's
works. He also corresponded with Philip Yorke and Thomas Secker.
(Gunther).

FOULIS, Robert (1707–76) and Andrew (1712–75). Printers and booksellers;
Robert Foulis set up as a bookseller in 1741 and two years later became the
printer to Glasgow University along with his brother Andrew. He requested
WW's permission to print AP's works in Scotland in 1754. (Gaskell,
Bibliography of the Foulis Press).

GARRICK, David (1717–79). AP saw him on stage as Richard III; a close
friend of Somerset Draper; acted as go-between for Sterne when WW heard a
rumour that he was to be satirized as Tristram Shandy's tutor; he urged WW
to support the booksellers' monopoly in 1774.

GOSLING, Robert (1684–1741) and Francis (*fl.* 1742–57; *d.* 1768). Father
(founder of Gosling's Bank, Fleet Street) and son (who established it from
1757), who had been booksellers. Account-holders included WW (1755–6)
and JK (Mar. 1751–May 1770) for whom ledgers recording their transactions survive. (Fleeman in *Studies in the Book Trade*; Melton in Myers and
Harris, *Economics of the British Booktrade*).

HARDWICKE, 1st Earl of, see YORKE, Philip

HARRIS, James (1709–80). Grammarian and close friend of Fielding; WW
read his *Hermes* (1751); he sent WW a copy of the second edition in 1765.
(Battestin; Probyn).

Hildyard (Hilliard, Hilyard), John (*fl.* 1731–57). York bookseller who
occasionally acted on behalf of WW and JK.

HILL, Sir John (1716?–75) Quack and miscellaneous writer; specialist in
popular treatments of scientific and medical topics. His offer to dedicate *The
Inspector* to WW early in 1753 was declined. (Nichol, 'A Warburton-Hill
Letter'; Rousseau).

Hitch, Charles (*fl.* 1733–64). Bookseller who ran a delivery service from
Holborn to Bath with James Leake. (Boswell, *Life*).

HOGARTH, William (1697–1764). Artist who was absent from AP's list of
acquaintances, possibly because of an early caricature of a paint-spattering
hunchback at Burlington Gate. His last work, 'The Bathos: Tailpiece'
(1764), owes much to the *Dunciad* and AP's 1744 sepia drawing used as a
frontispiece to posthumous editions of *An Essay on Man* (1745–55). WW
subscribed to his *Analysis of Beauty* against the prevailing opinions of Horace
Walpole and the Dilettanti. Hogarth supposedly satirized WW in 'The Five
Orders of Periwigs'. (Paulson).

HORSFIELD, Robert (*c.* 1723–98). 'Mr Horsfield died March 4, 1798, aged
75. —— He had been for several years a Bookseller in Ludgate-street; where

he succeeded to the extensive business of Messrs. Knapton' (*LA*, 3: 607). He was one of the executors of JK's will.

Hume, David (1711–76). WW attacked his *Four Dissertations* (1757); Millar published Hume and WW at the same time; Hurd addressed an attack on Hume to WW in 1757, rpt. 1777. (Mossner; Price).

Hume, Hugh, see Marchmont

HURD, Richard (1720–1808). Bishop of Worcester who was WW's protégé and eventual editor. He paid a compliment to WW in his edition of Horace's *Ars Poetica* (1749) which was returned in a footnote to *An Essay on Criticism* in the 1751 *Works*. Hurd dedicated his 1753 edition of Horace to WW who then presented Hurd with a gift set of the 1753 edition of AP's *Works*. He bought WW's library including most of the books bequeathed by AP to WW and Ralph Allen (who had left his share of AP's books to WW in 1764) and housed them in his new library at Hartlebury Castle when he was translated to Worcester in 1781. (Brewer; Hurd, *Correspondence of Richard Hurd and William Mason*, ed. Whibley).

JORTIN, John (1698–1770). WW's assistant at Lincoln's Inn from 1747 to 1751. With Birch, he proof-read the 1751 large octavo edition of AP's *Works*. He attended Jesus College, Cambridge. According to the *DNB*, 'While an undergraduate he was selected by his tutor, Styan Thirlby, to translate some passages from Eustathius for the notes to Pope's "Homer," and noticed an error in Pope's translation, which Pope silently corrected in a later edition.' A disagreement with WW's interpretation of book 6 of the *Aeneid* led to an estrangement in 1755.

Knapton, James (*d.* 1736?). Bookseller; father of John and Paul and founder of the business; he started his bookshop about 1687 at the Queen's Head in St. Paul's Churchyard, moving to the nearby Crown in 1690. The business moved to the Crown in Ludgate Street about 1735.

KNAPTON, John (1696–1770). Eldest son of James Knapton. He published AP's *Letters* in 1737 and appeared in another dozen AP imprints before the poet's death. AP recommended JK to WW shortly after the death of the latter's bookseller Fletcher Gyles in 1741. His name was first in the imprint of AP's *Works* (1751) and Johnson's *Dictionary* (1755). The Knapton share in the first five Warburton editions of AP's *Works* was 25·2%. He seems to have remained a bachelor all his life. WW regarded him as one of the most successful booksellers in London until the collapse in 1755, after which he only partially recovered. Most of JK's stock and copyrights were auctioned off at the Queen's Head Tavern on 25 September 1755.

KNAPTON, Paul (1703–55). Bookseller; he married Elizabeth Chalwell of Coleman Street who brought a dowry of £5000 on 14 February 1741 at Stevenage (*GM*, 11 (March 1741): 108). Rarely mentioned in WW's letters, he most likely had a small role in the day-to-day running of the shop. His death precipitated the financial crisis from which his brother eventually but only partially recovered.

LEAKE, James (1685?–1764). Bath bookseller and proprietor of its first circulating library. With Charles Hitch, he ran a parcel service between Bath and Holborn Bridge, London. He was Samuel Richardson's brother-in-law.

LINTOT, Henry (1703–58). Bookseller whose name appears in imprints of AP's *Works* between 1736 and 1764. Son of Bernard (1675–1736) who once vied with Jacob Tonson (1656?–1736) over AP's earlier works. Henry bought the copyright to the *Dunciad* in 1740 against AP's wishes. AP filed a complaint against him in Chancery. He tried again in 1755, but WW threatened to lay claim to his forthcoming edition of AP's Homer by furnishing commentaries. Lintot held a 12·9% share in WW's edition of AP's *Works* from 1751 to 1754.

LITTLETON, Sir Edward, 4th baronet (succeeded 1742; *d.* 1812). Lived at Teddesley, Staffordshire, and became Hurd's pupil at Emmanuel College, Cambridge, in 1744; Hurd dedicated the 1757 edition of *Ars Poetica* to him; he was the M.P. for Staffordshire, 1784–1807.

LYTTELTON, George (1709–73), 1st Baron Lyttelton (Lyttleton). AP hailed him in *Epistle I. i*, *Dialogues I* and *II*, and left him his marble busts of Spenser, Shakespeare, Milton and Dryden. Patron of Thomson, Mallet and Fielding (who dedicated *Tom Jones* to him in 1749). Secretary to the Prince of Wales in 1737. He discouraged WW from attacking Bolingbroke in his unpublished biography of AP. WW helped him with research for his long-delayed book on Henry II.

Major, Thomas (1720–99). Engraver; he completed Andrew Lawrence's 'Death of a Stag' in 1750, dedicating it to Lord Chesterfield. WW suggested JK commission him to make an engraving for the 1751 edition of AP's *Works*. Major engraved the Blakey design for the 1751 frontispiece which depicts WW as the principal figure.

MALET, Catherine (*fl.* 1769–74). Evidently a trusted friend in Gloucester; for Gertrude Warburton's correspondence with her, see BL: Add. MS. 41580, ff.3, 6 and 9.

MALLET, David (1705?–65). Scottish-born poet, dramatist and friend of AP. When Mallet recounted the story of AP's vision of Apollo leaping from his forehead into Mallet's own, WW rebuffed him. As Bolingbroke's secretary, he quickly became an enemy of WW; he was a likely candidate for the authorship of *A Familiar Epistle to the most impudent Man Living* (1749). WW withdrew a derisive footnote about him in the 1751 edition of AP's *Works*. As editor of Bolingbroke's *Works*, he again came into conflict with WW.

MANSFIELD, 1st Earl of, see MURRAY, William

Marchmont, Hugh Hume (1708–94), 3rd Earl of. Literary executor who was to take charge of AP's manuscripts and unprinted papers in the event of Bolingbroke's death. He wittily alerted AP to WW's pedantry.

MASON, William (1725–97). His *Musaeus: a Monody to the Memory of Mr. Pope in Imitation of Milton's Lycidas* (London: R. Dodsley and M. Cooper, 1747) brought him to WW's notice. As a poet and playwright he was encouraged by WW, but also advised not to mix clerical and poetical vocations. WW was influential in getting his *Elfrida* published by the Knaptons in 1752. (Hurd, *Correspondence of Richard Hurd and William Mason*, ed. Whibley; Gaskell, *First Editions of William Mason*).

MILLAR, Andrew (1707–68). Scottish-born bookseller who published the works of Thomson, Fielding and Johnson. His legal redress in copyright infringement of *Joseph Andrews* encouraged AP, although his attempts at eliminating piracy in Scotland proved ultimately fruitless. He seems to have curried WW's favour over a number of years, visiting him at Prior Park. He sent specimens of his forthcoming edition of Bolingbroke to WW hoping for approval, which never came. Although WW frowned on his involvement in the publishing of Bolingbroke and Hume, Millar published several editions of AP's works from 1756 and became WW's bookseller. He was succeeded by Thomas Cadell. (Amory).

MILLES, Jeremiah (1714–84). F.S.A. (1741); F.R.S. (1742); he succeeded Lyttelton as President of the London Society of Antiquaries from 1768 to 1784.

MURRAY, William (1705–93), 1st Earl of Mansfield. AP dedicated *Epistle I. vi* to Murray who had been tutored in oratory by AP. He was the Solicitor-General from 1742 to 1754 and served as the Attorney-General from 1754 to 1756 during the Newcastle ministry. He presided as Lord Chief Justice over the Wilkes trial. Murray at one time acted as counsel for Glasgow University which presented him with an honorary LL.D. in 1754, shortly before WW consulted him about the Foulis affair. His library was destroyed in the riots of 1780. (Fifoot).

NEWCASTLE, Thomas Pelham-Holles (1693–1768), 1st Duke of. Prime Minister (1754–6), long-time correspondent and patron of WW who secured the deanery of Bristol for him in 1757. WW sought to reconcile Newcastle with Pitt.

NEWTON, Thomas (1704–82). Attended Westminster School with Mansfield and served as Pulteney's chaplain; consecrated Bishop of Bristol on 28 December 1761. By 1775, eight editions of Milton earned him £735.

NOURSE, John (1730?–80). London bookseller who specialized in French literature and scientific works; WW ordered various books from him. (Feather, 'John Nourse and his Authors').

Osborne, Thomas (*fl.* 1738–67). Roguish but sometimes respectable bookseller, satirized in the *Dunciad*, who worked with – and occasionally against – the Knaptons.

PELHAM-HOLLES, Thomas, see NEWCASTLE

Pitt, John (1706–87). Minor politician and favourite cousin of William Pitt; Gertrude Warburton visited his wife in Dorset in August 1754.

Pope, Alexander (1688–1744). He recommended JK to WW when his bookseller, Fletcher Gyles, died in 1741. After AP's death, WW published editions of the *Dunciad*, *Essay on Man* and *Works* with JK.

RICHARDSON, Samuel (1689–1761). Aaron Hill told AP that Richardson was the printer of the pro-Walpole *Daily Gazetteer* which attacked the poet. Dr. George Cheyne relayed AP's 'warm compliments to the author of *Pamela*' (*Correspondence*, 4: 335 n.3). WW supplied the preface to the fourth volume of *Clarissa* in 1748, which Richardson subsequently dropped. While their friendship may have been strained by Richardson's association with Thomas Edwards, WW praised *Sir Charles Grandison* in 1753. He married the sister of James Leake.

ROSS, George (*fl.* 1754). London solicitor in Conduit Street engaged by Murray to correspond with Crawfurd in Edinburgh about possible legal action against Foulis.

ST. JOHN, Henry, Viscount Bolingbroke, see BOLINGBROKE

SAYER, John (*fl.* 1738–56). B.A., Balliol College, Oxford, 1738; M.A. 1741; clergyman and Latin translator who belatedly asked WW's permission to reprint AP's works in 1754. The text of AP's third epistle of *An Essay on Man* appeared in footnote form to Sayer's translation, *De homine* (Oxford, 1752). Sayer later published a Latin–English edition in quarto of AP's *Universal Prayer: Alexandri Popii, sive Universi Generis Humani Supplicatio* (London, 1756). Sayer was presumably the author of *A Vindication of the Power of Society to Annul the Marriage of Minors* (London, 1755); and translator of Montesquieu's *The Temple of Gnidus* (London: printed for G. Woodfall and sold by F. Knight, 1765).

Stanhope, Philip Dormer, see Chesterfield

STERNE, Laurence (1713–68). JK was involved in the publication of his sermon, *The Case of Elijah and the Widow of Zerephath, consider'd* (York: printed for J. Hildyard: and sold by Mess. Knapton; Mess. Longman and Shewell, and M. Cooper, London, 1747). According to Horace Walpole, WW recommended *Tristram Shandy* to his fellow bishops, praising Sterne as the 'English Rabelais', although shortly after the publication of the first two volumes of the novel, a rumour circulated that Tristram Shandy was to be tutored by a caricature of WW. 'What the devil! –' Sterne wrote to Garrick, 'is there no one learned blockhead throughout the many schools of misapplied science in the Christian World, to make a *tutor* for my Tristram?' During their brief correspondence, WW offered Sterne advice on his writing to which the novelist seems to have alluded – 'see you've splash'd a bishop' – although in the last volume of *Tristram Shandy* he favourably compared *The Divine Legation* to *Tale of a Tub*. The Knaptons also co-published two sermons or 'charges' of his uncle, Jaques Sterne. (Cash; New).

Strahan, William (1715–85). Printer-publisher who shared part of the printing of the 1752 edition of AP's *Works*; and appears in imprints of four editions of AP's *Works* from 1769 to 1776, on each occasion with Charles Bathurst among others. (Cochrane; Hernlund).

Tonson, Jacob (*d.* 1767). Great-nephew of 'genial' Jacob Tonson (1656?–1736), the first bookseller of that name, who published Dryden and AP; and son of Jacob Tonson II (*d.* 1735). He carried on the family business in the Strand upon his great-uncle's death. He paid WW £500 for editing Shakespeare in 1747. With his brother Richard and Somerset Draper, they owned a 6·7% share of AP's *Works* from 1751 to 1754. Between 1745 and 1764, their names appear on the imprints of at least thirteen editions of AP's *Works*. (Papali).

Tonson, Richard (*d.* 1772). Brother of Jacob Tonson III, above; he 'took little part in the concerns of the business' (Plomer); elected M.P. for Wallingford in 1747.

TOUP, Jonathan (1713–85). Philologist and classical editor; WW thought him 'the first Greek scholar in Europe'.

Upton, John (1707–60). Prebendary of Rochester from 1737. Editor of Arrian's *Epictetus* (1739–41) and Spenser's *Faerie Queene* (1758); he attacked WW's 1747 edition of Shakespeare in the second edition of *Critical Observations on Shakespeare* (1st ed. 1746; 1748). WW replied in the footnotes to the 1749 *Dunciad* and the 1751 *Works*.

WARBURTON, Gertrude, née Tucker (1728–96). Ralph Allen's favourite niece; married WW in 1745. After Mrs Allen died, she was left in control of Prior Park. Rumours that Thomas Potter was the father of their son Ralph Allen Warburton were suggested by Churchill and later published by Wilkes. After the bishop's death, she married WW's chaplain, the Reverend Martin Stafford Smith (nicknamed 'Gaffer Smut').

WARBURTON, William (1698–1779). AP's editor and literary executor, consecrated Bishop of Gloucester in 1760. He earlier carried on an extensive correspondence with Theobald criticizing AP's edition of Shakespeare, but later came to the defence of the *Essay on Man* against Crousaz's charges of deism. WW's *Vindication* brought him into AP's influential sphere. He had to cope with a barrage of attacks from critics of his editions of Shakespeare (1747) and AP (1751). A 50·5% shareholder in AP's *Works*, he helped JK recover after the setback of 1755.

Wilkes, John (1727–97). Responsible for the private printing of *An Essay on Woman*, passages of which were read in the House of Lords by the Earl of Sandwich in 1763. WW feebly condemned the effort and wrote to Ralph Allen of Wilkes' duel with Martin. He also planned his own edition of AP's works: his annotated set of the 1751 Warburton edition, specially bound with extra leaves, is in the BL. (Rudé).

Yorke, Charles (1722–70). The second son of Philip Yorke; he carried on a long correspondence with WW. He was appointed Solicitor-General (1756–61), Attorney-General (1762 and 1765–7), Lord Chancellor and Privy Councillor (1770). He was also a trustee of the Warburtonian Lecture.

YORKE, Philip (1690–1764), 1st Earl of Hardwicke. Attorney-General in 1727 when WW helped Samuel Burroughs with *The Legal Judicature in Chancery*. With his help, WW was appointed to a prebend of Gloucester Cathedral in 1753.

LIST OF WORKS CITED

[See Appendix C for Pope and Warburton titles published by the Knaptons.]

Allen, Brian. *Francis Hayman*. New Haven and London, 1987.

Allgemeine Deutsche Biographie. Berlin, 1970.

Alumni Oxonienses (1715–1886), ed. Joseph Foster. 4 vols. Oxford, 1888.

Amory, Hugh. 'Andrew Millar and the first recension of Fielding's *Works* (1762)', *Transactions of the Cambridge Bibliographical Society*, 8 i (1981): 57–78..

Barber, Giles. 'Bolingbroke, Pope, and the *Patriot King*', *The Library*, 5th ser., 19 (1964): 67–89.

Barker, Nicolas. 'Pope and his publishers', *TLS* (3 September 1976), p. 1085.

Battestin, Martin, with Ruth Battestin. *Henry Fielding: a Life*. London and New York, 1989.

Belanger, Terry. 'Booksellers' Trade Sales, 1718–1768', *The Library*, 5th ser., 30 (1975): 281–302.

——. 'Publishers and writers in eighteenth-century England', *Books and their Readers in Eighteenth-Century England*, ed. Isabel Rivers. Leicester, 1982, pp. 5–25.

Black, Jeremy. 'Bolingbroke's Attack on Pope: a Lawyer's Comment', *N&Q*, 231 (1986): 513–14.

Blanchard, Frederic T. *Fielding the Novelist*. New Haven, 1927.

[Bolingbroke, Henry St. John, Viscount.] *A Familiar Epistle to the Most Impudent Man Living*, ed. Donald T. Siebert, Jr., Augustan Reprint Society, no. 192. Los Angeles, 1978.

Boswell, James. *The Journal of a Tour to the Hebrides* (with Samuel Johnson, *A Journey to the Western Islands of Scotland*), ed. Peter Levi. Harmondsworth, 1984.

——. *Life of Johnson*, ed. R. W. Chapman, rev. J. D. Fleeman, introd. Pat Rogers. Oxford, 1980.

Boyce, Benjamin. *The Benevolent Man: a Life of Ralph Allen of Bath*. Cambridge, Mass., 1967.

Brewer, Sarah. 'The Early Letters of Richard Hurd from 1739 to 1762'. 4 vols. Unpublished Ph.D. thesis, University of Birmingham, 1987.

Brumfitt, J.H. 'Voltaire and Warburton', *Studies on Voltaire and the Eighteenth Century*, ed. Theodore Besterman, 18 (Geneva, 1961): 35–56.

Carnie, Robert Hay, and Ronald Paterson Doig. 'Scottish printers and booksellers 1668–1775: a supplement', *Studies in Bibliography*, 12 (1959): 131–59; Carnie, 'Supplements', *Studies in Bibliography*, 14 (1961): 81–96; and *Studies in Bibliography*, 15 (1962): 105–20.

Carruthers, Robert. *Life of Alexander Pope*. London, 1857.

Carter, Harry. *A History of the Oxford University Press*, vol. 1. Oxford, 1975.

Cartwright, Graham. 'Pope's Books: a postscript to Mack', *N&Q*, 231 (1986): 56–8.

Cash, Arthur H. *Laurence Sterne: the Later Years*. London, 1986.

Chomsky, Noam. 'Aspects of the Theory of Syntax', *Readings in the Theory of Grammar from the 17th to the 20th Century*, ed. Diane D. Bornstein. Cambridge, Mass., 1976, pp.218–40.

Clifford, James L. *Dictionary Johnson*. London, 1979.

Cochrane, J.A. *Dr. Johnson's Printer: the life of William Strahan*. London, 1964.

Colvin, H.M. *A Biographical Dictionary of English Architects*. London, 1954.

Cradock, Joseph, ed. *Literary and Miscellaneous Memoirs*. London, 1824.

Crane, Eva. *A Book of Honey*. Oxford, 1980.

Dickinson, H.T. *Bolingbroke*. London, 1970.

Dickson, P.G.M. *The Sun Insurance Office 1710–1960*. London, 1960.

Doddridge, Philip. *Letters to and from the Rev. Philip Doddridge*, ed. Thomas Stedman. Shrewsbury and London, 1790.

Dodsley, Robert. *The Correspondence of Robert Dodsley 1733–1764*, ed. James E. Tierney. Cambridge, 1988.

Dunton, John. *Life and Errors of John Dunton*, 2 vols. London, 1818; rpt. New York, 1969.

Eaves, T.C. Duncan, and Ben D. Kimpel. *Samuel Richardson: a Biography*. Oxford, 1971.

Eddy, Donald D. *A Bibliography of John Brown*. New York, 1971.

Evans, A.W. *Warburton and the Warburtonians*. Oxford and London, 1932.

Feather, John. *Book Prospectuses before 1801 in the John Johnson Collection*. Oxford, 1976.

——. *A History of British Publishing*. London, 1988.

——. 'John Nourse and his Authors', *Studies in Bibliography*, 34 (1981): 205–26.

——. *The Provincial Book Trade in Eighteenth-Century England*. Cambridge, 1985.

——. 'The Publishers and the Pirates: British Copyright Law in Theory and Practice, 1710–1775', *Publishing History*, 22 (1987): 5–32.

Fielding, Henry. *The History of Tom Jones*, ed. R. P. C. Mutter. Harmondsworth, 1966.

Fifoot, C.H.S. *Lord Mansfield*. London, 1936.

Fleeman, J.D. '18th-century Printing Ledgers', *TLS* (19 Dec. 1963), p.1056.

——. 'The revenue of a writer: Samuel Johnson's literary earnings', *Studies in the Book Trade In Honour of Graham Pollard*, OBS, ns vol. 18. 1975, pp.211–30.

Foxon, David. *English Verse 1701–1750*, 2 vols. Cambridge, 1975.

Fraser, George S. *Alexander Pope*. London, 1978.

Garrick, David. *The Letters of David Garrick*, ed. David M. Little and George M. Kahrl, 3 vols. Cambridge, Mass., 1963.

——. *Private Correspondence of David Garrick*, ed. James Boaden, 2 vols. London, 1831–2.

Gaskell, Philip. *A Bibliography of the Foulis Press*, 2nd ed. Winchester, 1986.

——. *The First Editions of William Mason*, Cambridge Bibliographical Society, monograph no. 1. Cambridge, 1951.

Griffith, R.H. *Alexander Pope: a bibliography*, 1 vol. in 2 pts. Austin, 1922–7.

Guerinot, J.V. *Pamphlet Attacks on Alexander Pope, 1711–1744*. London, 1969.

Gunther, A.E. *An Introduction to the Life of the Rev. Thomas Birch, D.D., F.R.S., 1705–1766*. Halesworth, 1984.

Hammelmann, H.A. 'Eighteenth-Century English Illustrators: Samuel Wale, R.A.', *Book Collector*, 1 (1952): 150–65.

Hammond, Brean. *Pope and Bolingbroke: a Study of Friendship and Influence*. Columbia, Miss., 1984.

Hanmer, Thomas. *The Correspondence of Sir Thomas Hanmer*, ed. H. Bunbury. London, 1838.

Harris, Michael. 'Periodicals and the Book Trade', *Development of the English Book Trade, 1700–1899*, ed. Robin Myers and Michael Harris. Oxford, 1981, pp.66–89.

Heal, Ambrose. 'London Booksellers and Publishers, 1700–1750', *N&Q*, 161 (1931): 328 and *passim*.

Hepworth, Brian. *Robert Lowth*. Boston, 1978.

Hernlund, Patricia. 'William Strahan's Ledgers: standard charges for printing, 1738–1785', *Studies in Bibliography*, 20 (1967): 89–111.

——. 'William Strahan's Ledgers II: charges for papers 1738–1785', *Studies in Bibliography*, 22 (1969): 179–95.

Hill, John. *The Letters and Papers of Sir John Hill 1714–1775*, ed. G. S. Rousseau. New York, 1982.

Hodgson, Norma, and Cyprian Blagden, ed. *The Notebook of Thomas Bennet and Henry Clements (1686–1719)*, OBS, ns vol. 6. Oxford, 1956.

Hume, David. *A Treatise of Human Nature*, ed. Ernest C. Mossner. Harmondsworth, 1985.

Hume, Henry. *A Selection from the Papers of the Earls of Marchmont*, ed. Sir G. H. Rose. 3 vols. London, 1831.

Hurd, Richard, and William Mason. *The Correspondence of Richard Hurd & William Mason*, introd. E. H. Pearce, ed. Leonard Whibley. Cambridge, 1932.

[——.] *A Discourse, by Way of General Preface to the Quarto Edition of Bishop Warburton's Works*. London, 1794.

Jarrett, Derek. *The Ingenious Mr Hogarth*. London, 1976.

Johnson, Samuel. *A Dictionary of the English Language*. 2 vols. London, 1755.

——. *Lives of the English Poets*, ed. G. Birkbeck Hill. 3 vols. Oxford, 1905.

——. *Samuel Johnson on Shakespeare*, ed. H. R. Woudhuysen. London, 1989.

Jones, Wendy L. *Talking on Paper: Alexander Pope's Letters*, English Literary Studies, no. 50. Victoria, B.C., 1990.

Kilvert, Francis. *Memoirs of the Life and Writings of the Right Rev. Richard Hurd*. London, 1860.

Knapp, Elise F. 'Community Property: the Case for Warburton's 1751 Edition of Pope', *Studies in English Literature*, 26 (1986): 455–68.

Lippincott, Louise. *Selling Art in Georgian England: the rise of Arthur Pond*. New Haven, 1983.

MacDonald, W.L. *Pope and his Critics: a Study in Eighteenth Century Personalities*. London, 1951.

MacDougall, Warren. 'Gavin Hamilton, John Balfour and Patrick Neill: a study of Publishing in Edinburgh in the 18th century'. Unpublished Ph.D. thesis, University of Edinburgh, 1974.

——. 'Gavin Hamilton, Bookseller in Edinburgh', *British Journal for Eighteenth-Century Studies*, 1 (1978): 1–19.

——. 'Copyright Litigation in the Court of Session, 1738–1749, and the Rise of the Scottish Book Trade', *Edinburgh Bibliographical Society Transactions*, 5th part, 5 (1988): 2–31.

Mack, Maynard. *Alexander Pope: a Life*. London and New York, 1985.

——. *Collected in Himself: Essays Critical, Biographical, and Bibliographical on Pope and Some of His Contemporaries*. Newark, 1982.

—— (ed.). *Essential Articles for the study of Alexander Pope*. Hamden, Conn., 1968.

McKenzie, D.F. *Stationers' Company Apprentices 1641–1700*, OBS, ns vol. 17, 1974.

——. *Stationers' Company Apprentices 1701–1800*, OBS, ns vol. 19, 1978.

McKitterick, David. *Four Hundred Years of University Printing and Publishing in Cambridge 1584–1984*. Cambridge, 1984.

McLaverty, J. 'Lawton Gilliver: Pope's Bookseller', *Studies in Bibliography*, 32 (1979): 101–24.

——. *Pope's Printer, John Wright: a preliminary study*, OBS Occasional Publication no. 11. 1977.

——. 'A Study of John Wright and Lawton Gilliver, Alexander Pope's printer and bookseller'. Unpublished Oxford University B. Litt. thesis, 1974.

Maslen, K.I.D. *The Bowyer Ornament Stock*. OBS Occasional Publication no. 8. 1973.

——. 'New Editions of Pope's *Essay on Man* 1745–48', *PBSA*, 62 (1968), 177–88.

——. 'Works from the Bowyer Press 1713–1765: a supplement to John Nichols'. Unpublished Oxford University B. Litt. thesis, 1952.

Maxted, Ian. *The British Book Trades 1710–1777*. Exeter, 1983.

Melton, Frank. 'Robert and Sir Francis Gosling: Eighteenth-Century Bankers and Stationers', *Economics of the British Booktrade 1605–1939*, ed. Robin Myers and Michael Harris. Cambridge, 1985, pp.60–77.

Morrison, Blake. 'Self-portrait with poet', *TLS* (7–13 July 1989), p.740.

Mossner, E.C. *The Life of David Hume.* Oxford, 1954.

Munby, A.N.L., gen. ed. *Sale Catalogues of Libraries of Eminent Persons.* 12 vols. London, 1971–5.

Murray, David. *Robert & Andrew Foulis and the Glasgow Press.* Glasgow, 1913.

Musgrave's Obituary, ed. Sir George J. Armytage. 6 vols. London, 1900.

Myers, Robin. 'John Nichols (1745–1826), Chronicler of the Book Trade', *Development of the English Book Trade, 1700–1899*, ed. Robin Myers and Michael Harris. Oxford, 1981, pp.1–35.

Neale, R.S. *Bath 1680–1850: A Social History.* London, 1981.

New, Melvin. 'Sterne, Warburton, and the Burden of Exuberant Wit'. *Eighteenth-Century Studies*, 15 (1982): 245–74.

Nichol, Donald W. 'A Misplaced Plate in Warburton's *Pope* IV', *N&Q*, 228 (1983): 34–5.

——. 'Pope, Warburton, Knapton, and Cole: a longstanding connection'. *N&Q*, 234 (1989): 54–6.

——. ' "So proper for that constant pocket use": Posthumous Editions of Pope's *Works* (1751–1754)', *Man and Nature*, vol. 6, ed. Kenneth Graham and Neal Johnson. Edmonton, 1987, pp.81–92.

——. 'A Warburton-Hill Letter: a supplement to Rousseau', *Études Anglaises*, 42 (1989): 185–7.

Nichols, John. *Illustrations of the Literary History of the Eighteenth Century.* 8 vols. London, 1817–58.

——. *Literary Anecdotes of the Eighteenth Century.* 9 vols. London, 1812–15.

Nuttall, Geoffrey F. *A Calendar of the Correspondence of Philip Doddridge, D.D. (1702–1751)* Historical Manuscripts Commission, JP 26. London, 1979.

——. *Handlist of the Correspondence of Mercy Doddridge 1751–1790*, Dr. Williams's Trust Occasional Paper no. 12. London, 1984.

The Oxford Dictionary of Quotations, 2nd ed. Oxford, 1953.

P. T. P. 'Pope and Woodfall', *N&Q*, 11 (19 May 1855): 377–8.

Papali, G.F. *Jacob Tonson, Publisher: his life and work (1656–1736).* Auckland, 1968.

Pattison, Mark. *Essays by the late Mark Pattison*, ed. Henry Nettleship. 2 vols. Oxford, 1889.

Paulson, Ronald. *Hogarth's Graphic Works: first complete edition.* 2 vols. New Haven and London, 1965.

Percy, Thomas, and Edmond Malone. *The Correspondence of Thomas Percy and Edmond Malone*, ed. Arthur Tillotson, in *The Percy Letters*, gen. ed. D. N. Smith, C. Brooks *et al.* 9 vols. New Haven, 1944–88.

Plomer, H.R. *et al. A Dictionary of the Printers and Booksellers who were at work in England, Scotland and Ireland from 1726 to 1775.* London, 1932; rpt. 1968.

Plutarch's Lives, trans. John and William Langhorne. London, 1890.

Pope, Alexander. *The Correspondence of Alexander Pope*, ed. George Sherburn. 5 vols. Oxford, 1956.

——. *The Prose Works of Alexander Pope*, vol. 2, ed. Rosemary Cowler. Oxford, 1986.

——. *The Twickenham Edition of the Poems of Alexander Pope*, ed. John Butt *et al.* 11 vols. in 12. London, 1938-69.

——. *The Works of Alexander Pope*, ed. Whitwell Elwin and W. J. Courthope. 10 vols. London, 1871–89.

Price, John Valdimir. *David Hume.* Boston, 1969.

Prior, James. *The Life of Edmond Malone, Editor of Shakespeare. With Selections from his Manuscript Anecdotes.* London, 1860.

Probyn, Clive. 'James Harris to Parson Adams in Germany: some light on Fielding's Salisbury set', *Philological Quarterly*, 64 (1985): 130–9.

——. *The Sociable Humonist: the life and works of James Harris 1709–1780*. Oxford 1991.

Ratchford, Fannie E. 'Pope and the *Patriot King*', *University of Texas, Studies in English*, 6 (1926): 157–77.

Richardson, Samuel. *The Correspondence of Samuel Richardson*, ed. Anna Lætitia Barbauld. 6 vols. London, 1804; rpt. New York, 1966.

——. *Selected Letters of Samuel Richardson*, ed. John Carroll. Oxford, 1964.

Rogers, Pat. *Hacks and Dunces: Pope, Swift and Grub Street*. London, 1972; abridged 1980.

Rousseau, G.S. 'Science Books and their Readers', *Books and their Readers in Eighteenth-Century England*, ed. Isabel Rivers. Leicester, 1982, pp.197–255.

——. 'Seven New Hill Letters', *Études Anglaises*, 39 (1986): 174–87.

——. 'Six New Hill Letters', *Medical History*, 28 (1984): 293–302.

Rudé, George. *Wilkes and Liberty*. Oxford, 1962.

Ryley, Robert M. *William Warburton*. Boston, 1984.

Seary, Peter. *Lewis Theobald and the Editing of Shakespeare*. Oxford, 1990.

Shakespeare, William. *Complete Oxford Shakespeare*, general ed. Stanley Wells and Gary Taylor. Oxford, 1987.

Shenstone, William. *The Letters of William Shenstone*, ed. Marjorie Williams. Oxford, 1939.

Sherbo, Arthur. *The Birth of Shakespeare Studies*. East Lansing, 1986.

Sherburn, George. *The Early Career of Alexander Pope*. Oxford, 1934.

Smallwood, Frank T. 'Bolingbroke *vs*. Alexander Pope: the Publication of the *Patriot King*', *PBSA*, 65 (1971): 225–41.

Spence, Joseph. *Observations, Anecdotes, and Characters of Books and Men*, ed. James M. Osborn. 2 vols. Oxford, 1966.

Stephen, Leslie. *History of English Thought in the Eighteenth Century*, 3rd ed. 2 vols. London, 1902; rpt. New York, 1962.

Sterne, Laurence. *Letters of Laurence Sterne*, ed. Lewis Perry Curtis. Oxford, 1935.

Straus, Ralph. *Robert Dodsley: Poet, Publisher & Playwright*. London, 1910; rpt. New York, 1968.

Sutherland, James R. 'The Dull Duty of an Editor', *Review of English Studies*, 21 (1945): 202–15.

——, ed. *The Oxford Book of Literary Anecdotes*. Oxford, 1976.

Templeman, William Darby. 'Warburton and Brown Continue the Battle Over Ridicule', *Huntington Library Quarterly*, 17 (1953): 17–36.

Thornbury, George Walter. *Old and New London*. 6 vols. London, 1873–8.

Tierney, James E. '*The Museum*, the "Super-Excellent Magazine"', *Studies in English Literature*, 13 (1973): 503–15.

——. '*Museum* Attributions in John Cooper's Unpublished Letters', *Studies in Bibliography*, 27 (1974): 232–5.

Treadwell, Michael. 'London Trade Publishers 1675–1750', *The Library*, 6th ser., 4 (1982): 99–134.

Wallis, Philip. *At the Sign of the Ship: notes on the house of Longman, 1724–1974*. Harlow, 1974.

Walpole, Horace. *The Yale Edition of Horace Walpole's Correspondence*. ed. Wilmarth S. Lewis *et al*. 48 vols. New Haven, 1937–83.

Warburton, William. *Essai sur les hiéroglyphes des Égyptiens*, traduit par Léonard des Malpeines, édition et notes par Patrick Tort, précédé de SCRIBBLE (pouvoir/écrire) par Jacques Derrida. Paris, 1977.

——. *Horace Walpole's Political Tracts 1747–1748 with Two by William Warburton on Literary Property 1747 and 1762* in *The English Book Trade 1660–1853*, ed. Stephen Parks. 42 vols. (no vol. number). New York, 1974.

[———.] *A Letter to the Editor of the Letters on the Spirit of Patriotism, &c.* rpt. with *A Familiar Epistle to the Most Impudent Man Living*, ed. Donald T. Siebert, Jr., Augustan Reprint Society, no. 192. Los Angeles, 1978.

———. *Letters from a Late Eminent Prelate to One of his Friends*, ed. Richard Hurd. Kidderminster, [1808].

———. *Letters from the Reverend Dr. Warburton, Bishop of Gloucester, to the Hon. Charles Yorke, from 1752 to 1770.* London, 1812.

———. *A Selection from Unpublished Papers of the Right Reverend William Warburton, D.D.*, ed. Francis Kilvert. London, 1841.

———. *Works*, ed. Richard Hurd. 7 vols. London, 1788–94; rpt. Hildesheim, 1978–80.

'Warburton's letters', *The Wesleyan Journal, the Methodist Magazine*, 41 (1818): 35–8.

Watkins, Leslie. *Barclays: a Story of Money and Banking*. London, 1982.

Watson, George, ed. *The New Cambridge Bibliography of English Literature*, vol. 2, 1660–1800. Cambridge, 1971.

Watson, John Selby. *The Life of William Warburton, D.D., Lord Bishop of Gloucester, from 1760 to 1779: with Remarks on his Works.* London, 1863.

Wilkes, John. *The Correspondence of the late John Wilkes*, introd. John Almon. 5 vols. London, 1804; rpt. New York, 1970.

Wimsatt, W.K. *The Portraits of Alexander Pope*. New Haven and London, 1965.

Wood, Frederick T. 'Notes on London Booksellers and Publishers, 1700–1750', *N&Q*, 161 (1931): 186 and *passim*.

Wooll, John, ed. *Biographical Memoirs of the Late Revd. Joseph Warton, D.D.* London, 1806.

INDEX

211